EUROPE AFTER 1815

By René Albrecht-Carrié

About the Author

1. Present Position: Professor Emeritus of History in Barnard College and School of International Affairs, Columbia University.

2. Publications: *Italy at the Paris Peace Conference* (Columbia University Press, 1938); *Italy from Napoleon to Mussolini* (Columbia University Press, 1950); *A Diplomatic History of Europe Since the Congress of Vienna* (Harper, 1958); *France, Europe and the Two World Wars* (Harper, 1961); *Europe Since 1815* (Harper, 1962); *One Europe* (Doubleday, 1965); *The Concert of Europe* (Harper & Row, 1968); *Britain and France* (Doubleday, 1970). Has written articles and reviews dealing with history, international affairs, and issues of contemporary interest for *American Historical Review, Journal of Modern History, Journal of Central European Affairs, South Atlantic Quarterly, Political Science Quarterly, The American Scientist, The Scientific Monthly, The Annals, Orbis,* etc.

About the Book

1. Material has been systematically arranged with varying sizes of type and numbers or letters to emphasize the organization of the outline.

2. In addition to giving the essential factual infomation, the arrangement of chapters and the division of the whole into three parts is designed to give a more connected and coherent picture of the entire story.

3. An average of some ten books per chapter has been selected among the most useful, dependable, and (when possible) recent books. But in order to avoid repetitions, these references have been grouped together before each major Part of the outline.

EUROPE
After 1815

By René Albrecht-Carrié
PROFESSOR EMERITUS OF HISTORY
BARNARD COLLEGE AND COLUMBIA UNIVERSITY

FIFTH EDITION

A HELIX BOOK

ROWMAN & ALLANHELD
Totowa, New Jersey

ACKNOWLEDGMENTS

In addition to the original maps prepared especially for this Outline, several others have been reproduced, by permission, from other sources. The publisher and author gratefully acknowledge this courtesy.

The maps appearing on pages 2, 114, 132, and 187 have been reproduced from *A History of the Modern World* by R. R. Palmer, by permission of Alfred A. Knopf, Inc.

The maps appearing on pages 154, 179, 182, 258, 267 and 270, have been reproduced from *The War In Maps* by Francis Brown, by permission of the Oxford University Press.

The maps appearing on pages 289, 323, and 331 have been reproduced from *History of Europe After 1815,* Revised Edition by René Albrecht-Carrié, by permission of Harper & Row, Publishers.

The chart of *The United Nations System* on pages 296 and 297 has been reproduced by permission of United Nations Press.

Copyright 1972
BY LITTLEFIELD, ADAMS & CO.
Library of Congress Catalog Number 55-26420

First Edition 1952
Second Edition 1955
Third Edition 1958
Reprinted 1961, 1962
Fourth Edition 1964
Reprinted 1965, 1967, 1968
Fifth Edition 1972

Reprinted in 1984 as A HELIX BOOK, published by Rowman & Allanheld, Publishers (a division of Littlefield, Adams & Company) 81 Adams Drive, Totowa, New Jersey, 07512

Printed in the United States of America

Preface

The purpose of an outline is to facilitate the study of a subject. Most history texts inevitably tend to be voluminous, and the wealth of detail which they are likely to contain, while important and even in some respects essential, has the effect of burdening the student's memory and blurring the outlines of the total picture that is formed from reading them.

An outline is not a substitute for a text. Its function is to simplify and clarify by emphasizing the essentials, arranged in such a way as to bring out the "outline" of a skeleton.

To this end, short sections with headings set in different type and numbering are designed to call attention to the underlying structure of the outline. Details not indispensable to this purpose have been eliminated, save on occasion when they may serve to sharpen or illustrate a point.

The result of such treatment is not, however, a mere accumulation of fact. Such a collection, even when reduced to essentials, would merely defeat its purpose of aiding memory. Despite the task of simplification, therefore, the outline has been so written as to tell a story which, when read by itself, presents an organized picture of the whole course of the history that it covers.

The retention of factual information by memory is indispensable. But it is only a first step and a beginning which, if one should stop at that stage, would be of little interest or value. Such a subject as history especially would have little justification unless pursued to the point of understanding. This understanding tends to be at first in the light of contemporary experience which is perhaps the reason why there is no finality in history and why history is rewritten by each successive generation.

This is both inevitable and proper, but an effort should be made in addition to place oneself as much as possible outside the context of immediate and limited experience into the different framework of other times and places. This caution applies especially to the American student of European history, since Europe presents within itself such great diversity in both time and locality.

But the process of understanding cannot be divorced from that of interpretation. It is indeed the intention of the present outline to convey certain major themes that run through the entire period and over the whole of Europe. Having mastered a sufficient body of fact, and formed a coherent picture of their relationship and significance, the student should then proceed to develop his own critical views. This is the purpose of the reading lists which have been appended at the beginning of each part of the outline.

This device has been used in lieu of indicating references at the end of each chapter for the sake of avoiding repetitions. It also fits the "natural" chronological division into segments of a comparable order of magnitude: from 1815 to 1870; from then to the outbreak of the First World War; finally our own age of transition. The student can easily select from these lists a book dealing with the particular period, country, or aspect of development about which he wishes to enlarge his knowledge.

The careful student who wishes to benefit most from these features should follow a standard procedure in studying for any examination. First, he should read thoroughly and carefully the text and collateral material assigned in the course he is taking, making notes on the outside reading. Then he should study this outline, noting that certain facts and interpretations are in both the text and the outline, while others are in the text alone. These latter are less essential than the former, but should be remembered if possible.

Next, the student should prepare an outline of this outline by copying out the topics in bold type in the chapter or chapters he is studying. This is recommended because most of us have visual memories; by writing something down we store that information in our minds. Moreover, that skeleton outline, which will fill less than a sheet of paper, will be easy to remember. Having learned that outline thoroughly, the usual student in an examination will be able to recall the more detailed treatment of the subject in this fuller outline, and from that most of the subject matter in the text.

PREFACE

From the textbook to the outline, from this outline to the student's own outline; the whole rounded out with some additional reading, is the best procedure to obtain the knowledge and understanding which history has for its purpose.

Preface to the Fifth Edition

The twenty years that have elapsed since the first publication of this outline have witnessed in the whole world, in Europe in particular, substantial changes which, in economic terms at least, have produced a remarkable recovery. The interval has been a period of peace, in the sense at least that open conflict has not occurred among the major powers, although there have been numerous clashes involving others. These have been limited and contained for the reason that the United States and the Soviet Union have recoiled before the possibility of mutual involvement. This condition is known as the balance of terror, a reasonably dependent equilibrium so long as leadership remains in responsible hands. This in turn puts a high premium on the desirability of an understanding, some agreement on the limitation and control of nuclear weapons, and the effort to prevent their spread. Here lies one of the most important issues of the present time. It is one on which but very limited progress has so far been registered, but the outcome of which is of vital importance for all.

The passage of time has also brought a considerable modification in the former sharp divisions of Europe. At the same time the bipolar division of the world into two hostile blocs and the resultant climate of Cold War between them has undergone a notable modification. The new countries which have emerged to independence out of the demise of the colonial empires do not wish to be involved in the quarrels of the superpowers, least of all to be treated as pawns; they have not, however, succeeded in organizing an effective Third Force, any more than has Europe herself. The nearest candidate for that role has been The People's Republic of China, now an acknowledged member of the international community with her accession to the United Nations.

Where Europe is concerned, her recovery has also had the effect of inducing a greater assertion of independence on the part of her component units. This tendency is perceptible on both sides of an increasingly flimsy Iron Curtain. The Russian hand has been far heavier than the American in countenancing these manifestations of independence, as witness the events of 1956 in Hungary and of 1968 in Czechoslovakia in contrast with the impunity of France's withdrawal from NATO. In any event there can be little question about the progressive erosion of the blocs that emerged in the immediate aftermath of the second World War. There is little prospect of their revival, but there has developed instead an increasingly fluid condition in which more centers of power develop. The emergence of China is so far the most significant development in this direction, which has had in addition the effect of shifting to Asia the focus of international tensions. This may be taken as further confirmation of the diminished importance of Europe. For that formerly dominant part of much of the world the issue remains, as it has been since the war, that of possible unity. The enlargement of the Common Market with the possible accession of four new members puts new life into that possibility, the unfolding of which is likely to constitute the most important aspect of the course of European affairs in the coming decade.

CONTENTS

CHAPTER   PAGE

PREFACE v

PREFACE TO THE FIFTH EDITION...................................... viii

PART I: REACTION, LIBERALISM AND NATIONALISM: 1815-1870

1   THE STRUGGLE BETWEEN LIBERALISM AND REACTION: 1815-1848 3
Europe in 1815. The Restoration, 1815-1830. The Eastern Question. Liberal Successes and Failures. Europe in Mid-century. The Intellectual Climate of the Period.

2   THE REVOLUTION THAT FAILED: 1848-1852 29
The Second French Republic. Revolutions in Central Europe. The Balance Sheet.

3   TRIUMPHS OF NATIONALISM: 1852-1870 42
The Crimean War. The Unification of Italy. Germany on the Road to Unity (to 1867). Eastern Europe. The Western Countries. The Showdown Between France and Germany. The Progress of Europe.

PART II: THE APOGEE OF EUROPE 1870-1914

4   GENERAL CHARACTERISTICS OF THE PERIOD: 1870-1914   69
The Significance of 1870. The Economic Scene. Social Change. The Political Forces. The Intellectual and Moral Climate of Europe.

5   THE INDIVIDUAL NATIONS OF EUROPE: 1870-1914 83
The Western Democracies. The Central European Powers. Autocracy in Eastern Europe.

Chapter		Page
6	THE EUROPEAN FAMILY OF NATIONS: 1870-1914 General Considerations. The Bismarckian Period. The Period of Realignment. The Last Decade: The Road to War.	120

PART III: THE PASSING OF EUROPE'S SUPREMACY: 1914-1939

7	THE FIRST WORLD WAR The Outbreak of War. The War (1914-1918). Mortgages on the Peace: The Diplomacy and Ideology of the War.	155
8	THE SETTLEMENTS FOLLOWING THE FIRST WORLD WAR The Peace Conference of Paris. The Peace Treaties. Appraisal and Reception of the Peace.	172
9	THE FALSE RECOVERY The Economic Consequences of the War. The Democratic West. New Political Experiments. The Power Vacuum of the Succession States. The European Community of Nations.	193
10	THE RETURN TO WAR The World Economic Crisis. The Rise of Nazi Germany. The End of the League. France's Final Surrender of Leadership. The End of the Versailles System.	230

PART IV: EUROPE IN THE MODERN AGE

11	THE SECOND WORLD WAR The European War. The World War.	261
12	BETWEEN WAR AND PEACE The World After the War. The Cold War. Europe in the World Today.	281
	INDEX	346

MAPS

	PAGE
Europe, 1815-1859	2
Unification of Italy	45
Unification of Germany	62
Dissolution of the Ottoman Empire	114
Africa in 1898	132
Europe in the First World War	154
The World of Versailles	179
Europe After 1919	182
Languages of Europe	187
Central and Eastern Europe, 1914-1938	214
Partition of Poland (1939)	260
The Allied Blockade	267
Lend Lease in War Strategy	272
State of Europe in 1955	283
Germany After World War II	289
The Emergence of the Dependent World	323
The Integration of Europe	331

PART I

Reaction, Liberalism, and Nationalism 1815-1870

SELECTED READINGS

Albrecht-Carrié, René, *A Diplomatic History of Europe* (1958); Allison, J. M. S., *Thiers and the French Monarchy* (1926); Artz, Frederick B., *Reaction and Revolution, 1814-1832* (1934); Binkley, Robert C., *Realism and Nationalism, 1852-1871* (1935); Brinton, Crance, *English Political Thought in the XIX Century* (1950); Brogan, D. W., *The French Nation, 1814-1940* (1957); Bury, John, P. T., *France, 1814-1840: A History* (1940); Clapham, John, *The Economic Development of France and Germany, 1815-1914* (1928); Chapham, John, *An Economic History of Modern Britain*, vol. I, (1926); Clough, Shepard B. and Charles W. Cole, *An Economic History of Europe* (1941); Darmstaedter, Friedrich, *Bismarck and the Creation of the Second Reich* (1949); Dietz, F. C., *The Industrial Revolution, 1750-1927* (1927); Eyck, Erich, *Bismarck and the German Empire* (1950); Fisher, H. A. L. *Bonapartism* (1914); Florinsky, Michael T., *Russia: A History and an Interpretation* (2 vols., 1953); Friedjung, Heinrich, *The Struggle for Supremacy in Germany, 1859-1866* (1935); Guérard, Albert, *Napoleon III* (1943); Halévy, Élie, *History of the English People, 1815-1841*, 3 vols. (1924-1928); Halévy, Élie, *The Growth of Philosophic Radicalism* (1950); Kissinger, Henry, *A World Restored: Metternich, Castlereagh and the Problem of Peace, 1812-1822* (1957); Laski, Harold J., *The Communist Manifesto, a Socialist Landmark* (1948); Mack Smith, D., *Italy* (1959); Marriott, J. A. R., *The Eastern Question* (1940); Marx, Karl and Engels, Friedrich, *Revolution and Counterrevolution, or Germany in 1848* (1919); May, Arthur, *The Age of Metternich, 1814-1848* (1933); Merz, J. T., *A History of European Thought in the Nineteenth Century* (4 vols., 1896-1914); Namier, Lewis B., *1848: the Revolution of the Intellectuals* (1946); Pascal, Roy, *The Course of Modern Germany* (1946); Pinson, Koppel S., *Modern Germany* (1954); Robertson, C. G., *Bismarck* (1919); Robertson, Priscilla, *The Revolutions of 1848* (1952); Ruggiero, Guido de, *The History of European Liberalism* (1927); Schenck, H. G., *The Aftermath of the Napoleonic Wars: the Concert of Europe—an Experiment* (1947); Seton-Watson, R. W., *The Southern Slav Question in the Habsburg Monarchy* (1911); Taylor, A. J. P., *The Course of German History* (1946); Taylor, A. J. P., *The Habsburg Monarchy, 1809-1918* (1943, 1948); Thayer, William R., *The Life and Times of Cavour* (1911); Thompson, J. M., *Louis Napoleon and the Second Empire* (1954); Valentin, Veit, *1848: Chapters in Germany History* (1940); Webster, Charles, *The Congress of Vienna, 1814-1815* (1920); Whitridge, Arnold, *Men in Crisis: the Revolutions of 1848* (1949).

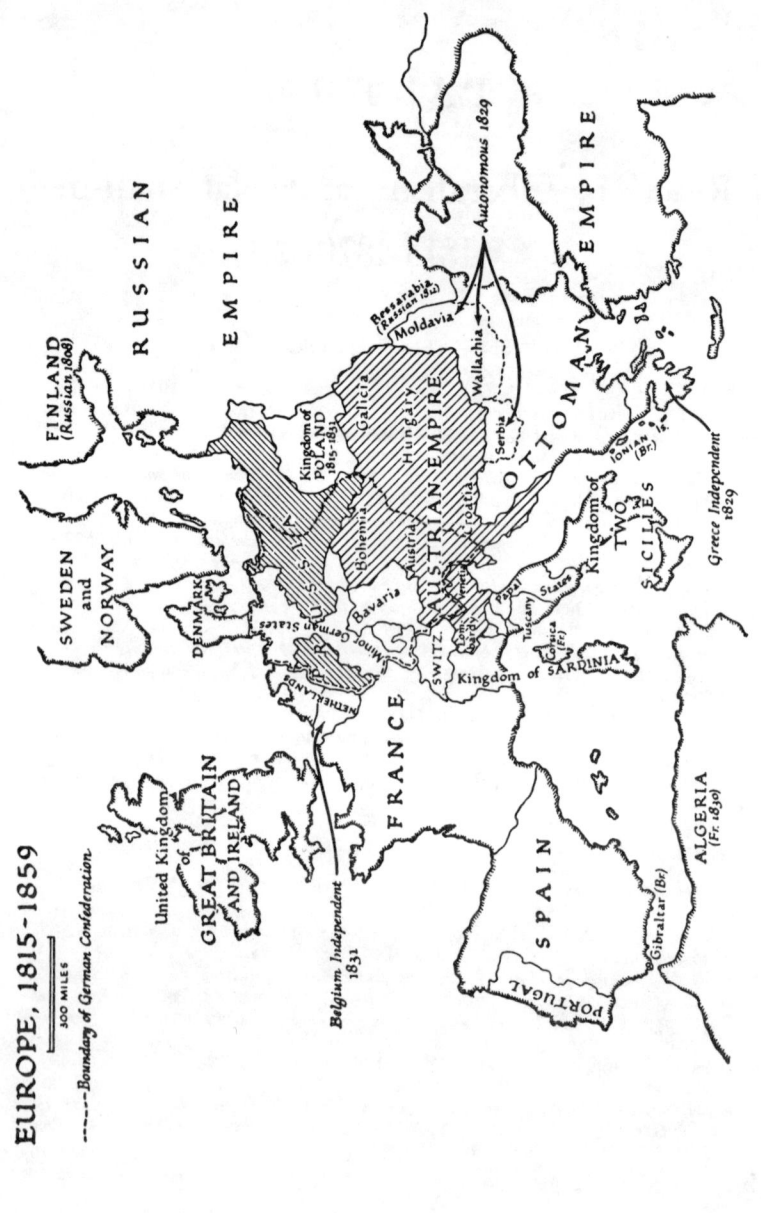

CHAPTER 1

The Struggle between Liberalism and Reaction: 1815-1848

I. EUROPE IN 1815

Napoleon had been an autocrat, in actual fact rather more arbitrary and powerful than his divine-right predecessors on the French throne. Yet Napoleon had called himself a son of the Revolution, and there is no denying that his armies had carried abroad with them some of the fundamental aspects of that upheaval. The example in practice of "the career open to talent," the recognition of individual merit irrespective of birth, and the institution of up-to-date constitutions on much of the continent, had given the *ancien régime* blows from which, after a quarter of a century, it could not wholly recover.

But the natural tendency, especially after a long and arduous conflict, is to equate the restoration of peace with that of "normalcy," interpreted in turn as synonymous with the *status quo ante*. The whole nineteenth century is filled with the struggle between the old (absolutism, reaction) and the new (liberalism, democracy, or progress), a contest in which, viewing the century as a whole, the old will appear to be fighting a retreating action. The battle was fought out in France as elsewhere, but it was only natural that in France should be found the greatest strength of the new and that France should be its standard bearer and the weather vane of change. Especially during the first half of the century, until 1870, this state of affairs is adequately expressed in the quip, "When Paris sneezes, Europe catches cold."

A. France and the Coalition

Napoleon had been defeated in 1814, and peace with France had been promptly made by the first Treaty of Paris (March,

1814). Napoleon had abdicated (Treaty of Fontainebleau) and the Bourbons had returned to France, in the person of Louis XVIII, brother of the executed king. France was not punished for the misdeeds of Napoleon; she was confined to the frontiers of 1792 and no indemnity was imposed upon her.

Obviously, however, the danger stemming from France could not be considered destroyed for all time, and the successful coalition had cemented its bonds by the Treaty of Chaumont (March, 1814). Also, while it was relatively simple to deal with France alone, the map and the status of much of Europe had to be re-examined. This the allies proposed to do at a subsequent meeting which took place in Vienna from the autumn of 1814 to June, 1815.

1. The Hundred Days. From March to June, 1815, Napoleon made a sensational, but short-lived, reappearance upon the scene. Waterloo definitely marked his exit from history. Peace had to be made again with France (second Treaty of Paris, November, 1815), setting her frontiers at those of 1790, imposing upon her an indemnity of 750,000,000 francs, and occupation for a time by foreign troops.

B. The Settlement of Vienna

The arrangements made at Vienna were not affected by the Hundred Days. The task of the Congress of Vienna had not proved easy. All Europe, the rulers and their delegates that is, was at Vienna, but decisions were largely in the hands of the four chief allies (Russia, Prussia, Austria, and England) in whose discussions, taking advantage of their differences, the wily Talleyrand soon managed to insert himself. France had an important voice in Vienna. With the addition of Sweden, Portugal, and Spain, the five became the eight.

1. The Leaders, the Issues, and the Guiding Principles. Metternich was host and guide to the Congress. He sincerely held the Jacobin ideal to be a dangerous fallacy, under whose guidance no society or state could hope to function; restoration of the old regime was not only necessary, but the preservation of the "ideology," as we should call it now, was the proper concern of all, not the purely domestic task of individual states and rulers. In addition to this, the European community as a whole could best function under the aegis of the principle of the balance of power. In this last view, he found support from Castlereagh, the British representative; Tsar Alexander was more responsive to the former. Well-meaning, but impressionable and unstable, the Tsar was easily swayed by the contradictory influences that attracted his shifting fancy. Talleyrand, biding his time, made a telling point with his concept of legitimacy; in defeat, this was the best defense of French interest. Prussia, under the guidance of the timorous Frederick William, was not an initiator of ideas or policies.

Legitimacy, however, could be restored only up to a point. The outmoded structure of the defunct Holy Roman Empire, for example, could not be resurrected; Napoleon's job of simplification was in large measure allowed to stand. Also, the balance of power did not necessarily preclude the effort on the part of its participants to secure individual benefits. Tsar Alexander was desirous of securing all Poland for himself; he would assuage his liberal leanings of the moment by making it a separate kingdom and giving it a constitution. For a price (cession of Saxony), Prussia was willing to acquiesce in this. But neither Metternich nor Castlereagh could see the virtue of having destroyed excessive French power merely to replace it by Russian. The Polish-Saxon issue proved the most difficult problem that faced the Congress; for a time it threatened its continuance, and it was the wedge through which Talleyrand reinserted France in the councils of the powers. [1]

The outcome of these circumstances was ultimately compromise. The settlement of Vienna was made under the aegis of the principles of legitimacy and restoration, qualified by compensation.

2. The Results. The principal results were these:

Britain—since 1801 the United Kingdom of Great Britain and Ireland—had no direct territorial interests on the continent. She wished, however, to retain some of the overseas territories conquered during the recent wars. This was facilitated[2] by the

---

[1] In January, 1815 a treaty of alliance was made between Britain, France, and Austria to oppose, by force of arms if necessary, the Russo-Prussian coalition.

[2] Britain acquired, as a result of the Napoleonic wars, some Caribbean islands, Mauritius, Guiana, and South Africa. In the Mediterranean, she took from temporary French control and retained Malta and the Ionian islands. These last she relinquished to Greece in 1863.

fact that her continental allies had generally little appreciation of or interest in colonies.

Holland was the chief sufferer from British acquisitions, but she was compensated by the incorporation of the former Austrian Netherlands. This had the additional advantage of creating a stronger barrier against France in the north, and specifically of keeping Antwerp and the mouth of the Scheldt out of French hands.

The same purpose of blocking French expansion was served by consolidating the conglomeration of minute states in the Rhineland, now a solid block of territory turned over to Prussia.

This arrangement, in turn, served to compensate Prussia for her failure to incorporate Saxony, only three-fifths of which she acquired. There was no compensation for Saxony, faithful until too late to the Napoleonic cause.

Austria was willing to relinquish the awkwardly distant Netherlands in exchange for nearer possessions in Italy; Venice was not restored, but instead, with Lombardy, became Austrian. This served to confirm the predominant Austrian influence in the Italian peninsula (members of the Habsburg house also ruled in the Duchies) where otherwise restoration was the order of the day, save that, like Venice, Genoa was not revived, being instead incorporated into the Kingdom of Sardinia. [3]

In place of the old Holy Roman Empire, a comparable German Confederation was set up within roughly the same boundaries. Austria, by right, was to have its presidency, and paramount Habsburg influence was thus presumably insured from the Baltic to Sicily.

Tsar Alexander of Russia did not get all, but only the major part, of Poland, substantially more than in the last partition of 1795. Russia also retained Bessarabia, acquired in 1812 from the Turks, but the Congress did not otherwise concern itself with the Ottoman Empire. In the north also, Finland, acquired in 1809, was retained by Russia.

---

[3] In 1814, Murat, King of Naples, had thought to save his throne by abandoning Napoleon. Metternich accepted Murat's assistance, and the Neapolitan question might have been an awkward one at Vienna had not Murat conveniently eliminated himself by throwing his lot with Napoleon during the Hundred Days.

There was no reason, however, to punish Bernadotte's Sweden for this loss. It was made up by the adjunction of Norway, detached from her hitherto Danish allegiance. Denmark, like Saxony, had not deserted Napoleon early enough.

Spain and Portugal were restored, but the problem of their revolting American colonies was not dealt with.

3. *Appraisal of the Settlement.* The settlement of Vienna[4] was essentially a political one. It is a measure of the changed conditions that a century was to bring that, by contrast with modern treaties, those of Vienna were virtually unconcerned with matters economic.

The peoples had no voice at Vienna. Nationalism was ignored, and this has often been considered a valid criticism of these arrangements. There is no question that nationalism, like democracy, was to prove one of the guiding currents of the nineteenth century, much of the history of which can be written in terms of ultimately successful efforts to undo the charter of 1815. To the rulers of the day, nationalism meant little; and nationalism at the beginning of the century was not the sort of thing that we have come to know. In the context of its own time, the settlement of Vienna was a reasonable and moderate compromise. It proved rather more lasting than attempts of comparable scope in our own century.

4. *The Holy and Quadruple Alliances.* More important than nationalism in the eyes of the rulers was the matter of preserving the social and political structure of the various European states. Tsar Alexander, combining in his own inimitable fashion the various tendencies at work in him, contrived the Holy Alliance (November, 1815). This was a vague and pious declaration, of elusive content, entered into by the rulers under the aegis of the Holy Trinity, for mutual assistance and protection. What significance it would have, if any, would depend upon whether and how it was implemented when suitable circumstances arose.

The British monarch, on the plea of his constitutional status, declined to join in this "nonsense." Britain was more interested in a more concrete instrument, the Quadruple Alliance, which provided specific guarantees against a recurrence of French aggression, and also for further meetings of the powers.

---

[4] The final Act was signed in June, 1815, a few days before Waterloo.

II. THE RESTORATION, 1815-1830

The period following the Congress of Vienna has sometimes been labeled the Era of Metternich. If Metternich is regarded as the most consistent and staunchest advocate of the old order, hence of reaction, the label for a time is suitable.

A. The United Kingdom

The constitutional structure of Britain had been unaffected by events of the past quarter of a century. Victory over Napoleon redounded to the credit of the Tory administration, and the general revulsion toward the "excesses" of revolutionary France hampered the influence of the able but small band of "radicals" in and out of Parliament. Economic problems, those deriving from an already well-developed industry, and fiscal ones arising from the debts incurred in financing the war, loomed large. England was still devoted to protection of her still important agriculture and to an increasingly outmoded system of political representation. Unrest growing out of the economic crisis of 1819 was met by the repressive Six Acts, curtailing the traditional British liberties.

The private affairs, or scandals, of the Regent, who became George IV upon the death of George III in 1820, did not enhance the prestige of the Crown. If Britain had not joined in the Holy Alliance, the policies of her government were satisfactory to Metternich.

B. The Germanies

In the German Confederation, the enthusiasm of the war of liberation had much abated. In Prussia, the reforming zeal of Stein had yielded to conservative rule, and the king had conveniently forgotten his promise of a constitution. The ferment of a romantic liberalism was still at work, especially in the universities; student societies, the *Tugendbund* and the *Burschenschaft*, were its chief expressions. The murder of the writer Kotzebue, an agent of the Tsar, by an exalted fanatic, provided Metternich with a suitable pretext for calling together the representatives of the various states. The Carlsbad Decrees, in 1819, inspired by the same spirit as the British Six Acts, were the result.

C. France

In France, Louis XVIII, anxious not to set out on further travels and realizing the irreversible imprint of the past twenty-five years, had granted a charter, or constitution, that provided representative institutions, albeit with a very limited franchise. The reactionary party was strong, and the episode of the Hundred Days was followed by a White Terror and the election of the so-called *Chambre introuvable*, more royalist than the king, by whom it was dissolved in 1816. The new chamber had a majority of the center in favor, like the king, of the charter and constitutional monarchy.

1. The Congress of Aix-la-Chapelle. France was under enemy occupation. The seeming restoration of stable government, the fulfillment of her financial obligations to the allies, and the fear of these lest their troops become "infected" with revolutionary ideas, induced a reconsideration of France's status at the Congress of Aix-la-Chapelle in 1818. The result of this meeting was to reinstate France to the status of a member in good standing of the Concert of Europe. She joined the Holy Alliance, but the Quadruple Alliance was also secretly renewed.

This apparent stabilization was interrupted by the assassination of the Duc de Berry, the king's nephew. This was the signal for a new instalment of reaction, endorsed by the elections of the same year. The split between right and left was thus accentuated, and the latter, under persecution, tended to resort to the conspiratorial activity of secret societies.

D. The Concert of Europe; The Issue of Intervention

1. The Revolutions of 1820 in Italy. Activity of this nature was particularly flourishing in the Italian peninsula where the *Carbonari* and other similar groups had their main strength. The slogan of liberals at this time was "Constitution," a word which seemed to carry an aura of magic attributes. In Naples, King Ferdinand I of the Two Sicilies, was setting an example of thoroughgoing and blind reaction. In July, 1820, a virtually unopposed rising extorted from him the grant of a constitution, modeled after the Spanish one of 1812. The Neapolitan situation had echoes throughout Italy, and particularly in Piedmont.

2. The Congresses of Troppau and Laibach. Intervention in Italy. Here was a potentially dangerous situation, in Metternich's view, a proper subject for consideration by the Concert of Europe. A meeting was held at Troppau in Silesia, in November, 1820 and reconvened at Laibach the next month. It was about this time that Tsar Alexander, frightened away from his uncertain liberalism by the spectacle of plots, conspiracies, and assassinations, yielded to Metternich's guidance and gave his support to a policy of armed intervention. Britain assumed an ambiguous position of formal opposition, while Castlereagh privately reassured Metternich. France also hedged, refusing to associate herself formally with the decisions of Troppau and Laibach.

In these circumstances, the appearance of Austrian troops in Naples restored the situation with ease. The triumph of reaction was assured throughout Italy. Its manifestations were particularly brutal in Naples, but suppression was also severe in the Papal States, in the Austrian territory of Lombardo-Venetia, and in Piedmont. In that state, the abortive rising of 1821 had resulted in the abdication of Victor Emmanuel, and its success had been hampered by the gyrations of the temporary regent, Charles Albert. Many liberals were imprisoned, while others sought the safety of exile, pursued where possible by the long arm of Metternich acting through the Concert of Europe.

3. The Congress of Verona. Intervention in Spain. Spain had been the scene of rebellion even earlier than Italy, to whom she set an example. The trouble began in January, 1820 among the troops gathered at Cadiz for embarkation to South America, where the colonies were fighting for independence. King Ferdinand had been forced to grant a constitution which operated after a fashion between the pressures of the extremes of the left (*exaltados*) and right (*apostolicos*). After the Italian situation, nearer the center of Europe, had been dealt with, Spanish affairs came up for consideration at the Congress of Verona (October, 1822). No one was anxious to entertain the Tsar's offer of his armies for service in Spain. If Europe were to intervene in that peninsula, the logical agent of its mandate was France. After some hesitation on the part of the French government, somewhat uncertain of the spirit of its armies, French forces entered Spain in 1823. They met with little resistance, and King Ferdinand was restored to full and arbitrary power, of which he made the same abusively repressive use as his Neapolitan namesake.

4. The Monroe Doctrine and England. The Spanish affair had other repercussions. England eyed with suspicion the French intervention. When it came to the possibility of Europe assisting Spain in the recovery of her American possessions, not only would she not join, but she actually opposed such intervention. It was useful, for British purposes, that the support of the desire for independence in South America should fit with her commercial interests. The United States found itself in essentially the same position. But sufficient suspicion on the American side still tinged Anglo-American relations to prevent overt concerted action. In December, 1823, President Monroe sent to Congress the famous message containing the declaration associated with his name since then. The Monroe Doctrine was an American statement; its effectiveness would inevitably depend for a considerable time to come upon British maritime supremacy, and Canning, who had meantime succeeded Castlereagh after the latter's suicide, claimed ample credit for the successful birth to independence of the South American republics.

E. The Decembrist Rising in Russia

At the other extremity of Europe from Spain, the liberal ferment had made some impression, especially among army and educated circles. There was no sufficient basis for revolution in Russian society, however, and the Tsar, though wedded by now to reaction, did not seriously interfere with the impotent talk and scheming of secret societies. His death, in 1825, followed by an interval of uncertainty over his succession, was the occasion for an ill-planned and hopeless rising in December. Tsar Nicholas, once on the throne, dealt severely with the "Decembrists" and their following.

By the mid-twenties, Metternich could contemplate with satisfaction the state of Europe, largely under the rule of reliable conservative governments.

III. THE EASTERN QUESTION

A. Nature of the Problem

1. *Ottoman Decline.* The story of the Ottoman Empire during the eighteenth century had been one of gradual territorial recession, mainly under the joint pressure of Austria and Russia. In addition, France had long-standing interests, economic and cultural, in the empire of the sultans, and the imperial and commercial growth of Britain caused her to take increasing interest in its affairs. The Turks had lost their former expanding vigor, and instead of keeping up with the modern world, their state, beset by maladministration, was in a condition of advanced decay.

Although the Congress of Vienna, partly in deference to Russian wishes, had not dealt with Ottoman affairs, it was clear that the fate of the still vast Ottoman domain would be of concern to the powers, particularly the four just mentioned. This is the essence of the eastern question.

2. *The Straits.* More narrowly, in the purely European sphere, the traditional Russian push toward warm and open waters, had become clearly focused on some form of control of the straits (the Bosporus and the Dardanelles), a desire generally opposed by the other powers and by the Turks themselves. In their weakness, the sultans consistently pursued the policy of seeking to prevent agreement among the powers, not too difficult a task.

3. *The Balkans.* The problem was further complicated by local considerations. The bulk of the European possessions of the Turks—roughly the Balkan peninsula—was inhabited by Christians, mainly of the Greek Orthodox persuasion. Religion playing the central role that it did among Moslems, by contrast with the secular West—the Sultan was also Caliph of Islam—the fact of Christianity had been the chief agency in preserving the distinct identity of the Balkan peoples. The Greek Patriarch of Constantinople, head of this Christian community and regarded by the sultans as its representative, was in effect an important official of the Ottoman state.

B. The Independence of Greece

1. The Greeks. This personage was normally drawn from the Greek community of Constantinople (Phanariotes). This community was important because of its wealth, largely drawn from commerce, an activity in which the Turks took little share. To a considerable extent also, Greeks, always a seafaring people, manned the fleets. This contributed to give the Greek element, as distinct from Bulgarian, Serb or other, a special position in the Ottoman Empire. The Greeks, moreover, however low and sad their current estate, especially in Greece proper, had the memory and example of "the glory that was Greece" to look back to. For some time there had been a revival of the Greek national spirit, in great part literary in its manifestations, as is normally the case with nationalities awakening after a long eclipse. The echoes of the French Revolution, though muffled, had reached distant Greece, and the revival began to take on political overtones, a desire for independence. [5]

2. The Greek Revolt. Active trouble began in 1821 with simultaneous action in the Danubian Principalities and in Greece proper (Morea). The Tsar, despite his sympathies (Ypsilanti had been allowed to prepare his filibustering expedition in Russia), refused to give the hoped-for support, and even disavowed Ypsilanti. Metternich's view that this was a rebellion against legitimate authority, the Sultan, a revolt moreover taking place "beyond the pale of civilization," prevailed, and the attempt in the Principalities was a failure. It went otherwise in Morea where the movement initiated a ten-year period of brutal and ferocious warfare.

3. The Powers Intervene. In western Europe there was much sympathy, largely romantic, for the revolting Greeks, but little concrete aid at first, despite such individual instances as that of Lord Byron. But as the war dragged on, European chancelleries began to concern themselves with the problem. The Sultan had appealed for help to his vassal, Mehemet Ali of Egypt. The new Tsar, Nicholas I, abandoning in 1826 the restraint of his predecessor, began to interfere more actively.

---

[5] As early as 1804, there had emerged a principality of Serbia, endowed with a degree of autonomy, but still under Turkish suzerainty.

By the Treaty of London (July, 1827), Russia, Britain, and France agreed to put an end to hostilities, and an Anglo-French fleet sailed for Greece.

By accident rather than design, this fleet became involved in action which resulted in the destruction of the Turco-Egyptian fleet in Navarino Bay in October, 1827. Greece, hard pressed, had been saved, but the issue was more than ever an international one. In April, 1828, losing patience with the tergiversations of the Sultan and of diplomacy, Russia declared war on Turkey.

The campaign proved more difficult than expected in Russia, but in the spring of 1829 Turkish resistance was broken, and the frightened Sultan signed the Treaty of Adrianople (September, 1829) which, in addition to providing for Greek independence, secured advantages for Russia in the Principalities.

This independence of Greece was formally sanctioned by the powers meeting in London (February, 1830). It was a very small Greece, leaving out much Greek-inhabited territory, but its sovereignty was unfettered by any limitations. All that remained was to give the new state a ruler, whom the three powers finally agreed should be Otto, the second son of the King of Bavaria, who thus became the first king of modern Greece.

IV. LIBERAL SUCCESSES AND FAILURES

The successful emancipation of Greece was as much a triumph of nationalism as of liberal forces, sympathetic to it. Despite the seemingly secure hold of reaction in the twenties, there were other instances of liberal successes at this time.

A. The Revolution of 1830 in France

In France, Charles X had succeeded his brother Louis XVIII in 1824. He was a thoroughgoing reactionary and acted accordingly, creating much discontent and opposition among a people whose wishes he willfully ignored. The climax came when he dismissed an uncongenial and relatively liberal ministry in 1829, arousing strong protests in the Chamber and in the press. Elections merely confirmed the strength of the opposition. The king's answer, in the form of four ordinances that dissolved the Chamber, curbed the press, and further restricted the franchise, produced an explosion at the end of July, 1830.

Three days of barricades and street fighting in Paris were sufficient to overthrow the government. Charles X took the road to exile, and the Chamber invited Louis Philippe, of the Orléans branch, to mount the throne. When the smoke of battle had cleared, the French revolution of 1830 proved to be a success of political economic liberalism. The Charter of 1814 was essentially maintained, but the fact is important that, instead of that document deriving its validity from the will of the ruler, it was he who derived his power from the will of the nation. This was given expression in his title, Louis Philippe I, King of the French—no longer of France.

A lowering of the property qualification widened the franchise, but the electorate was still not much above 200,000. The influence of the old aristocracy was weakened in the upper house through the abolition of the hereditary peerage. The year 1830 was definitely a triumph of the commercial, moneyed bourgeoisie, and Louis Philippe has been properly dubbed the bourgeois king, a role which he himself emphasized.

B. The Reform Bill of 1832 in England

The same forces that had won the day in France were clamoring for greater recognition in England. They were even stronger in the latter country, where industry was more advanced. The hold of reaction had been weakening in England despite the continued tenure of the conservatives. Legislation, economic and social, began to be enacted: partial repeal of navigation acts; freedom of association (1824). Catholic emancipation took place in 1829.

The advent of Louis Philippe in France was well received in England, especially when it became apparent that the orientation of the new government was moderate in its domestic as well as in its foreign policy. In the same year 1830, the accession of George IV to the throne weakened the support that the Tories had received from the Crown, and an election returned them to power with a much diminished majority. All this combined to give a fillip to the agitation for reform which had been going on for many years.

The issue was essentially, as in France, confined to the dominant layers of society; the rising, and by now powerful, industrial bourgeoisie wanted a recognition that the antiquated system of representation granted in disproportionate measure to the landowning aristocracy. The "rotten boroughs" were the clearest expression, most easily attacked, of the inadequacy of the representation. The Whigs, led by Grey, espoused the cause of electoral reform, to which the Prime Minister, Wellington, opposed an uncompromising refusal. Grey formed a ministry of Whigs and Canningites, and the defeat of a Reform Bill led to a dissolution of Parliament. The new House of Commons (1831) was favorable to reform, which was blocked by the Lords. Feeling ran high in the country, where agitation, enlisting the working class, reached impressive proportions. But in contrast with France, Britain's revolutions were too far in the past and had given way to an evolutionary tradition of political change.

The crisis was ultimately resolved through the device of threatening to create a sufficient number of new peers to procure an amenable majority. On this, as on other comparable occasions, when faced with inevitable defeat, the Lords yielded rather than destroy the exclusiveness of their order. In 1832, the great Reform Bill became law. It redistributed representation and increased the electorate from some 500,000 to about 800,000. The election of December, 1832 overwhelmingly endorsed the reform. Henceforth Whigs and Tories became known as Liberals and Conservatives. The British tradition of peaceful change had been further entrenched, and when the king sought to impose a Tory ministry in 1834, Robert Peel, calling an election, declared that the Reform Bill was accepted by the Tories. The Liberals were returned in the majority and in 1835 regained the prime-ministership.

C. Repercussions of 1830 Elsewhere in Europe

The liberal ferment which had achieved success in France and in Britain was not confined to those countries.

1. The Independence of Belgium. The former Austrian Netherlands, modern Belgium, which had in 1815 been incorporated with Holland, was largely different from that country. King William I showed little wisdom in imposing an essentially

Dutch administration in Belgium instead of allowing some scope for autonomy in a territory that was economically advanced and politically conscious of its diversity. The difficulties of the Dutch administration might have come to a head even earlier had it not been for the Belgian division between Catholics and Liberals.

These tendencies managed to come together in 1830. Encouraged by the example of events in Paris and confronted with the stubborn intransigeance of the Dutch ruler, they made revolution in Brussels in August 1830, and the movement culminated in a Belgian proclamation of independence. Not until 1839 did Holland recognize the irreversible fact, but Belgium was in effect independent from 1830.

This result was made possible by the action of the powers. The Belgian issue was an important one in the eyes of Europe. France, for reasons of ideology as well as of national interest, looked upon Belgian freedom with a kindly eye. Britain was not averse, with one proviso, that it be not a prelude to renewed French expansion. Metternich would have been inclined to respond to King William's appeal to the powers against this breach of the settlement of 1815, but Prussia would move only in the event that France threatened the Rhine. The Tsar was prepared to send armies which, however, found more pressing tasks nearer home, in Poland.

In these circumstances, the powers responded to an invitation to meet in London, where the Belgian problem was essentially solved at the beginning of 1831 through their recognition of the new state. An important part of their agreement was the declaration that they would henceforth respect Belgian neutrality, an engagement which held good until the German aggression of 1914. As in the case of Greece, there remained the question of finding a king for the new country. Peacefully inclined Louis Philippe made the solution easier by withdrawing the candidacy of his second son to whom the crown had been offered. Eventually, Prince Leopold of Saxe-Coburg, uncle of the future Queen Victoria, became King of the Belgians, a constitutional ruler, founding the reigning dynasty of Belgium.

2. Revolution Fails in Poland. The Greek and Belgian successes had no counterpart in central Europe. Poland, redivided since 1815, was under three different rules of varying quality and liberality. In the largest portion, the Russian Tsar Alexander had allowed considerable autonomy, constitutional practice, a separate administration and army. Nevertheless, opposition to the Russian connection, or a simple desire for moderate reform, persisted and came to a head in 1830 with the proclamation of a completely separate government. The revolution was inadequately led, it nourished illusions devoid of foundation on the likelihood of British and French assistance, and Russian armies put down the rebellion. The disillusioned Poles were subjected to brutal repression, lost their constitution, and, worst of all, became the objects of a deliberate policy of Russification. Many sought refuge in exile. With greater mildness, the Russian example was emulated in the Austrian and Prussian parts of the nation.

3. *Revolution Fails in Italy*. The hope of foreign assistance, specifically French in this case, likewise disappointed Italians whose risings achieved some initial and misleading successes in 1831. The bourgeois government of Louis Philippe was bent on reassuring Europe of its peaceful intentions. [6] Soon reaction was seemingly secure in the saddle again in Italy.

D. Europe, East and West

By 1830, or 1832, the ideological cleavage had been accentuated between western Europe and the rest of the continent. With the advent of Louis Philippe in France and the passage of the Reform Bill in England, these two countries had taken further steps along the democratic path, far though they still were from the ultimate goal of full political democracy.

As against this, in Prussia, in Austria, and in Russia, the agitation for reform had been a failure. Whether among their own peoples, or among alien populations whom they ruled, as in Poland and Italy, those governments had been able to withstand any concession to liberal demands, or had in some cases retrogressed. Metternich and the Tsar could take heart again and feel that the spirit of the Holy Alliance, albeit deprived of British and French cooperation, was still dominant over much

---

[6] The Italian situation became one of rivalry between France and Austria. The latter country sent forces into Italy, which France matched by landing troops in Ancona. Both countries withdrew their armies in 1838.

of Europe. It was destined to remain such until the signal came again from France for a renewal of revolutionary outbursts.

V. EUROPE IN MID-CENTURY

The revolutionary fever of 1830 abated, Europe remained undisturbed until the outbreaks of 1848. This was due in considerable measure to the fact that domestic change and growth absorbed the energies of its peoples. This economic growth and the thought that accompanied it will shortly be surveyed. We may briefly look first, however, at the relations and controversies among the powers, for these disputes, though subdued, remained important.

A. International Rivalries and Conflicts

1. The Eastern Question. The successful independence of Greece had left unsolved an issue between the Sultan and his vassal Mehemet Ali of Egypt. The rivalry of the powers over the Near East made this internecine Ottoman quarrel a European question.

a. THE RISE OF EGYPT. Mehemet Ali was an able and successful adventurer, whom the backward semifeudal condition of the Ottoman Empire had furnished with an opportunity to establish personal power in Egypt. No liberal, Mehemet Ali was progressive in that he understood the elements of power in a changing world. He provided Egypt with a more efficient administration, developed her economy, and modernized her armed land and naval forces. The technicians to whom he appealed for assistance were in large numbers French. Egypt for a half century was to become a Franco-British problem, for Britain, if she had no designs of her own on Egypt, did not wish her to fall under predominantly French influence.

Mehemet Ali wanted to consolidate and extend his power from the Sudan to Syria, and possibly into Arabia. Had it not been for outside interference, he would have been able to subdue for the Sultan the rebellious Greeks. From the fact that he wanted his price for assistance, regardless of the outcome in Greece, there developed a quarrel which degenerated into war. By the end of 1832, the Egyptian forces had conclusively shown their superiority over the Turkish.

At this juncture, the Sultan's appeal to the powers was eagerly answered by the Tsar. The appearance of Russian forces in Constantinople for his protection overshadowed Anglo-French differences. A compromise was effected with Mehemet Ali, and the Russians withdrew, but not until they had extorted from the Sultan an ostensible alliance (Treaty of Unkiar Iskelessi, July, 1833), whose secret terms made it tantamount to a Russian protectorate. There matters rested for a time, until Sultan Mahmud II, eager for revenge against his vassal, and thinking that he had adequately reorganized his forces, took the initiative of renewing hostilities. The military outcome in 1839 was the same as in 1832. This time Constantinople became the scene of rival British and French intrigues.

b. <u>Anglo-French Rivalry</u>. The French Prime Minister, Thiers, thought to effect a compromise favorable to his protégé, Mehemet Ali, and then to confront the powers with a *fait accompli*. Before this could be done, he was himself confronted with another *fait accompli*, the work of his nemesis, Palmerston, the British Foreign Minister, in the form of a four-power agreement, excluding France, for concerted action in the East (Treaty of London, July, 1840). Feeling ran high in France over the prospect of the revival of the 1814 alliance, and there was talk of war. Bellicose Thiers was dismissed by the more peacefully inclined Louis-Philippe; Guizot, an anglophile, succeeded him, a compromise was arranged for the Near East, and the crisis blew over. In the process, Britain had scored a definite diplomatic victory over France, and incidentally over Russia, for a revised international Convention of the Straits (July, 1841) went far to undo the unilateral Russian advantage of Unkiar Iskelessi.

Anglo-French rivalry cropped up in many quarters. There had been virtually no British opposition to the French occupation of Algiers in 1830, just before the fall of Charles X, an occupation which, after some hesitation, the government of Louis-Philippe decided to make permanent and extend, thus laying the basis of the future vast African holdings of France. But in Spain the two powers eyed each other with suspicion.

2. The Spanish Marriages. Spain was troubled by civil war during the thirties between the partisans of the claimant

Don Carlos, brother of Ferdinand, who had died without male issue, and those of Ferdinand's daughter Isabella. By 1839, the Carlist forces were defeated. A similar situation had developed in Portugal, and there also, Maria Christina won out against her uncle Don Miguel. These results were, in a measure, successes for liberalism, and served to emphasize the cleavage between East and West in Europe. There was made in 1834 a quadruple alliance [7] involving Britain, France, Isabella, and Maria Christina, against which agreement the three eastern powers manifested their displeasure by simultaneously withdrawing their representatives from Madrid. The presence in office of Aberdeen in England and of Guizot in France made for superficially better relations between the two countries. The expression "first Entente Cordiale" has even been used, but it is premature. Differences between them over Isabella's prospective spouse were complicated by the intrigues of their respective ambassadors in Madrid and the return of Palmerston with his highhandedness to the Foreign Office in 1846. The affair of the Spanish marriages restored Anglo-French relations to their normal state of suspicious acrimony.

3. Imperial Expansion and Conflicts. These two powers began to meet as well on the opposite side of the planet. The quarrel of rival missionaries in Tahiti ended with French control of that Pacific island, but not until much feeling had been aroused, feeling which incidentally, forecast of more recent occasions, ran higher among peoples than governments. British Far Eastern interests, through India, were of long standing and growing. They led to the Opium War with China, as a result of which the Treaty of Nanking in 1842 opened certain Chinese ports to foreign trade. China was soon compelled to extend similar privileges to France and to the United States.

The shadow of Russia's expansion in the Far East, and more especially in central Asia, was also beginning to enter British imperial calculations.

The pressure of imperial conflict was, however, a relatively minor factor during the first half of the century, mainly because there were still vast unpre-empted areas in the world and because economic developments nearer home absorbed the bulk of the nations' energy.

---

[7] Palmerston had initially sought to exclude France from the alliance.

B. Changes in Economic Practice and Thought

1. *The Industrial Revolution.* This phase, of relatively recent coinage, constitutes an apt recognition of the importance of the new phenomenon, industry, in shaping the course of mankind during the last century and a half.

Clearly, no specific date can be assigned to an obviously gradual change, but it may be said that the last third of the eighteenth century is the period in which the new development assumed recognizable shape. This it did first in England owing to the simultaneous existence of a suitable set of circumstances. The presence in close proximity of deposits of coal and iron, basic materials to this day, is one. But of equal importance are the prior economic growth of England, the progressiveness of her commercial class, the accumulation of capital, the fiscal policies of the state, and last but not least, a number of specific inventions and technical developments such as those associated with the name of James Watt.

By the time Napoleon was overthrown, English industry had assumed substantial proportions. Britain was launched on the path that was to make her the most highly industrialized nation in the world and had achieved a primacy that she was to retain throughout the century.

a. THE SECOND PHASE. The period from 1830 to 1870, sometimes described as the second phase of the industrial revolution, is that during which Britain effected the transformation to a virtually exclusively industrial economy. It is the period during which the application of steam to transportation, in the form of the railway engine, for the first time enabled man to overcome the limitations of his traditional modes of transportation depending upon animal power. Steam also began to displace sail on the seas. By mid-century, Europe was well launched on the building of its extensive railway system.

This growth of industry was uneven in space and time. Launched in England, it may be said to have gradually spread on an eastward course. Across the Channel, in Belgium and northern France, industry was next to be developed, and thence to the Rhineland and into Germany, whose level of development, by 1870, was roughly comparable with that of France. In the Habsburg domain proper (Bohemia) and in progressive

Piedmont, some industry began to grow, but the rest of Europe was still an overwhelmingly agrarian society by the middle of the century.

The growth and spread of industry went hand in hand with the expansion of financial activity. Industry created much wealth and in turn drew upon accumulated capital for its expansion. The importance of banking paralleled that of industry.

2. Economic Thought. Laissez Faire and Free Trade. These developments were accompanied by a changing outlook in economic thought. Already in the preceding century, Adam Smith and the Physiocrats had expounded the *laissez faire* philosophy. The new class in society, whose activity centered in industry, tended to be in favor of economic liberalism. Finding irksome the fetters of the mercantilist system, it thought it could best prosper under a system of free competition and enterprise. This tendency was particularly marked in England where it meant, in addition, the advocacy of free trade. The battle was fought out during the thirties and forties, led by such men as Richard Cobden and his Anti-Corn Law League. The repeal of the Corn Laws in 1846 [8] and of the last of the Navigation Acts in 1849 marked the definite victory of free trade, to which England remained long devoted thereafter. One consequence of this was the virtual destruction of English agriculture.

The continent did not enjoy the English advantage of earlier beginnings and, on the whole, remained devoted to protectionism. After a time, it became clear that the dream of a free-trade world was not to be realized. But the domestic aspects of economic liberalism flourished on the continent as well.

3. The Impact of Industry upon Society. The effects of the industrial phenomenon upon the structure of society were gradual and uneven, but deep. More and more the old putting-out system gave way to factories where the machines were

---

[8] The failure of the potato crop in Ireland in 1845 and the ensuing famine gave a fillip to the agitation for the repeal of the Corn Laws. It is worth noting that the population of Ireland was 8,500,000 in 1845. It had declined to 6,500,000 in 1851 and continued to decrease thereafter as a result of large and sustained emigration.

gathered, although it must be stressed that the farther back in time one goes, the more one finds of industry in the form of small undertakings, organized and directed by an individual owner-manager.

The labor force that tended the machines and manned the factories, small and large, naturally was in large part recruited from the fields. This labor force congregated in urban centers, with the result that the ratio of urban to rural population steadily increased. The growth of cities, especially in England first, was such as to warrant the expression "mushroom cities." With it went the customary problems of early urbanization.

But industry also introduced a new element of instability in the economy of nations. No longer were famines and the vagaries of the forces of nature to be feared so much as the fluctuation of prices and the operation of the market. The industrial worker, unlike the peasant growing part at least of his own prime necessities, was wholly dependent for his livelihood on money wages. Industry could not but accentuate the alternating cycle of boom and depression resulting from the ever-shifting balance between production and consumption.

An important aspect of the doctrine of economic liberalism was the belief in freedom of contract applied to labor. This meant that labor was to be regarded as a commodity, the value of which would be determined by the operation of the law of supply and demand, not interfered with by extraneous controls and regulations so familiar to our day. Such views may seem inhuman to a later age, and the conditions of British labor were truly miserable. Dickens and Marx have both, with different motives, depicted them.

The free-contract view was bolstered by analyses like that of Malthus at the beginning of the century, which stressed what they believed to be the inescapable effects of the constant pressure of population upon available resources. And it is indeed true that the enormous and unprecedented growth of Europe's population—roughly trebled during the nineteenth century—was in large part made possible by Europe's drawing on the food and raw material resources of the whole world, for which it paid with manufactures.

a. POLITICAL REPERCUSSIONS. The gloomy Malthusian outlook could hardly be expected to be supinely accepted by the victims of its operation. From the growing working class of England, to whom the Reform Bill of 1832 had brought no benefits, emerged the Chartist agitation. The core of the People's Charter was political: universal suffrage would provide the means to institute reforms. The small, but articulate, band of radicals espoused the extension of democratic practice. This agitation failed, and by 1848 the movement had virtually collapsed. This failure had much to do with the subsequent and long-adhered-to tendency of British labor to stress trade unionism rather than politics.

The Reform Bill of 1832, and the repeal of the Corn Laws in 1846, were triumphs of political and economic liberalism, manifestations of the growing power of the new capitalist industrial bourgeoisie in competition with the older landowning aristocracy. It was essentially the same group that reaped the benefits of the July days in Paris in 1830. Despite the devotion of this class to the ideal of noninterference by the state in matters economic and social, there began to be enacted in England a modicum of factory legislation.[9] But this was likely to be at first Tory rather than Liberal legislation.

The liberal outlook prevailed in matters imperial as well, and this is one reason why imperial rivalry was at a relatively low ebb prior to 1870. The view was held by many that colonies, like children, were eventually destined to abandon the family fold when they would reach maturity, and that coercion was therefore futile. To this view the example of American independence gave strength. Lord Durham's Report of 1839 laid the bases for self-government in the Canadian colonies.

4. The Victorian Compromise. In the case of England, the battles between Conservatives and Liberals were fought within the bounds of a wide area of agreement, sometimes described as the Victorian Compromise:[10] neither party questioned either the fundamentals of the British constitution or the fact that it was the proper appanage of an élite to govern society.

The greater strength of reaction and the precedent of the

---

[9] The first of these acts, dealing with children's employment and hours of labor, dates from 1819. This was extended and strengthened in 1833. There was a Mines Act in 1842 and another Factory Act in 1844.

[10] Queen Victoria came to the throne in 1837 and reigned until 1901.

French Revolution made for sharper divisions on the continent. In France especially, there flourished certain movements that are called socialistic. This socialism was of the utopian variety, in part derived from the Rousseau approach, and was concerned with broad schemes of social reorganization with a large humanitarian content. It produced some interesting experiments, but had little effect in practice.[11]

Of greater moment was the influence of the "utilitarian" approach associated with Jeremy Bentham (1748-1832). Such "radicals" as he, James Mill, and Richard Cobden were the standard-bearers of the early agitation for reform in England.

Later in the century, John Stuart Mill (1806-1873), influenced by both Bentham and Comte, carried on the tradition under the banner of the "new liberalism," stressing the need for social reform along with the devotion to individual liberty. Mill's *Essay on Liberty* remains a classic to this day.

VI. THE INTELLECTUAL CLIMATE OF THE PERIOD

The concern with economic growth and political change did not monopolize the thought of Europe, whose activity flourished in many directions. Scientific development was not at this time, as it was to become later, closely connected with the industrial, but science was well launched on its astounding career of expansion, which the twenty-five years of warfare at the turn of the century did not interrupt. Perhaps the most significant aspect of this phenomenon is the rapid accumulation of a vast store of knowledge, an accumulation the rate of which was destined to increase with time. The very quantity of information, as well as its diversity, made for enforced specialization. More and more, the scientist and the scholar were compelled to devote their efforts to the study of a particular field of knowledge, and often to some branch of a particular field.

One consequence of this scientific growth was the progressive encroachment of science into the domain that traditionally had belonged to philosophy. Science is not philosophy, but the latter had to take increasing notice of the contributions,

---

[11] Saint-Simon and Fourier in France, Robert Owen in England belong in this development. Utopian socialism also flourished in the United States.

presumably less speculative, of the former. Fact tended to be worshipped. The positivism of Auguste Comte (1798-1857) is an apt expression of this state of affairs.

The brilliant eighteenth-century contribution to mathematics was continued, especially in France and Germany, though by no means confined to those countries. In astronomy, physics, and chemistry important new discoveries were made and theories propounded. Most significant of all was the new organization of scientific inquiry which came to center in the universities. Mainly under state sponsorship, except in England, these ancient institutions became the modern centers of learning that we know, and new ones came into existence. The victory of the eighteenth century enlightenment was made manifest in their secularization.

The natural sciences, hitherto less advanced than the exact and physical, also made progress preparatory to the great blossoming later in the century.

The so-called social sciences, disciplines with a large literary content, sought to emulate the qualities of precision usually associated with scientific disciplines. The desire for accurate knowledge of man's past led to the search into the extant records of that past. German scholarship led the field, emulated by others. The vast collection *Monumenta Germaniae Historica* is a typical product of the activity of the new historical school whose aim was best expressed by Ranke's ideal of writing history *wie es eigentlich gewesen* (as it actually occurred). Beyond the written record of man, archeology, prehistory, and anthropology undertook a great task of reconstruction and analysis. The work of Champollion in Egypt, that of Schliemann at Troy, are instances of this activity in its most spectacular form.

Such discoveries have a romantic quality. And the early part of the century was the romantic age. From its original eighteenth-century home in Germany and England, the movement penetrated in France and elsewhere on the continent. It was a reaction against eighteenth-century rationalism, and its manifestations were outstanding in the pictorial arts, in music, and in literature. Along with scholarship, it rehabilitated the Middle Ages, considered dark since the Renaissance.

There was also a revival of interest in religion after the great revolutionary upheaval. But in this case the part of scholarship worked in a contrary direction, for the new Higher Criticism, where again German scholarship took the lead, tended to weaken the hold of holy books and of tradition. Such an approach could logically best prosper in the Protestant atmosphere of free inquiry or in the hands of free thinkers; the Church of Rome had little part in it.

The economic and political changes brought ever larger masses of men in contact with the forces that molded a changing world. Education and the demand for it at the lower levels were spreading, a phenomenon that gave sharpness to the long-term issue of the control of education. The church, traditional dispenser of education, fought to retain this privilege. The issue is not settled to our day, but, allowing for many vicissitudes in the contest, the tendency was to increase the area of control of the secular state.

All these developments went on apace. Literary, artistic, and scientific production flowed on uninterrupted, reflecting and in turn acting upon the intellectual climate of the time. The direction of thought gradually altered. In the political realm a major upheaval was to shake most of Europe at the exact middle of the century.

CHAPTER 2

The Revolution that Failed: 1848-1852

I. THE SECOND FRENCH REPUBLIC

A. Background and Causes of the Revolution of 1848 in France

Britain and France led Europe on the road of political progress—or change—the chief agency of which in the middle of the nineteenth century was the capitalist bourgeois class.

The instauration of Louis Philippe in France was an instance of bourgeois success, and the July Monarchy was a thoroughgoing bourgeois regime well represented by the king's chief ministers, Guizot and Thiers. There was considerable economic growth in France under the bourgeois king.

The further victory of this same class in England in 1846 has been mentioned. But there were other, and different, elements in the French situation. For one thing, there was in France, a "legitimate" claimant to the throne, hence a legitimist party unreconciled to the Orléans ruler. For another, the actual carrying of revolution in 1830 had been, in part at least, the work of the proletariat of Paris. This group had reaped few benefits from a regime dedicated to the laissez faire ideal. It did not have the vote, but the tradition of the barricades belonged to it. There were Republicans in France, and among them a left wing of radical reformers.

Catholics felt at best lukewarm toward a regime which had tampered with the Catholic hold on education. The uninspired foreign policy of the king commanded little enthusiasm in any quarter: his genuine devotion to peace had caused him to take action that opinion regarded as ignominious surrender to England.

Faced with increasing opposition, the administration of Guizot, chief minister from 1840 to 1848, had taken on an increasingly dictatorial character. The economic crisis of 1847 helped to increase the mounting discontent.

B. The Revolution

1. *The First Phase.* Unable to voice its grievances in a muzzled press, the opposition resorted to the device of holding large banquets at which its demands, primarily electoral reform, were aired. The government's ban of one of these occasions, on February 12, 1848, was the signal for demonstrations which, when fired upon, turned into revolution.

The work of revolution was brief. Even the national guard had joined the demonstrators, and on the 24, Louis Philippe took the road of exile to England after abdicating in favor of his grandson. The provisional government proclaimed France a republic, for the second time in her history.

Like the revolution of 1830, that of 1848 was the work of a conglomeration of forces that had little in common beside their opposition to the existing system. But it took somewhat longer for the smoke of battle to settle than in 1830. The influence of the Parisian proletariat was paramount at first, and the Second Republic reflected this fact in its initial radical orientation. Elections were decreed for a National Assembly by universal manhood suffrage, in itself a very radical measure for the time. Moreover, social problems loomed equally large with political, and the socialist Louis Blanc obtained the creation of "national workshops," an institution implying the recognition—premature as it turned out to be—of responsibility of the state in securing the right of employment. [1]

2. *The Second Phase.* At this point there occurred a phenomenon repeated more than once in France. The initial shape of the Second Republic was to a large extent the result of Parisian influence. But Paris is a very large urban agglomeration, unrepresentative of the country at large. [2] The latter

---

[1] Unemployment was severe at this time. In actual practice, the national workshops, hastily set up, turned out to be a device for providing a temporary dole to the unemployed.

[2] The discrepancy between Paris and other urban centers in France has no counterpart in any other European country. This phenomenon, and the consequent primacy of Paris, is a consequence of the long tradition of high centralization of the French state.

returned a National Assembly far more conservative in its composition than the original provisional government.

One of the first acts of this Assembly upon meeting in June was to abolish the socialistically inspired national workshops. For the second time barricades rose in Paris. But the workers were alone this time, and the second revolution (June 24-26) was ruthlessly crushed by armed forces under the command of General Cavaignac, entrusted with full powers by the Assembly. This thorough defeat of radicalism was correspondingly a triumph for the moderate forces (Catholic, peasant, and bourgeois) henceforth in control of the Second Republic.

There remained to elect a President, which was done in December. General Cavaignac was a candidate and might have won the office but for the intrusion of an unexpected rival in the person of Prince Louis Napoleon.

3. Louis Napoleon. This personage was the son of Louis Bonaparte, one of Napoleon's brothers, who was king of Holland at the time of Louis Napoleon's birth. With the death of the Duke of Reichstadt, Napoleon's own son, in 1832, Louis Napoleon assumed the headship of the family and appropriated the inheritance of the Napoleonic claim and tradition, the latter fast becoming legend by this time. The lack of clarity in Louis Napoleon's thought, either before or after 1848, has made him to this day a highly controversial figure, object of widely varying estimates. In his youth he had been active with Italian *carbonari;* the principle of nationality ever appealed to him. He had taken an interest in social questions, as his *Extinction of Poverty* indicates. More important perhaps, his *Napoleonic Ideas* contained an interpretation of the work of his famous uncle, thwarted, he claimed, by the forces of reaction. The first Napoleon had indeed, among other things, called himself a son of the Revolution, which in a sense he was, and whose ideas he had more effectively spread abroad than the initial revolutionaries themselves.

In 1836 and 1840, Louis Napoleon had attempted abortive putsches at Strasbourg and at Boulogne. Imprisoned, he had escaped to England where his residence in 1848 had had the advantage of preventing his involvement in the initial phase of the French turmoil. Returning to France, he knew how to put to best use a very modern aptitude for demagoguery which he possessed in high degree. As a candidate for the presidency, he managed to be all things to all men: a defender of order to conservatives, a hope of reform to the workers, a restorer of French glory to all. The prestige of the Napoleonic name was great, and the outcome of the free consultation of the French electorate was that Louis Napoleon received 5,400,000 votes to 1,500,000 for Cavaignac. [3]

The election of Louis Napoleon to the presidency of France posed a great question mark, both in regard to the future domestic course of the country and to the role that it might seek to play abroad. But in the year 1848 much of Europe was involved in upheavals the course of which must first be traced.

II. REVOLUTIONS IN CENTRAL EUROPE

A. The Habsburg Domain in 1848

If France, and especially Paris, was in the eyes of the rest of the continent the standard bearer of revolutionary change, asserting the principle that the nation, rather than the ruler, was the repository of sovereignty, Vienna may be regarded as the opposite ideological pole to Paris. In Vienna Metternich was ruling, and since 1815 he had been able to ride successfully whatever storms had broken out.

The Habsburg influence was paramount through central Europe. In addition to the Austrian Empire proper, Austrian leadership asserted itself through the presidency of the German Confederation where the Prussian challenge of its primacy had been relatively weak during this period, and throughout most of the Italian peninsula, by means of dynastic connections and as the main bulwark of reaction. The prime directive of Austrian policy was the preservation of this state of affairs.

Though weaker than in the two leading western countries, liberal agitation was not unknown in the central European world. Constitutionalism was its slogan: somewhat naively perhaps, liberals tended to endow the word *constitution* with inherently magic properties.

---

[3] There were two other candidates, Ledru-Rollin and Lamartine, but their role was confined to that of "also rans." They received 370,000 and 18,000 votes, respectively.

1. Nationalism in Central Europe. But the situation in the central European area of Habsburg dominance was complicated by an entirely different factor, the force of nationalism. In Italy especially, the desire for unification could easily be identified with that to rid the land of the dominant Austrian, hence alien, influence: liberalism and nationalism went hand in hand in Italy.

It was slightly otherwise in the German Confederation, for Austria was, in part at least, Germanic. From the German liberal point of view, Vienna and Berlin were equally reactionary; from the nationalist point of view, the question was whether German unity should be confined to purely German lands or not, the so-called *klein-deutsch* versus the *gross-deutsch* solution. More concretely, should or should not Austria be included in a united Germany? The bulk of the Austrian domain was not German. The leading German state was Prussia. Prussia included non-German lands, but, unlike Austria, its greater bulk was German. The issue between the advocates of *klein-* and *gross-Deutschland* grafted itself therefore on the old dynastic rivalry between Habsburgs and Hohenzollerns.

In the Habsburg domain proper, among the non-German peoples there were, in addition to the Italians of Lombardo-Venetia, Hungarians, and various groups of Slavs, Czechs, Poles, and diverse South Slavs.[4] Here also, liberalism and nationalism could go hand in hand. Metternich and the Austrian government, quite consistently from their point of view, were inimical to nationalism, which they considered a threat to the very existence of the Empire. More narrowly, within the Germanic world, they felt it to be a potential asset to the Prussian position and correspondingly detrimental to their own.

This is the background of the central European situation.

B. The Italian Revolutions

1. The First Phase. Revolutionary outbreaks in Italy had actually preceded those in France. They first occurred in

---

[4] There were also Roumanians in Transylvania. Their agitation for independence was not an issue at this time, and in any event remained an essentially Hungarian problem.

Naples at the end of January and in Turin in February. In both places they resulted in the grant or promise of constitutions. The Sardinian charter, or *Statuto*, promulgated on March 4, was destined to have a long history and lasting consequences.

When news was received in Italy that revolution had succeeded in Vienna, the very stronghold of reaction, a wave of revolutionary enthusiasm swept the entire peninsula. In Milan, the Austrian forces were expelled by the people, and the same was done in Venice under Manin's leadership. The movement took on the color of one for national liberation and unification. On March 23, Sardinia declared war on Austria. The initial response was widespread in Italy, contingents from all quarters moving to join the Sardinian forces. Hard pressed at home, the Austrians were reduced to a holding action in the shelter of the Quadrilateral fortresses. It soon appeared, however, that the Sardinian army would receive little effective assistance; the Pope, for instance, refused to engage in offensive war against a Christian ruler. Although the Sardinian army gave a good account of itself in the field, its strategy was faulty; the Austrians, led by Radetzky, had time to retrieve themselves, and in June, at Custozza, the Piedmontese were defeated, after which an armistice was signed.

2. Attitude of the Powers. The attitude of the powers, especially France, was important at this juncture. As early as March, the French government took the position that it would not intervene in Italy which, for that matter, had proclaimed through Charles Albert the intention to proceed unaided (*Italia farà da sè*).

In England, Palmerston had watched the initial outbreak with more sympathy than concern, but as the movement spread he thought it prudent to seek its containment. He urged compromise in both Turin and Vienna. England, at this time, wanted neither the destruction of Austria nor a united Italy, but was more concerned lest France become involved in Italy or Russia gain some advantage in the East.[5] With the defeat of Piedmont in the field, both England and France sought to

---

[5] Russia herself was unaffected by the revolutionary outbreaks of 1848. She assumed an attitude of neutrality, conditional upon others doing the same, but proceeded to occupy the Danubian Principalities.

mediate between her and an Austria that was regaining confidence.

C. The Revolution in Austria and Germany

The successful liberal uprising in Vienna in March has been mentioned. It resulted in the final withdrawal of Metternich and the calling of a constitutional assembly that met in July. But revolution was not confined to Vienna. In Budapest and Prague as well, similar triumphs of liberalism were registered. In the latter city, there convened in June a Pan-Slavic Congress representing the various Slav elements of the Habsburg Empire; a cleavage had begun to appear among Viennese and Hungarian liberals on the issue of freedom for the Slavs.

In the German Confederation, the frightened princes were found yielding to the usual liberal demand for constitutions in state after state. Rioting in Berlin induced unstable Frederick William IV to display momentary enthusiasm for the movement.

The defeat of Metternichism in the Germanic world gave a fillip to the idea of German unification which liberal reformers espoused with enthusiasm. The Diet of the Confederation at Frankfort sanctioned the somewhat irregular call for a German National Assembly, elected by universal suffrage, to draw up plans for a federal government.[6] This Assembly, the Frankfort Parliament, met in May and proceeded to adopt a typical expression of mid-nineteenth century European liberal nationalism in the "Fundamental Rights of the German Nation."

D. The Turning of the Tide

By mid-1848 the tide of revolution seemed to be running full and the whole Metternichian structure, whether in terms of antiliberal institutions or in those of Habsburg power, looked as if it might be swept away. As it turned out, Metternich had given up too soon. The Habsburgs were saved by two things: the army, which remained loyal, and the rivalries of the nationalities that they were able to exploit. In addition, it has been pointed out that the revolution was the work of cities

---

[6] The Diet itself was rather a congress of diplomats representing the states. The call for an election was the initiative of a group of liberals whose agitation preceded the revolution in Berlin.

where liberalism had most of its strength among bourgeois and intellectual groups. In the still predominantly agrarian world of central Europe, the broad masses had been little touched as yet by the liberal ferment.

1. Prague, Vienna, and Italy. The tide turned quite sharply in June. During that month, Prince Windischgrätz restored "order" in Prague, dispersed the Pan-Slavic Congress, and put Bohemia under martial law. Radetzky, reinforced in Italy, inflicted the above-mentioned defeat of Custozza on the Piedmontese. The more conservative government issued from the French elections was less than ever likely to assist liberal movements outside of France.

These developments heartened conservatives in Austria. In October, Vienna was subdued by the combined pressure of armies under Prince Windischgrätz and under the governor of Croatia, Jellacich. The following month saw the appointment of Prince Felix Schwarzenberg, a true and capable successor of Metternich whose tradition he reinstated.

2. Hungary. The Croatian army of Jellacich had been intent on crushing the Hungarian movement, a fact illustrative of national rivalries. While he cooperated with Windischgrätz, the liberals in Budapest and in Vienna had sought correspondingly to effect an alliance. The fall of the latter city was therefore a setback for the former. In January, Budapest was occupied by Austrian forces.

But this was not the end of the Hungarian movement which, instead of collapsing, took on a new lease on life under the vigorous leadership of Louis Kossuth. A republic and complete independence were proclaimed in Hungary in April, 1849, while new forces were being organized. At this point, the Tsar responded to the Austrian appeal for assistance. Foreign intervention from some other quarter could alone have saved Hungary at this juncture. But no such was forthcoming, in spite of desperate appeals, and the republic collapsed in August after the country had been overrun by Austrian and Russian armies.

3. The German Question. While the Habsburgs were restoring their position in their own domain, the Austrian government had temporized on the German problem. This proved to be sound policy.

The example of successful reaction in Vienna was not lost on the Prussian king. Taking heart from it, he installed a reactionary ministry in Berlin in the autumn of 1848, having previously put an end to the conflict with Denmark.[7]

The triumph of reaction in both Austria and Prussia was awkward for the Frankfort liberals. They had considered the Austrian emperor as their first choice to wear the German crown. After protracted and wordy debates, they finally agreed upon the draft of a constitution in April, 1849 and proceeded to offer the crown to the Prussian king. He hesitated for a while, but finally refused the offer of a crown from the "gutter," meaning liberal and popular in origin, and because of the perhaps more serious factor of opposition from other German states and from the powers, most of all from the Habsburgs.

a. OLMÜTZ. This yielding was a humiliation for Prussia. Frederick William sought to retrieve it by inviting the other German states, except Austria, to form a union under Prussia's presidency. The representatives of seventeen German states that accepted the invitation met at Erfurt in March, 1850. But by now Schwarzenberg felt that Austria was sufficiently secure and strong to enforce a veto. For a time the prospect of war loomed as a possibility when Prussia mobilized, but Frederick William recoiled before an Austrian ultimatum, and in November, 1850, accepted the treaty of Olmütz, a long-rankling humiliation to Prussia, which restored the *status quo ante* in the Germanic world.

4. *The Second Phase in Italy.* Matters in Italy did not completely subside after the defeat of Piedmont in 1848. While the situation was being restored in the north, new and more violent outbursts occurred elsewhere. At the end of 1848, Pope Pius IX had to flee from Rome, where a republic was proclaimed in the following February. Mazzini was its leading

---

[7] The Duchies, Schleswig and Holstein, had since 1815, been ruled by the King of Denmark. Holstein was German in population and part of the German Confederation. The Danish King's attempt to incorporate Schleswig into Denmark, following a liberal revolt in the Duchies in 1848, resulted in war between Denmark and the Confederation, a war which was fought by Prussia in behalf of the latter. Russia, Britain, and France put pressure on Frederick William to respect the treaties of 1815. In August, 1848, a truce was concluded and Prussian forces withdrawn.

spirit. Similar situations developed in Florence and in Naples, and threatened in Turin. Yielding to pressure, Charles Albert renewed the war with Austria in March, 1849. The move was ill-advised, for by the end of the month he had met disaster at Novara. He abdicated in favor of Victor Emmanuel II, his son, and Piedmont was fortunate to escape with a humiliating but not punitive peace.

With Austrian help, the former rulers and status were also restored in Tuscany and in the Two Sicilies, while Venice was being finally reduced. The Roman situation presented greater complexity. It was the one instance of French intervention. For reasons of domestic politics (the pressure of Catholic opinion) and of balance of power (counterbalancing Austrian influence in Italy), Louis Napoleon sent a force which overthrew the Roman Republic and reinstated the Pope in Rome in June, 1849.

III. THE BALANCE SHEET

By the middle of 1849, the various states of Europe were all restored to order. The revolutionary fever had spent itself and the revolutions had failed.

A. Gains of Liberalism

Some traces of the upheaval nevertheless remained. In Britain and in France, the tradition of constitutionalism and representative institutions was confirmed and strengthened. In some small countries of the West, there had been progress in the same direction: Switzerland emerged with a federal democratic constitution; in Holland and in Denmark, the rulers also granted constitutions, and in Piedmont, despite Austrian threats and pressure, the *Statuto* of 1848 was maintained as the law of the state. These liberal gains in these small states were destined to be permanent. Nowhere, however, save in France, was the practice of universal suffrage adopted, but the granting of a franchise, however initially restricted, was clearly a step in the long-term direction of universality.

For the longer term, the effects throughout Central Europe were deep and lasting. Despite such remnants as the Prussian constitution of 1850, the victory of reaction in that part of Europe may be said to have been complete. The fact remained, nevertheless, that the threat to the established order had been serious; far more so than at any time since 1815.

B. The Workers and Socialism

One important and new—new at least in degree—aspect of the outbreaks of 1848 was the part played in them by the industrial working class. The workers and the liberal bourgeois had little in common besides their opposition to existing regimes. The case of France is a good illustration of how the second group deprived the first of participation in the benefits of change. Where liberalism succeeded in asserting itself at all, it was still essentially the same economic liberalism described earlier.

Socialism, which hitherto had been for the most part of the utopian variety, was about to take a novel orientation, so-called "scientific." The thought and influence of Louis Blanc were important factors in the initial stages of the second French Republic. It was in January, 1848 that Marx and Engels published their *Communist Manifesto*.

To be sure, this famous document attracted little notice and had no influence at the time. It was none the less an apt and vigorous criticism of the existing state of affairs and a harbinger of change. Reduced to its simplest and most effectively attractive form, Marx's argument, largely based on his analysis of the conditions prevailing in English industry, asserted that the workers could and would liberate themselves from the operation of the presumably inexorable iron law of wages. "Workers of the world unite, you have nothing to lose but your chains," was destined to become a slogan the power of which has by no means evaporated yet.

This Marxian approach, whatever its merits on other scores, was representative of a tougher and more realistic outlook than the utopian. The romantic age of revolution, barricades, flag waving, and speeches, was passing. Revolution, too, was to become "scientific," consciously guided by economic fact and thought instead of by a vague humanitarian wish for justice and the good society. These last aims, to be sure, would also be realized, but rather as ultimate by-products. The thing to do meanwhile was to concentrate on correct economic and historic analysis. [8]

---
[8] For a further discussion of Marxism, see Chapter IV.

C. The Second French Empire

The election of Louis Napoleon to the presidency of France at the end of 1848 and the combination of circumstances that made that result possible have been indicated: briefly, Louis Napoleon had succeeded in gathering the support of disparate opinion by contriving to mean all things to all men. The question mark about him remained.

For a time Louis Napoleon continued to please widely divergent groups: social legislation (old age insurance) showed his solicitude for the workers; industry was encouraged at the same time; the restoration of the Pope through the agency of French arms and the education act of 1850 pleased the Catholics. The Assembly, elected at the same time as the President, reflected a predominantly conservative temper. By 1850, it proceeded to enact legislation restricting the franchise. Out of this action grew a conflict with the President, who shrewdly took the position of defender of popular rights. A year later, after an ultimatum to the Assembly, Louis Napoleon effected a *coup d'état*, dissolving that body, and proclaiming a temporary dictatorship.

A consultation of the electorate [9] endorsed the action of the President by 7,500,000 to 640,000 and empowered him to revise the constitution of 1848. The chief feature of the new constitution, of January, 1852, was the strengthening of the executive. The situation was reminiscent of that of 1799, and the similarity continued to hold after the *coup d'état* of 1851. The year 1852 was spent by Louis Napoleon in preparing the ground for the final step: traveling the length and breadth of the country, he successfully managed the role of appealing to a wide variety of opinion. On December 2, 1852, with the sanction of a new plebiscite, Louis Napoleon became Napoleon III, Emperor of the French.

The assumption of the imperial title meant little in actual fact. It was nevertheless a gesture of which Europe could hardly fail to take notice. In France, Napoleon III sought to present the Empire as the successful culmination of the revolution. But the First Empire was inextricably associated, at home and abroad, with visions of conquest and military glory. To be

---

[9] The government did its best to prevent opposition activity, but despite this pressure it may fairly be said that the electorate acquiesced in the coup.

sure, Napoleon III had proclaimed that the Empire meant peace, and he had also reinstated the Pope in Rome. In 1852, Napoleon was still an enigma. Would he seek to emulate his famous uncle, or would he join the ranks of those other rulers who by this time seemed safely restored to their positions threatened in 1848, and work with them to keep Europe on the paths of conservatism and peace?

In a sense, the enigma was never to be clarified. If Napoleon III did not embark on a career of military conquest, for the eighteen years that the empire lasted, France, or rather the Emperor, pursued a very active foreign policy that often held the center of the European stage.

CHAPTER 3

Triumphs of Nationalism: 1852-1870

Whether by the standards of political or of national liberalism, the revolutions of 1848 had been failures. But the setback was only temporary. By the time two decades had elapsed, the map of central Europe was to have been completely remade, to a considerable extent in accordance with the wishes of successful nationalism, and in part at least under the aegis of liberal institutions.

The story of these two decades and of these nationalistic successes might be written around the foreign policy of the Second French Empire which was deeply involved in them. Napoleon III was sympathetic to the principle of nationality; but the application of this principle in central Europe threatened to be detrimental to the position of France in Europe as a whole. Hence the never-resolved contradictions among which the Emperor's policy floundered. It soon became clear that he was not bent on duplicating his uncle's career of conquest. He was anxious, however, to enhance French prestige abroad, for this would consolidate his position at home. An opportunity for action was soon to be at hand.

I. THE CRIMEAN WAR

A. Background and Immediate Origin of the War

This episode, which started as "a quarrel of monks," soon developed into an important chapter in the everlasting Near Eastern question.

Matters had been on the whole quiescent in the Ottoman Empire since the early forties. In Palestine, part of the Turkish province of Syria, there were, for religious reasons, shrines of especial sentimental interest to the great faiths that had originated in the Near East: Judaism, Christianity, and Islam, especially the first two. In the course of time, Christianity had split into a variety of sects, two of which, the Roman Catholic and the Greek Orthodox, enjoyed special privileges in the holy places, under the relatively impartial and indifferent Turkish rule. For centuries, France had filled the role of protector of western (Catholic) Christians in the Ottoman Empire; in the eighteenth century, Russia had achieved a similar position for those of the eastern persuasion, a fact that could be put to good use in her general policy of southward encroachment. Behind the often undignified and petty quarrels of the rival monks there stood therefore the rival influences of Russia and of France.

Prior to 1850, the Orthodox monks had been extending their influence at the expense of western missions. Napoleon III, become Emperor, and in addition irritated by the unfriendly attitude of the Tsar toward him, thought to achieve a small diplomatic success by restoring the situation in the holy places. Caught between rival pressures, the Sultan sought to gain time by giving satisfaction to both sides through the issuance of contradictory decrees. This merely confused the situation further, but by this time the powers, especially Britain, had become interested in the question. When Prince Menschikoff appeared in Constantinople and sought to intimidate the Sultan, Britain assumed the role of chief resister to the Russian demands.

B. The War

Protracted negotiations involving the powers and the Porte broke down with the Russian refusal to evacuate the Danubian Principalities which had been occupied, the Turkish initiation of hostilities, and Russian naval action in the Black Sea which incensed public opinion, particularly in England. By early 1854, Britain and France joined Turkey in war against Russia. A year later, they had induced Sardinia to join them.

Austria having meantime replaced the Russians in occupation of the Principalities, the "unnecessary" war was fought in the Crimea. The allies suffered their greatest losses from difficulties of supply and faulty organization, but managed nevertheless to score successes against the Russians. By 1856, the accession of a new Tsar in 1855, Russian setbacks, weariness on all sides, the growing French conviction of the futility of the enterprise, had prepared the ground for termination of hostilities and the elaboration of a settlement to take place in Paris. Because of the cost it involved in both blood and treasure, and because of the logistics problems which had to be solved, the Crimean war has been called the first modern war.

C. The Congress of Paris (1856)

This congress represented the Concert of Europe in successful operation. Diplomatically well prepared, the congress worked expeditiously. The peace was not punitive, registering mainly the negative result of having blocked Russian expansion, to which the demilitarization of the Black Sea constituted an important setback. Much stress was placed on the principle of international action, the integrity of the Ottoman Empire being jointly guaranteed by the powers, who likewise substituted themselves collectively to Russia in regard to the Principalities. The status of Serbia was similarly guaranteed. The powers, professing to accept the Sultan's word at face value, henceforth renounced the right to interfere in behalf of any of his subjects.

Other matters of international interest were taken up and provided for at the congress: the navigation of the Danube, and the freedom of the seas. The congress marked a peak in European harmony. France's, and Napoleon's, prestige stood high.

II. THE UNIFICATION OF ITALY

The only power which did not fare well at Paris was Austria. This was largely due to a clumsy diplomacy which, seeking to derive advantage from a war fought by others, had contrived to elicit the discontent of all. Even more specifically, Cavour, representing Sardinia at the congress, had managed to raise before it the Italian "question" as one of European concern.

A. The Italian "Question"

This question had two aspects: increasingly, the nationalistic one of unification; but also that of the repressive nature of most of the regimes in the Italian states, regimes depending in varying degrees upon Austrian support.

The risings of 1820, 1830, and 1848 have been mentioned. They had all failed, but the last failure had served to clarify the situation. Italy still fitted Metternich's description of "a geographical expression," but the idea of national unification had made considerable progress since the first Napoleon had given it its initial modern impulse. It had been an important aspect of the agitation of 1848.

1. The Risorgimento. The half century after 1815 is known as the *Risorgimento* in Italian history. The desire for unity, drawing upon ancient historic memory, was largely confined to the relatively small educated and literate middle class. Diverse currents ran through it. Mazzini, representing the most radical view, wanted a republic; he spent most of his

life in exile, unsuccessfully plotting and agitating for the realization of this premature ideal. Gioberti envisioned a federal structure under the presidency of the Pope. A third group looked to Piedmont, the only truly independent state, to lead the movement. All those in favor of unification were opposed to the existing regimes and, inevitably, to Austria.

By 1850, the Mazzinian and the Giobertian solutions were substantially discredited. There remained Piedmont whose king, though defeated militarily, had refused to abrogate the *Statuto* of 1848. The events of 1848 also resulted in the emergence to the prime ministership of Sardinia of Cavour, one of the outstanding statesmen of the century.

B. Cavour

Count Cavour has been correctly described as a typical mid-nineteenth century liberal of the English school. In the context of his time, he was an essentially progressive and modern man, fully aware of the importance of economic factors and of the trend toward constitutionalism and representation. The uncongenial nature of the Piedmontese state prior to 1848 had caused him to withdraw into private activity where he had made a conspicuous financial success. Following the new orientation of 1848, he entered the Cabinet in 1850; by 1852 he was Prime Minister. Within less than ten years—he died in 1861—Italian unity was a virtually accomplished fact.

1. Cavour's Policy and Diplomacy. With single-minded devotion to the new constitutional order of Piedmont, he first embarked on a program of domestic reform designed to modernize and strengthen the state. Cavour, in addition, clearly understood these things: unification meant war with Austria, which Italy unaided, let alone Piedmont, could not successfully wage; England would supply sympathy, but no power; France, therefore, must be his ally.

In 1855, Cavour brought Piedmont into the Crimean war where Piedmont had not the remotest direct interest. But this provided him, as hoped, with the opportunity to air the Italian question before the powers assembled in Paris in 1856. He presented himself there as the defender of order; it was Austria and the regimes that she supported whose reactionary tendencies were the most likely cause of revolutionary disorder.

Cavour was a great success in Paris, with everybody save Austria.

a. PLOMBIÈRES AND THE WAR WITH AUSTRIA. Within two years, in 1858, he managed to arrange with Napoleon an alliance for purposes of joint war against Austria. In exchange for assisting in the formation of a kingdom of northern Italy, evicting Austria from the peninsula, France would receive Savoy and Nice. Obligingly, Austria allowed herself to be goaded into taking the initiative of hostilities in April, 1859. The war went well for the Franco-Sardinian forces, until Napoleon unexpectedly made separate terms at Villafranca with the Austrian Emperor on the basis of his relinquishing Lombardy alone, but not Venetia. [1]

To Cavour, this development was as unforseen as it was unwelcome; unable to pursue the war alone, Piedmont must acquiesce. But for the spontaneous risings in central Italy he was fully prepared, if Napoleon was not. The new situation offered the basis of a new compromise: by the treaty of Turin of March, 1860, France received Savoy and Nice as originally planned, after plebiscites had been held in both territories, and acquiesced in the annexation to Piedmont of the Duchies and of Papal Romagna in lieu of Venetia.

C. The Kingdom of Italy

But the end was not yet. Taking advantage of the ferment pervading all Italy, Garibaldi's picturesque filibustering expedition of the Thousand was allowed to sail for Sicily in May, 1860. There he was soon in control of the island. Crossing to the mainland, Garibaldi proceeded toward Naples where he met the Sardinian army led by Victor Emmanuel. Allowing his patriotic feelings precedence over his republicanism, for the sake of unity Garibaldi yielded to the king. The Two Sicilies thus became part of Italy, as well as the major portion of the Papal domain. [2] In March, 1861, the new Kingdom of Italy was proclaimed.

---

[1] See below, p. 56, for the motivation and domestic aspects of Napoleon's policy.

[2] Rome and some surrounding territory were preserved to the Pope as the result of French intervention.

1. Venice and Rome. The kingdom still lacked Venice and Rome. Taking advantage of the Austro-Prussian embroilment, Italy joined Prussia in the war of 1866, with the result that, despite her own poor military performance in that war, Austria's defeat enabled her to acquire Venetia. Rome alone was still lacking, owing to the veto enforced by French Catholic opinion. Similarly taking advantage of the Franco-Prussian war, Rome was entered by Italian forces in September, 1870.

This left but a relatively minute *irredenta* still under Austrian rule. Until the first world war the slogan of Italian irredentism was Trento and Trieste.

The newly formed Italian kingdom had many problems. From 1861 until 1870 its activity was taken up in considerable measure by the issues of Venetia and Rome. But there was also the less dramatic, if not less fundamental, task of creating and getting to function the essential organs of the state, as distinct from the fact of proclaiming unity. Cavour was no longer there, but his associates and the impulse he had provided continued to dominate the Italy of the sixties. The solution adopted was that of making a unitary, strongly centralized state, after the French model, through the outwardly (but deceptively) simple device of extending the Piedmontese system of law and administration to the entire realm. The operation of this solution will be examined in the next chapter.

III. GERMANY ON THE ROAD TO UNITY (to 1867)

A. Germany and Prussia after 1848

The period that witnessed the final achievement of Italian unity saw a similar accomplishment in the Germanic world. In Germany as in Italy, the final achievement of unity was in large measure the work of one man. Bismarck and Cavour stand out as the leading statesmen of the period, both masters in the field of diplomacy, both accepting the view that war is an instrument, not the end, of policy.

Little happened for nearly a decade, but the accession of William I to the Prussian throne, as Regent in 1858, in full power in 1861, impressed a steadier direction on Prussian policy and leadership. Army reorganization received priority under the able management of von Moltke and von Roon. This undertaking led to a clash between the ruler and his parliament, where liberal sentiment was strong enough to assert itself on the specific issue of military appropriations. The impasse was resolved by the entrance on the stage of Bismarck in the capacity of chief minister.

B. Bismarck

Otto von Bismarck, typical representative of Prussian junkerdom, was by this time a thoroughgoing conservative. For the liberal efforts at unification and constitution drafting he had nothing but contempt; the Prussian constitution of 1850 he regarded in a similar light. Not by speeches and resolutions, but by blood and iron were results to be achieved. From 1851, he had held various diplomatic posts where he obtained good training and experience for his coming task.

1. Bismarck's Policy. When Bismarck was called to office in 1862, his solution for the constitutional deadlock was simple: set the constitution aside—a significant point of contrast with Cavourian methods. For four years he succeeded in imposing arbitrary rule upon Prussia. Bismarck's plan for making a united Germany under Prussian leadership was also simple in conception, and masterful in execution. The first big step was to settle conclusively the age-old issue of Austro-Prussian rivalry. This must be done by force of arms. Bismarck felt that he could settle scores with Austria with Prussian arms alone; unlike Cavour, he had no need of powerful allies, but merely of the neutrality of other powers.

2. The Danish War. The question of the Duchies, Schleswig and Holstein, which had already caused hostilities in 1848, provided him with a convenient pretext to initiate his scheme. The attempt in 1863 of the new Danish king, Christian IX, to assimilate the institutions of the Duchies to those of Denmark led to war in which Prussia and Austria, jointly defending German nationality, inevitably overpowered the little country in 1864. [3]

3. The Convention of Gastein. The question of the disposition of the Duchies could easily, as indeed Bismarck had

---

[3] Denmark, vainly relying on the intervention of the same powers that had interfered in 1848, found herself alone in this instance.

intended, be made to develop into an Austro-Prussian quarrel. A temporary, and purposely awkward, solution was embodied in the Convention of Gastein in August, 1865. Preparing for the showdown, Bismarck, already on good terms with the Tsar, scored an important success when he lulled the suspicions of Napoleon III whom he visited in Biarritz, through nebulous promises of compensation. For good measure, he entered into an alliance with Italy.

Using the situation in the Duchies as a wedge, Bismarck simultaneously accused Austria of violating the Gastein Convention and submitted to the Diet a reorganization scheme that excluded Austria from the Confederation. The expected defeat of the plan was pretext for secession on the part of Prussia and the Diet's decree of mobilization in defense of Austrian rights in the Duchies enabled Bismarck to pose as the victim of aggression. All this had been so skillfully contrived that when hostilities were opened Prussia enjoyed the sympathy of much public opinion both in Germany and outside.

4. The Austro-Prussian War. The war, which lasted seven weeks, showed the superior quality of Prussia's military preparations. Bismarck struck so quickly at the main enemy that any possible assistance to Austria from the smaller German states sympathetic to her was nullified. The decisive victory of Sadowa, in Bohemia, on July 3, 1866, virtually ended hostilities, and the subsequent treaty of Prague in August registered Austria's defeat.

5. The North German Confederation. The peace was not punitive, though its results were far-reaching. The most significant was Austria's consent to the dissolution of the German Confederation, in place of which was created a North German Confederation, headed by Prussia, from which were excluded Austria and the south German states.[4] This North German Confederation was overwhelmingly Prussian, for as the result of territorial incorporations, Prussia now constituted a solid block stretching from France to Russia, and the remaining twenty states could carry little effective weight in the whole. Appearances were saved, however, through the in-

---

[4] Austria ceded Venetia to Italy, and Holstein, that she had held, to Prussia. The promised plebiscite in partly Danish Schleswig was conveniently forgotten and did not take place until after Germany's defeat in World War I.

stitution of a Bundesrat, or federal council, representing the states, in addition to a Reichstag popularly elected in the Confederation as a whole.

Having accomplished these results, Bismarck restored to Prussia the constitution without the benefit of which he had governed since 1862. What could be done but sanction his illegal rule, especially in view of the nature of his achievement?

Bismarck was now ready to embark on the execution of the second part of his grand design: incorporation of the four south German states of Bavaria, Württemberg, Baden, and Hesse-Darmstadt, and the probable accompaniment to this of a showdown with France. Before considering this last phase of German unification, it will be best to bring abreast the situation in other parts of Europe.

IV. EASTERN EUROPE

A. The Habsburg Empire

1. Austria after 1848. The Habsburg state was by its very existence the denial of nationality. It had shown astonishing resilience, emerging virtually unscathed from the storm of 1848. If certain changes could not be undone, such as the emancipation of the peasantry, the orientation of the reconstituted state was frankly conservative. The new Emperor, Francis Joseph, mediocre but conscientious, was thoroughly steeped in antiquated notions of his position and function. But the task of restoration was largely Schwarzenberg's. His death in 1852, though a serious loss, left control of affairs in the hands of associates he had chosen.

Buol at the foreign office showed little distinction, but Bach instituted the "system" named after him, an effort at centralization designed to counter the disruptive force of the various nationalisms. The defeats of 1849 did little but temporarily suppress these nationalisms, of which the Magyar was the most highly developed and articulate. Hungarian sympathies were not with Austria in the Italian war of 1859, and the course of German affairs as guided by Bismarck was considered favorable to the Magyar cause.

2. Austria after 1866. The Ausgleich. The seven weeks' war irrevocably excluded the Habsburgs from Germany as well as from Italy, and obviously called for reconsideration of the structure of the purely Habsburg domain. A solution based on a partnership of five members, German, Magyars, and three Slavic groups (Bohemian, Galician, and South Slavic) was rejected. In its place, Deák's idea, which had come to supersede Kossuth's in Hungary, of a dual monarchy won the day.

From 1867 dates the *Ausgleich,* or compromise. Henceforth, one must speak of the Dual Monarchy, Austria-Hungary, consisting of two equal members: Austria, comprising the Germanic part of the state, the northern Slavs, and reaching down the Adriatic coast; Hungary, including besides the Magyars, Transylvania and the bulk of the southern Slavs.[5] Despite some Austrian concessions to Galician Poles and the Magyar grant of a Croatian constitution in 1868, the Slavs remained discontented; Roumanians and Italians felt likewise, and the problem of nationalities was to remain the central issue of the Dual Monarchy for the rest of its existence.

B. Liberalization and Reaction in Russia

1. Russia after 1855. Tsar Alexander II. The Tsar had not been troubled in 1848, but had instead given assistance to his brother Austrian Emperor in 1849. The Crimean war, however, had marked repercussions in Russia, which found herself worsted in the test of force by the more advanced western countries. Coming to the throne in 1855, Tsar Alexander II proceeded first of all to liquidate the Crimean episode.

If backwardness were the cause of Russia's inferiority, this could be remedied by adaptation to the more effective ways of the west. Alexander II soon embarked upon a policy of reforms. The most outstanding of these, in 1861, was the abolition of serfdom, under which status the vast majority of Russian peasants were still held. But the abolition of serfdom in Russia, like the contemporary abolition of slavery in the American South, was not a simple matter of legislation. In many instances, the lot of the peasants was little altered, their obligations being transferred to the state instead of to their

---

[5] Some Italians in the southern Tyrol and around Trieste were also still under Austrian rule.

landlords. Despite disappointment, the act was a progressive measure. So was the reform in the administration of justice in 1862 through the institution of courts of western European type. Two years later, *zemstvos* or local representative assemblies, were created in the "governments", or provinces, into which Russia was divided.

2. The Return to Reaction. The Tsar's liberalism, such as it was, had done little to soften the disgruntlement of the Poles. In 1863, insurrection broke out in Warsaw and soon spread to the entire country. The Polish rising could have little hope of success unless outside help were forthcoming. Diplomacy busied itself with the issue but did not go beyond the sending of notes by some of the powers to the Tsar. Bismarck gathered 60,000 men on his Polish frontier in case the Tsar should need assistance. They were not put to use, for, though the rebellion was stubborn, the Russians crushed it in the end. By 1865, the Tsar's reforming zeal had largely evaporated, and "Holy Russia" was back on the path of reaction, free to exercise her "mission" of conservation, eschewing dangerous western innovations.

C. The Balkans

1. Roumania. As a consequence of the Crimean defeat also, Russia's influence in the Ottoman Empire received a notable setback. European guardianship was substituted for Russian in the Danubian Principalities of Wallachia and Moldavia. The desire for union of these provinces, favored by some powers and opposed by others, led to a temporary compromise that gave them similar constitutions while maintaining their separateness. This last provision was largely nullified by the election, in 1861, of the same person, Prince Alexander Couza, to head both provinces. When union was formally proclaimed in 1862, and Roumania thus born, the powers tacitly acquiesced. This was a minor success for Napoleon III, who had favored the union.

2. Greece. At the opposite end of the Balkans, the force of nationalism was also at work in Greece, so far consisting of but a fraction of the Greek people. The normally turbulent operation of Greek politics resulted in the dethronement of King Otto and in the search for a new ruler in 1862. Britain, having obtained the election of her candidate, was content with the diplomatic victory over Russia that this represented, and allowed him to decline the offer of the Greek throne. A compromise candidate was found in the person of Prince George of Denmark, and Britain turned over to Greece the Ionian islands that she had held since Napoleon's time. No outside help was forthcoming to assist the revolt in Crete against Turkish rule, and the Cretan rebellion of 1866, like the Polish of 1863, was allowed to "burn itself out."

V. THE WESTERN COUNTRIES

A. The Steady Progress of Britain

This is the period during which the "Victorian compromise" prevailed in Britain. Between Conservatives and Liberals the area of agreement was large. The influence of the Manchester school was well established, and the combination of humanitarian liberalism and evangelical fervor was eminently satisfactory to the powerful commercial class. Under the laissez faire ideal Britain was prosperous, and her power was universally acknowledged and respected.

1. The Reform of 1867. The passing in 1865 of Palmerston, representative of the more conservative tendency within the Liberal camp, was the signal for a new instalment of reform. It was the Conservatives, under the leadership of Disraeli, who put through the Reform Bill of 1867 which nearly doubled the electorate, to some 2,500,000. The tradition was well rooted in Britain that major reforms, by whichever party enacted, were not to be undone.

2. The Irish Question. The Irish problem began to intrude at this point in the restricted form of the issue of disestablishment of the Anglican Church in Ireland. In the elections of 1868, the Conservatives did not even carry their stronghold, England proper, and from these elections emerged a rejuvenated and more radical (by contrast with 1865) Liberal majority. Having put through the disestablishment measure in 1869, Gladstone, personification of the British liberalism that he led, now at the height of his prestige and power, proceeded to attack the Irish land problem. The law of 1870 proved disappointing in its results, and the Irish land question was to continue long after to plague and distort the functioning of British politics.

3. Imperial Developments. Prosperity under laissez faire was reflected in imperial matters as well. The urge toward imperial expansion was at a low ebb in this period, and toward the existing empire the general liberal attitude prevailed. The same year 1867 witnessed the formation of the Dominion of Canada [6] from the federation of the four provinces of Upper and Lower Canada (Ontario and Quebec), New Brunswick, and Nova Scotia. The Dominion, where British authority was represented by a Governor General, was allowed to manage its own affairs under a political system similar to the British. The federal structure resembled that of the neighboring United States, but the central power was somewhat stronger. Canada was launched on her career of western expansion, also comparable with that of the United States, and was to be the model for later similar creations within the Empire. The large French element, nearly a third of the whole population, retained its laws and institutions in the Province of Quebec.

B. The Second Empire at Home

The restoration of the Empire in France had undoubtedly received popular endorsement, for all that there had been thorough suppression of the opposition when the plebiscite was held.

The institutions of the Second Empire were modeled after those of the first. It was a personal dictatorship, but it must be recognized that Napoleon III was a modern man, in advance of his time in the sense that his views and methods were those that our own time has seen flourish.

Universal suffrage was retained, but the representatives of the people had no power. Napoleon seems to have been genuinely sincere in his desire to promote the general good. This was to be achieved through order and progress, under

---

[6] Thirty years earlier, following rebellion in Lower and Upper Canada, Lord Durham, sent to investigate, had issued the famous report bearing his name in 1839. That report, recommending virtual self-government, save in matters of foreign policy, became the basis of British policy in Canada with the appointment of Lord Elgin as Governor in 1846.

the guidance of his government, not through free, and sterile, political agitation and bickering. The task of government was to be equated with the act of enlightened administration.

1. *Economic Progress*. In many respects, the Empire was progressive and brought material benefits to the country. By contrast with the laissez faire philosophy prevailing across the Channel, a more paternalistic attitude was adopted. Road and railroad building proceeded on a large scale, and manufacture was greatly encouraged to expand through the development of credit institutions.

To a large extent these policies were successful. If industrial wages did not quite keep up with the inflationary tendency that accompanied expanding business activity, the country as a whole was prosperous, and, as usual in such circumstances, acquiesced in large measure in the direction of the regime whose motto might have been: "order and progress, but no politics." Dictatorships are usually given to ambitious public works and embellishments: the modern face of Paris is, to a large extent, a legacy of the Second Empire.

2. *The Impact of Foreign Policy*. This eminently satisfactory state of affairs was disturbed mainly because of the foreign entanglements in which Napoleon III became involved and in which his lack of decisiveness caused him to make the worst of both worlds. When the Congress of Paris was held in 1856, the prestige of the Empire stood high both at home and abroad, and the costs of the Crimean war could be eclipsed by the outcome. Thereafter the situation changed.

The course and outcome of the Italian war have been outlined. Successful in its military aspects, politically and diplomatically it was a failure. The territorial gains of France, Nice and Savoy, were no compensation for the antagonism aroused in France among liberal supporters of Italian unity on one hand, and conservative backers of the Pope on the other. The Roman question was to remain thereafter an ever-festering sore in French politics. The same year, 1860, that saw Italy made was the one when the commercial treaty with Britain antagonized French commercial interests.

3. *The "Liberal" Empire*. Opposition from the right and from the left had one point in common: the wish to curb the personal power of the Emperor in favor of the representative bodies. From 1860, there began a steady evolution of the Empire in a more liberal direction, allowing increasing scope to criticism and political opposition. These concessions, fully taken advantage of by an opposition that did not consider them sufficient, did not serve to strengthen the Empire, while its foreign policy likewise continued a source of dissatisfaction. By 1867, Napoleon, weakened by illness, had a strong sense of failure: he had witnessed, if not aided, the Prussian defeat of Austria; he had been forced to send again to Rome the forces he had withdrawn the year before;[7] and the Mexican episode (of which more presently) could be judged a costly and discreditable adventure.

Hopelessly torn between the influence of the strongly Catholic Empress and her party and the opposite liberalizing anticlerical tendency, Napoleon was less than ever able to decide and direct, and the Empire drifted toward catastrophe. At the eleventh hour, in 1869, Ollivier was called to power. This substantial instalment of liberalism seemed to give the Empire a new lease on life; it was endorsed by the electorate in May, 1870 by a nearly five to one majority. But the foreign situation again was about to intervene. The Empire could not survive Sedan four months later.

C. Europe and North America

The year 1860 was a turning point in the fortunes of the Second Empire. Napoleon III who, during the preceding decade had succeeded in allaying the fears entertained by Europe upon his accession, was now embarked upon a series of adventures that caused him to be looked upon as an irresponsible meddler rather than a prop of peace. The decade of the sixties was to witness important developments on the North American continent which had marked repercussions in Europe.

1. The Mexican Question. Ever since her emancipation

---

[7] In 1864 an agreement had been made whereby, in exchange for an Italian promise to respect Rome, French troops were to be withdrawn from that city. The capital of Italy was transferred to Florence in 1865, and the French left Rome in 1866. But an attempted coup by Garibaldi led to their return in 1867.

from Spanish rule, Mexico had followed in relative isolation the checkered course of her affairs.[8] As a consequence of one of her violent changes of rule, there developed the issue of debts owed some European states, Spain, Britain, and France. This led, in 1862, to the despatch of a joint expedition for the purpose of enforcing debt collection. The United States, fully occupied with her own Civil War, was not in a position at the time to oppose this European intervention.

a. NAPOLEON'S MEXICAN SCHEME. It soon appeared that French policy had designs far exceeding the limited scope of debt collection, for an enlarged French force, acting alone, proceeded to Mexico City where, in 1864, the Archduke Maximilian of Austria was installed Emperor. The flimsy Mexican Empire of Maximilian, a wholly artificial creation, was entirely dependent for its existence on the support of French bayonets.

The combination of local opposition in Mexico, that of the United States, which could become effective once the Civil War had been liquidated, and looming complications in Europe, induced Napoleon to abandon this ill-advised attempt at planting French influence across the Atlantic. French forces were withdrawn in 1866, but the luckless Maximilian, choosing to stay behind, was soon captured and executed in 1867. The episode redounded to the discredit of the Second Empire, at home as well as abroad.

2. *The American Civil War.* This episode also had some repercussions in Europe, mainly in Britain and France. In both countries the textile industry suffered from the deprivation of its American cotton supply, and the governments were not unsympathetic to the prospect of secession, which would have served to weaken the growing power of the United States, even though that country was not at this stage in a position to threaten either Britain or France. Still largely absorbed in the process of expansion and consolidation within her continental boundaries, the United States was pursuing her course in essential isolation from the outside world; but her potentialities of growth were even then obviously very great.

---

[8] Relations with the United States were of considerable importance (e. g., the Mexican War in 1846) but do not belong in this treatment.

There was friction between the government of Washington and the British, mainly over the issue of the rights of neutrals at sea, but eventually these differences were amicably settled. Hints of possible mediation between North and South, whether of British or French origin, were firmly discouraged by Washington and consequently abandoned. With the victory of the North, the French abandonment of Mexico served to strengthen the Monroe Doctrine.

VI. THE SHOWDOWN BETWEEN FRANCE AND GERMANY

In 1867 there took place in Paris a great international exposition which many European rulers visited. But the atmosphere of peace and cordiality thus superficially engendered was no accurate measure of the unresolved tensions that made the peace precarious. The foci of unrest were two: Bismarckian policy moving toward the last phase of its goal of complete German unity, and the French search for means either to prevent this achievement or alternatively to secure some compensation for its accomplishment. The story in brief is one of steady purpose under skillful guidance, crowned by success on one side, contrasted with uncertain purpose and fumbling that led to disaster on the other.

A. French Policy after 1867

The quick performance of the Austro-Prussian war of 1866 had destroyed any possibility of French intervention or mediation that a prolonged stalemate would have yielded. Napoleon fell back on the prospect of compensations dangled before him by Bismarck while the latter was preparing for war. But he had little to bargain with.

Bismarck did not discourage the discussion, during or after the war, but rather led it on to good purpose. The possibility that France might seek some German territory on the Rhine was used to frighten the south German states, otherwise not overly friendly to Prussia, into making an alliance with him against the danger of French aggression.

1. The Luxembourg Question. Napoleon's eyeing of Belgium would merely have served to arouse British alarms.

For a time, Luxembourg was considered by him. Luxembourg had been a member of the now dissolved German Confederation, and was under the personal rule of the King of Holland. The negotiation for the acquisition of the Grand Duchy by France seemed to prosper until a calculated outburst of national feeling in Germany [9] caused it to be abandoned, and the issue was resolved by international compromise in London that neutralized Luxembourg after the Belgian model.

2. *Austria and Italy*. Napoleon turned to Austria, where he found a certain amount of guarded response. The negotiation was prolonged and reached the point of discussion of the text of a treaty of alliance which, however, was still pending when war broke out. A tripartite alliance between France, Italy, and Austria was likewise considered, but Napoleon found himself caught in the usual dilemma of the Roman question, for Italy would join only on the condition that she obtain Rome.

3. *The Spanish Question*. While these various prospects were being considered and talk of war was sometimes heard, a new and, as it turned out, fatal complication arose from an unexpected quarter, from Spain. In that ill-governed country, the year 1868 had seen another revolution, the expulsion of Queen Isabella, which led to the search for a new ruler. Eventually, the choice fell upon Prince Leopold, a member of the Catholic branch of the Hohenzollern family, brother of the ruler whom Napoleon himself had assisted mount the Roumanian throne. The news of this possibility, which became public in July, 1870, created much excitement in France where visions of a revived empire of Charles V were played up. [10]

B. The Franco-Prussian War

1. *The Ems Despatch*. The French objections were

---

[9] A deputy rose in the Reichstag to question the "abandonment" of Luxembourg by Germany. That intervention, as subsequently revealed, had taken place with Bismarck's connivance.

[10] Prince Leopold had little interest in the Spanish crown, but Bismarck, sensing the possibilities of the issue in goading France, induced him to change his mind and accept the offer.

generally considered valid, and the issue was regarded as solved when the Hohenzollern candidate was withdrawn with the approval of the Prussian king. Bismarck was badly disappointed, but once more Napoleon played into his hands. Ill-advised by irresponsible counselors, he elected to push his advantage by seeking to extract from the Prussian king a formal declaration of renouncement. The very insistent French ambassador could obtain from the king only a noncommittal answer. The account of the meeting at Ems, where the king was vacationing, which was sent to Bismarck, was given out by the latter in an abridged form that made it appear a record of mutual discourtesies between the ambassador and the king. The edited Ems despatch had the desired effect on French opinion. With irresponsible levity, the initiative of a declaration of war was taken in Paris.

2. The War. On the basis of the potential strength of the belligerents, there was no inevitable reason why victory should favor either side. But strength in being and quality of management were as inferior on the French side as had been diplomatic preparations. As a result of these, France found herself without allies and with little sympathy in any quarter.

Militarily, the war falls into two phases. From the first, the French suffered severe reverses, which incidentally destroyed any lingering possibilities of Austrian assistance. Instead of reforming their forces nearer Paris, for internal political reasons, Napoleon himself and Marshal MacMahon marched their inferior forces to the rescue of the beleaguered garrison of Metz. They were trapped at Sedan, where the Emperor and his army surrendered at the beginning of September.

3. Fall of the Second Empire. The humiliation of Sedan brought down the Empire. A provisional "government of national defense" was set up in Paris and exerted itself with great vigor to raise new armies. But with Sedan, also, the French military machine was broken past retrieving. After a siege, Paris was starved into surrender at the end of January, 1871. Further resistance was futile, and an armistice was signed. It made possible the holding of elections, and peace negotiations were conducted between Thiers and Bismarck.

The latter's terms had to be accepted and peace was signed at Frankfort in May, 1871.

4. The Treaty of Frankfort. The first provision of the peace was an indemnity of 5,000,000,000 francs ($1,000,000,-000), large by the standards of the time, but by no means unmanageable. By 1873 this obligation had been discharged. Of greater consequence were the territorial arrangements by which France lost Alsace and a part of Lorraine. This was undoubtedly a violation of national feeling, and was looked upon as a moral wrong in France. The representatives of the territory protested the annexation, in the French National Assembly first, later in the German Reichstag. Outside the belligerent countries, the impression was widespread that the annexation was unwise, and the consequences of the legacy of bitterness that this act left behind it were accurately forecast by Gladstone, prime minster of Britain at the time.

C. Consequences of the Franco-Prussian War

1. The Completion of German Unity. Apart from the military outcome and the treaty of peace, the war acted as the cement of final German unity. The German Empire was proclaimed in Versailles (another symbolic act of unwisdom) on January 18, 1871, and the crown offered, no longer "from the gutter," but on motion of the King of Bavaria, to the Prussian king, henceforth William I, German Emperor. The Second Reich had come into existence, and at the same time emerged as the first power on the continent of Europe. This was the outstanding consequence of the Franco-Prussian war, a consequence which at the time seemed no cause for alarm to the other powers. Bismarck with blood and iron had reaped the fruits of his masterful diplomacy.

2. The Black Sea Convention. There were some other, incidental but important, consequences of the war. In October, 1870, Russia sent a note to the powers denouncing the clauses of the treaty of 1856 that affected the status of the Black Sea (neutralization). As France was impotent and Bismarck was willing to support the Russian claim for the sake of Russia's benevolent neutrality, the English protest remained purely formal. However, a conference was held in London, where the powers gave their assent to the Russian desire. If Russia had her way, the fiction was preserved that international instruments could not be modified by unilateral action.

3. Italy Acquires Rome. There had been some feeling in Italy, not least on the part of Victor Emmanuel, for coming to the assistance of France in the war.[11] But the everlasting Roman impasse and the early French setbacks served to insure Italian neutrality. The collapse of the Second Empire was used, perhaps speciously, as an argument for considering invalid the Italian commitments with respect to Rome, and the withdrawal of the French garrison from the city made possible its entry by Italian forces after the Pope had upheld the principle of his rights by a token show of resistance. In 1871 the Italian government moved to Rome, henceforth the capital of Italy.

---

[11] Garibaldi raised a volunteer legion which joined the French forces around Dijon.

VII. THE PROGRESS OF EUROPE

A. The Political and Economic Balance Sheet

The appearance of Germany and Italy as solid blocks on the map of Europe constitutes the outstanding triumph of nationalism in the whole nineteenth century. The fact that Germany was welded together through blood and iron under the guidance of Bismarck, while Cavour in Italy was a typical mid-nineteenth century liberal, was to have important consequences for the future. In both cases, however, the force of nationalism was at the heart of the development. That is one reason why Bismarck and Cavour, working with that force, had both been successful.

These political developments, which naturally dominate the scene, did not impede the continued progress of Europe while they were taking place. Britain stood at the acme of her power, confident and secure in her imperial position, even though the urge to expand the empire was in this period weak. In events on the continent she took a dispassionate interest, not devoid of a superior attitude.

The Second Empire in France had meant prosperity at home and had pursued a relatively more vigorous imperial policy than Britain. This policy had resulted in the Mexican fiasco, but in north Africa, the Far East, and the Pacific, expansion was successfully pursued. The year preceding its demise, 1869, had witnessed the opening of the Suez Canal, built by a French company under the guidance of the enterprising Ferdinand de Lesseps. Half-hearted British opposition had allowed this accomplishment, the importance of which for the future, whether economic, political, or strategic, was to be great. To a degree, the Mediterranean could now revive, emerging from the limbo which it had entered in the sixteenth century.

Industrial growth went apace, transportation and communication systems were spreading their networks over Europe in generally decreasing density as one went from west to east. If Britain had become firmly devoted to free trade, this ideal had failed on the whole to convert continental states to its practice.

B. The Thought of the Period

This industrial growth of Europe went hand in hand with fertile activity in the realms of the intellect and the arts, although the link between scientific development and technological progress was not yet the more intimate connection that it was to become in a later age.

1. Comte, Marx, and Darwin. The growth of scientific knowledge had an inevitable impact on the broader field of ideas. Auguste Comte died in 1857 having reflected this impact in his *Positive Philosophy*, seeking to bring "social science" within the scope of "natural." Karl Marx's most important work, also ostensibly "scientific," was being done during this period. But perhaps the most impressive contribution was in the field of natural science. Charles Darwin's *Origin of Species* was published in 1859, and his *Descent of Man* dates from 1871. The concept of evolutionary change in living matter through the process of selection was one ranking in importance with the Marxian doctrine: both rate among the seminal ideas which have deeply affected the course of human thought.

2. Secular versus Religious Thought. The expression of such views as those of Comte, Marx, or Darwin betokens an intellectual climate of thoroughgoing freedom. This liberalism of the mind could not help but have an impact upon religious thought.

Among the churches, that of Rome took an equally thorough and uncompromising position of opposition to liberalism. Pope Pius IX's short-lived experiment with liberalism had thoroughly immunized him against such an outlook. Whether in politics, religion, or philosophy, the Roman Church under his guidance refused to compromise with change or progress. If the *Syllabus of Errors*, issued in 1864, was a logically consistent document that saw in the principles of the Enlightenment the root of modern thought, hence of current evil, it was nevertheless a shock to many, not excluding Catholics, who felt such a position was one that meant withdrawal from the world that was. Undeterred, Pope Pius proceeded to call the Vatican

Council in 1869, which sanctioned the dogma of Papal infallibility.[12]

But, for good or evil, Europe was launched upon a course that could not be altered. The active forces of change which had set the direction of this course were entrenched more powerfully than ever. They were to continue in control for the next half century, during which period Europe was to reach the apogee of her power and influence.

---

[12] The last previous universal Council of the Roman Church had been that of Trent (1545-1563). The lapse of time and the action of the Vatican Council put the final seal on the position of supremacy of the papacy in the Roman Church.

PART II

The Apogee of Europe: 1870-1914

SELECTED READINGS

Albertini, Luigi, *The Origins of the War of 1914* (3 vols., 1953-1957); Beer, Max, *Fifty Years of International Socialism* (1937); Bowden, W., Karpovich, M. and Usher, A. P., *An Economic History of Europe since 1750* (1937); Branbenburg, Erich, *From Bismarck to the World War* (1927); Brogan, D. W., *France under the Republic* (1940); Carr-Saunders, A. M., *World Population: Past Growth and Present Trends* (1936); Charques, Richard, *The Twilight of Imperial Russia* (1959); Croce, Benedetto, *A History of Italy, 1871-1915* (1929); Dangerfield, George, *The Strange Death of Liberal England* (1936); Dawson, William H., *The German Empire, 1867-1914* (1930); Ensor, R. C. K., *England, 1870-1914* (1949); Fay, Sidney B., *The Origins of the World War* (1928); Feis, Herbert, *Europe, the World's Banker, 1870-1914* (1930); Figgis, John N., *Churches in the Modern State* (1914); Gooch, G. P., *Germany* (1927); Halévy, Élie, *History of the English People* (1949 ff.); Hobson, John A., *Imperialism: a Study* (1948); Hoskins, Halford L., *European Imperialism in Africa* (1930); Isaac, Julius, *Economics of Migration* (1947); Jaszi, Oscar, *The Dissolution of the Hapsburg Empire* (1929); Kantorowicz, Hermann, *The Spirit of British Policy and the Myth of the Encirclement of Germany* (1931); Karpovich, Michael, *Imperial Russia, 1801-1917* (1932); Kohn, Hans, *A History of Nationalism in the East* (1929); Langer, William L., *The Diplomacy of Imperialism, 1890-1902* (1936); Langer, William L., *European Alliances and Alignments* (1939); Lenin, V. I., *Imperialism, the Highest Stage of Capitalism* (1916, 1939); Mansergh, Nicholas, *The Coming of the First World War; a Study in the European Balance 1878-1914* (1949); Masaryk, Thomas G., *The Spirit of Russia* (1919); May, A. J., *The Habsburg Monarchy, 1867-1914* (1951); Miller, William, *The Ottoman Empire and its Successors, 1801-1927* (1936); Moon, Parker T., *Imperialism and World Politics* (1926); Neff, Emery, *The Poetry of History* (1947); Pribram, A. F., *Austrian Foreign Policy, 1908-1918* (1923); Redlich, Joseph, *Emperor Francis Joseph of Austria* (1929); Renouvin, Pierre, *The Immediate Origins of the War* (1928); Rosenberg, Arthur, *The Rise of the German Republic* (1951); Russell, Bertrand. *Proposed Roads to Freedom: Socialism, Anarchism and Syndicalism* (1919); Schevill, Ferdinand, *A History of the Balkan Peninsula* (1933); Schuman, Frederick, *War and Diplomacy in the French Republic* (1931); Schumpeter, Joseph A., *Capitalism, Socialism and Democracy* (1950); Seton-Watson, Hugh, *The Decline of Imperial Russia* (1952); Seton-Watson, R. W., *Sarajevo* (1926); Sontag, Raymond J., *European Diplomatic History, 1878-1932* (1933); Sprigge, J. C. S., *The Development of Modern Italy* (1945); Stavrianos, L. S., *The Balkans Since 1453* (1958); Stolper, Gustav, *German Economy, 1870-1940* (1940); Taylor, A. J. P., *The Struggle for Mastery in Europe* (1954); Thomson, David, *Democracy in France: the Third Republic* (1946); Trevelyan, G. M., *British History in the XIX Century* (1934); Trevelyan, G. M., *English Social History* (1943); Veblen, Thorstein, *Imperial Germany and the Industrial Revolution* (1939); Webb, Sidney and Beatrice, *History of Trade Unionism* (1920).

CHAPTER 4

General Characteristics of the Period 1870-1914

I. THE SIGNIFICANCE OF 1870

In the period of exactly one hundred years that elapsed between the end of the Napoleonic wars and the opening of the era of conflict and transition which is ours, the year 1870 marks an important and convenient stopping point. Large as it was, the Franco-Prussian war was in itself of limited scope; but the consequences that derived from it went far beyond the circle of its immediate participants. Most important of all was the final achievement of German unity, simultaneous with the emergence of the German Empire to the front rank of European powers. That fact and its results, which dominated the relations of the European community for the next half century, must, because of their magnitude, be given separate treatment.

There is much diversity among the European nations and states. This diversity, the peculiar developments and problems that distinguish their several courses during this period, will also be dealt with separately. But first it may be worth considering those aspects of the European community which give it unity—forces and trends operating throughout the whole complex of Europe. Such developments are bound to be uneven in time and place, but here again the date 1870 is a suitable one to mark change, alteration in the rate of change, or the coming to fruit of ferment earlier at work.

II. THE ECONOMIC SCENE

A. The Spread of Industry

The period around 1870 has sometimes been described as initiating the second industrial revolution. Certainly it ushered in a considerable spread of the industrial process. An expansion and acceleration of it, comparable with the simultaneous post-Civil War phenomenon in the United States, took place in Germany. Not much later, Japan, entering the field and making rapid strides in it, was to be reckoned among world powers, whose influence Europe would have to take into her calculations.

The spread and rate of the development were uneven. The rapidity of it in Germany made that country, within twenty years, a contender for the place of primacy traditionally held by Britain. France, by contrast, fell relatively behind in the industrial race, but east and south of Germany, industry became increasingly important: in Austria proper and in Bohemia, in Sweden, even in poorly favored Italy, and in Russian Poland.

B. Technological Developments

The development was characterized, not only by its geographical spread, but by the changes brought in it by a host of technical alterations. Iron definitely gave way to steel; new sources of power, such as electricity, became increasingly important; chemistry grew to be the basis of an entirely new set of industries and manufactures. By 1870, much of the European network of communications was in existence, but there was still room for much construction of railway and telegraph lines. The telephone was soon to be invented, and by the end of the century the first automobiles had made their appearance. Flying was not a significant industrial factor before the first world war.

C. The Two Europes

Along with this, the rate of productivity was also increasing, giving Europe an enormously greater degree of mechanical power than any other part of the world, save the United States. Within Europe, industry and the efficiency of industry may be said to have roughly diminished as one moved from northwest to southeast.

A similar phenemenon was apparent in agriculture, where technological improvements were decreasingly in evidence as one moved away from the North Sea and the Channel. It has been pointed out, in fact, that there were two Europes: an "inner" Europe, or "Europe of steam," bounded by a line running from Glasgow to Stockholm, Danzig, Trieste, Florence, and Barcelona, where heavy industry was largely concentrated, and an "outer" zone, primarily agricultural. The "inner" region was ever tending to expand its boundaries.

D. Finance Capitalism

The phenomenon of growth in industry was paralleled by changes in the structure of its organization and management. This is the age when the large corporation came into its own, drawing for its capital needs on the savings of myriad investors. Rapidly accumulating wealth forever sought profitable employment, which meant steady expansion and growth of enterprise. To an unprecedented degree, management of capital became a specialized activity, reflected in the growing importance of banking and financial manipulation.

The management of growth, left to free enterprise, made the rate of development unsteady, marked by the classical alternation of the cycles of prosperity and depression. There were recurrent economic crises, but they were soon surmounted, and the alternating rhythm came to be looked upon as the normal manner in which the upward moving (over a long period) curve unfolded itself; just as the law of supply and demand was the fundamental regulator of the exchanges of mankind.

E. International Trade and Investment

These exchanges were growing ever more voluminous, for industry means trade. Inner Europe, instead of Britain alone as formerly, was now the workshop of the world, though London was still its financial capital. Intra-European commercial exchanges were large (Germany came to be Britain's first customer), but inner Europe supplied in manufactures, and in exchange drew upon for food and raw materials, not only outer Europe, but the rest of the world as well.

A vast and intricate network of connections, of which Europe was the nerve center, was built and encompassed the entire globe; fluctuations in the price of wheat in Liverpool would affect its primary producers in Argentina, Russia, and Australia. This delicate machinery was kept in smooth operation mainly by two factors, expansion and stability. The case of Britain, still leader in the process and its most perfect or extreme example, is illuminating. Britain had become an almost exclusively manufacturing nation, and looked ever farther afield for new markets for her manufactures. There was a steady outflow of British capital meanwhile which went to right the unfavorable balance of trade on which the successful operation of the British economy was based.

A great boon to the functioning of the system was the gold standard. The currencies of European nations bore a fixed relation to gold, so that the transactions of international trade were not impeded by exchange barriers and difficulties. The existing equilibrium was not a static one, but because it was equilibrium the prevailing state of affairs came to be regarded as normal and stable. The breakdown of it after 1914 had revealed its precarious temporarity.

III. SOCIAL CHANGE

A. The Growth of Europe's Population

Economic growth went parallel with that of the basic element of society, human material. The old Malthusian view seemed to be invalidated by the record of actual performance. During the second half of the century, the population of Europe increased from some 250,000,000 to about 400,000,000, not counting some 50,000,000 who emigrated from Europe, and this increase was relatively more rapid than that of the rest of the world, excluding the New World. It was made possible by a variety of factors: improved medical knowledge steadily lowered the death rate while the birth rate continued generally high; food for the added numbers was provided by increased productivity at home and by drawing on the resources of the non-European world, while industry provided employment for many.

Here also the development was uneven. The death rate fell and the expected span of life was lengthened, more rapidly in the technically more advanced countries of inner Europe. But even there there were differences, of which the case of

France is the most striking. For a long time, France had been far the most populous state of Europe, but her population hardly increased at all in the half century before 1914 when it was 40,000,00. Germany, with about the same population as France in 1870, had 65,000,000 in 1914; Britain had passed France in the nineties, and Italy was catching up with her. The relation between population and power is obvious, although the new factor of industrial development increasingly tended to alter the balance of mere numbers.

B. Urbanization

By far the larger portion of the increased population was absorbed in the cities, many of which grew to unforeseen and unprecedented size. To say nothing of the myriad problems that the mere physical existence of a modern large city presents, the result was a profound change in the composition of society, hitherto predominantly rural. The change had started earliest and went farthest in Britain, and it remained, even by 1914, largely confined to inner Europe. The English development, being earliest, was also the least planned, and led to the horrible conditions already noted earlier in the century. During the second half of it, the necessity of some organization and planning gained greater recognition, but slums were still highly prevalent. The emergence, then vast increase, of a numerous, propertyless urban proletariat, wholly dependent on jobs and wages, the conditions of which were dictated in turn by those of industrial production and world markets, became one of the most pressing problems of European society.

Despite much misery and uneven progress, progress there was, at least if measured by the standard of the material conditions of existence, higher in any case than in Asia or Africa. Within the area of Europe, there were again vast differentials, standards being generally higher in inner Europe, and much higher in Germany, for instance, than in Italy. Most significant perhaps, was the altered composition of the population in the new industrial nations, now made up in considerable measure of a relatively unattached, more fluid, and more volatile mass. This was bound to have profound social and political repercussions.

IV. THE POLITICAL FORCES

A. The Growth of Socialism

Bearing some important qualifications in mind, it may be said that the political expression of industrial development, resulting at the human level in the formation of a large industrial proletariat, is to be found in socialism, which saw its heyday in the period under consideration. There is, in fact, a rough correlation between the degree of industrial development and the strength of socialist parties. By 1914, they were the second largest single party in the French Chamber and the largest in the German Reichstag.

To this state of affairs, the British scene offers an important exception, for while Britain was the foremost industrial nation, there were virtually no British socialists before 1914. This is to be accounted for by the unique nature of the British political evolution: the long-established parliamentary tradition, the two-party system, the Chartist failure, and the subsequent tendency of British labor to concentrate on nonpolitical organizational activity. But on the continent, the correlation largely holds.

This is not to say that all workers were socialists. The Catholic Church, for instance, especially under Leo XIII, realizing the novel conditions, made an effort to organize the workers in Christian syndicates or unions. Its success was relatively small. In the Latin countries especially, such tendencies as anarchism had some attraction. But, on the whole, socialism was the one organized and significant force that could speak for the workers.

1. Socialist Theory. This socialism was of Marxian derivation. The *Communist Manifesto* had been issued in 1848 and the publication of *Das Kapital* was completed in 1867. In simplest terms, Marx thought he had found the key to the law of historic development in the economic interpretation of it. Armed with this tool, he could not only explain the past, but foretell the course of the future. The French Revolution had marked the triumph of the bourgeoisie over the old landholding aristocracy. This bourgeoisie now found the chief source of its power in the new industry. The next phase would consist in the displacement of the exploiting capitalist class by the real producers of wealth, the hitherto dispossessed proletariat. This last phase of social evolution was inevitable in any event, and would take place when the proletariat, conscious of its grievances and of its strength, would rise to take power. To the development of this consciousness, Marx with his analysis made an important contribution.

These views appealed to many, intellectuals like Marx himself for the most part at first, who proceeded to organize the movement of which they constituted the general staff. It would of course take time for the proletarians to achieve consciousness of their historic role and their power, and, needless to say, such views found little favor with the established holders of power. But, despite opposition and attempted suppression, the Marxist view succeeded in establishing itself alongside with the recognition to labor of the right to organize for purposes of collective action.

For socialism, church and state were both enemies, tools in the hands of the ruling class. "Religion is the opiate of the people," went the slogan. The only struggle that mattered was that between classes, not nations. The second Socialist International was founded in 1889.

2. Revolutionary versus Reformist Socialism. The present-day distinction between socialist and communist has no validity prior to 1917, but the seeds of it were present in all the pre-First World War socialist parties. Some took the view that the ruling class would never peaceably yield power, hence would have to be evicted by violence; others put their faith in a less bloody, if slower, evolutionary process of education. The struggle between revolutionaries and reformists went on, however, within the various sections of the International.

B. The Progress of Democracy

One important factor in the reformist tendency was the influence of that force, older than socialism, which, for the continent at least, largely stemmed from the French Revolution, that is, democracy. Especially after 1870, the progress of democracy was uninterrupted and steady in all its aspects. First and foremost was extension of the suffrage toward its ultimate goal of universality. France had inaugurated universal manhood suffrage in 1848, and in 1914 there were still restrictions on it in most countries, but the trend had assumed the character of inevitability. Even Russia had begun a timid essay in representative institutions after 1905.

Alongside with the widening franchise went the spreading of education. Free compulsory education, at least at the elementary level, provided by the state, became the order of the day, and its influence was apparent in the spread of literacy, complete or nearly so in the area of inner Europe, but making progress outside it also. Increased literacy in turn increased the power of the printed word. The press was now a potent agency for influencing opinion, a tool which held equal possibilities of enlightenment and of corruption of this opinion.

If social classes still had reality, European society was undoubtedly moving in the direction of equality of opportunity, albeit with considerable differences according to locale. At the opposite extremes, politically as well as geographically, may be said to have stood France and Russia. The latter was still an autocracy while the former was a republic, an exception among governments, the normal form of which was monarchical. The slogan of the First World War, "to make the world safe for democracy," was the expression of the prevailing view of the trend of social and political evolution. Put into different words, Europe was increasingly liberal.

C. Nationalism

Along with democracy, nationalism is often mentioned as the main driving force of the nineteenth century. To a large extent this is true, for this force, old in its basic components, was given modern shape by the French Revolution. However, by mid-century it had begun to undergo considerable transformation. The final accomplishment of Italian and German unity was its most outstanding triumph.

But the latter was unfortunately achieved through the effectiveness of Bismarck's blood-and-iron methods instead of through the impotent talk of liberal forty-eighters. It is not surprising that German nationalism should have become annexed by its successful military sponsors. But not in Germany alone was the tendency increasingly noticeable of nationalism to become aggressive and the monopoly of the conservative elements of society. The difference is only one of degree, but the degree is marked. In France, a long tradition had associated liberty and country (*patrie*); but if the settlement of Frankfort rankled among all groups, *revanche* was increasingly the slogan of an otherwise reactionary "integral" nationalism as expounded by such writers as Maurras and his *Action française*. Even in Italy, unlike Germany united under liberal auspices, with the turn of the century there began to appear the same type of aggressive and noisy assertion of national rights and destiny.

The broad trend of nationalism, tending to identify nation and state, in other words self-determination, was generally at work. In those parts of Europe where there were still peoples under alien rule—Austria-Hungary, the Balkans, the western regions of Russia—liberty and liberalism could still be identified with the basic struggle for national independence. In these regions nationalism was therefore a disruptive force. This nationalism, also, while claiming for itself the benefits and rights of freedom, could be intolerant of them where others were concerned. Hungary is a good example of this dual aspect: the *Ausgleich* of 1867 had given her nationalism satisfaction within the Dual Monarchy; but Hungary was thoroughly intransigeant when it came to the similar wishes of the Slavs within her borders.

D. Militarism and Imperialism

1. The Nation in Arms. The emphasis put by the French Revolution on the people as the basic element in the nation was a democratic concept. But it also had the logical consequence of the armed nation, for the state was no longer the property of its God-appointed ruler, but the common patrimony of its members. The practice of conscription therefore stems from democratic origins, a fact often insufficiently realized in the English-speaking world. This practice became universal among continental states.

Large armed forces, once in existence, tend to a degree of autonomous behavior, and they can be used as an instrument in the implementation of the foreign policy of the state as well as for purposes of domestic policy. The army, meaning by this its permanent directing officer corps, tends to be a conservative force, and the dangers of militarism, both domestic and foreign, were realized by many. As armies grew ever larger, so likewise the issue of militarism assumed growing importance, and the divergence between the needs of defense and the dangers of militarism was one of the basic issues of pre-1914 European politics. The military were used at times to suppress the workers, and, logically, the socialists were antimilitaristic.

2. The Connection between Nationalism, Militarism, and Imperialism. They were antiimperialistic as well. The long process of the conquest of the world by Europe, begun in the sixteenth century, now received a new impetus and was about to reach its climax. Allowing that the basic motivating force of imperialism is economic, the factor of armed power is obviously important. The sharp renewal of colonial activity from about 1880, and the fact that, in general, the military were allied to whatever forces made for expansion, must be registered at this point. One consequence of this state of affairs was that imperial rivalries and national prestige became entangled, and we shall observe the repercussions of the former in the formation of national foreign policies. The intertwining of nationalism, militarism, and imperialism is one of the characteristic aspects of pre-1914 Europe and a basic factor in its collapse.

V. THE INTELLECTUAL AND MORAL CLIMATE OF EUROPE

This great expansive outburst of Europe was a manifestation of power. For a proper understanding of this phenomenon, the deeper roots of this power must be examined. First and most important among them must be placed scientific development.

A. Science and Technology

It is not necessary to make a catalogue of scientific discoveries in this period, but rather to examine briefly the effects of the state of scientific development at this stage. Modern science begins with the Renaissance. Its progress, necessarily slow at first, created in the seventeenth century a revolution in thought which, in the eighteenth century, may be said to have been popularized at the level of the educated groups of society, still a very small section of the community.

With the nineteenth century, a new phase opens in the development. The mathematical and physical sciences, which had been its initial basis, while continuing their progress, no longer hold exclusive primacy, for the natural sciences come into their own. There is, in addition, the fact that scientific development overflows into the field of practical application, and this, combined with the spreading of education, produced fruits which are ripening in our period.

Invention is distinct from science, but becomes increasingly integrated with it. The very growth of the mass of scientific knowledge makes easier the organized procedure of further search into directed channels, until technological may be regarded as a by-product of scientific development to which it gives in turn additional motivation. Some of Pasteur's work illustrates this point. In terms of the practical living of men, industrial growth is therefore, at one remove perhaps, a consequence of scientific knowledge, while the great progress of medicine shows an even closer connection between practice and theory. The whole process may be summed up as that of the conquest by man of the forces of nature and of his putting these forces, as a result of his understanding of them, at his service.

Undeniably, more things and services were becoming available to ever greater numbers of people. The novelty of the process was accompanied by concentration of control of the sources of power and wealth mainly in private hands, instead of putting emphasis on the equable distribution of plenty to which the twentieth century may be arriving. To repeat again, the sources and the consequences of the phenomenon—increased scientific knowledge as well as industry and higher living standards—were largely concentrated in inner Europe.

B. Material Progress and Materialism

The most conspicuous manifestations of this development were material. It is not surprising, therefore, that the concept of progress should have taken deep root and its tone been materialistic. If man could conquer nature, the millennium, traditionally situated in some remotely past Garden of Eden from which man had once been expelled, could now be placed in a measurable future which it was within man's power to reach. Unlimited progress became a commonplace phrase of Fourth of July type of oratory, and optimistic materialism is an apt description of the prevailing atmosphere. The further away one went from the sources of the new development, the greater the naive confidence with which such views were accepted.

C. Science and Religion

At the higher levels of understanding and contemplation, the effects were no less important. Confidence in the unlimited possibilities of science was bolstered, though the outlook was broader than the limited one of eighteenth-century Newtonian mechanism. The tone of the *Zeitgeist* was set by the natural sciences, and here the work of Darwin stands on a par with, and had greater immediate influence than, that of Marx. If eighteenth-century mechanism had run into conflict with traditional religion, new and more solid bases of attack had been developed in the first half of the nineteenth century: geology and anthropology bearing out the antiquity of the earth and of man; philology, archeology, and history leading to Higher Criticism.

This last especially, starting from the premise that the sacred writings of Christianity should be examined in the same manner as any texts of antiquity, had flourished among German theologians when Renan's popular *Life of Jesus* (1869) awakened a wide public across the Rhine to the new development. Higher Criticism penetrated Britain also, and everywhere the narrower exegetical controversy merged into the broader issue of the relation, or conflict, between science and religion, on which the influence of Comte's positivism was also brought to bear.

Science by now had conquered the seats of learning, and increasingly the prevailing attitude of the educated public became agnostic when not antireligious. The state remained indifferent and passive while the process of laicization went on. To a large degree, Europe—the continent somewhat faster than Britain—was becoming de-Christianized.

1. *Modernism*. In this atmosphere, the churches were fighting a losing battle. The Church of Rome, little aware of the challenge, sought with Pius IX to meet it with a bland denial of change and a blanket condemnation of liberalism. Leo XIII (1878-1903) was a more enlightened and supple Pope, but after him modernism was condemned anew and the Church of Rome abstained from participation in the movement of ideas of the time. Thereby it lost much of its hold among intellectuals as well as among the industrial proletariat; more than ever anticlericalism flourished in Catholic countries.

The less rigidly organized Protestant churches, often linked to the state as in Britain, Prussia, or the Scandinavian countries, found it easier to come to terms with the impact of new scientific ideas, but in Protestant countries also polite agnosticism became highly prevalent. If organized religion retained a considerable hold, though often voided of spiritual content, this was in part owing to the belief in its value as a preserver of social order.

The Eastern Church, wholly subservient to the state and operating in much more backward surroundings, was little affected by these controversies.

D. The Impact of Europe on the World

1. The Power and Prestige of Europe. In view of what has just been said, it would hardly be expected that Christianity should make much progress outside of Europe. In fact, its successes were negligible, whether in Asia or in Africa (Mohammedanism was much more successful in making converts in Africa), although missionary activity was substantial. Also, this activity was impeded by the bewildering (to non-Christians) rivalry among Christian sects, and suspicion, often in part correct, that it was a mere cloak for the colonial activity of European powers.

But the potency of these powers was not to be denied and they commanded for that reason influence as well as respect, if not affection. Europe, especially inner Europe, exported the products of its factories as well as its ideas. From outer Europe and from outside Europe there was a steady influx of students to the centers of European learning and technique.

Japan is the one successful example of emulation of Europe in this period. The Young Turks, nourished in western thought, tried but failed to renovate their decadent empire before 1914. The movement had already begun which is coming to fruition in our time, but it was still neither conspicuous nor alarming. Whether through forcible conquest or willing imitation, this is the age when European influence in the world reached its apogee.

2. Progress and Peace. Europe was highly conscious of and took pride in the accomplishments of her civilization and her culture, material as well as moral. Under the latter rubric, in present retrospect ironical, went the widespread belief that the age of peace had arrived. This belief rested in part on awed respect for the effectiveness of the then existing weapons of destruction—another aspect of the worship of science. Colonial wars there might still be, or even Balkan wars, but these occurred essentially beyond the pale of civilization. To be sure, the great civilized states of Europe had differences among themselves, but the very ability to compose these differences, which led to numerous and repeated crises, was used as justifying the hope that these same powers would not allow to break out among them an open conflict in which their common civilization would be wrecked. What has become of this optimism, not universally shared at the time for that matter, will be seen in the last section of this outline.

3. The United States. Much of what has been said was paralleled in the United States between the Civil War and the First World War. By the beginning of the twentieth century, America had become an industrial giant, but her influence was not yet commensurate with her resources and power. This was largely because the American development had been essentially self-contained, Americans being fully occupied with settlement and exploitation at home. For that reason, also, America remained relatively a stranger to the relations and conflicts among European powers. Moreover, and precisely because of the degree of absorption of her energies in the endeavor of physical growth, America in such fields as those of ideas and scientific development, still largely looked to Europe.

CHAPTER 5

The Individual Nations of Europe 1870-1914

It has been pointed out in the preceding chapter that while there is much that justifies speaking of a European community, there are also many differences among the constituent members of that community. Since, in the last analysis, the operation of the community as a whole is bound to be considerably influenced by the peculiar concerns of its component units, it is to this set of considerations that we shall now turn our attention. Broadly speaking, whether one thinks of degree of political evolution, technical development, standard of living, productivity of new ideas, leadership in brief in all those things which constitute the modern world, one may note a gradation from west to east, or better from northwest to southeast.

I. THE WESTERN DEMOCRACIES

A. Form of Government

By the end of the nineteenth century a group of countries had developed a form of government which may be described as parliamentary democracy. These countries were the United Kingdom, France, Italy, Belgium, Holland, Switzerland, and the Scandinavian countries; Spain and Portugal might be added also. For convenience and brevity, the main features of this type of government are outlined here and will not be rehearsed for each separate country.

The traditional division between executive, legislative, and judiciary is found in all these countries, but different in this from the American case, there is no balance between these powers.

1. The Executive. The executive, normally a king, but a president in France and in Switzerland, has been shorn of all effective power and been reduced to a figurehead. The British crown thus resembles more closely the French than the American presidency.

2. Parliament or the Legislative. Effective power is in the hands of an all-powerful legislature, normally consisting of two houses: a popularly elected lower house, and an upper house, hereditary or appointed (Britain, Italy), or else elected under restricted or indirect suffrage (France). Within the legislative, the lower house is dominant, the upper house acting as a brake on, but not an initiator of, legislation. The steady extension of the franchise makes the lower house ever more representative of the people, and the system thus ever closer to full democracy.

3. The Cabinet. The business of government is conducted by a committee of the legislature, the Cabinet or Council of Ministers, under the chairmanship of a prime minister, technically appointed by the executive, but responsible to the legislature with whose approval alone he may remain in office. Legislation must have the approval of both houses and of the executive who, however, has no power of veto.

In the event of the ministry receiving a vote of no confidence in the legislature, it resigns, whereupon a new cabinet is formed which enjoys the confidence of parliament, or else new elections are decreed. Normally, the elected part of the legislature holds office for a fixed term of years, but practice came to vary. In Britain or Italy, elections were held on the occasion of some important new issue or circumstance arising, whether in connection with the fall of a cabinet or not, but in France no elections were held save at the regular four-year intervals. [1]

4. The Constitution. All these countries had constitutional government. The constitution is usually a written document, but in Britain it is made up of the accumulation of laws, traditions, and practices which have collected through the ages. Unlike the American, these constitutions can easily be modified

---

[1] For the single exception to this rule, which served to strengthen it, see p. 91.

by simple vote of the legislatures, new legislation merely superseding older in the event of conflict. There is no organ comparable to the American Supreme Court.

5. *Parties and Politics*. In the United Kingdom, politics operates normally under the two-party system. But this practice, characteristic of the English-speaking world, is found nowhere on the continent, where government therefore must perforce be by coalition. The greater looseness of this arrangement is likely to result in more frequent crises and to produce ministerial instability. This is very marked in France, where the average life of a ministry is less than a year. But the obvious disadvantages of governmental discontinuity are mitigated by the fact that the new coalition which will sustain the successor to a fallen cabinet is likely to differ but little from its predecessor, and much of the same personnel remains in office, though portfolios are reshuffled. Also, considerable continuity is provided by the very important permanent civil service and administration.

Within this group of countries we may now look at individual problems and differences.

B. The United Kingdom of Great Britain and Ireland

This is a period of continued growth and progress and on the whole of prosperity for the United Kingdom. The population increases from some 27,000,000 to over 40,000,000. Still *the* workshop and banker of the world *par excellence* at the beginning of the century, that position meets an increasingly severe challenge. There is great wealth in Britain, but it is highly concentrated, and there is also deep poverty. In this oldest of democracies, class distinctions are in some ways more marked than in some countries with less advanced forms of government.

1. British Politics

a. <u>Conservatives and Liberals.</u> For Britain, the period opens more properly with the Reform Act of 1867 rather than with 1870. Put through by a conservative majority, the act led to a liberal triumph and Gladstone's rule for six years (1868-1874). For all their differences, Conservatives and Liberals have a large area of agreement between them, representing essentially segments of the ruling class.

One great difference between the two parties is that the Liberals are relatively more concerned with the domestic scene. They are the party of peace abroad, and this period of Gladstone's tenure of office witnessed the passage of the Education Act (1870), whereby the state provided increased educational facilities, and the Trades Union Act (1871) legalizing those associations. The relatively passive foreign policy of Gladstone was one of the causes of the success of the Conservatives under the leadership of his great and more colorful rival Disraeli who retained the prime ministership until 1880.

b. THE LIBERAL SPLIT OF 1885. Gladstone was in office again for the next five years, but found it increasingly difficult to resist the rising tide of nationalism and imperialism. In order to remain in office he was led to enter into an alliance with the Irish members, on the basis of a compromise which would grant the latter their desideratum of home rule. This raised an issue within Liberal ranks and resulted in a split in the party. Under the leadership of Joseph Chamberlain, the Liberal Unionists opposed greater freedom for Ireland. With this new group, in addition to the Irish faction, British politics became less stable, and the next ten years, though mainly dominated by the Conservatives, represent a period of transition.

c. THE LIBERAL UNIONISTS. Having separated from Gladstone, Joseph Chamberlain drifted further away from the Liberal fold. Reacting to the changing economic situation, he came increasingly to stress the bonds of empire and even the imposition of tariffs as a solution to the growing competition that was confronting Britain in the world. His evolution was completed with the logical step of his joining the Conservatives, into whose ranks he instilled new life. For ten years, until 1905, the latter were in full control of the government.

d. THE NEW LIBERALISM. But the Liberals, too, were evolving in the meantime and became advocates of the New Liberalism. This meant the rejection of much that had been fundamental in the Liberal faith of the earlier part of the century, and accounts for much of the confusion that attaches to the present use of the term. Liberalism retained its belief in free trade, but instead of defending the virtues of unrestricted free enterprise and competition, now came to advocate a large program of state intervention in the form of state-sponsored social services; the New Liberalism became the exponent of social reform.

The Conservatives meantime found their strength impaired by such things as the divergences raised within their ranks by Chamberlain's advocacy of tariffs and the reactionary and unpopular Taff Vale decision.[2] Late in 1905, the Liberal leader Campbell-Bannerman succeeded the Conservative Balfour upon the latter's resignation, and the ensuing election at the beginning of 1906 was a Liberal landslide. The Liberals were still in office when war broke out in 1914, having vigorously pressed during that decade their announced social program.

e. SOCIAL REFORM. The climax of this program came in 1909 when Lloyd George, the Chancellor of the Exchequer, introduced his famous "war budget." The now familiar, but then novel, conception of financing social services through direct taxation of wealth aroused bitter controversy, and the rejection of the budget by the Lords precipitated an election. The result was that the Liberals could maintain themselves in office only with the support of the Irish Nationalists and the Labor members.[3]

f. THE PARLIAMENT BILL. The issue now changed to a constitutional conflict, for as the Lords refused to bow to the decision of the electorate, a Parliament Bill was introduced in 1910 which would withdraw financial bills from their competence and limit their power of veto on others. Again an election was held in December, 1910 which confirmed the same coalition in power. The Parliament Bill became law in 1911 when the peers, as in 1832, yielded to the threat of swamping their body with a sufficient number of new members that would insure passage of the legislation. The British political system had survived this crisis, thereby confirming its reputation for adaptability to circumstances.

2. *The Irish Question.* Except in the northeastern corner

---

[2] A decision of the House of Lords, in 1901, considered a blow at the right to strike, because of its holding a union liable for damages resulting from a strike.

[3] Labor unions were powerful, but socialism had made little headway in Britain. Not until the election of 1906, when it elected 29 members, can one speak of a Labor party in Britain.

of the island, where settlers in sufficient numbers from Britain had altered the character of the population, British attempts to assimilate or coerce the Irish have yielded nothing but a legacy of bitterness and hatred. One important consideration is that, during the course of the nineteenth century, while the population of Britain was rising from some 15,000,000 to 40,000,000, that of Ireland decreased from 8,000,000 to less than 4,000,000. This, together with the prevailing liberalism of the time, caused Britain to turn to a softer policy toward the island which was legally an integral part of the realm.

a. HOME RULE. In the middle seventies, Parnell organized with other members of the British Parliament the Irish Nationalist party whose first aim it was to restore "home rule" to the island. [4] The size of this group—about 80 members in 1880—made it a factor in British politics. Gladstone, generally sympathetic, put through in 1881 his second Land Act, granting the "three F's" (fixed tenure, free sale, fair rents). This did not satisfy the Irish, whose opposition continued. Gladstone's attempt to retain their support, in the form of submitting a Home Rule bill in 1886, resulted in his downfall and the above-mentioned desertion of the Liberal Unionists. [5]

A similar situation arose in connection with the passage of the social legislation and the Parliament Bill. In payment for Irish support of these measures, the Liberals put through a Home Rule bill in 1912. This was rejected by the Lords. The Lords' suspensive veto would have lapsed after two years, but matters were complicated by the indicated determination of the Protestant minority in Ulster to offer armed resistance to the enactment of Home Rule. However, the issue did not have to be faced at this time, for the outbreak of war in 1914 caused it to be postponed until after the termination of hostilities.

3. The Empire. With a large empire already in existence, Britain naturally was a prime participant in the renewed colonialism of this period. The details of this expansion and its international repercussions will be considered later, along with the imperial activity of other powers. The nature and evolution of the large conglomeration of lands that constituted

---

[4] The Act of Union of 1801 had abolished a separate Irish parliament.

[5] He renewed the attempt in 1893, during his last ministry. The bill, passed in Commons, was rejected by the Lords.

the Empire and came to embrace one-quarter of the world's surface and one-fifth of its population is alone being considered here.

One striking fact is the great diversity of the component parts and of their administration. They may be divided into three chief categories.

a. THE DOMINIONS. The British North America Act of 1867 had joined the eastern North American possessions of Britain, except Newfoundland, into the Dominion of Canada, which was granted self-government with a constitution similar to the British. The growth of the Dominion was rapid; by 1878, it included all British territory north of the United States [6] and its constitutional charter became the model for others. In 1900, the Commonwealth of Australia Act federated the various colonies of that continent, and New Zealand attained dominion status in 1907. After the successful conclusion of the Boer war in 1902, an act of 1909 established the Dominion of South Africa.

The characteristic feature of the Dominions was self-government, the common crown represented by a governor general constituting the chief link with the rest of the Empire. The few remaining rights retained by the mother country were destined to be whittled away in time, and the Dominions were set on the path of full sovereignty. It will be noticed that the Dominions were those lands predominantly settled by Europeans, with the exception of South Africa where Europeans, though a minority, constituted nevertheless a substantial nucleus.

b. INDIA. Larger by far in population than all the rest of the Empire put together was the subcontinent of India, under direct rule of Britain since 1858. In 1876, Queen Victoria assumed the title of Empress of India. India presented a great diversity within herself, and for purposes of administration fell into two parts: so-called British India, ruled directly by Britain; and a congeries of some 600 native states of all dimensions, with their own rulers in alliance with Britain, whose suzerainty they recognized. In actual practice, Britain ruled all India through a viceroy. To India, Britain brought peace and good administration, but also the seeds of nationalism

---

[6] Except Newfoundland, a separate dominion.

which began to voice its opposition to alien rule.

c. THE REST OF THE EMPIRE. In addition to the Dominions and India, a large number of territories, scattered over the face of the earth, colonies in the proper sense, were ruled directly from London. They were for the most part inhabited by backward populations, often at the tribal stage of development. There were also protectorates, in regions where a more advanced civilization existed. These included large sections of Africa, numerous islands, and far-flung strategic outposts of empire.

Egypt. There was finally the special case of Egypt. Following the opening of the Suez Canal in 1869 and subsequent complications with incompetent rulers, the British sent a force to Egypt in 1882. The "temporary" occupation led to ever deeper involvement, although Egypt continued nominally to retain her tenuous Ottoman connection. Not until after the outbreak of war in 1914 was the situation clarified through proclamation of a British protectorate.

C. The Third French Republic

By contrast with the smooth British record of change, France since the great revolution presents a picture of violent discontinuity. The last abrupt upheaval, the fall of the Second Empire in the midst of military disaster, had once more opened the issue of governmental form.

The provisional government, set up after Sedan, proclaimed the Republic, but the final outcome would have been difficult of prediction at the time. The story of the next forty-four years might be summed up as that of the continuing struggle, legacy of 1789, between the forces of conservation and those of change, between right and left, the French electorate in its majority invariably supporting the latter when it came to a crucial test. The issue assumed different guises with the passing of time, but was in essentials unchanged. In the context of pre-1914 Europe, France was the radical state of the continent, somewhat looked askance at by presumably more stable and respectable monarchical governments. More than any other European country she was the ideological battleground of the day and, in the eyes of many, still the standard bearer of the revolutionary ideal.

1. Establishment of the Republic

a. THE NATIONAL ASSEMBLY AND THE COMMUNE. A truce after the fall of Paris in January, 1871 was arranged to permit elections. The National Assembly which issued from this consultation was monarchist in its majority, but the monarchists were divided into two factions: Conservative Legitimists, whose candidate was the Count of Chambord, grandson of Charles X; and the Liberal Orleanists, favoring the Count of Paris, grandson of Louis Philippe. Unable to compromise their differences, the situation was left unsolved while the veteran statesman Thiers headed the government.

The outcome of the war was clear, and Thiers proceeded to negotiate peace. There was in fact little negotiating for Bismarck dictated his terms. The territorial annexation and the five-billion franc indemnity were both unwise, especially the former. The Assembly was faced, in any event, with a major task of internal reorganization, complicated at the outset by the bloody episode of the Paris Commune, suppressed with efficient but needless brutality.[7]

b. MACMAHON. The National Assembly continued in existence until 1875. In 1873, Thiers, having expressed his belief that the Republic was the only possible form of government, was forced to resign by the Royalist majority who replaced him by the more amenable Marshal MacMahon. The legislation enacted by the Assembly became the French constitution, a task completed by 1875. MacMahon bore the title of President of the Republic, and, in 1875, by a one-vote margin, a law providing for the election of future presidents was passed—a measure of the growing but still uncertain republican strength.

The election of 1876 returned a republican Chamber and a monarchist Senate. This precipitated a struggle between the executive and the legislature when, in 1877, a royalist ministry was appointed and the Chamber dissolved. The memory of

---

[7] As in 1848, the National Assembly turned out to be much more conservative than the Parisian government. While the victorious German forces stood aside, Paris underwent a second siege and was taken by the army loyal to the National Assembly. Large-scale executions took place, and the episode left a legacy of bitterness.

earlier *coups d'état* has registered deeply among the French electorate, and the tradition of fear of a strong executive is deep. Its answer was a decisive republican victory, and when, in 1879, the Senate too became republican the President resigned and the Republic had become securely established.

c. <u>Colonialism and Clericalism.</u> The country meantime had made an excellent recovery and was ready to begin reasserting its power. Gambetta, the hero of the struggle for the Republic, died in 1882, and politics reverted to the mere divisions of numerous groups. One important issue of the eighties was that of colonialism, favored by some, opposed by others, such as the radical leader Clemenceau, who thought that French forces should concentrate at home with an eye on the German danger. Under the leadership of the moderate Jules Ferry, the Third Republic embarked on an eventually vast and successful program of empire building, second only to the British.

Clericalism was another important issue. Catholics had, in their large majority, been supporters of a monarchical restoration. It was Gambetta who had coined the phrase, "Clericalism, there is the enemy." Moderates and radicals could agree on this issue, and the Ferry school laws, as well as other "laic" measures, asserted the nature and control of the state against clerical interference.

2. *The Republic and the Army.* France was on the whole rich and prosperous at this time. Her industry, though expanding, was growing at a slower rate than either the German or British, and much accumulated saving was available for investment. In the field of foreign investment also, France was second only to Britain.

a. <u>The Issue of Personal Power: the Boulanger Episode.</u> If the Republic seemed safe, the issue of the strong executive, "the man on horseback," seizing power through a *coup d'état*, was not dead. It reappeared this time in the form of General Boulanger who, from his appointment as war minister in 1886, began to build up a personal following. Though forced to resign in 1887, by playing on the patriotic chord, hinting at revenge against Germany, he achieved considerable popularity and political success by 1889. The danger produced a rallying of Republican forces. When Boulanger was ordered arrested and tried for conspiracy, he merely fled to Belgium, whereupon the movement collapsed. The Republic was further strengthened by the *"ralliement,"* its acceptance by sections at least of the Catholic opposition, although some Catholics remained more Papist than Pope Leo XIII who had suggested the *ralliement.*

b. <u>THE DREYFUS CASE</u>. Shortly thereafter, in 1894, an army captain, Alfred Dreyfus, was convicted of having sold military secrets to Germany. At about the same time there broke the Panama scandal involving improper dealings between politicians and financiers, some of whom were, like Captain Dreyfus, Jewish. These events were conveniently exploited by the exponents of a newly developed antisemitism.

It soon developed that the trial of Captain Dreyfus might have been a miscarriage of justice, but the army was loath to admit the possibility of error on its part, and the Dreyfus affair became the *cause célèbre* of the end of the century, not only in France, but outside. The country became bitterly divided between *dreyfusards* and *antidreyfusards*—with little regard to the actual facts in the case—roughly along the lines of pro- and anti-Republic. The former, counting among them such names as Clemenceau and Zola, formed in Parliament a Bloc of Republican Defense.[8] The relatively minor case of espionage had grown into a trial of strength between the Republic and the army, the outcome of which was that the former definitely vindicated the supremacy of the civilian power. The army was "republicanized," and in the heat of battle, the process was not devoid of petty individual persecution.

3. *The Republic and the Church.* Despite the *ralliement*, only moderately successful, active Catholics tended to be *antidreyfusards*. Anticlericalism received new impetus from the *affaire*, and, in 1901, the Republican bloc put through an Association Law severely restricting the activity of religious congregations and particularly obnoxious to the teaching orders. Anticlericalism was the particular hobby of the

---

[8] Captain Dreyfus was tried and found guilty anew, but pardoned and finally reinstated. The case was conclusively cleared with the disclosure of the guilty parties.

Radicals, one of whose members, Emile Combes, enforced the law with stringency while he was prime minister. The quarrel grew into a larger one, until, in 1905, the Concordat of 1801 was abrogated, and church and state were formally separated in France. The bitter feeling engendered by the dispute somewhat abated after 1907, but here also the Republic had triumphed.

The Third Republic, if politically radical, was definitely bourgeois in character and relatively conservative in matters economic. Social problems began to assume increasing importance after the settlement of the army and church issues. In 1905, under the leadership of Jean Jaurès, the various Marxist groups amalgamated into the Unified Socialist party, an increasingly important factor in French politics; its representation of 56 in 1906 had nearly doubled by 1914.

By that year, there was no longer any threat to the Republic, the monarchists constituting a noisy but insignificant fringe. The Republican bloc had served its function, but the continuing cleavage between right and left was prevented of clarification along new lines by the increasingly dominant role of the foreign situation.

D. The Kingdom of Italy

"We have made Italy; all that remains is to make Italians." This quip of an Italian statesman of the time expresses the dominant fact that the central problem facing Italy after unification was one of integration and organization. The story of her first half century as a united nation may be summed up as just that of integration while at the same time seeking to find her proper place in the European family of nations. In this, she continued to be broadly guided by the liberal Cavourian legacy of the *Risorgimento*.

Outwardly, the problem of integration had been solved as early as 1861 through the simple device of merely erasing the old boundaries and extending to the entire peninsula the rule of the House of Savoy and the constitution of the Kingdom of Sardinia. Upon the great diversity that was Italy was suddenly superimposed a highly centralized administration. A greater recognition of regionalism might, for the longer term, have been preferable.

1. The Economic Backwardness of Italy

a. THE NORTH AND THE SOUTH. The chief difference was between North and South. The North, consisting of Piedmont, the former Austrian provinces of Lombardy and Venetia, the Duchies, and the Papal Legations, had in common the fact that these sections had been participants in the main stream of European life; it was part of inner Europe. The same could not be said of the South, made up of the former Kingdom of the Two Sicilies, Sardinia, and the bulk of the Papal states, where not only had government been reactionary, but administration had ranked with the most corrupt and backward in Europe. The difference in some respects is reminiscent of the American division between North and South. No mere legislative act could produce the results that time alone could effect. This cleavage has, to our day, remained one of the central facts and problems of Italian life and politics.

b. ECONOMIC CONDITIONS. Taken as a whole, Italy is unusually deficient in natural resources. Largely mountainous, much of her territory is not fit for cultivation. Her subsoil is likewise virtually devoid of any of the resources that are needed for industry; of water power alone is she well endowed. Despite this handicap, she contrived to build up a substantial amount of industry, situated almost exclusively in the north. But, even under more enterprising and efficient management than she had in the direction of her economic life, the problem of mere existence was bound to be difficult, even with her generally low standard. Her rapidly growing population could sustain itself only through increasingly large emigration. In turn, the growing emigrant remittances came to be an important asset in redressing an otherwise unfavorable balance of trade. Unlike Britain or France, Italy had no large accumulation of capital for investment abroad, being rather herself a field for foreign investment.

2. The Politics of Italy

a. THE RIGHT AND THE LEFT. This economic backwardness, combined with the background of the political experience of the major part of the country, imposed definite limitations on the operation of the democratic government which nominally was Italy's, and the practice of which had to be learned. Illiteracy was high, and the franchise at first highly restricted. For a time, the country carried under the impetus of the *Risorgimento* and the leadership of Cavour's lieutenants. But this group, known as the Right, fell from power in 1876 and the so-called Left came into office. Italy had neither the British tradition nor the French experience of political struggles and she also lacked the reservoir of a sufficiently large middle class. The personal element loomed inordinately large in her politics, in lieu of abstract principle, and the distinction between Right and Left tended to evaporate.

b. <u>Democratic Dictatorship.</u> The use of patronage was perfected into the practice of "making elections." The result was the emergence of certain dominant individuals, "democratic dictators" as they have been called, who, whether in or out of office, virtually ruled the country.

Depretis, first leader of the Left in power, filled this role until succeeded upon his death in 1887 by Crispi, a strong and somewhat erratic personality. Save for an interim in the early nineties, Crispi's rule lasted until 1896, when his ill-advised attempt at playing the imperial game resulted in military disaster at the hands of the Abyssinians and the termination of his career. The country was not ready for an imperial role.

c. <u>The Transition of the Nineties.</u> The period of the nineties was troubled by social unrest which attempted suppression did little to allay. The socialists made their appearance in this period, and while still too weak to be politically effective, they instilled a fresh leaven into the political life of the nation. The turn of the century witnessed the appearance of a similarly energetic and able, though small, group of nationalists.

But the last decade before the war saw the emergence of Giolitti as the third "democratic dictator." Thoroughly versed in the art of politics and the manipulation of men and parties, Giolitti was enlightened and steadily led the country along the path of democratic practice. In retrospect, and despite all the corruption and abuses of his tenure, many have come to believe that he gave Italy the best administration she could have in the circumstances, and that, had not war intervened to interrupt her progress and distort its course, she would have continued in the steady improvement of democratic practice.

3. *The Roman Question*

a. THE LAW OF GUARANTEES. The incorporation of Rome into the Italian kingdom in 1870 provided a radical and final solution of the problem which its status had presented. But there could be no question of interfering with the functions of the Papacy. The Pope, Pius IX, taking the position that he was victim of an act of force, shut himself up in the Vatican and refused to deal with the Italian state. The latter, therefore, unilaterally enacted in 1871 the Law of Guarantees which it had hoped to make into a treaty. This document recognized the sovereign prerogatives of the Pontiff and insured all facilities for the exercise of his religious functions and for his dealings with other sovereigns. It also provided financial compensation which, however, the Pope refused to accept.

b. THE VATICAN AND ITALIAN POLITICS. The situation was in a way anomalous, and remained so until 1929. In practice, it soon appeared that the Roman question would not be a likely cause of foreign intervention, and a *modus vivendi* was tacitly established. Pius IX had forbidden Italian Catholics to participate in politics, a prohibition which had some effect and tended to enhance the influence of those inimical to, or suspicious of, the Holy See. Anticlericalism was a force in Italy, though never in full control as in France. With the passing of time and the growing importance of social questions, the ban was gradually relaxed, until by 1904 Giolitti was able to reach an understanding which threw the influence of the Vatican to the side of the forces of conservation. This compromise was all the easier to reach as Leo XIII, while maintaining the formal stand of his predecessors, had recognized already in the nineties (encyclical *Rerum novarum*) that, if socialism ought to be combated, the grievances on which it fed likewise ought to be acknowledged and at least mitigated. On the whole, the Roman question turned out to be less of a factor than it might have been expected to be.

E. The Smaller Democracies of Western Europe

The case of Italy may be cited as illustration of the fact that the form of institutions is not necessarily synonymous with their practice, though few would have claimed that she was not riding the dominant democratic wave of the period or that her institutions were endangered.

1. *Spain and Portugal.* The qualification just made applies even more in the case of the two countries that occupy the Iberian peninsula. Constitutional monarchies in form, with the customary trappings of elections and parliaments, these institutions had there little significance. Parties, dubbed conservative and liberal in Spain, corresponded to no reality. In both countries, a reactionary church exerted considerable influence, and the power of the army was likewise strong.

The decline which had started in the seventeenth century, or earlier, had not been arrested. Both countries were essentially agricultural, though Spain began to develop a certain amount of industry in Catalonia and in the Basque region, and they conspicuously lacked that backbone of a modern progressive state, a substantial middle class.

What there was of intellectual and political activity tended to extremism in one direction or another. Anarchism and individual acts of violence are a conspicuous feature of the Spanish political landscape. In the nineties, Spain was stunned by the loss of almost the last remnants of her once vast empire in connection with war with the United States.

The intellectual stirrings which flowered into "the generation of '98" produced some eminent writers, philosophers, and scientists but did not result in the renovation of Spain. Sinking back into conservative inertia, yet unable completely to escape the impact of the modern world, the Spanish monarchy was tottering at the beginning of the century. Spain was also troubled by the problem of separatism, or at least the demand for regional autonomy, conspicuous in the same more advanced and industrialized northern regions of Catalonia and the Basque country.

Portugal's course was generally similar to Spain's. Her becoming a republic in 1910 did little to change substantially the tenor of her life.

2. *The Low Countries.* The small kingdoms of Belgium and the Netherlands were in sharpest contrast to the Iberic countries. Next to Britain, Belgium had been the scene of the most intensive and earliest industrial development, while Holland retained with her valuable empire the commercial prosperity of trade. Both countries, very densely populated, had economic importance altogether out of proportion with their diminutive dimensions.

a. BELGIUM. Ethnically, Belgium consists of two parts: the French-speaking Walloon, and the Flemish. The latter conducted a steady, and eventually successful, struggle for recognition of cultural parity, until the country became bilingual, officially as well as in fact. The constitutional monarchy functioned satisfactorily and so did representative government. The Catholics appeared in Belgian politics as a distinct party, in opposition to the Liberals, who dominated the scene until 1884. Benefiting from the intrusion of socialism, and its rivalry with the Liberals, thereafter the Catholics ruled the country, though not in unprogressive fashion.

The Congo. One particular feature of the Belgian record was the acquisition of the Congo. Leopold II, as much business man as king, organized in the seventies a private company for exploitation of that vast region. In 1885, he received international sanction for the creation of the Congo Free State under his personal rule. In response to widespread criticism of the practices of the administration of the Free State, and in exchange for substantial compensation, King Leopold, in 1908, turned over the territory to his somewhat reluctant country.

b. HOLLAND AND LUXEMBOURG. The record of Holland was generally smooth, prosperous, and uneventful. Despite the constitution of 1848, under the House of Orange the tone of politics was much more conservative than in neighboring Belgium. The question of education absorbed the attention of the country; in 1889, a combination of Protestant Conservatives and Catholics secured state support for denominational schools.

Until 1890 the Grand Duchy of Luxembourg was joined in personal union with Holland. The two became separated upon the death of William III and the accession to the Dutch throne of his daughter Wilhelmina.

3. *The Scandinavian Countries.* These countries which have much in common, historically and culturally, standing outside the main stream of power politics, provide an example of progressive conservatism and good management.

a. DENMARK. In Denmark, the long reign of Christian IX (1863-1906) was largely taken up with the struggle of the lower house to assert its power against that of the monarch and of the upper house. The government could hardly be called constitutional until the liberal success of 1901 which was followed by a struggle to enhance democratic control of the government, a struggle crowned with success in 1914-1915. The constitutional dispute did not impede the economic progress of the country, characterized by the progressive nature of its farming.

b. SWEDEN AND NORWAY. These two countries had been joined under the rule of Bernadotte at the Congress of Vienna. But they differed socially as well as politically. The important Swedish aristocracy had no counterpart in Norway, whose constitution was correspondingly much more liberal than Sweden's. This continued to be the case even after a bicameral parliament superseded the old Estates General in the latter country in 1863. Differences were further accentuated by the growing industrialization of Sweden, not duplicated in Norway.

The Swedish desire for closer integration was countered by Norway's wish for greater independence, reflected in her parliament. This body, in 1905, voted in favor of complete separation, and the Swedish government, though reluctantly, agreed, thus furnishing the world with a rare example of peaceful secession. There followed, in 1907, important liberalizing constitutional amendments in Sweden, where meantime socialism had made its appearance.

4. *Switzerland.* One more state must be mentioned to complete the roster of western democracies, far the oldest among them in terms of governmental methods. Switzerland offers the rare example of a successful multinational state. Divided between German, French, and Italian-speaking sections, divided also between Protestantism and Catholicism, the federation of Swiss cantons had been for a long time a thoroughly integrated nation.

Political democracy, long a practice in Switzerland, was extended by constitutional revision in 1874 which introduced the referendum while increasing the federal power in such matters as education. The initiative in legislation was adopted in 1891.

Following a steady course, Switzerland, little endowed in natural resources, managed to develop a balanced and prosperous economy.

As indicated earlier, the countries which have been so far listed constituted the core of democratic Europe. This statement needs strong qualification in the marginal case of the Iberic countries; and one finds a much more conservative tendency in Denmark, Sweden, and Holland than in Norway, Belgium, or Switzerland, while class distinctions remain important in Britain. But the trend is everywhere the same and unmistakable. The same forces were at work elsewhere but they had not yet achieved comparable successes.

II. THE CENTRAL EUROPEAN POWERS [9]

A. The Second Reich

On January 18, 1871, in the Hall of Mirrors of the palace of the French kings at Versailles, on motion of the King of Bavaria, William I, King of Prussia, was proclaimed German Emperor. The Second Reich had come into existence.

1. The Structure of the Government. The new state was a federation, consisting of twenty-five members, plus the "imperial territory" of Alsace-Lorraine. Each member retained its own governmental structure, but a new constitution had to be provided for the whole.

a. THE CONSTITUTION. At the top, the Prussian king, German Emperor by right, retained the attributes of autocratic power, since the federal chancellor was responsible to him and not to the representative bodies of the state. These bodies were two, the Bundesrat, or federal council, made up of representatives of the rulers, and the Reichstag, popularly elected by all males of twenty-five years of age. Unlike the British Commons, the German Reichstag did not learn to make use of the power of

[9] Geographically, Italy may be said to belong with central rather than western Europe, but by reason of her political practice and cultural affinity has been included in the preceding section.

the purse as the lever through which to establish its supremacy in the state.

Among the German states, Prussia, by sheer weight of size and numbers (she comprised roughly two-thirds of the territory and population), plus the prestige of her role in the wars of unification, was bound to dominate the whole, as in fact she did.

b. THE PARTIES. The political parties which had existed prior to unification continued to function. Among them, the Conservative remained narrowly provincial (Prussian) and fearful of Bismarck's "liberal" tendencies. The Free Conservative party drew its chief support from the Prussian landed aristocracy, while the National Liberals tended to put more emphasis on the first than on the second adjective in their name. Like these parties, the Progressives naturally approved of unification, but, as their name implies, were concerned with securing a more liberal constitution.

Dissatisfaction with, or at least reticent acceptance of, the new state of affairs was more scattered. Representatives of the Danish and Polish minorities, and those from Alsace-Lorraine, were naturally concerned primarily with the fact of their national divergence. There were some "Guelf" deputies wishing to restore Hanoverian autonomy.[10] All of these, together with a few socialists at first, amounted to insignificant numbers. The representatives of the southern states, in large part Catholic, were interested in addition in what may be called the issue of states rights.

2. The "Reign" of Bismarck. Bismarck's prestige was inevitably high in 1871. King William I did the logical thing in retaining him at the helm, where he remained another twenty years to mold and direct his creation. There were no frequent ministerial crises in Germany, and Bismarck had relatively little difficulty in securing the cooperation of the Reichstag, where the first three above mentioned parties formed the core of his support.

a. DOMESTIC INTEGRATION. As in the case of Italy, formal unification was not synonymous with integration. Bismarck

---

[10] Hanover was joined in personal union with Britain from 1714 to 1837, when the accession of Queen Victoria, unable to rule in Hanover, owing to the male law of succession, severed the connection.

was aware of this, and if the federal solution gave greater scope to regionalism than was the case in Italy, he was anxious to encourage uniformity. Much legislation was directed to this end.

The Kulturkampf. Out of this grew a quarrel with the Catholic Church whose universal character was considered a potential obstacle to the national allegiance of its adherents. The struggle, grandiosely dubbed the *Kulturkampf*, began with a Prussian diplomatic break with the Vatican in 1872, followed during the next two years by the "May" or "Falk Laws" designed to strengthen Prussian state control over the Catholic hierarchy. The clearest result of this effort was the consolidation of a Catholic, or Center, party, advocate of religious freedom and social reform, which elected 90 deputies in 1874. Wisely, Bismarck decided not to press the issue, which was allowed to die a quiet death after 1878.

Socialism. One reason for Bismarck's decision was his belief that a potentially more threatening force was that of socialism. Repressive legislation may have retarded, but did not prevent, the growth of socialism, and Bismarck essayed different tactics. Partly with the idea of stealing the socialist thunder, but also in conformity with the paternalistic tradition of the Prussian state, he undertook to sponsor a whole program of social legislation in the eighties. If this also failed to halt the growth of socialism, it put Germany in the forefront of progressive states in this respect.

Economic Development. The paternalistic state extended its interest to the direction of the economic life of the country, encouraging the great outburst of industrial activity characteristic of the period, to the value of which in terms of military power Bismarck was not blind. Thus Germany pursued an economic policy which may be described as mercantilistic, or neomercantilistic, in contrast to the British devotion to free enterprise and trade. This meant protection, and the alliance of eastern landowners with western industrialists, the "marriage of steel and rye," came to be an important factor in German politics as well. There was much of enlightened despotism, with orderly efficiency in the tradition of Frederick the Great, in the conduct of the German state, where the old landed aristocracy, backbone of the army, retained a large measure of prestige and power.

Emperor William died in 1888. The three-month reign of Frederick III was followed by the accession of William II, destined to be the last Kaiser. Young, unsure of himself, and jealous of his power, William II soon found it difficult to put up with the ways of Bismarck, grown old and used to the unquestioned acceptance of his decisions. His resignation was demanded in 1890.

3. William II's Germany. What the record of Wilhelmine Germany would have been had she had a Bismarck to guide her makes for interesting speculation. Certainly, Kaiser William II was an unfortunate director of her policies. Albeit well intentioned, he was unstable and erratic, enamored of the flamboyance of military display. Yet, in some ways, he well personified the nation, too rapidly arrived at too great power, hence displaying some of the characteristics of the *parvenu*, given to power worship, oversensitive, and easily resentful of the calmer assurance of older, longer-established, even if weaker, nations. Certainly also, foreign relations assumed increasing importance: German imperialism and navalism loomed large in the affairs of Europe. These will be dealt with later.

a. THE CONTINUED GROWTH OF GERMANY. At home, the most characteristic feature was the continuation of the astounding record of growth, industrial and demographic, the bases of the former having been laid in Bismarck's time and by him encouraged. Despite a growing demand for liberalization, the structure of the state was unaltered. The same chief political parties continued in existence, but while the Progressives declined, the socialists or Social Democrats made great progress. In 1912, they polled 4,500,000 votes, more than twice as many as their nearest rivals, the Centrists. This growth of socialism was accompanied by an increasing tendency toward conservatism in the party, reform rather than revolution. The political picture was one of stability. By contrast with the kaleidoscopic succession of ministries across the Rhine, there were only four chancellors in Germany from 1890 to 1917.[11] To be sure, none of them approached Bismarck in stature.

---

[11] These were Caprivi (1890-1894), Hohenlohe (1894-1900), Bülow (1900-1909), and Bethmann-Hollweg (1909-1917).

Proud in its power, accomplishments, and growth, the Second Reich was the most modern state of Europe, in terms at least of technique and efficiency. This very record of success redounded to the prestige of the conservative forces under whose aegis it had been achieved. The liberal forty-eighters and their heirs could not compete with this, and the forces of political change were consequently impeded, or at least retarded, in their action. Yet the German electorate was highly literate and politically conscious, though relatively uneducated in the responsibilities of power. The Second Reich was a halfway house between the more democratic west and the purer autocracy in the east.

B. The Dual Monarchy of Austria-Hungary

The ancient House of Habsburg had for long played an important part in the affairs of Europe. Despite steady decline, it still headed one of the great states of this period, the story of which may be summed up as that of the failure to adapt itself successfully to the new conditions of the modern world, with the twin consequences of the disintegration of the state and the demise of the dynasty.

1. The Forces of Disruption: the Subject Nationalities. Nationalism was the central problem of the Habsburg empire, amounting to the basic issue of survival. The *Ausgleich* of 1867 had satisfied the demands of Hungarian nationalism. With the eviction of the Habsburgs from dominant influence in both Germany and Italy, and the constitutional reorganization of 1867, and with the continuing decline of Ottoman power, their function as outposts against Slavdom assumed clearer and more exclusive importance. While this determined the foreign policy of the state, it created at the same time its chief domestic problem. For Austrians in the limited sense, German Austrians that is, and Magyars, together constituted a minority of the population, some twenty million out of fifty in 1914. The rest was predominantly Slavic. [12]

These nationalities were subject, and in their own eyes, oppressed peoples, looked down upon by the dominant groups. If Austrian rule was more lenient than Hungarian, granting

---

[12] See above, p. 52 for the enumeration of these subject nationalities.

concessions to Czechs and Poles, both states were characterized by the tendency to "divide and rule" their subjects. What concessions were made were too little and too late, and a bolder policy of trialism—transforming the dual into a tripartite partnership by giving the Slavs equal status—while advocated by some, was prevented of trial by the vested dominant national interests. The struggle of the subject nationalities grew more intense and bitter with the passing of time, attempts at suppression added fuel to their discontent, and the specter of complete disruption of the empire assumed growing reality.

2. *The Forces of Cohesion.* That the Dual Monarchy held together as long as it did was due to certain traditional and cohesive elements in its structure.

a. THE EMPEROR. The Crown was one such, commanding wide respect, and the personality of the Emperor assumed particular significance. Francis Joseph, come to the throne in 1848, endured until 1916. In his own person and ideas a link with the *ancien régime*, conservative and narrow, but conscientious and hard-working, particularly unfortunate in his personal life, the passing years had given him an aura of fatherliness in the eyes of many of his people.

b. THE ARMY, THE BUREAUCRACY, AND THE CHURCH. The nobility was loyal to the Crown. From its ranks were drawn the officer corps of the army, another major prop of the state. Recruits were of course drawn from all the people, but it became a deliberate practice to garrison contingents of one nationality within the territorial confines of another.

The faithful and likewise loyal bureaucracy, though less rigidly efficient than the German, kept the machinery of the state functioning. The Habsburgs were Catholic and so were the majority of their subjects. Despite occasional differences, it proved to their and to the Church's mutual advantage to adopt a policy of cooperation. [13]

3. *The Evolution of Austria.* The power of the Emperor was constitutionally supreme, but there grew up in Austria a

---

[13] The fact might be added here that, while Austria and Hungary had separate governments, they had in common, besides the Emperor-King, the army and the conduct of foreign affairs. The Delegations, representing the Austrian and Hungarian parliaments, met yearly to discuss these common interests and vote appropriations for them.

fair amount of industry, especially in Austria proper, in Bohemia, and in Silesia, which brought with it the usual concomitants of a commercial bourgeoisie and a proletariat. The former, together with intellectuals allied with it in the Liberal party, dominated the political scene from 1867 until 1878.

Taaffe's Administration. Taaffe came to power then for the next fifteen years. His policy was one of balancing as best he could the various forces in existence. The newly arisen Christian Socialists, nationalistic and antisemitic, could be countered by seeking Czech support. This was not an easy policy to implement, and there was often much confusion and obstructive tactics in parliament as the policy of keeping some sort of equilibrium between warring nationalities became entangled with the effort to deal with the rising Social Democrats.

Taaffe's proposal of granting universal suffrage in 1893, in an effort to divert attention from other difficulties, aroused much opposition and lost him the confidence of the Emperor. Suffrage was nevertheless extended in 1896 and, with some qualifications, made universal in 1907, when the Social Democratic representation rose to 87 members in the lower house, the Christian Socialists having meantime lost strength. Even Austria could not remain immune to the rising democratic tide.

4. Hungary. The Austrian Emperor was King of Hungary, which operated under her own constitution. The fact that Hungary remained essentially agricultural, while industry developed in Austria, made for a healthy economic balance in the state as a whole, while it simplified the politics of Hungary. The government, parliament and ministry, was securely in the hands of the landed aristocracy, many of whom ruled over vast estates. By 1910, in a country of twenty million there were only one million voters.

In some respects, Budapest enjoyed a privileged position with respect to Vienna, whose difficulties it was not loath to exploit on occasion. The narrowness of outlook of the ruling class, successful in preserving the appearance of order, served to increase the mounting pressure of discontent. Not only would Hungary not allow scope to the wishes of her subject peoples, she sought instead to curtail the limited concessions granted the Croatians in 1868, strove to Magyarize the Slovaks, and destroyed the local autonomy enjoyed by Roumanian-speaking Transylvanians.

The unity of the Habsburg domain, from the economic point of view, served a highly useful function. But for all the importance of economic factors, other forces operate as well to mold the collective existence of peoples. Nationalism was such a force in nineteenth-century Europe. In history as in biology, forms of life unable to adapt themselves to changing circumstances are doomed to extinction. Of this, the Dual Monarchy may be considered an example.

III. AUTOCRACY IN EASTERN EUROPE

A. The Empire of the Tsars

1. The Complex That Was Russia

a. RUSSIA BETWEEN EAST AND WEST. Whether Russia belongs to Europe or not will not be argued here. This much is clear, however, that it is as a result of the policy of imitation of western (and central) European ways inaugurated by Peter the Great that she advanced and succeeded in making herself an increasingly important factor in the affairs of Europe.

But Russia also claimed, through Byzantium, the heirship of Rome, as the title of her rulers (Tsar=Caesar) betokened, and there was a strong current in Russia, best represented by the Orthodox Church, which had always maintained that the ways of the West were the ways to perdition, adding the corollary that it was Russia's mission to restore the world to the path of salvation. The name of Dostoevsky may also be cited in this connection.

That tendency should not be either minimized or underestimated, however odd it may seem to westerners impressed by such facts as the backwardness of Russia, the subservience in her of the church, mere organ of the state in a way that bears no comparison with other state churches in Europe, plus the consideration that Russia has been effective in proportion to the extent that she has imitated the West.

b. THE PEOPLES OF RUSSIA. The operation of these contending tendencies has resulted in a rhythm of alternation between eastern and western orientation characteristic of

Russian policy, domestic as well as foreign. Russia's expansion, comparable to the American in its eastern course, has usually concentrated its pressure in one direction at a time. As a result of largely successful efforts, the Russian state, while Russian in its core, had come to include vast numbers of alien population. The whole western fringe in Europe consisted of a variety of non-Russian nationalities: Finns, Esthonians, Latvians, Lithuanians, Poles, and Roumanians.

c. THE RUSSIAN STATE. But in any case, whatever the direction of her policy, it was the result of direction from the top. The Tsar, properly styled "autocrat of all the Russias," was responsible to no one, and did not even have a Reichstag where public opinion could make itself felt. Such public opinion can, in fact, hardly be said to have existed, for the overwhelming mass of the population consisted of illiterate and ignorant peasants, not formally emancipated from serfdom until 1861. The nobility acquiesced in the system. What opposition there was came from intellectual circles—Russia produced able individuals who do not suffer by comparison with their western compeers—but these, inevitably scarce in numbers, could hardly be effective, and, if too vocal, were likely to be driven into forced or voluntary exile. What there was of a middle class was likewise too restricted in numbers to be able to play a significant role.

So retrograde a system is likely to depend upon obscurantistic suppression. The circulation of ideas, justly feared, was carefully watched, and the police was an important prop of the state. Such suppression produces a typical reaction to itself: unable to make itself heard in the open, what opposition there is is driven underground and assumes extreme forms. The system can be destroyed only by violence, and terrorism was the frequent answer to suppression. To the Russian political climate, the British tradition of free debate, peaceful acceptance of majority rule, and gradual but extensive change, was thoroughly alien at all levels. In such circumstances, the personality and policies of the ruler assume paramount importance.

2. *Alexander II (1855-1881).* This Tsar, come to the throne during the Crimean war, and whose first act it was to liquidate that war, exemplified in his own person the alternating rhythms of Russian policy. Impressed by western effectiveness, he had introduced some reforms during the early sixties, but the Polish insurrection of 1863 set him back on the path of reactionary suppression. After the new setback of 1878, [14] he seems to have toyed again with the idea of constitutionalism, and he had had a project of a constitution drafted when he met violent death in 1881.

3. *Alexander III* (*1881-1894*). His successor was of different mettle and entertained few doubts about the proper course his state should follow. Thoroughgoing reactionary, his police minister Plehve, assisted by Pobyedonostsev in the post of Procurator of the Holy Synod, saw to it that Russia did not stray from the proper path. Even the mild beginnings of Alexander II were in part undone; arbitrary imprisonment and exile flourished. The non-Russian nationalities of the empire were subjected to an intense effort at Russification, and the numerous Jews (about 5,000,000) were made the object of specially restrictive measures and even outright persecution.

4. *Nicholas II* (*1894-1917*). The next Tsar pursued on the whole the same policies as his father, whose ministers he retained in office. Much milder and weaker, however, strongly under the less than fortunate influence of his wife, he was not the person to cope with the difficulties that beset his reign and culminated in disaster to the country and to himself.

The natural resources of Russia are vast and one can get a measure of her backwardness by comparing the failure to develop them and the consequently low standard of her people with the development of the United States, possessed of comparable endowment, during the same period. Yet, for all the deliberate isolation from dangerous western ideas and ways, some industrial development had taken place, mainly in western Russia. Count Sergei Witte belonged to the school of "westerners." Put in charge of the ministries of communication and then finance in 1892-1893, he sought to promote industrial development and economic expansion; largely with French capital, much railway building took place. Not surprisingly, the "liberal" Witte aroused much opposition, and was forced to retire in 1903, although his policies were generally continued.

---

[14] See below, pp. 123, 124 for the Russo-Turkish war and the Congress of Berlin.

a. The Revolution of 1905

The Russo-Japanese War and the Revolution. The system might have gone on indefinitely but for the impact of foreign complications. In the course of her eastern expansion, Russia came to cast her eyes upon Manchuria, where she began to infiltrate her influence. But she encountered there a similar penetration on the part of Japan, who, having begun to westernize herself, along with other western ways adopted those of economic and imperial expansion. The rivalry of influences led to war in February, 1904. There was no little surprise, in Russia and elsewhere, when, during the course of the following year, the despised "little yellow men" inflicted a series of decisive reverses, on land as well as on the sea, upon the mighty Russian colossus.

Allowing for the Russian logistic difficulties and Japan's corresponding advantage, the result, confirmed in the treaty of Portsmouth of September, 1905, seemed altogether ignominious. At home, it definitely tarnished the glories of the regime and unleashed a storm of criticism and discontent which the absence of the army made it difficult to deal with.

In July, 1904 Plehve was assassinated, and the similar stamp of his successor did not put a stop to political murders. The government was frightened, and when an inoffensive procession of strikers, led by a priest, proceeded toward the Tsar's palace to submit a petition, it was fired upon by the troops. The episode (January 5, 1905) has become known as "Red Sunday."

The October Manifesto. As unrest seemed to grow rather than subside, the Tsar resolved to make some concessions. Reactionary ministers were dismissed, Witte was recalled to office, and finally was issued the October Manifesto, prelude to a constitution, while a Duma was to be elected, at first under restricted, then nearly universal, suffrage. At the same time, Finland regained her own Estates General, suppressed in 1899, which proceeded to endow the Grand Duchy with a modern constitution.

The Opposition. If unrest was widespread, the organized forces that wanted to reform the state commanded but a small following and were moreover in disagreement among themselves. Russia would hardly seem to have been ripe for the penetration of Marxist ideas, which had nevertheless gained some adherents. A Social Democratic party [15] had come into existence in 1898, while a group attaching greater importance to agrarian problems, as would seem logical in Russia, styled themselves Social Revolutionaries.

Social Democrats, whether Bolshevik or Menshevik, Social Revolutionaries, and those more moderate liberals favoring the establishment of a western type, constitutional, parliamentary state, could agree on the need of reform, but quarreled on its nature, thus weakening the strength of the forces of change. The liberals themselves were divided between "Cadets," under the leadership of Miliukov, and "Octobrists" on the issue of the respective powers of the Tsar and the Duma.

The Dumas. By the time this body first met in May, 1906, the Tsar had already decreed some restrictions on its powers. Witte had been dismissed, and Stolypin, a conservative of the Plehve school, was in charge of the ministry of the interior. With the war liquidated, the frightened forces of reaction had begun to recover. When the Duma sought to assert itself, it was simply dismissed and new elections ordered.

The second Duma, of March, 1907, still proved unsatisfactory to the Tsar. Dismissed like its predecessor, a new constitutional law, restricting and qualifying the suffrage, produced an amenable body in the third Duma of October, 1907. This body, though possessed of little power, did exert a noticeable influence, and there were those who felt that Russia, too, had at last embarked on the western path of representative government along which she was taking the first faltering steps. Economically, too, she was developing, and all that was needed was the gradual labor of time to bring her abreast of the more evolved and advanced countries of the West.

This might have been the case had time been granted. But it was not. When Russia had to meet again the test of arms, the evolution of her structure had not gone very far. A vacillating Tsar, easily swayed by his wife and his court, to say nothing of the less credible doings centering around the strange

---

[15] At a congress, appropriately held in Prague, that is outside Russia, in 1903, a split occurred between the two sections of the Social Democrats on the usual issue, plaguing all socialist parties, of tactics. Henceforth, a left-wing Bolshevik (majority) and a right-wing Menshevik (minority) were in existence, and the present day nomenclature came into use.

figure of Rasputin, did not provide the backbone of material and moral strength needed for survival.

B. The Ottoman Empire and the Balkans

1. *The Empire of the Sultans*

a. <u>Decline of the Ottoman Empire.</u> The Turks had at one time penetrated to the very heart of Europe and for long been a major factor in the affairs of the continent. But the long and uninterrupted decline of their power and the steady retreat of the line of their control had earned their empire the name of "the sick man of Europe." We are dealing here with a state that cannot be described as European by any standards, save the one that its European territory was still substantial, amounting to the greater part of the Balkan peninsula. The rest of the empire, mainly Asiatic, but still extending its dubious suzerainty over much of north Africa, was still very extensive.

The decline of the Ottoman Empire was related to its backwardness. The Turks had shown little understanding of matters economic. The standard of life was low and its level primitive, even representing decline from earlier centuries. What trade there was was in the hands of either Europeans or non-Turkish subjects of the Sultans—Greeks, Armenians, and Jews—to an almost exclusive degree.

b. <u>The Ottoman State.</u> The state was a complete autocracy, with the Sultan at its head. Able and vigorous Sultans had long since given way to incompetent or indifferent rulers, likely to come and go as a consequence of palace intrigues, or assassination when necessary. In theory, and in practice sometimes, the Sultan was absolute and arbitrary master of the lives of his subjects. The army, too, once pride and chief prop of the state, had lost its former qualities. What there was of administration, crude, inefficient, and corrupt, was partly in the hands of non-Turks. Even the writ of Constantinople did not go unquestioned in parts of the empire, a condition to which the nineteenth-century rise of the Egyptian dynasty bears witness.

c. <u>The Role of Religion.</u> The Sultan in addition was

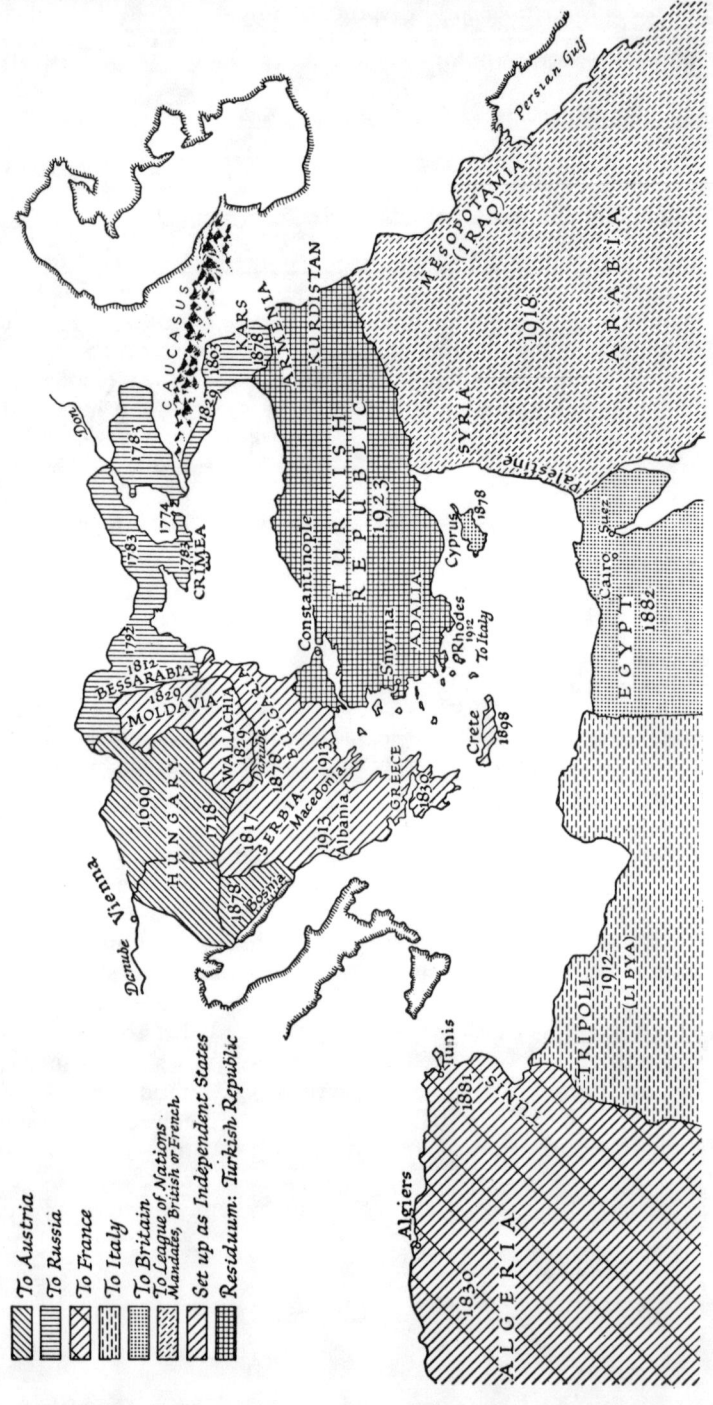

Caliph, that is, religious head of all Moslems. Here was not a case of the church being allied or subservient to the state; one can hardly speak, in fact, of a Moslem church. It was rather a case of identity, the Koran being the basis of all law. Whatever the theoretical virtues of such an arrangement, the whole tendency of the modern world asserting itself in this period, was in the direction of the secular state. Such being the situation, religion rather than nationality had traditionally been the basis of distinction in the Ottoman Empire.

Christians and Jews were on the whole not persecuted on religious grounds; Islam's record of tolerance is rather better than Christianity's. They were different and inferior subjects, liable to certain discriminatory taxation, but otherwise left free to manage their own affairs on the basis of the religious allegiance that was theirs.

Not that Moslem fanaticism could not on occasion be aroused, as attested by the instances of Bulgarian and Armenian atrocities which shocked Christian Europe and caused Gladstone to use the phrase "unspeakable Turk." Such outbursts were likely, however, to have political and economic overtones, easily made to overflow into religious, somewhat comparable to Jewish pogroms in Russia. Christian Europe, though shocked, in actuality did little, mainly for political reasons, to succor persecuted Christian brethren.

d. THE ISSUE OF REFORM. The bulk of the European territory of the Ottoman Empire was inhabited by Christians, mainly of the Orthodox persuasion. The fact that they had resisted conversion to Islam, and that religion played the central role that it did in the Ottoman world, had served to preserve the distinct identity of the Balkan peoples. In Europe, around Constantinople alone were the Turks in a majority; some isolated groups, in Bosnia, in the Dobrudja, Pomaks in Bulgaria, had alone embraced Islam. But it was rather the general maladministration, the exactions of local government, which caused unrest and occasional uprisings in the Balkans and induced the powers to urge reforms upon the Sultan. This demand for reform found some authentic echo among a few Turks. Kemal Pasha was one such, around whom gathered a group of enlightened and liberal Turks who would have emulated the model of the western states. In 1896, he lost his place as grand vizier, or chief minister, to the well-entrenched forces of conservation.

The troubles of 1875-1876 [16] had resulted in the installation of a new Sultan, Abdul Hamid II, and the proclamation by him of a constitution of western type. The constitution was no sooner proclaimed than it was suspended. Abdul Hamid proved a thoroughgoing reactionary, relying upon the crude weapons of suppression and persecution which earned him the nickname of "Red Sultan," and playing the time honored game of trading upon the divergences among his rival "protectors," the powers.

The Young Turks. Such a state of affairs, as in Russia, put a premium on change by violence, if change there was to be. The military are the best-indicated agency of such change. For some time, French revolutionary ideals had influenced a group of army officers, mainly young, hence the description "Young Turks." Their agitation of necessity was secret, and the headquarters of their societies were abroad, in Geneva, then Paris. The most famous of these groups, the Committee of Union and Progress, executed a coup in Salonika in 1908, as a result of which the Sultan resurrected the old constitution, which became the constitution of 1908. Kemal was recalled to office, and a parliament was even elected.

The Revolution of 1908. The result at home was chaos, on top of which foreign complications ensued. There were differences, moreover, between the more liberal and older Kemal and the younger military man, Enver Bey, inclined to stress the factor of nationalism. Under his leadership, another coup took place in April, 1909; the Sultan was deposed and replaced by his elderly and innocuous brother, and the new faction were thereafter in power.

Their promise of renovation, which had initially evoked a surprisingly favorable response among Christian subjects, soon proved to have been a false hope. The accent was put on militarism, nationalism, and Turkification. Appropriately enough, Enver Bey turned increasingly toward a German connection.

2. *Emancipation of the Balkans.*

a. THE BALKAN PEOPLES. The last act, or perhaps the act

---

[16] See below, pp. 123, 124.

before the last, in the story of the Ottoman Empire began in 1878 rather than 1870. It was a continuation of the tale of national emancipation of the Balkan peoples, another chapter in the development of nineteenth-century nationalism. These Balkan peoples, mainly Greek Orthodox in religion, had in common the desire for emancipation from Turkish rule. They consisted, however, of diverse national groups whose mutual rivalry assumed larger importance in proportion as they made progress in the solution of the first and more basic problem of gaining freedom from their common masters.

There is a long and complicated tale of power politics and balance, duplicating on the smaller Balkan stage the politics of the powers on the larger European. What makes it especially involved is the intermingling of the rival Balkan nationalisms with the imperial rivalries of the powers over the entire Ottoman inheritance.[17]

b. THE CONGRESS OF BERLIN, 1878. Prior to 1878, only Roumania, very small Greece and Serbia, and minuscule Montenegro had achieved complete or nearly complete independence. The rest of the territory south of the Danube and the Save, except the Adriatic littoral other than the Albanian coast, was Turkish. The arrangements of the Congress of Berlin recognized the full sovereignty of Montenegro, Serbia, and Roumania. These last two states, and Greece in 1881, were somewhat enlarged territorially; a small Bulgaria was created, and Eastern Roumelia received a degree of autonomy. Among the great powers, Austria-Hungary was placed in occupation of Bosnia-Herzegovina (in compensation for Russia acquiring southern Bessarabia from Roumania, which in turn obtained the Dobrudja), while Britain occupied the island of Cyprus.[18] The integrity of the Ottoman Empire, thus curtailed, was reasserted by the powers. The settlement may be called equitable, as far as the Balkans were concerned, in that it effected a fairly even distribution of discontent.

c. BALKAN GOVERNMENTS AND POLITICS. The Balkan

---

[17] Arab nationalism, copied on western models, began to appear in this period, but still played a minor role by comparison with the situation in the Balkans.
[18] The French occupation of Tunis in 1881 may be regarded as part of the same process of compensation and equilibrium among the powers.

countries developed generally similar institutions. They were monarchical in form,[19] the ruling dynasty usually drawn from one of the numerous German ruling houses. They had representative institutions, to which a sturdy and independent peasantry might eventually give authentic democratic shape. But they were long destined to suffer the effects of the prolonged period of degradation under Turkish rule. Four of them, Greece, Bulgaria, Serbia, and Montenegro, entertained overlapping irredentist grievances against Turkey, as well as toward Austria-Hungary in the case of the last two. Roumania with a better economic potential—wheat, and oil in her subsoil—looked to unredeemed brethren in Hungarian Transylvania and Russian Bessarabia alike. *Coups d'état* and assassination were not rare occurrences in Balkan politics.

The Individual States. Roumania made progress in the development of her resources during the reign of Charles I (1881-1914). The union of Bulgaria with Eastern Roumelia was allowed to take place in 1885, and a change occurred in the reigning dynasty in 1887. Greece's war against Turkey in 1897, though unsuccessful, eventually resulted in the virtual withdrawal of Crete from Turkish control, and, perhaps more important, brought to the fore the Cretan Venizelos destined to play a very large role on the Greek and Balkan stages.

Serbia and Montenegro were exceptions to the practice of imported ruling dynasties. In the long feud between the rival Serbian houses of Obrenovitch and Karageorgevitch, the former had been in power since 1859. Domestic factions, an unpopular pro-Austrian policy, and the complications of the private life of Alexander I (1889-1903), resulted in one of the more spectacular and gruesome Balkan coups, involving the king's assassination. Unwitting Peter I, heir of the Karageorgevitch line, became king, while his minister Pashitch presided thereafter over the destinies of the country.

d. THE BALKAN WARS OF 1912-1913. By 1912, the stage was set for the last scene while Turkey was involved in war with Italy. Partly as a result of foreign, chiefly Russian, interference, the differences between Bulgaria on the one hand, and Greece and Serbia on the other, were momentarily composed. The

---

[19] The ruling dynasties, in most cases, assumed the royal title at some time subsequent to the emergence of the country into independence.

Balkan allies waged successful war against Turkey, as a result of which the latter was virtually evicted from Europe, save for a narrow strip along the Straits. One problem, that of Turkey in Europe, was and has remained settled.

But the powers intervened to impose upon the Balkan allies a settlement in closer conformity with their own views of the proper balance of power, which differed greatly from the plans drawn up by the successful belligerents. War broke out anew, with Bulgaria alone this time against Turkey and all her former allies, joined in addition by Roumania. Bulgaria had to yield and gained little ultimate advantage from these troubled events. Peace was finally restored, Serbia and Greece dividing between them the bulk of what had been Ottoman territory in the Balkans prior to 1912, while an independent Albania was created along the southern entrance of the Adriatic.

For the Ottoman as for the Habsburg empire, the war of 1914 was to usher in the last act, ending in the complete distintegration of the state.

CHAPTER 6
The European Family of Nations 1870-1914

I. GENERAL CONSIDERATIONS

The end of the Napoleonic wars had seen a reassertion of the idea that it was the common responsibility of the powers to preserve the European community from disturbances within or among its members. If the effort to prevent domestic constitutional change was challenged by the opposite doctrine of nonintervention, the desirability of peace, despite failures to preserve it, was not.

A. The Concert of Europe

The Franco-Prussian war was one of these failures, the most important in the nineteenth century. It resulted in a substantial readjustment of power, but the concept of the Concert of Europe continued to play an important part in her affairs until 1914. Two things must be remembered about this Concert of Europe. One, it consisted of the great powers only, of which there were six in Europe: Great Britain, France, Germany, Russia, Austria-Hungary, and Italy, and rested on the theory that the responsibility for peace could not be divorced from the effectiveness of power. The other, the belief that the proper way to preserve the peace was through maintenance of the balance of power.

B. Sovereignty

All states had a right to existence, and none should become disproportionately strong. This concept applied equally under any view of the state, whether it be the property of a God-appointed ruler, or whether the nation be the repository of sovereignty. In addition, the state, large or small, was sovereign.

The anarchy that sovereignty implies was held in check by the balance of power. This is the framework, become traditional, within which European diplomacy operated. Within this framework, such basic forces as democracy, nationalism, industrial growth introduced stresses and strains with which it was the task of foreign offices to deal.

C. Chronological Division

The period from 1870 to 1914 may, for convenience and with a minimum of arbitrariness, be divided chronologically into three parts. During the first twenty years, Germany and Bismarck dominate the scene. From 1890, with his passing from office, there follows a period of readjustment and realignment lasting some fifteen years. From 1904 or 1905, the increasingly uneasy balance between two rival groupings of powers constitutes the prelude to the final catastrophe, or better the epilogue to the nineteenth century.

II. THE BISMARCKIAN PERIOD

The Franco-Prussian war represented not only a victory of German arms; it was a triumph of Prussian diplomacy as well. Not only had Napoleon III been maneuvered into taking the initiative of hostilities, but France found herself thoroughly isolated. The peace settlement was less than wise, for it destroyed any possibility of reconciliation within any foreseeable future. If its terms were judged unduly harsh, and not in France only, the good relations which Bismarck had established with the other European powers continued to prevail after the war.

A. Bismarck's Policy

To Bismarck war was a tool, not an end. Having achieved his goal with blood and iron, he was now satisfied. Germany had nothing to gain by further adventures and could better profit by turning her energies to consolidation of the newly erected structure and internal development of her resources and potentialities. With justly earned prestige, Bismarck was in effect unchallenged ruler of the country.

His foreign policy was simple in conception: be on good

terms with everybody; Bismarck was now a man of peace. Even defeated France could have his friendship, provided she accepted the outcome of the war and genuinely gave up any thoughts of revenge. As to the likelihood of this Bismarck had few illusions, and this had been one reason for a settlement that would cause France the greatest possible injury.

1. *The Western Countries*. If France would not be reconciled, she must be neutralized, that is prevented from entering into alliances; isolated, she was no cause for concern to Bismarck. In 1871, prospects were promising. Britain was not unsympathetic to the new Germany. Traditionally, Britain did not enter into peacetime alliances. Moreover, there would be no foreseeable source of conflict if her imperial structure were not threatened. Britain's destiny was imperial, and Bismarck saw Germany's role limited to the continent. Britain's traditional imperial rivals were Russia and France, a condition wholly satisfactory to Bismarck.

Italy was of no great consequence as a power, and the Roman question would probably—as in fact it did—stand in the way of her making any connection with France. Also, Britain and Italy were, like France, ruled by democratic governments at the mercy of fickle popular majorities: one could not make dependable arrangements with such states.

2. *The Eastern Powers*. The east offered a more congenial prospect. Like Germany herself, the empires of Austria-Hungary and Russia were stable regimes where the ruler had power. For reasons both domestic and foreign, an alliance of conservative states seemed attractive, and toward the formation of it Bismarck directed his efforts. Friendship with Russia had been confirmed by the events of 1863 and 1870.[1] As to Austria-Hungary, excluded from the rest of central Europe in 1866, the war of 1870 had closed the door to any possibility of re-establishing her lost position.

a. <u>Alliance of the Three Emperors.</u> Moreover, farseeing Bismarck had treated her with leniency in 1866. Taking advantage of a strong current in the Dual Monarchy which,

---

[1] In 1863, Bismarck had offered help to the Tsar in putting down the Polish insurrection. During the Franco-Prussian war, Russia had maintained a benevolent neutrality, and Bismarck had been sympathetic to the modification of the status of the Black Sea.

accepting the *fait accompli*, saw in a German connection the best, if not the only, support that the Habsburgs could find abroad, Bismarck succeeded, as early as 1872, in bringing together the three emperors in a joint undertaking to cooperate in the preservation of peace and with a view to a common course of action.

3. *The War Scare of 1875*. There was a minor flurry in 1875, the year of a so-called "war scare." Bismarck was worried by the too rapid recovery and reorganization of France, whom he thought he should have more severely injured. France, on her side, was desirous of testing the international situation. The war clouds were easily dissipated, but the incident served to bring out some inklings of concern in Britain and in Russia over German power and methods.

The task of preserving the peace was, in the seventies, made easier by the fact that, save for Britain and Russia, the powers were largely concerned with their various problems of domestic reorganization.

B. The Eastern Question

1. *Austro-Russian Rivalry in the Balkans*. It was easy for Germany herself to remain on good terms with both Russia and Austria, with neither of whom she had outstanding issues. The problem for Bismarck was rather how to drive the Austro-Russian team. For by his own exclusion of Austria from much of central Europe he had caused that country to concentrate more exclusively her attention toward the southeast, the Ottoman Balkans. This was an area of traditional Russian interest, and if Bismarck did not deem the Balkans worth the bones of a Pomeranian grenadier—for Germany—the Balkan situation was outside his control, as events were to prove.

2. *The Russo-Turkish War*. Trouble began in 1875 in the form of revolts in Bosnia and Bulgaria, growing out of Turkish maladministration. As the troubles increased, the ponderous machinery of the Concert of Europe went into action, but, fettered by the rival interests of its components and the use that the Sultan made of these rivalries, proved incapable of restoring order and peace.

Losing patience with the inconclusive tergiversations of diplomacy, Russia took matters into her own hands and went to war with Turkey in 1877. Having finally broken an unexpectedly effective Turkish resistance on the Danube, the way was open to Constantinople, where the frightened Sultan submitted to the treaty of San Stefano in March, 1878.

a. THE TREATY OF SAN STEFANO. This treaty effected far-reaching rearrangements in the Balkans, its chief feature being the creation of a large Bulgarian state, reaching from the Black Sea and the Aegean to Albania, and including all Macedonia.[2]

b. INTERVENTION OF THE POWERS. Russia's impatience had not been unjustified, but the war, and especially the treaty, laid her open to the charge of unilateral action in clear violation of international agreements designed to prevent just that. The powers could not remain indifferent to the reopening of the eastern question, and Britain, followed by Austria, was the most definitely opposed to the new status created for Russia's benefit. Under Disraeli's leadership, she asserted her position most vigorously. Russia recoiled before a repetition of the Crimean episode, and, though disgruntled, consented to the re-examination of the issue by the powers.

3. The Congress of Berlin. This meeting, diplomatically well prepared, quickly produced a fresh settlement in July, 1878. This was based on the theory of the balance of power, on the European as well as on the smaller Balkan stage. A much reduced Bulgaria emerged, separated from Eastern Roumelia in the south, the latter to be ruled by a Christian prince under Turkish suzerainty. Macedonia and the Aegean coast remained Turkish.[3] Bosnia and Herzegovina, by way of compensation, were to be occupied and administered by Austria, placed in military occupation also in the Sanjak.[4] Having trimmed the Ottoman Empire, the powers reasserted its integrity and even admitted it to their circle.

---

[2] Russia secured some territory in Armenia, part of Bessarabia for which Roumania was compensated by the Dobrudja, and a probably impossible indemnity which might furnish cause for future intervention. The Straits were to be open to all commercial vessels. Nominally, Bulgaria was to remain under Turkish suzerainty, while the full independence of Roumania, Serbia, and Montenegro was recognized.

[3] See above, p. 117 for the local Balkan rearrangements and Cyprus.

[4] This was intended to prevent territorial contiguity between Serbia and Montenegro.

The settlement of Berlin was a neat exercise in the balance of power formula, but caused little satisfaction among most of its beneficiaries. Bulgarians were thoroughly disgruntled, and the fleeting vision of "Greater Bulgaria" has since then troubled the Balkans. Serbs now would nourish irredentist grievances toward the Habsburgs as well as toward the Turks. Among the larger powers, Russia who had fought and won the war, was largely deprived of its benefits, while Britain and Austria had profited. Nevertheless, peace among the great powers had been preserved.

C. Bismarck's New System of Alliances

1. The Austro-German Alliance. Germany sought and received no compensations at Berlin. Bismarck, ostensibly the "honest broker," solely concerned with preserving the peace, was in reality mainly interested in preserving the *Dreikaiserbund*. But Russia's disgruntlement from feeling that he had not adequately supported her, put an end to that tripartite connection.

Faced with a breakdown in the Austro-Russian team, rather than remain alone, and for the sake of the Germanic position in central Europe, Bismarck opted for the former member. In 1879, the Austro-German alliance was made. This was a formal military alliance, specifically promising Austria the assistance of German arms in the event that she should be attacked by Russia, but in that event alone; in form and intent the alliance was defensive. Henceforth that treaty became the fixed cornerstone of German foreign policy and continued in force for the rest of the life of the two empires.

2. The Renewed Dreikaiserbund. But Bismarck, who had no quarrel with Russia, had not abandoned the hope of renewing the tripartite partnership. Second thoughts on Russia's part, the accession of the new Tsar Alexander III in 1881, plus the fact that the time was not yet ripe for a Franco-Russian connection, gave him the opportunity of reviving the alliance of the three emperors. In this same year 1881, Serbia entered into an alliance with Vienna. Bismarck's view of how to compose Austro-Russian rivalry in the Balkans was the reasonable one that each member should recognize the other's legitimate interests in that region. This could be done most simply by drawing a line in the middle: thus Serbia would be within the Austrian sphere of influence as Bulgaria would be in the Russian. Neither power should interfere in the other's preserve.

3. *The Triple Alliance*

a. <u>The French Occupation of Tunis</u>. Neither France nor Italy, though both present, played a significant role at the Congress of Berlin. The Italian representative boasted, in fact, of Italy's clean hands, which some remarked at home were also empty. For a long time, Italy had cast eyes on the Tunisian province, still vaguely connected with the Ottoman Empire. Tunisia was adjacent to French Algeria and therefore a natural goal of further French expansion. France had received assurances from both Britain and Germany that they had no objection to her taking possession. This France did in 1881, producing an explosion of frustrated resentment in Italy.[5]

b. <u>Italy Joins the Triple Alliance.</u> More important than Tunisia in Franco-Italian relations was the Roman question, natural cause in Italy, in view of recent history, of fear of possible French intervention. The Tunisian episode enhanced in Italy the feeling that it would be desirable to have some connection among the powers. Despite Bismarck's scant esteem, he was willing to have Italy as an ally, but, as he put it, "the key to Berlin lies in Vienna." Overcoming the traditional dislike of Austria and the difficulty of the still existing irredenta, in 1882, Italy joined the Austro-German partnership, which thus became the Triple Alliance.

In 1884, Roumania also joined the grouping of central European powers. A network of alliances had thus been woven, the threads of which centered in Berlin. Britain, by choice, remained aloof, and France, by necessity, isolated.

4. *The Serbo-Bulgarian War of 1885.* But the small Balkan countries, though clients, could not always be controlled by the powers. The year 1885 saw war between Bulgaria and

---

[5] Bismarck thought that an interest in colonies would help divert France from the German question. Tunis had, in addition, from his point of view, the virtue of possible Franco-Italian estrangement.

Serbia. The latter country was saved from defeat only by the threat of active Austrian intervention. These events which, to his regret, Bismarck could not control, led to a renewal of the Austro-Russian friction and to the Russian refusal to renew the tripartite arrangement in 1887.

5. *The Year 1887*

a. THE REINSURANCE TREATY. Bismarck would not go back on the decision of 1879 where Austria was concerned. With complete frankness—candor may at times serve better than dissembling—he showed the Russians the text of the Austrian alliance (valid in case of Russian aggression only) and concluded with that country the so-called Reinsurance treaty: just as Germany would aid Austria against Russia, so likewise Russia might, if she wished, come to the aid of France in case that country were victim of German attack. Put otherwise, in the event of French aggression, Russia promised her neutrality, all that Bismarck needed to allay his nightmare of the war on two fronts. In addition, Germany promised Russia her support in Bulgaria and at the Straits.

b. THE GENERAL EUROPEAN SITUATION IN 1887. This, be it remembered, was the year 1887, a year when the European situation was unusually beclouded: Bulgarian affairs were hardly clarified, while Boulanger's rising star in France gave grounds for misgivings about that country's future policy. It was also a year of economic crisis. The Italian alliance was also renewed in this same year, and, partly for the above-mentioned reasons, Italy obtained more favorable terms which recognized her claims in north Africa and gave her a voice in Balkan affairs.

c. THE MEDITERRANEAN AGREEMENTS. In 1887, again, were concluded the Mediterranean agreements. These were not alliances, but a series of bilateral exchanges involving Britain, Italy, Austria, and Spain, ostensibly proclaiming the desire of all these countries to preserve the *status quo* in that sea. Germany, not a Mediterranean power, was not involved, and France, definitely such a power, was excluded. The German system of alliances and the system of Mediterranean guarantees meshed through the common points of Rome and Vienna.

D. The Quality of Bismarck's Diplomacy. This is sometimes presented as the high point of Bismarckian diplomacy. Yet the Bismarckian system began to crumble three years later. What would have happened had not Bismarck been dismissed from office by Kaiser William II is a nice question, but it may be said that the very elaborateness and intricacy of the structure erected by 1887 was a reflection of a changing state of affairs, of stresses and strains connected in large measure with Germany's own changing position.

The Reinsurance treaty might also be described as a tightrope walking act; it did nothing for instance to soften the friction with Russia growing out of Germany's tariff policy. Formerly anticolonialist Bismarck had not been able to resist the pressure of internal economic growth: during the eighties, Germany began to acquire extra-European possessions. Relations with Britain were friendly, but some of the seeds of conflict had been planted. This same force of economic expansion likewise was about to lead Germany to become a major factor in her own right in the affairs of the Ottoman Empire. When Bismarck left the chancellorship in 1890, one of the great issues of German foreign policy was whether or not to renew the Russian Reinsurance treaty of 1887.

III. THE PERIOD OF REALIGNMENT

Before tracing the further evolution of the relations of the European powers among themselves, it will be useful to follow the course of a development which, while not new, was destined to play a much increased role in these relations, namely the imperial expansion of Europe.

A. The New Imperialism

1. The Situation until the Seventies. The great outburst of European expansion which began in the sixteenth century and which in varying form and fluctuating rhythm has been going on ever since, is one of the chief threads that run through the so-called modern period of history. The roots of this expansion are many, but it may be granted that the single most important one is economic.

The first half of the nineteenth century had witnessed the arrival of industry which, quite naturally, concerned itself at first with the needs of the domestic market. European expansion during this period was at a relatively low ebb, and, correspondingly, the imperial rivalries of the powers were relatively mild. The eastern question, a European as much as a colonial issue properly speaking, was the object of the three-cornered rivalry involving Russia, Britain, and France. The Spanish and Portuguese empires were finally virtually destroyed in the early part of the century. Of the great French empire of the eighteenth century barely some token remnants were left and, by 1870, France had done little more than lay the bases of her Algerian possession. The Dutch, despite their losses during the Napoleonic wars, still retained the important archipelago vital to their economy.

Britain alone, among the major powers, was truly imperial, her empire having steadily grown from its beginning, at the expense or through the elimination of successive rivals, Spanish, Dutch, and French. But, even in Britain, during the first half of the century, imperial growth was relatively neglected and even its validity at times questioned.[6]

2. Bases for the Renewal of Imperialism. By 1870, the conditions which made for this state of affairs were about to change.[7] The steady growth of industry in its original home and its spread to new regions had the effect of filling the home and near markets while causing competition to increase. The search for new markets beyond the bounds of Europe was one of the motive forces of the new imperialism about to resume its course of expansion. To it may be added the search for raw materials and the desire to control their source, as well as the pressure of accumulating wealth looking abroad for profitable fields of investment.

a. BRITAIN. To see in these economic forces the sole cause of the renewed imperial expansion of this period would be a misleading oversimplification. The effect of their action is

---

[6] The loss of the thirteen colonies made a deep impression and gave strength to the view that colonies were in any case fated to ultimate emancipation from the mother country.

[7] Russia's imperial expansion, like Britain's, had also been continued and steady. But Russia's expansion constitutes a special type of imperialism, owing to the territorial contiguity and relative emptiness of much of the Asiatic territory. In these respects, it bears considerable resemblance to the westward expansion of the United States.

best illustrated by the British case, for the very basis of Britain's economic life was the fact that the country had become the workshop of the world, making herself over into an almost exclusively manufacturing nation. [8]

Britain also illustrates the importance of the strategic factor. Committed as she was to empire, she found herself involved in a steady process of expansion for reasons of security, either local, or because of the threatened encroachments of European rivals. This explains the consistency of her policy, dictated more by national need than by differences of political philosophy. It was liberal Gladstone who went to Egypt in 1882.

b. FRANCE. The case of France is other. French industry had not developed as rapidly as British, and French capital could have found ample scope for industrial expansion at home. But France had behind her a long tradition of power and of empire. The factor of prestige is an important one in this case. It may seem a contradiction in some respects that the democratic Third Republic should be the one to build an imperial structure second to the British alone. It must be remembered that the French Empire was the work of a handful of individuals and that it was built amidst considerable apathy and not a little opposition at home.

c. GERMANY AND ITALY. Both of these countries entered the colonial race, but they were latecomers in it. In the case of the former, the economic motivations which have been mentioned were effectively present; they and the factor of prestige were responsible for the growth of an important colonial party. It is worth noting, however, that, by 1914, German trade with her colonies accounted for a mere ½ of 1 per cent of her foreign trade. As to Italian colonialism, it had no sound basis. Italy had neither the resources nor the tradition of France, for instance, to sustain her activity in this field. European considerations of power, strategy, and prestige alone explain such an undertaking as the Libyan war of 1911-1912.

d. THE PRESSURE OF POPULATION. This has often been advanced as an argument for colonial expansion, especially in Germany and Italy. Such pressure did exist and from both

---

[8] It should be pointed out, however, that Britain, more than any other country at this time, was devoted to free trade.

there was considerable emigration. But this emigration was overwhelmingly directed to the temperate countries, such as the United States; it could not and did not find its way to tropical countries, unsuited to Europeans. The argument has therefore no economic validity, but is nevertheless a factor, political and psychological, in the operation of the domestic scene.[9]

B. The Partition of Africa

A map of Africa around 1870 shows the bulk of that continent as *terra incognita*, unexplored, let alone pre-empted. Thirty years later, virtually the whole of Africa appears in neat patches of color indicating possession by various European powers. This is a measure of the vigor of the new imperialism, the chief results of which will be enumerated.

1. Egypt. It has been pointed out that the decade of the seventies found most powers devoting their energies to problems of domestic reconstruction and reorganization. Britain was free of this, and the arrival of Disraeli to the prime ministership in 1874 put a conscious and determined imperialist in office. Understandably, Britain had watched with misgivings the building of the Suez Canal by a French company. Palmerston's opposition had failed, and the predictions of unsuccess proved false: the Canal soon proved to be a financially highly rewarding undertaking.

But the poor financial management of the Egyptian ruler gave Disraeli, in 1875, an opportunity to purchase the Khedive's block of shares in the Canal. Continuing Egyptian difficulties resulted in joint Anglo-French intervention in the financial affairs of the country. By 1882, matters were further complicated by rising xenophobia in military circles, and Gladstone found himself compelled to send armed forces to Egypt. The British intervention[10] was intended to meet a temporary emergency, but proved the beginning of ever deeper involvement in the country itself and eventually in its southern extension, the Sudan.

---

[9] Much has been said and written, with considerable response at home, in a country like Italy for example, about the "rightful" colonial claims of a "have-not, proletarian" nation.

[10] At the last moment, France withdrew her fleet.

AFRICA IN 1898

2. *Africa During the Eighties*. By the early eighties, colonial activity began to grow more intense. The French established themselves in Tunis in 1881, and the Germans laid the bases of their four African colonies: Togoland, the Cameroons, German East Africa, and German Southwest Africa. The Italians established themselves on the shores of the Red Sea, while the British and French were pushing in from various points around the periphery of Africa. King Leopold of Belgium had established the Congo Free State, and even Portugal was extending her old coastal holdings in Angola and Mozambique.

a. THE BERLIN COLONIAL CONFERENCE OF 1885. There was ample room in Africa and these penetrations had not yet begun to interfere with each other. In 1885, the powers, meeting in Berlin, gave international sanction to the Congo Free State and agreed to certain procedures (e. g., effective occupation) with a view to introducing order in the process. Thereafter, one may speak of a colonial race, intensified by the desire of each power to forestall possible claims by others. By the end of the last decade of the century the colonial policy of the powers in Africa was shaping along grandiose lines.

3. *The Boer War*. The British had long been established at the Cape of Good Hope, whence the original Dutch settlers had moved northward (the Great Trek) to establish the Boer republics of Orange and Transvaal. The discovery of diamonds and gold in the Transvaal had the customary result of bringing an influx of outsiders (uitlanders) and of upsetting the internal life of the country. From this situation and from the imperial dreams of such men as Cecil Rhodes and Milner developed the conflict with Britain.

The Boer war proved more arduous than expected in London, and the world's sympathy was not on Britain's side on that occasion, but the outcome could not be in doubt once Britain decided to prosecute the war in earnest. By 1902 the Boer republics were subdued and their acquisition gave added impetus to the ambitious scheme which envisioned a large block of British controlled territory running the whole length of Africa and was symbolized by the Cape-to-Cairo railway project.

4. *Other Imperial Projects of the Powers*. The French

meantime had secured control of the bulk of the great bulge of Africa, and were pushing their influence toward the Sudan. Using the small, but important, base of French Somaliland at the entrance of the Red Sea, the scheme, comparable with the British, of an empire covering the entire width of Africa began to take shape. British and French projects could and did collide.

The Germans likewise entertained the idea of a consolidation of their possessions to form a large solid block in central Africa. The Italians, too, briefly entertained a large vision of empire. Starting from Eritrea and Italian Somaliland on the Indian Ocean, their ambitions focused on the Abyssinian uplands. But a setback at Adowa at the hands of the Abyssinians in 1896 produced in them a reaction opposite to that of the British when they met reverses in South Africa. The dream of an Italian east African empire was not revived until forty years later.

These imperial dreams had inevitably important repercussions in the foreign offices of Europe, which will be traced presently. By the opening of the present century, the only portions of African territory not pre-empted by European powers consisted of Libya and Morocco in the north, Abyssinia, and the small Liberian republic.

C. Imperialism in Asia

The story of the impact of the western world upon Asia is different from the African chapter. For one thing, Asia was a densely populated continent, save in her deserts, and the home of highly developed civilizations, older than the European. For another, as against the sudden overrunning of Africa, the Asiatic development was more continuous and gradual.

1. The Dutch Possessions. These have been mentioned. The nineteenth century witnessed the consolidation, expansion, and reorganization of what had been primarily trading posts. Important as it was, the Dutch empire was essentially maintained for the same reason that smaller European states continued to exist, namely the balance among the greater powers.

2. India. The British, long established in India, had reorganized the structure of that subcontinent after the Sepoy mutiny of 1857. The British government, rather than the Company, took control. Both India and Indonesia were prime examples of the functions of nineteenth-century colonialism: markets for home manufactures, valuable sources of raw materials, profitable fields for investment and for good positions for the sons of the ruling class. Dutch and British rule insured law, peace, and order, and also made possible a large increase in population. British rule in India had marked effects on the social structure, and toward the end of the century began to produce the reaction of anti-European nationalism; the Indian National Congress was founded in 1885, and the Moslem League twenty years later.

3. Russian Expansion. The peculiar nature of Russian expansion has also been noted. In many respects it was a manifestation of the Russian effort to reach warm water outlets. The city of Vladivostock had been founded in 1860. In their push in central Asia, it was inevitable that the Russians should meet British interests. Afghanistan provided the first such contact, and was neutralized by agreement in the eighties.

4. The Penetration of China. But the largest single Asian unit was China. The Sons of Heaven, proud of their ancient culture, looked down upon barbarous westerners whose contact they eschewed. They successfully isolated themselves from the currents of the western world—and from the sources of its power. In addition, the ruling Manchu dynasty, quite apart from external forces, was in a state of decadence. European commercial influence had asserted itself in the forties. The Opium War and the treaties of Nanking (1842) and of Tientsin (1857) forced China to open some of her ports to British and French trade first, then to others. The Taiping rebellion in 1850, an internal disturbance, was a measure of China's disintegration. The European powers elected to support the reigning dynasty in a state of suitable weakness.

If the body of China proper was not partitioned, annexations took place on its periphery, in regions of traditional, if loose, Chinese influence: Burma to Britain in 1885, Annam to France in 1883, following some earlier penetration in what was to become French Indo-China. The British were also established in the Malay States.

5. Japan. A new factor meanwhile appeared upon the

scene in the shape of a reformed and rejuvenated Japan which, from 1868, deliberately embarked upon the path of European imitation, economic and military. One result of this imitation was the appearance of a Japanese imperialism. Japan went to war with China in 1894. Chinese contempt was of little avail against Japanese arms which eventually secured Japan possession of Korea and Formosa (treaty of Shimonoseki, 1895).

6. *Further Penetration of China.* Japan's success startled the western powers. There was renewed activity on their part around 1898 which took the form of extracting long-term concessions from China: Kiao-Chao to Germany, Port Arthur to Russia, Kwang-Chao to France, Wei-hai-wei to Britain.[11] The Boxer rebellion in 1899, an antiforeign outburst among other things, resulted in joint foreign intervention, some shocking manifestations of western "barbarism," and the renewed confirmation of Chinese impotence.

a. THE RUSSO-JAPANESE CLASH. It was only natural that Japanese imperialism should cast covetous eyes upon Manchuria. It was equally logical that Russia should object to any foreign influence other than her own, in this region jutting between Vladivostock and Siberia in the great arc of the Amur River. Here was a ready made occasion for a clash which, compromise attempts having failed, occurred in 1904 with a sudden Japanese attack on Port Arthur.

In the largest land engagements hitherto recorded, the Russian forces were decisively worsted by the Japanese, and the ill-considered Russian naval attempt, in the form of sending their Baltic fleet half around the world to the Far East, merely procured a thorough defeat at Tsushima Strait. Peace was made at Portsmouth in 1905. The concrete Japanese gains were perhaps less significant than enormously enhanced prestige; for the first time, a non-European power had defeated a European one in a large and prolonged test of power.

D. The European Realignment

The Russo-Japanese war cast interesting light upon the state

---

[11] The United States had long been interested in the China trade. She did not participate in the scramble for concessions, taking her stand on the open-door principle, meaning that whatever terms of trade were imposed upon China should be available to all.

of the relations of European powers among themselves, for, at the time of its occurrence, Japan was allied to Britain, while Russia was allied with France. Neither Britain nor France entered the conflict; indeed this is the very time when they were liquidating their own imperial differences. The fifteen years elapsed since Bismarck's dismissal had witnessed a thoroughgoing reshuffling in European relationships, now on the point of crystallizing into a new alignment. This story must now be traced.

1. *The Franco-Russian Alliance*

a. THE RUSSO-GERMAN ESTRANGEMENT. The first important break in the Bismarckian system had to do with matters purely European rather than imperial. Bismarck's delicate balancing act of 1887 has been described. During the three-year course of the Reinsurance treaty, relations between the two countries were beclouded as a result of Russian land policy, injurious to German interests, and of German tariff policy, inimical to Russia. In addition to this, or in connection with it, Russia encountered difficulties in the Berlin money market. Two Russian loans were launched instead, with considerable success, in the Paris market. France had for long been anxious to emerge from her isolation, and further cultivated Russia through arms contracts. All this was not yet conclusive, but the German refusal in 1890 to renew the Reinsurance treaty gave a fillip to those forces and persons who favored a Franco-Russian connection.

b. THE FRANCO-RUSSIAN CONNECTION. The connection was not easy to make, for the Russian dislike of France's democratic ways and fickleness was deep. In addition, the interests of the two countries diverged. France's great obsession was Germany, with whom Russia might be annoyed but had no real quarrel, looking as she did either to the Far East or the Balkans. In this last region she met Austria, with whom in turn France had no differences. Basically, the atmosphere created by Germany's too boisterous growth and diplomacy helped to overcome the difficulties. In 1892, the Franco-Russian alliance was formed. It was a military alliance, directed against Germany, but like the Austro-German alliance of 1879, a fundamentally defensive instrument.

It could indeed be argued, and it was, that the new alliance, balancing the tripartite central European connection, made for a better equilibrium and reinforced the prospects of peace. To repeat, both alliances were defensive and could be used, as in fact they were, by one partner to restrain the other rather than egg him on to adventures.

2. *Anglo-French Relations.* The situation of balance may in fact be said to have been reinforced by the position and interests of Britain. That country and France had been traditional enemies, and the vigorous colonial policy of the Third Republic gave rise to a situation reminiscent of earlier days when the influences of the two countries had met and clashed over the globe.

a. <u>Fashoda</u>. The two met in Siam, between Indo-China and Burma, but the tension created by that issue in 1893 was relieved. More serious was the conflict between their overlapping schemes in Africa. Captain Marchand had started a west-east crossing of the continent in 1896 and reached the Nile at Fashoda in 1898. There he was met by Kitchener, operating in the Sudan to redress earlier British setbacks. The meeting aptly symbolized the clash of the two countries, and feeling rose to such a pitch that war seemed likely. At this point, France, in the person of her foreign minister Delcassé, made a wise decision. Judging correctly that British enmity added to German was a luxury that French power could no longer afford, Delcassé accepted the humiliation of yielding. If hostilities were avoided, feeling was not improved for the moment.

3. *Germany and Britain.* In her age-long conflict with France, Britain had tended to look to Germany (or Prussia) as a useful counterweight to French power. Despite the relative decrease of this power, and a certain amount of annoyance at Bismarck's methods, the tradition of friendship lived on in Britain. A colonial agreement in 1890 amicably adjusted relations at various points of contact.

a. <u>Weltpolitik and Navalism</u>. But the Germany of William II, if she continued the progress and growth initiated earlier, lacked the skill of a Bismarck to guide her. Economic growth may be regarded as a process that had to run its course, and German commercial rivalry the world over began to be a serious concern to Britain. The policy of prestige of William II was another matter. William, ever fond of making startling pronouncements, began talking *Weltpolitik* and using such phrases as "our future lies on the water." Translated in concrete terms, this meant a vigorous colonial policy, the right to a voice in any "world" problem, and most of all the launching of an ambitious naval program. This last especially could not leave Britain unmoved, although she did not challenge Germany's right to colonies or to a fleet, so long, however, as vital British interests did not seem threatened, a position that Bismarck had fully recognized.

b. <u>British Approaches to Germany.</u> The whole world situation led Britain to realize that she, too, was suffering a relative decline of power and to re-examine the traditional bases of her policy of splendid isolation. Again, logically in the light of past history, she was led to conclude that a German connection was the most suitable. What nascent rivalry there was could be, in British eyes, amicably composed by reasonable compromise. Joseph Chamberlain, chief champion of this view in Britain, was entrusted with the conduct of negotiations at the turn of the century. To sum up a long story, German suspicions, touchiness, and lack of diplomatic suppleness caused the attempt to fail.

4. *The Entente Cordiale*

a. <u>The Anglo-French Rapprochement.</u> This failure gave an opportunity to the alternative tendency in Britain which felt that, for all past historic rivalry, France no longer presented a serious threat—had she not yielded at Fashoda?—indeed might have much in common with Britain. The new king, Edward VII, coming to the throne in 1901, was favorable to this orientation. On the French side, Delcassé was bold enough to orient his policy toward Britain. The result of this conjunction of circumstances and personalities was the formation in 1904, a bare six years after war had seemed imminent, of the so-called *Entente Cordiale* between the two countries.

b. <u>Nature of the Entente.</u> This understanding, properly named, was no alliance. Wiser than Bülow, his German counterpart, Delcassé did not seek to extract from Britain political commitments in Europe, but was content instead with a purely colonial agreement, trusting to time to complete his work. The agreement registered liquidation of all outstanding differences in the imperial field; the heart of it dealt with Africa where France gave Britain a free hand in Egypt in exchange for a like undertaking by Britain toward France where Morocco was concerned. In the context of the imperialism of the day, this was an eminently reasonable transaction. Naturally, it aroused German suspicion while marking a second defeat for a policy founded of the twin false premises that a Franco-Russian, and even more an Anglo-French, connection were not realizable possibilities.

In her suspicion, Germany thought to put the reality of the Anglo-French understanding to a test. Bülow's blundering diplomacy opens the last section of the present story. But before surveying it, two more things remain to be considered in order to bring the story up to date.

5. *The Role of Italy.* Since 1882, Italy had been a member of the Triple Alliance. In 1887, Crispi became prime minister in Italy. He was a man of ambition, large vision, but insufficient balance. His badly managed imperial plans led to the Adowa disaster and his downfall in 1896. Crispi himself was a strong adherent of the Triple Alliance and very suspicious of France, which heartily reciprocated his dislike. Relations between the two countries deteriorated and a tariff war ensued in 1888. [12]

a. THE FRANCO-ITALIAN RAPPROCHEMENT. This condition prevailed until Crispi's final downfall. This was followed by a reconsideration of her policy on Italy's part. France was willing enough to have Italian friendship if it could be obtained. A limited agreement in 1896 dealt with Tunisian problems, and a commercial treaty in 1898 reestablished normal economic relations. Delcassé, ably seconded by his ambassador in Rome, Barrère, pursuing this advantage, obtained an agreement in 1900, similar with the later one with Britain in 1904, and the terms of which were Tripoli (to Italy) versus Morocco (to France).

b. ITALY ON THE FENCE. Better still, from the French point of view, in 1902 there took place a Franco-Italian exchange of

---

[12] The repercussions of this are interesting. It was one reason for the flow of French capital to Russia, instead of Italy, and correspondingly, this is the period when German financial interest in Italy became important.

notes the ambiguous gist of which was that Italy might remain neutral in the event of a Franco-German war. Almost simultaneously, Italy renewed the treaty of the Triple Alliance.[13] What this meant in effect was that Italy, ever sensitive barometer of the fluctuations in power relationships, was reserving her freedom of action, taking a position on the fence between two rival camps, instead of being solidly aligned with either.

6. *The Ottoman Empire and the Balkans.* This region, transitional between Europe proper and the area of imperial rivalry of the powers, was relatively quiescent during this period. Problems and issues there were, the Serbian coup of 1903, a Greco-Turkish clash in 1897, the perennial issue of reforms in Turkey made the object of much talk, but nothing but talk, by such episodes as Armenian massacres. None of these led to major power clashes. One reason for this was the softening of the Austro-Russian rivalry which "put the Balkans on ice" for a time while Russia was concentrating her energies in the Far East.

a. GERMAN INTEREST IN THE OTTOMAN EMPIRE. A new factor, however, entered upon the scene. Here also, Wilhelmine Germany, reversing Bismarck's lack of interest, became involved in her own right rather than indirectly through the Austrian connection. William II's visits to Palestine, to the Sultan, accompanied by suitable (or not so suitable) speeches, were a manifestation of his role as Germany's foremost salesman. Germany developed substantial economic interests in Turkey, second only to the French and British, which took primarily the form of railroad-building concessions. Starting from Constantinople toward the Anatolian interior, the great Berlin-Bagdad scheme gradually began to take shape.[14]

7. *The Fluidity of International Relations.* The foregoing survey of the evolution of international relations at the turn of the century purposely gives the picture of an unmistakable drift. This is a picture of retrospect, and it must be

---

[13] These treaties and agreements were generally secret at the time. Their existence, but not their terms, were known.

[14] These German railway schemes were the object of much diplomatic activity involving Germany, Britain, France, and Russia. This activity was carried on up to 1914, and ultimately resulted in peaceful compromises.

remembered that the trend of the present is never so clear in its own eyes. At the time, there appeared to be much fluidity and confusion and no inevitability of outcome. To repeat again, the alliances were defensive and by no means exclusive; there was talk of their interpenetrability. Might not Russia, allied to France, be the agent for bringing that country and Germany together? Such an outcome was one of William II's dreams; he envisioned beyond it a grand continental alliance. William was also fond of holding up the Yellow Peril as an inducement to European unity: when Japan defeated China in 1894, she was forced to relinquish some of her gains by the combined pressure of Russia, Germany, and France.

When Britain was seeking to obtain a strip of the Belgian Congo that would establish territorial continuity between her northern and southern African possessions, the deal was blocked by joint French and German opposition. Franco-German cooperation, extending to a continental league, was a possibility to which Britain, ever opposed to European unity, could not remain indifferent. The best way to prevent such a development would be to make a connection with some one of its members; Britain's courting of Germany failed, and the connection with France began to take shape in 1904. But Britain also had a long-standing imperial rival in Russia and it is of interest that the first formal alliance into which she entered was with another imperial rival of Russia: the Anglo-Japanese alliance was made in 1902.

Even the Anglo-French agreement of 1904 was one the results of which the future alone could tell. In the perspective of the past, its solidity might seem questionable at the time of its making. If Delcassé built large hopes upon it, in British eyes it certainly was an understanding of clearly limited scope which by no means committed Britain to an unalterable course. The story of the evolution of British policy and the other developments of the European scene will now be surveyed.[15]

---

[15] It will be noted that the whole question of imperialism has been treated exclusively from the point of view of the European powers. The rights and wrongs of imperialism from the point of view of the subject peoples are another matter which is, however, purposely excluded as extraneous to this treatment.

IV. THE LAST DECADE: THE ROAD TO WAR

The last decade of European peace was characterized by an increasing hardening of the connections hitherto described. The lessening fluidity of relations made the balance of power ever more precarious and tenuous. In such a situation, relatively minor issues assume disproportionately large importance, suspicion thrives, and the factor of prestige becomes itself a major consideration, reflection that it is of power standing. This, in turn, lies at the root of the accelerating rhythm of crises that confronted Europe during these ten years.

A. The First Moroccan Crisis

1. Morocco before 1904. By the beginning of our century, Morocco, the northwestern corner of Africa bordering on the Atlantic and the Mediterranean, was still an independent entity. Such a state—if so it can be called—could not hope to withstand in independence the pressure of European imperial expansion. No decree of Providence, however, assigned Morocco to France, and the region was fairly open to the penetration of all. But, wholly surrounded as it was by French possessions, [16] it was logical that it should some day be absorbed in the French empire. Italy, in 1900, on the basis of a *quid pro quo*, had taken such a view, and Britain had done likewise in 1904. Fundamentally, Germany also agreed with this. She had certain economic interests in Morocco, but some day would consent to French political control in exchange for suitable French concessions elsewhere. This was the eventual solution of the problem, but before it was reached, in 1911, Moroccan developments were the source of two major international crises.

2. Bülow's Tactics. Wishing to test the Anglo-French agreement of 1904, Bülow, the German Chancellor, proceeded to assert unspecified German claims. This was a tactical move: the vaguer the claims, the higher the price France might be induced to pay. Dark hints that military action might be

---
[16] Spain asserted some claims which were made the object of a Franco-Spanish agreement, also in 1904.

considered should further enhance the price and bring out the precise position of Britain in regard to France. Bülow's bluff, for such it was, was in a sense successful and had consequences far beyond those intended. He managed to frighten the French government to a point where Delcassé, who favored a determined policy on resistance, had to resign. Bülow took foolish pride in his victory, and instead of cashing in on his advantage, by trying to pursue it further contrived to unite French opinion in the belief that Germany was bent on sabre-rattling intransigeance. He conveyed a similar impression in Britain.

3. The Conference and Act of Algeciras. Germany won the first hand. While France wanted a bilateral agreement with her, Bülow, with ostensible propriety, insisted on holding an international conference to consider the affairs of Morocco.[17] The conference met in January, 1906, and its result was the Act of Algeciras. This reaffirmed the international status and the open-door situation in Morocco, but at the same time recognized France's right to insure order, if necessary, in the country. Most significant, Germany found herself isolated at the meeting, receiving lukewarm support from Austria alone. She had indeed tested the Anglo-French agreement of 1904 to which her own policy had given, within a year, truly the nature of *Entente Cordiale*.

4. The Björkö Episode. There is a footnote to this episode. In 1905, Kaiser William met his cousin Tsar Nicholas on a Baltic cruise at Björkö. Playing on their personal friendship, and on such things as the lack of French support for Russia in the Far East, William induced Nicholas to initial a Russo-German agreement.[18] It is revealing that, in the midst of the Moroccan imbroglio, the Kaiser should have genuinely considered a Russian threat to desert France a likely means to induce that country to join his cherished continental league. Needless to say, nothing came of the project to which the advisers of the two rulers were equally opposed.

---

[17] The international status of Morocco had been regulated by the Convention of Madrid of 1880.

[18] The original draft of this agreement dated from the preceding autumn, when it had been considered and abandoned. The discussion itself is an indication of the continued fluidity of relationships.

B. The Triple Entente

1. The Anglo-Russian Rapprochement. It was in the year after Algeciras that another of the basic assumptions of German policy was proved invalid. In 1907, Britain and Russia came together in a manner similar to that in which France and Britain had three years earlier. The Anglo-Russian agreement was an exclusively imperial one, dealing with Asia, across the whole length of which, from Turkey to China, the interests of the two countries met and clashed. The problem of the Straits, covered by existing conventions, did not apear in this agreement, the subjects of which were China, Tibet, and Persia. The line of the Yang-Tse-Kiang in China would delimit respective spheres of economic interest; both countries would stay out of Tibet, and also of Persia. This last was divided into three zones: a Russian in the north and a British in the south, separated by a neutral middle region.

2. The Triple Entente and the Einkreisung. France was naturally pleased at this development toward the realization of which she had striven. Facing the Triple Alliance there was now a Triple Entente, consisting of one formal alliance, the Franco-Russian, and two *ententes* involving England. For the long run, basic community of interest is likely to be a stronger binder than formal written charters. This common interest was created in large measure by German policy, or at least by the impression that policy gave of itself abroad. The unmistakable trend could not but alarm Germany. The Pyrrhic victory of Algeciras, followed by the Anglo-Russian agreement, were shocks to German opinion, and it is around this time that there began to be talk in Germany of the famous *Einkreisung*, or encirclement. To a point this was so: to the extent that Germany would convince others that she was a potential, irresponsible threat to peace she might induce them to join in restraining her.

C. The Bosnian Annexation Crisis

1. Austria and the South Slavs. The Russian setback in the Far East had the effect of shifting the alternating interest of Russian policy back toward Europe again. The Balkans, "on ice" since 1897, were no longer so. On the Austrian side, the problem of nationalities was increasing in acuteness. So long as Bosnia and Herzegovina were merely under Austrian occupation and administration, the door was not irrevocably closed on the possibility that these lands might join their South Slav Serbian cousins. The coup of 1903 in Belgrade had given free rein to the expression of South Slav irredentism now that Serbia was no longer, even only formally, Austria's client where foreign policy was concerned. The idea of annexation of the provinces, often considered before, was taken up once more.

2. *The Buchlau Bargain and the Annexation.* But Russian interest must obviously be considered. The foreign ministers of the two countries, Aehrenthal and Izvolsky, meeting at Buchlau in the autumn of 1908, discussed a possible *quid pro quo:* Austrian wishes in Bosnia-Herzegovina, Russian ones at the Straits. However, no formal written agreement was made. Izvolsky went on to a tour of other European capitals and felt that he had been taken advantage of by his Austrian counterpart when he was apprised that Austria had formally proclaimed the annexation.

The move was a clear violation of international agreements, however inept Russia may have been in abetting it, just as her own unilateral action in 1878 had been. The subject was one for joint consideration by the powers, but Austria had deliberately committed herself in public, and now insisted that her action could not be submitted to outside intervention. For reasons of prestige, Germany took the position that she must stand by her ally, whose humiliation would otherwise reflect upon herself. In this crisis, Russia found herself alone: the response in Paris and in London had been unsympathetic to Izvolsky's desire to alter the status of the Straits, and these capitals, though disapproving Austria's action, did not see in it a sufficient cause for hostilities. Russia, moreover, had not yet recovered from the Japanese war and was militarily unprepared.

3. *The Solution of the Crisis.* Face was saved, ostensibly, for all concerned through the agreement of the powers to accede to this modification of the treaty of Berlin of 1878, so that legality was preserved.[19] No one was blind to the reality the Austro-German combination had definitely scored a victory, albeit a purely diplomatic one. Russia was frustrated and embittered, Serbia was incensed, and the feeling of uneasiness at German methods was reinforced. The crisis of 1908 has been considered by many as a preview to that of 1914. But it could also be argued that, however awkwardly, another crisis had been peacefully surmounted.

a. <u>The Racconigi Agreement.</u> Italy had thoroughly disapproved of the action of her ally, and even sought, without success, to invoke compensation of the basis of the terms of the alliance. Her response, in 1909, was the conclusion at Racconigi of the Tittoni-Izvolsky agreement which laid the basis for future Italo-Russian cooperation in the Balkans, therefore implicitly directed against Austria.[20] Italy was drifting still further away from the Triple Alliance which, formally at least, remained nevertheless in force.

D. The Second Moroccan Crisis

1. French Intervention in Morocco. Following Algeciras, Moroccan affairs receded into the background, but the passing of the years made clear, as was to be expected, that France would find it necessary to intervene in that country. In 1911, she notified the powers that a force would be sent to Fez. The restoration of order is an operation presumably limited in both scope and time. But there was good reason to believe—witness Britain in Cyprus or Egypt—that a "temporary" occupation would be easier to initiate than to terminate. There were few illusions on this score, least of all in Germany, where the feeling was that the time had come for a final liquidation.

---

[19] This was the time of the Young Turk revolution in Turkey. Formally, the Porte renounced all sovereign rights in Bosnia-Herzegovina, in return for a money payment by Austria. It was this Austro-Turkish agreement that the powers endorsed.

Note that the fiction of the intangibility of international obligations had similarly been preserved by the retroactive sanction given by the powers to the unilateral Russian alteration in 1870 of the Convention of the Black Sea of 1856.

[20] Russia on her side agreed to the Italian claim to Tripoli.

As in 1905, the motivation was reasonable and sound; as in 1905, the diplomacy was faulty.

2. The "Panther" Incident and the Franco-German Agreement. It took the form this time of sending a warship to Agadir (hence the Agadir crisis), ostensibly for the protection of German nationals in Morocco. The move created all the sensation that its planners may have desired, and elicited a very strong public warning from Britain, which in turn caused irritation in Germany. Though desirous of negotiations with France, Germany used again the same tactics as in 1905, a sphinxlike attitude designed to create uncertainty and enhance the price of agreement. A long and difficult negotiation finally produced a Franco-German agreement in November, 1911, whereby Germany received territory in the French Congo and France was free to establish a protectorate over Morocco.[21] This she proceeded to do in March, 1912.

From this point on, the accelerating rhythm of crises kept Europe in an almost perpetual state of tension. The Ottoman Empire once again became the focus of disturbance.

E. The Italo-Turkish War

1. Italy's Preparations. The ambiguous position of Italy has been mentioned. Ever since the French acquisition of Tunisia by France, she had determined that French influence must not extend eastward over Tripoli. In this, she had obtained the promise of support of her allies, and even, implicitly, of Britain (in 1887). In 1900, France had agreed that Tripoli should be Italian, and Russia in 1909 took the same view. Italy held therefore a blank check from all the powers where Tripoli was concerned. Fear of the changing European situation, of growing German interest in the Mediterranean among others, caused Giolitti to decide that the check had better be cashed. Tripoli had no economic value, but to have it fall to any other power would certainly have been a serious blow to Italian prestige.

2. The War. Tripoli—more precisely the vilayets of

---

[21] Economic interests of other nations were not affected by this arrangement, just as they had not been by other similar colonial compromises, such as the Anglo-French of 1904.

Tripoli and Cyrenaica—was still nominally Turkish. In 1911, before Moroccan affairs were fully settled, Italy declared war on Turkey. Giolitti's management was better than Crispi's, and within a year, the Sultan had agreed to the cession to Italy of what came to be known as Libya.[22]

The war was a relatively minor affair, hostilities being largely confined to Africa, but the delicacy of the European situation made it unpopular with all the powers. Greatest concern was felt by Italy's own formal allies: Germany was in process of building up her influence, political and military in addition to economic by now, in Constantinople; Austria actually invoked the terms of the alliance in order to prevent Italy from extending hostilities to the Adriatic and the Aegean. Italy on her side urged that the best way to terminate a disturbance involving the Ottoman Empire was for the powers to exert pressure on the Porte to yield to Italian desires.

F. The Balkan Wars

One factor which induced the Sultan to put an end to the Italian war was the need to gather forces nearer home to meet brewing Balkan trouble. The small, and new, Balkan states presented a small-scale replica of the larger European canvas, highly nationalistic and very jealous of each other. Turkish territory in the Balkans was still extensive, reaching to the Adriatic. This territory was the object of irredentist claims of the Balkan nations. Bulgarian, Serb, and Greek ambitions overlapped and clashed in Turkish Macedonia, for years a concern of European diplomacy.

1. The Balkan League. Serbo-Bulgarian enmity was of long standing and intermingled with the rivalry between Russia on one side, Austria and Germany on the other. It was a measure of Russia's diplomatic success—and of her reckless irresponsibility some would say—that she helped contrive an understanding between Serbia and Bulgaria in 1912. With the addition of Greece, the Balkan League was formed, whose purpose was joint war against Turkey. The powers took

---

[22] The conquest and pacification of the interior took another twenty years. Italy also occupied "temporarily" the Dodecanese islands pending fulfillment by Turkey of the modalities of cession.

alarm at these intrigues, but their attempted intervention came too late to prevent the outbreak of hostilities in October, 1912.

2. The First Balkan War and the Intervention of the Powers. The successes of the Balkan allies were unexpected in both their extent and rapidity. Turkey had to sue for peace, the price of which was her virtual expulsion from Europe, where she has since been confined to Constantinople and the European side of the Straits. At this point new complications arose from the fact that the arrangements for the division of Turkish spoils entered into by the Balkan states among themselves did not fit into the power balance calculations of the greater powers. Austria in the first place would not let Serbia have a sea outlet on the Adriatic. Serbia, accordingly, sought concessions from the Bulgarian share in Macedonia, for which the latter country showed little inclination.

3. The Second Balkan War. Albania. When Bulgaria, unwisely, attacked Serbia, she found herself confronted by a new Balkan coalition; Roumania joined the fray, which Turkey re-entered. The second Balkan war resulted in the swift and thorough crushing of Bulgaria, which was dealt with in the treaty of Bucharest of August, 1913. There remained the matter of Serbia, Montenegro, and Greece, on whom the Concert of Europe, effective for the last time, imposed its views. The heart of the compromise, worked out by the conference of ambassadors in London, was the creation of the new independent state of Albania. Such a people as Albanians indeed exists—some 1,000,000 of them—but whether an Albanian state was a viable creation was another question again.

4. The Aftermath. Peace was restored, though not until Serbia had yielded to an Austrian ultimatum. It was a settlement that showed the great powers desirous of peace and willing to compromise among themselves, but which left a trail of rancor and dissatisfaction in the Balkans. Bulgaria, for one, was thoroughly disgruntled. Most important perhaps was the effect on Serbia: Serbian nationalism was at once elated at the successes of Serbian arms and frustrated by the final outcome. The focus of its rancor was henceforth the Dual Monarchy. Less than a year after these events, the pistol shot at Sarajevo, incident in the story of Balkan emancipation, was to set fire to the powder keg of Europe.

G. Europe on the Eve

It is easy enough, in retrospect at least, to see that these recurring crises and increasing tensions were but steps on a path leading logically to a result that one may be tempted to call inevitable.

1. The Armament Race. There is no doubt, for instance, that growing tensions were reflected in vastly increasing armaments. The armament race in which Europe had been engaged for some years before 1914 was not so much a token of aggressive intent as a vicious circle that the powers found no way to break. The piling up of arms is a result rather than cause of insecurity.

Economically, the burden of arms was not unbearable; Europe was on the whole prosperous and creating ever-increasing wealth. The role of diplomacy, in a situation of delicate balance, where prestige assumes disproportionate value, had become extremely important. But, just because of the tensions in existence, the diplomatic and military arms of the states became ever more closely entangled, particularly in the case of the nondemocratic states.

2. Britain and France. This is also illustrated, however, in the case of Anglo-French relations. Ever since the conclusion of the 1904 agreement, France had sought, with skillful and persistent patience, to obtain a clearer definition of British commitments in Europe proper. This effort Britain steadily resisted, but it was a losing battle. By 1912, arrangements were made by the two countries, whereby the British fleet was to concentrate in the Atlantic and the French in the Mediterranean, each to look after the interests of both countries in its respective sea. German navalism lay at the root of this arrangement.

The military staffs had meantime been holding conversations and making plans on how to handle such things as a joint campaign in the event of a German march through Belgium. These were strictly technical discussions, not treaty obligations, but to maintain in the face of it all, as Grey did to Cambon as late as 1912, that Britain's hands were wholly free, was perhaps less than realistic. It has been argued, and officially accepted in Britain, that the country would have better served the cause of peace by taking a definite position instead of entertaining a state of misleading confusion.[23]

3. The Relaxation of Certain Tensions. This British behavior was the result of historic tradition, and expressed the fact that Britain refused to accept as irrevocable the division of Europe into enemy camps. In 1912 again, Lord Haldane, the war minister, went to Germany to discuss the perennial issue of German naval programs. If no fruitful conclusion was reached, the discussions were frank and friendly. It was in 1914 that the last of a series of agreements was made, between Britain and Germany, which provided for an amicable liquidation of differences over the Berlin-Bagdad railway scheme.

4. The "Inevitable" War. As against the interpretation of inevitability, such things must be considered as the fact that the succession of crises just surveyed was evidence of the possibility of peaceful compromise. Even such a deep-rooted source of enmity as the issue of Alsace-Lorraine, though still alive, had lost much of its virulence with the passing of the years. There were voices warning of danger, but there was also much confidence abroad that these great civilized powers had in effect succeeded in outgrowing so crude a method as war in settling differences among themselves. Also, it was unthinkable that civilized man should encompass his own destruction, which a general war, it was believed, would have entailed.

War, as we know, occurred, but to those living in 1914 it came as a shock and surprise rather than as the working out of inevitable fate. It has been rightly said that, in 1914, Europe blundered into a war which she did not want. The task of history, however, is not primarily that of speculation on might-have-beens, but rather that of exposition and explanation of the record of things that have been. Having traced the course of Europe toward catastrophe, we must now observe the outbreak of this catastrophe, its course, and its consequences.

---

[23] On the other side, it could be argued in favor of the British policy that the very uncertainties surrounding the English position could serve as a deterrent to rash action by others.

PART III
The Passing of Europe's Supremacy 1914-1939

SELECTED READINGS*

Albrecht-Carrié, René, *Italy from Napoleon to Mussolini* (1950); Albrecht-Carrié, René, *France, Europe and the Two World Wars* (1962); Albrecht-Carrié, René, *One Europe* (1965); Ardagh, John, *The New French Revolution* (1968); Arendt, Hannah, *The Origins of Totalitarianism* (1951); Aron, Raymond, *The Century of Total War* (1954); Bailey, Thomas A., *Woodrow Wilson and the Lost Peace* (1945); Beloff, Max, *The Foreign Policy of the Soviet Union, 1929-1941* (1947-1949); Bergmann, Carl, *The History of Reparations* (1927); Birdsall, Paul, *Versailles Twenty Years After* (1941); Bowman, Isaiah, *The New World* (1928); Brenan, Gerald, *The Spanish Labyrinth* (1944); Brzezinski, Zbigniew K., *The Soviet Bloc: Unity and Conflict* (2nd. rev. ed., 1964); Bullock, Alan, *Hitler: A Study in Tyranny* (rev. ed., 1964); Carr, E. H., *The Soviet Impact on the Western World* (1947); Carr, E. H., *The Twenty Years' Crisis, 1918-1939* (1939); Chamberlin, William H., *The Russian Revolution, 1917-1921* (1935); Churchill, Winston S., *The World Crisis (1923-1927)*; Churchill, Winston S., *The Second World War* (1948-1954); Cruttwell, C. R. M., *History of the Great War, 1914-1918* (1934); De Gaulle, Charles, *War Memoirs of Charles de Gaulle* (1955-1960); Deutscher, Isaac, *Stalin: A Political Biography* (1949); Diebold, William, *The Schuman Plan: A Study in Economic Cooperation* (1959); Duverger, Maurice, *The French Political System* (1958); Fainsod, Merle, *How Russia is Ruled* (1953); Falls, Cyril, *The Great War* (1959); Feis, Herbert, *Neither War nor Peace: The Struggle for Power in the Post-War World* (1960); Furniss, E. S., *France: Troubled Ally* (1960); Finer, Herman, *Mussolini's Italy* (1935); Fuller, J. F. C., *The Second World War, 1939-1945* (1948); Gathorne-Hardy, G. M., *A Short History of International Affairs, 1920-1939* (1942); Gilbert, G. M., *Nuremberg Diary* (1947); Goodrich, Leland M., *The United Nations* (1959); Grosser, Alfred, *The Federal Republic of Germany* (1964); Gurian, Waldemar, *Bolshevism, Theory and Practice* (1932); Harper, Samuel N., *The Government of the Soviet Union* (1938); Heiden, Konrad, *Der Fuehrer, Hitler's Rise to Power* (1944); Hitler, Adolph, *Mein Kampf* (Reynal & Hitchcock ed., 1940); Hodson, Henry V., *Slump and Recovery, 1929-1937* (1938); Holborn, Hajo, *The Political Collapse of Europe* (1951); Hoffman, Stanley et al., *In Search of France* (1963); Howard, Harry N., *The Partition of Turkey, 1913-1923* (1931); Jordan, W. M., *Great Britain, France and the German Problem* (1943); Kalijarvi, Thorsten, ed., *Peace Settlements of World War II* (1948); Keynes, John Maynard, *The Economic Consequences of the Peace* (1920); Kirkpatrick, Ivone, *Mussolini: A Study in Power* (1964); Kogan, Norman, *A Political History of Postwar Italy* (1966); Kulski, W. W., *De Gaule and the World* (1966); Lichtheim, George, *The New Europe—Today and Tomorrow* (1963); Liddell Hart, B. M., *The War in Outline* (1936); Luethy, *France Against Herself* (1955); Marston, Frank S., *The Peace Conference of 1919* (1944); Maurice, Frederick, *The Armistices of 1918* (1943); Maynard, John, *Russia in Flux* (1948); Monroe, Elizabeth, *The Mediterranean in Politics* (1938); Mowat, Charles L., *Britain Between the Wars* (1942); Namier, Lewis B., *Europe in Decay* (1950); Neumann, Franz L., *Behemoth: The Structure and Practice*

---

* In view of the time span covered, and in order to avoid repetitions and duplications, these readings cover both Parts III and IV.

of National Socialism (1942); Pickles, Dorothy, *France: The Fourth Republic* (1955); Pickles, Dorothy, *The Fifth French Republic* (1960); Robbins, Lionel, *The Great Depression* (1935); Rosenberg, Arthur, *A History of Bolshevism from Marx to the First Five Years' Plan* (1934); Rosenberg, Arthur, *A History of the German Republic* (1936); Rudin, Harry, *Armistice 1918* (1944); Seton-Watson, Hugh, *Eastern Europe Between the Wars, 1918-1941* (1945); Seton-Watson, Hugh, *From Lenin to Khrushchev* (1960); Shotwell, James T., ed., *Governments of Continental Europe* (1952); Shub, Daniel, *Lenin, A Biography* (1948); Taylor, A. J. P., *English History, 1914-1945* (1965); Thomas, Hugh, *The Spanish Civil War* (1961); Thomson, David, *England in the Twentieth Century* (1964); Thomson, David, *Democracy in France* (1965); Toynbee, Arnold J., *The World After the Peace Conference* (1925); Toynbee, Arnold J. and Veronica M., *The Realignment of Europe* (1955); Ulam, Adam B., *Expansion and Coexistence: The History of Soviet Foreign Policy, 1917-1967* (1969); Wheeler-Bennett, John W., *Brest-Litovsk, the Forgotten Peace* (1939); Wheeler-Bennett, John W., *Munich: Prologue to Tragedy* (1963); Willis, F. Roy, *France, Germany and the New Europe, 1945-1963* (1965); Wilmot, Chester, *The Struggle for Europe* (1952); Wiskemann, Elizabeth, *The Rome-Berlin Axis* (1949); Wiskemann, Elizabeth, *Europe and the Dictators, 1919-1945* (1966); Wolfe, Bertram D., *Three Who Made a Revolution* (1948); Wolfers, Arnold, *Britain and France Between the Wars* (1940); Wright, Gordon, *The Reshaping of French Democracy* (1950).

Europe in the First World War

CHAPTER 7

The First World War

I. THE OUTBREAK OF WAR

A. Sarajevo

It is a measure of the continuity of history that the 28 of June (St. Vitus day) should have been a day of commemoration for the South Slavs, harking back to the episode of the battle of Kossovo in 1386. It was less than tactful of the archduke Franz Ferdinand, heir to the Habsburg throne, to choose that day to attend a display of the empire's military strength in Sarajevo, the capital of Bosnia. A group of fanatical nationalist conspirators, preparing for just such an occasion, successfully carried out their plot: Franz Ferdinand and his wife were killed. The pistol shots of June 28, 1914 truly were destined to ring around the world. That date marks the end of the nineteenth century and the beginning of our own era of conflict and transition.

B. The Diplomatic Activity in July, 1914

1. The Central Powers. Whether or not directly involved in this particular event, Serbia was, by her very existence, a focus of danger in the eyes of the Vienna government, which reacted to the assassination with the determination to settle scores once and for all with the small Balkan nation. If Austria did not act at once, it was because of divided counsels at home (Hungary, whose premier, Tisza, it took time to convince) and because of the wish to implicate the Serbian government through the findings of a local investigation. But the whole European situation had to be borne in mind.

Little Serbia was not friendless. Russia, her prime if not disinterested protector, was determined that there should be no repetition of the Austrian success of 1908.[1] The intrusion of

---
[1] For the Bosnian crisis of 1908, see above, pp. 145-147.

the Russian factor brought into play the whole network of European alliances. Austria consulted her German ally who, with irresponsible levity, offered unqualified support, the so-called "blank check" of July 5. Her other ally, Italy, was carefully kept in the dark lest she should exert a moderating influence.

a. THE ULTIMATUM TO SERBIA. It was not until July 23, however, that Vienna sent Belgrade a formal ultimatum. This document was couched in such terms as would, it was hoped, insure its rejection, thus providing the pretext for military action. Much of the outside sympathy which had gone to Austria at the moment of the assassination had by this time evaporated. Wisely, Serbia sent back an unexpectedly conciliatory answer, accepting most of the Austrian conditions, and offering to submit the rest to arbitration. [2] On July 28, war was formally declared upon Serbia. But meantime the European chancelleries had witnessed a rising tempo of diplomatic activity.

2. The Russian Intervention. Russia had begun to prepare for mobilization, partial at first, then total. The significance of mobilization, in the case of land powers, must be stressed: it is difficult, and might be fatal, to attempt to stop in its tracks the military machine once set in motion; the military assume greater voice in state councils; and that is why mobilization is regarded by many as tantamount to war. In the event, France decided to stand firmly by her Russian ally. [3]

3. The Failure of Mediation. It logically fell to Britain, least directly involved, to sponsor efforts at mediation. These failed, partly because Germany, though regretting her initial rashness and now desirous to hold back her ally, did not feel that she could run the risk of a diplomatic setback for the

---

[2] Certain Serbian officials had assisted the conspirators and supplied them with arms.

[3] French diplomacy was partially handicapped by the absence of the French President, Poincaré, and the foreign minister, Viviani, in Russia at the time. At the same time, the very presence of these personages served to bolster the Russian position. The French motivation in standing by Russia is comparable with the German in standing by Austria. The Austrian ultimatum to Serbia was timed to coincide with the departure from Russia of the French delegation, who would thus be on the high seas at that crucial moment.

central European combination. This state of affairs Austria exploited to the full.

C. Declarations of War

Despite some lingering hopes of conciliation even after July 28, [4] impressed by the importance of the time factor, Germany, on July 31, sent a 12-hour ultimatum to Russia asking her to demobilize. This failing, she declared war upon Russia on August 1. A futile inquiry of French intentions resulted in a German declaration of war on August 3. Europe was at war save for two major powers, Britain and Italy.

1. Italy, Britain, and the Belgian Question. Taking the position that the action of her allies was a breach of the terms of the alliance—which it was—Italy declared her neutrality on August 3. Britain had no formal alliances, but her commitments to France put her in an awkward dilemma. There was uncertainty about her stand, but at this point Germany's action in avowed violation of her long-standing obligation to respect Belgian neutrality on the dangerous plea that necessity is the higher law, resolved the British dilemma. Britain declared war on August 5.

D. The Issue and Debate of War Guilt

1. Long- and Short-Term Causes of the War. From these events, from the increasingly ideological character of the war (especially after 1917), and from the assertion of German guilt written into the treaty of peace, has stemmed the acrimonious debate on the issue of responsibility for unleashing the catastrophe of war. The long-term causes lie in the history of power rivalries which may be traced to the formation of rival alliances, to 1870, or indeed as far back as one wishes. As distinct from these, there is the narrower question of responsibility for acts of commission or omission from June 28 on. The Austrian espousal of brutal suppression, in itself a confession of failure, is understandable; and so is the Russian

---

[4] At the eleventh hour Germany favored the so-called "Halt in Belgrade" scheme, whereby Austria would have been allowed to occupy Belgrade but would not have proceeded farther. The scheme failed of acceptance owing to the too great suspicions already existing and given further point by the Austrian behavior.

determination not to accept a repetition of 1908. Germany acted with levity at first and realized too late the implications of her blank check. She was not an immediate prime mover. In so far as one can speak of German responsibility, in the broader and deeper sense, it lies in the record of a too rapid German growth, guided, or rather misguided after Bismarck, by a crude and incompetent diplomacy which created the very coalition that it professed to fear; and deeper still, in the essential nature of the German state as molded by its architects.

2. *A Peoples' War*. But what is equally important to remember is that in such a war as broke out in 1914, where all resources, human and material, of the nation are called into play, it is essential to uphold the morale of the broad masses of the people. To that end, the conviction of fighting a just, because defensive, war is of prime importance; that conviction, however sound or false, was basically shared by all the initial belligerents.[5] The growing stress on moral values, moral earnestness at its purest and propaganda at its crudest, are concomitants of a peoples' war, manifestations of the spread of the nineteenth-century force of democracy.

In the heat of battle, the varying shades of grey became sharp blacks and whites. The battle over, disillusion leads to cooler appraisal by some and violent revulsion on the part of many. Thus the debate on war guilt has been not only an important historic debate but a prime factor in the practical politics of the postwar period, exploited—paradoxically enough —by American isolationism and by German Nazism alike.

II. THE WAR (1914-1918)

A. The Initial Phase of the War

1. German Strategy: The Schlieffen Plan. The war on two fronts, Bismarck's nightmare, had now become reality. The answer of the German military to this possibility had been the Schlieffen plan: by quick action, to eliminate the western

---

[5] Socialists everywhere had been antimilitaristic, antinationalistic, and antiimperialistic. But in 1914 they nearly all accepted the defensive interpretation of the war in whose patriotic furtherance they acquiesced. One result was the demise of the Second International.

foe, before the eastern could bring to bear his larger but slower moving forces. Speed was the essence of the scheme, which could not run the risk of delay before the French border fortresses. These must be turned, hence the necessity of passing through Belgium. Despite some useful delay from the Belgian refusal to allow unimpeded passage, Belgium was overrun, and the French pushed back from the Belgian border. In late August, the German armies were making rapid strides toward Paris.

2. The Battle of the Marne. At this point, the French forces, injured but not broken, decided to make a stand on the Marne. The successful Battle of the Marne (September 6-12), comparable in its effects to the Battle of Britain of World War II, was the first turning point of the war: despite considerable success, the German attempt was essentially a failure. There followed an equilibrium of forces, the contending armies seeking to outflank each other, and in the process extending the range of their operations to the Channel. The initial war of movement thus gave way to the trench warfare characteristic of the First World War. For four years, a solid front of opposing armies remained established from the Channel to Switzerland.

3. The War in the East. A similar situation developed in the east after a sooner than expected Russian offensive was successfully turned back in East Prussia at Tannenberg. The end of 1914 found a solid front established along a line roughly following the western frontier of Russia from the Baltic to Roumania. As to Serbia, inadequate Austrian forces were unable to dispose of her.

4. The New War. Position of the Belligerents. It had been a common expectation that the war must be of short duration. But the military situation in the autumn of 1914 compelled a revision of all calculations: preparations must be made for a conflict of unpredictable length while means were sought to break the stalemate.

    a. <u>The Central Powers.</u> The initial advantage lay with the Central Powers, better prepared militarily. For the longer term, they enjoyed moreover the advantage of interior lines of communication without the handicap of divided authority.

To all intents and purposes, the German high command controlled the situation and ran the war throughout its duration.

b. THE ALLIES. In terms of ultimate potential, however, the Allies commanded far greater resources, human and economic. Their superior naval power could blockade the Central Powers while insuring to themselves access to their own vast empires and to the whole wide world. But it would take time to convert this potential into actual tools of war, whether soldiers or guns.

c. THE DISLOCATION OF WAR. On the continent, the mere fact of mobilization of millions of men meant a sudden and drastic readjustment of the life, economic and social, of the belligerents. Britain had no conscript army; overseas the readjustments were slower still, but increasingly the demands of the fronts made themselves felt in widening circles throughout the world. Clearly, the Allies needed time. The Marne meant that they had survived the first round. It should be emphasized that no plans had been made on either side for a long war; the organization of it presented a whole new set of problems which were solved piecemeal as their urgency became apparent.

B. Two Years of German Successes and Continued Stalemate, 1915-1916

In the last analysis, the war was won by the greater weight of allied resources. But many unexpected events were to take place before this came to pass.

1. The Search for Allies. One obvious way to break the deadlock was to secure the assistance of additional help from the neutrals. Holland, the Scandinavian countries, and Switzerland retained their neutrality throughout the conflict. Spain did likewise, but the more turbulent eastern Mediterranean offered greater opportunities. [6]

a. THE INTERVENTION OF TURKEY. For the long term, the weak spot among the Allies was industrially backward Russia. Hence the importance of the Turkish Straits. German diplomacy, capitalizing on its prewar assets in Constantinople, secured first an alliance in August, then the actual intervention

---

[6] Japan entered the war late in August, but her activity, confined to the Far East, had no significant effect on the course and outcome of the war.

of the Ottoman Empire in November. Free passage through the Straits for the Allies could be secured only by force, and the Allies finally espoused the idea of opening the Straits. The conception was basically sound, but the execution of it defective, and the attempt, begun in February 1915, was a recognized failure by April.

b. THE INTERVENTION OF ITALY. Following the initial declaration of neutrality and the German failure in the west, the question soon became in Italy how best to profit from the conflict, whether from continued neutrality (for a price from Austria) or from what could be obtained for joining the Allies. The result of negotiations conducted with both sides was an Italian declaration of war on Austria in May, 1915. Italy's entrance into the war was to be coordinated with a Russian offensive, but the plan went awry. Some initial Russian successes soon turned into reverses, and the Italian intervention merely resulted in the creation of a new front from Switzerland to the Adriatic.

The Eastern Front. While the western front remained essentially stable and quiescent during 1915, the Central Powers registered notable successes in the east. Although the Russian forces were not annihilated, they suffered disastrous losses, and by the end of the year, the Austro-Germans were established along a line running from Riga to the Roumanian frontier.

c. THE INTERVENTION OF BULGARIA. Further successes were granted the arms and the diplomacy of the Central Powers. An offensive against Serbia from the north was synchronized with a Bulgarian attack in the rear. Between these pincers, the Serbian army was crushed, and its remnants, trekking through the desolate Albanian mountains during the dead of winter, were evacuated to Corfu. By the end of 1915, the German command controlled the resources of a solid block of territory stretching from the North Sea to the Persian Gulf: Berlin-Bagdad was a reality. It fell mainly to the British forces from the overseas empire to hold outposts on the periphery of the Ottoman Empire. Despite setbacks, Suez was held, as well as the Persian Gulf base.

2. *The War at Sea.* The war at sea was assuming growing importance. Some German raiders scattered throughout the world in August, 1914 caused a certain amount of damage to allied shipping but were eventually tracked down. On the surface of the seas the Allies held a clear superiority, but the very existence of a substantial German fleet immobilized in the North Sea a large section of the British navy. The commercial blockade was largely effective, save for what could be brought in through neutral countries. The issue of freedom of the seas was to become increasingly important, inevitably affecting the only important remaining neutral, the United States.

a. <u>Submarine Warfare.</u> In the circumstances, Germany bethought herself of intensifying the use of an essentially novel weapon, the submarine. This she did with considerable success, and there were anxious months in Britain when the rate of sinkings reached alarming proportions. From its very nature, there is a premium on the submarine not abiding by the then existing rules of war at sea as they applied to merchantmen. In this case also, the tendency was to take the position that necessity is the higher law. The sinking of the Lusitania in 1915 created a considerable stir in America. American protests, a relaxation of submarine warfare, allied shipbuilding and countermeasures made it possible to surmount the crisis.

b. <u>The Battle of Jutland.</u> The year 1916 witnessed the only surface naval engagement of importance, the battle of Jutland. It ended inconclusively, the German fleet making good its return to its home ports.

3. The War in 1916. In the continued stalemate, the German command returned to a modified version of its initial plan, the elimination of the western front.

a. <u>Verdun and the Somme.</u> An offensive of unprecedented magnitude and intensity was launched around the key French fortress of Verdun (February-July). The result was a failure to break through, but a huge carnage and expenditure of material resources, typical of what had come to be a struggle of attrition.

In an effort to regain the initiative while relieving the pressure on Verdun, an equally inconclusive offensive was launched by Franco-British forces on the Somme. British forces had been taking over an increasing portion of the western front; by January, 1916, necessity had driven Britain to resort to the unprecedented step of conscription.

b. <u>Other Theaters of War.</u> An Austrian attempt on the Italian front was contained, and helped the Russians in an offensive of their own in Galicia. But the Germans retrieved the situation there. Later, the Italians achieved some successes, but the situation remained basically unchanged on both fronts. In the Middle East, growing British forces, aided by the revolting Arabs, achieved some notable successes. Both Bagdad and Jerusalem fell to them in 1916.

c. <u>The Intervention of Roumania.</u> But the year was to end with another success for the Central Powers. Roumania declared war upon them in August. Initial advances into Transylvania soon turned into retreat. By the end of the year Bucharest had fallen and the country was overrun. Despite the considerable wear of their own resources, this success was used by the Central Powers to initiate a "peace offensive" in the form of vague proposals for the termination of hostilities. But neither side was sufficiently exhausted either to yield to the adversary or to find a possible meeting ground with him.

d. <u>War Weariness of the Belligerents.</u> The favorable appearance of the war map was not an accurate reflection of the position of the Central Powers. Their war losses and the blockade were beginning to tell on them, especially on the weaker structure of the Dual Monarchy. One effect was substitutions in the German high command, which more than ever dictated all aspects of government policy.

Weariness appeared in France as well, where it was reflected in freer politics and led to changes in the government as well as in the military command. In Britain, Lloyd George emerged in leadership at the end of 1916.

Socialists in various countries began to recover from the 1914 failure of their international structure. At Zimmerwald in 1915, and at Kienthal in 1916, they began to reassert their earlier interpretation of the capitalistic-imperialistic nature of the war, but their appeals to the belligerent masses met little effective response. War weariness was general and widespread, especially among the continental peoples, and might become an important factor in their staying power. At the end of 1916 the outcome of the war was an open question into which the year 1917 was to introduce unexpected components.

C. The Year 1917, the Crisis of the War

1. *Intervention of the United States.* The growing resources of the Allies had caused the German command to doubt the possibility of a decision on land. It decided to return to the use of unrestricted submarine warfare in the hope of eliminating Britain. The consequence of this decision was a renewal of differences with the United States.

a. <u>Background of the American Intervention.</u> While inevitably concerned from the first with the fact of war and the possibilities of its outcome, the United States, feeling that the quarrels of Europe were not her own, had adhered to strict neutrality. Much was heard of the promise to "keep us out of war" during the presidential election of 1916. President Wilson had entertained some hopes of mediation, but the visits of Colonel House to Europe in 1915 and 1916 had shown the lack of basis for a negotiated peace.

By 1917, moreover, the United States, while essentially cut off from commercial dealings with the Central Powers, had built up a substantial and growing trade with the western allies. The financing of this trade was beginning to raise serious problems, for the financial resources of these allies were seriously strained. It may therefore be said that the United States as a whole—labor, as well as bankers and farmers—had acquired a stake in an allied victory. There was, in addition, the more fundamental factor, from the point of view of the national interest, of the long-term consequences of a possible German victory resulting in the domination of the European continent by a strong military and militaristic power. These considerations doubtless served to condition American policy. But the immediate and specific occasion was Germany's unrestricted submarine warfare, which precipitated a rupture of relations followed by a declaration of war on April 6, 1917.

b. <u>Effects of the American Intervention.</u> Many problems, chiefly of an economic nature, were solved for the Allies by America's entrance into the war. The virtually immeasurable resources of the United States would now be available for the prosecution of the conflict. Militarily, America was unprepared; her contribution could not be significant at first. Should, however, the conflict be prolonged, the American military potential, once realized, could become a decisive factor. But perhaps the greatest immediate value of the American entrance into the war was the moral factor, the realization on the part of the increasingly wearied allied peoples that their cause had the unlimited American reservoir of power to draw upon.

2. The Collapse and Defection of Russia

a. SITUATION OF THE CENTRAL POWERS. Conversely, this same consideration might be expected to depress the morale of the Central Powers. The weaker partner, Austria-Hungary, showed such signs of fatigue that the new Emperor Charles [7] initiated, through the French, approaches to the Allies with a view to a negotiated peace. Nothing was destined to come of this attempt save an increasing control by Germany over the conduct of the war when the news of the attempt was revealed.

But America's intervention need not be fatal to the fortunes of the Central Powers, provided only that they could snatch victory before the American potential was realized. Time again, as in 1914, became of vital importance. These hopes and calculations were by no means unreasonable, for, despite the domestic difficulties that beset the Central Powers (food shortages and labor troubles) the Allies suffered no less from disaffection, especially after the failure of their offensives: strikes in Britain and France, mutinies in the latter country, growing defeatism in Italy.

b. THE RUSSIAN REVOLUTION

The March Revolution. But the chief hope of the Central Powers, of greater immediate consequence than the American intervention, lay in the Russian situation. Despite some successes in organizing war production, the essence of Russia's difficulty lay in her backwardness, economic, political, and social. Mismanagement and growing disorganization at all levels resulted in increasing unrest that culminated in the revolutionary outbreak of March, 1917 and resulted in the Tsar's abdication and the creation of a provisional government.

---

[7] Francis Joseph died in November, 1916.

The revolution was the result of two sets of forces joined in temporary agreement: the western-type, democratic, bourgeois group in the Duma, and the more radical soviet of workers and soldiers.

Revolution in the midst of war entails obvious risks, and the Russian situation was anxiously watched by all belligerents. Russia's allies thought at first that the revolution might have the advantage of setting up in Russia a government similar to their own; the Central Powers hoped that the revolution might follow a more extreme course of disintegration, destroying Russia's fighting power. To this end, the Germans made it possible for Lenin to go from Switzerland to Russia.

The forces that had made the revolution had little in common save the desire to overthrow the existing system; that done their relation became one of a struggle for control. The story of the next six months in Russia may be summed up in the lack of sufficiently strong leadership among the moderates, and increasing disintegration in the country and the army, whose weariness was successfully exploited by German and Bolshevik propaganda.

<u>*The October Revolution.*</u> By November,[8] the second revolution put the country in the hands of Lenin and his followers. Applying their revolutionary Marxist doctrine, the Bolsheviks denounced with equal impartiality all belligerent governments, and appealed indiscriminately to the masses everywhere to revolt against their rulers. They advocated immediate peace, and proceeded to withdraw Russia from the war. As a military factor, Russia had ceased to exist.

3. The Balance Sheet at the End of 1917. In the failure of immediate world revolution, the Russian collapse was of enormous significance, equally encouraging to the Central Powers and depressing to the Allies. It had perhaps deepest immediate repercussions in Italy, where the degree of disaffection lay behind the Caporetto disaster. It looked for a while, at the end of 1917, as if the whole Italian front might collapse. But the Italians managed to retrieve themselves, after

---

[8] The revolution occurred at the beginning of November according to the western Gregorian calendar. This was the end of October in the Russian calendar.

suffering heavy losses and yielding much territory, essentially by their own efforts.

The fortunes of war were still undecided at the close of 1917. However, in all three western allied countries stronger governments had emerged in control from the trials so far undergone. America was organizing, and time was running out for the Central Powers. It was, moreover, soon to appear that the depth of the Russian chaos would prove miscalculated their hopes of drawing substantially upon the asset of Russian resources.

D. 1918, The Year of Allied Victory

1. The Withdrawal of Russia and Roumania. As things stood at the opening of the year 1918, it was clear that the issue would be decided on the western front, where the Germans enjoyed a slight numerical edge. An all out offensive might yet win the war for them, but its failure would be fatal, for German reserves were nearing exhaustion while those of the Allies were steadily increasing. Summer would be the turning point. German prospects were such, in the estimation of the high command, that little interest was shown in the Wilsonian statement of war aims announced in January. Instead, harsh dictated peace terms were forced upon Russia and upon Roumania.[9] The Ukraine, recognized as a separate entity, was the object of a separate treaty. These arrangements aimed at consolidating the advantages of the Central Powers in the east.

2. The Last German Effort. In keeping with this state of affairs, Germany, which by now bore the overwhelming weight of military operations, launched her western offensive in March. The attempt was not abandoned until July, having registered a major success in April, when British and French forces stood momentarily in danger of being separated. It was this crisis that finally induced the Allies to set up a united command under Marshal Foch. German successes, if not conclusive, seemed substantial enough to open the possibility of negotiations, but the military overruled the government. July

---

[9] Peace was made with Russia at Brest-Litovsk in March, 1918 and with Roumania at Bucharest in May. The separate peace with the Ukraine was made in February, also at Brest-Litovsk.

witnessed the last German effort, which the Allies again withstood.

3. *The Turning of the Tide*

a. <u>THE WESTERN FRONT.</u> With the rapidly growing material and moral asset of American assistance, they in turn were now ready to take the initiative. Quite sharply, the tide of war turned in August. From September, the Allies kept pushing forward till the end. If Ludendorff's fear of a breakthrough failed to materialize, his armies were never again able to regain the initiative, steadily falling back instead toward the home territory. Rather than have it become a battleground, the German government accepted an armistice tantamount to surrender. Hostilities ceased on the western front on November 11, 1918. The Allies had won the war. [10]

b. <u>OTHER THEATERS OF WAR.</u> While events were moving toward the grand climax in the west, the other fronts had also become active. In the Near East, in Macedonia, in Italy, the Allies began or continued an unbroken advance. Bulgaria was the first to sue for a truce, ceasing hostilities at the end of September. Turkey followed suit just a month later. Caught between the allied armies advancing from the south and the Italians attacking from the west, Austria-Hungary literally disintegrated into her component national entities and was out of the war a week before Germany surrendered.

III. MORTGAGES ON THE PEACE. THE DIPLOMACY AND IDEOLOGY OF THE WAR

A. The Secret Wartime Agreements

The business of war is a simpler undertaking than the making of peace. Under the stress of war, commitments are made which, whether desirable or not, are none the less valid contracts. They constitute mortgages on the future peace. For the sake of simplicity, the wartime interallied agreements will be enumerated together.

Those arrangements made among the defeated enemies need not be considered since they could not be put into effect. The known plans of the Central Powers, the treaties of Brest-

---

[10] For the conditions of the German armistice, see below, p. 171.

Litovsk and Bucharest, are of significance as evidence of their intention to establish their—especially Germany's—unquestioned and far-reaching control of the European continent at least.

1. The Interallied Agreements

a. THE STRAITS AND OTHER RUSSIAN CLAIMS. On the allied side, a whole network of agreements was created. Despite the alliance, doubts persisted in the west on the score of Russia's enduring loyalty. These doubts, not altogether unfounded, were exploited by Russia. In March, 1915 she finally succeeded in extracting an Anglo-French consent to her control of Constantinople and the Straits, and later of a large sphere in Anatolia south of the Caucasus.

A Franco-Russian agreement in 1917 was based on the *quid pro quo* of a French free hand on the left bank of the Rhine in exchange for a corresponding Russian free hand on her western frontiers. All agreements involving Russia were repudiated by the Bolshevik government, hence vanished as potential factors in the peace settlement.

b. THE TREATY OF LONDON. In order to secure the assistance of Italy, the Allies made certain promises to her embodied in the treaty of London of April, 1915. Italy was to obtain roughly what came to be her land frontier after the war, up to but excluding Fiume,[11] the northern half of Dalmatia, Valona and some hinterland, and "adequate" colonial compensations.

c. THE PARTITION OF THE OTTOMAN EMPIRE. Likewise, in their effort to enlist Arab support against the Turks, the British in 1915 undertook to support Arab independence. This undertaking was qualified in 1916 by the Sykes-Picot agreement which defined British and French zones in the Near East. The treaty of St. Jean de Maurienne in 1917 defined an Italian zone in Asia Minor that was to include Smyrna. The Balfour declaration of 1917 expressed itself in favor of the establishment of a "national home" for Jews in Palestine.

d. THE COMMITMENTS TO ROUMANIA. In the Balkans, Roumania's intervention had secured for her the promise that she would acquire Transylvania, Bukowina, and the Banat.

e. THE FAR EAST. In the Far East, Japan having evicted

---

[11] The city of Fiume was specifically mentioned in the treaty, and excluded from the Italian claims, being reserved as a sea outlet for Croatia.

Germany, took advantage of the preoccupation of the European powers to force upon China her famous twenty-one demands embodied in a treaty of May, 1915. These advantages were acquiesced in by the Allies, but the Far Eastern situation was beclouded by the ambiguous Lansing-Ishii exchanges and by China's entrance into the war on the side of the Allies in August, 1917.

B. The Ideology of the War

From the very beginning, the Allies had made much of Germany's brutal disregard of treaties as shown by her violation of Belgium. Unrestricted submarine warfare caused the Central Powers to incur more of the same onus. In a general way, stress was put by the Allies on the nature and degree of Prussian militarism. But the various agreements just mentioned could lend color to the charge that the war was a clash of imperialisms between which there was little to choose.[12] This charge was indeed made by the Bolsheviks who, once in power, proceeded to support it with the disclosure of the secret agreements which they, for their part, renounced. This situation, in addition to the growing weariness of the belligerents, caused a novel stress to be placed on the issue of war aims.

1. Effects of the American Intervention.

In this respect, the most potent influence was the intervention of the United States, which worked to much the same effect as the Russian revolution. For the United States entered the war with clean hands, free alike of prior commitments and of ulterior motives. The slogan "to make the world safe for democracy," much derided since, was in large measure an accurate expression of the hopes of the masses, both in America and elsewhere. Conscious of her unique position, the United States was and remained an "associated" rather than an "allied" power.

2. The Fourteen Points.

These conditions, added to the fact of American power, resulted in the United States becoming the spokesman of the Allies before the world at large. This role President Wilson was not reluctant to assume, and the result was his famous speech to Congress on January 8,

---

[12] Agreements had also been made with a view to a division of the German colonies in Africa between Britain and France.

1918, wherein the allied war aims were stated in the form of the Fourteen Points. This declaration, the result of considerable prior study and preparation, asserted the validity of the principle of self-determination, and laid down some general principles, such as open diplomacy, the freedom of the seas, and others, which were to be the charter of the future. Their application, if it should come to pass, could not but be detrimental to the territorial integrity of the Central Powers and to the nature of their governments.

C. The Armistices

1. The German Request for an Armistice. For these reasons, little interest was evinced in the Fourteen Points by the governments and military commands of the enemy. It was not until Ludendorff had become convinced that the war was lost that he urgently pressed his government to put an end to hostilities. In the rapidly deteriorating situation, the German government, hopeful for a while that peace could be negotiated on a basis of equality, resolved to approach the American government for a settlement on the basis of the Wilsonian program. A regrettable confusion ensued from the fact that the American answer, raising the issue of the nature of the German government, gave ground to the German hope that the institution of popular government would be tantamount to exoneration from the consequences of defeat.

2. Acceptance of the Fourteen Points. To clarify matters beyond cavil, Wilson consulted the Allies. They committed themselves, with minor reservations, to the acceptance of the Fourteen Points as the basis of peace. This answer was communicated to the German government. As to the military terms of the armistice, they were naturally to be set by the Allied command. These terms were tantamount to a surrender of the German armies which, in any event, had no choice in the matter. Acknowledging defeat, the German command and government, hastily reorganized on a popular basis,[13] could do no other than accept them. The circumstances and exchanges which attended the conclusion of the German armistice were to have important repercussions on the future course of events.

---

[13] The Kaiser abdicated and fled to Holland on November 9.

CHAPTER 8

The Settlements Following the First World War

I. THE PEACE CONFERENCE OF PARIS

A. Background and Preparations

1. Popular Illusions. The First World War had been truly a peoples' war. The huge conscripted armies consisted in the main of civilians temporarily attired in soldier's garb. To them and to their relatives at home their task seemed completed with the cessation of active hostilities. The defeated could, indeed had to, dismantle their war establishments. But among the victors, the end of war popularly meant peace, a peace moreover naively equated with a better, if not a perfect, world. The formal writing of treaties of peace was the professional task of diplomats and statesmen. From November, 1918, the hopes of a return to "normalcy" and the popular pressures to achieve that end were strong behind the statesmen gathering in Paris.

Yet the task to be done was unprecedented in its magnitude and complexity. By comparison, Vienna a hundred years earlier had had an easy assignment. With the record of Vienna in mind, it was decided by the Allies that they might find sufficient difficulty in reaching agreement among themselves, hence should avoid the possibly divisive effect on intrusion in their proceedings of representatives from the enemy countries. In deference to France's wartime contribution and for reasons of practicality, the decision had been made to hold the peace congress in Paris. Two months elapsed before the formal opening of the gathering.

2. The Preconference Period. During this time an election was held in Britain in December. The result was an overwhelming endorsement of the government, but the emotional atmosphere which presided over the balloting earned it the description of "khaki election." Save from the narrow standpoint of immediate political advantage, the proceedings were less than wise.

a. THE ISSUE OF WILSON AND HIS STATUS. The various allied delegations would, as a matter of course, be led by their prime ministers. But there is no precise American counterpart to a European prime minister. Having considered the matter, the American President, despite some contrary advice, decided to head his own delegation. The mid-term American election of November, 1918 had returned a Republican Congress, with the unfortunate consequence of injecting domestic party politics into the international situation.

b. LACK OF A PROGRAM OF PROCEDURE. Some preparations for the peace there had been. The Fourteen Points themselves were in large measure abstracted from the report of "The Inquiry," a group of American technicians gathered by Colonel House for the very purpose of collating data relevant to the drafting of the eventual settlement. Similar studies had been made by the British and the French, but a detailed French plan for the organization and procedure of the coming congress was rejected by Wilson, who preferred greater flexibility and freedom of motion. [1]

When the peace conference formally opened in Paris on January 12, 1919 it was not committed to any previous plan of action. It was generally expected that a quick preliminary peace would be made, to be followed by a more leisurely and careful implementation of detail. But circumstances ordered otherwise.

B. The Process of Peacemaking

1. *Procedure of the Conference.*

a. THE TECHNICAL COMMITTEES. Of necessity, the business of the congress had to be broken up into segments. The

---

[1] During December and January, President Wilson paid state visits to Britain and Italy. His initial contacts with European statesmen did not dissipate their attitude of questioning uncertainty toward him, in some cases they even laid the bases for future misunderstandings.

major political decisions could be made only by the chief delegates, but there was much of a technical nature which was turned over for preliminary study and report to *ad hoc* committees of experts. It would take some time for this work to be ready. Meanwhile, in deference to President Wilson's predilections, the conference busied itself with the Covenant of the League of Nations.

Some time passed in these activities. By mid-February, Wilson had to visit the United States to attend to domestic matters. When he returned to Paris a month later, much of the basic technical groundwork had been done. The reports of the various committees were, to a large extent, embodied into the final drafts of the treaties. The major political problems were taken into consideration at the top level after Wilson's return in March. Thus it came to pass that by May so much had been done that the earlier idea of a preliminary treaty was superseded by the fact that a German treaty could be assembled from its component parts, while much work had also been done on the other settlements.

b. THE SUPREME COUNCIL. The technical committees could only report and advise. Final decisions were made at the political level. Obviously, a full assembly of some sixty nations was an unwieldy tool: the plenary sessions of the peace conference were few and of little importance. Quite early it appeared that the directing organ of the congress was to be the Supreme Council. This body, evolved from the wartime Supreme War Council, consisted at first of ten members: the prime and foreign ministers of the five victorious great powers, or powers with "general interests," the United States, Great Britain, France, Italy, and Japan.

c. THE BIG FOUR. This group of ten was soon reduced to five by the elimination of the foreign ministers. Moreover, as Japan had little concern with most of the issues since they did not involve her interests, the five became the four. Wilson, Lloyd George, Clemenceau, and Orlando were the Big Four of 1919. In so small a group, discussion can be both direct and expeditious. Clemenceau's easy command of English (Wilson and Lloyd George had little or no French) obviated the necessity of translation though it handicapped Orlando, innocent of English. Italy, besides, did not choose to play a significant role in matters not affecting her immediate and narrow interests. The Big Four were often the Big Three.

The Personalities. In such a group, personalities became important. Wilson, conscious of his position of power, high-minded but unbending Messiah of the New Order, was little versed in the problems of Europe or in the practice of diplomacy. Sincerely devoted to the ideal of justice, but having little patience with the concrete complexities that surround the abstract ideal, he was influenced not a little by the widespread American distrust of European statesmen and their craft—or craftiness. From a dangerous readiness to equate his own views with moral right, he could easily draw the fallacious inference that opposition to them was synonymous with moral wrong.

Lloyd George was in most respects the direct antithesis of Wilson: the management of men, the art of politics, were second nature to the supple Welshman. Full of geniality and guile, little troubled by inconsistency, he was a born and useful compromiser—within the limits of major British interests. He had the advantage of a well-organized delegation including personalities of stature of whose advice he knew how to make use. This in contrast with Wilson who, to an unfortunate degree, dominated his own delegation.

Clemenceau was the strongest personality of the group. Close to eighty, his lifelong experience in the harsh school of French politics where his abilities and tactics had earned him the nickname of "the Tiger," had made him a disillusioned realist of the Bismarckian school, though he had often fought for ideals higher than Bismarck's. A sincere patriot, his ambition in 1919 was to crown his stormy career by making good for some decades the fruits of victory for his country. Clear-headed, powerful, and ruthless, his very realism caused him to appreciate the definition of politics as the art of the possible and to act accordingly. Depending in large measure on his right-hand man, Tardieu, he too dominated his delegation.

Of the Big Four, the most attractive in terms of personality may well have been Orlando. But he was also the weakest among them, representing the weakest national unit. His much stronger willed foreign minister, Sonnino, like Wilson in some respects, stubborn, self-righteous, and uncompromising, was no asset in the circumstances.

C. The Problems of Peacemaking

1. The Covenant of the League.

Wilson took little interest in the details of the multitude of often petty issues that had to be resolved. As he put it to his experts, "Tell me what's right, and I'll fight for it," was a fair statement of his simple approach. But in a future association of nations he had great hopes and the attachment of fatherhood toward the idea. The first major accomplishment of the high delegates was the drafting of the Covenant. Agreement on this was not reached until the issue had been brought up, on French initiative, of the law-enforcing powers of the future League. In the long debate, the more evasive American or Anglo-American view essentially won out, but only at the cost of evading a basic issue. [2]

2. The French Problem.

There were some other major political issues that had to be resolved, and these were taken up by the Council after Wilson's return to Paris in mid-March. First among these was the French problem. The essence of this problem can be simply stated. First and foremost, France wanted security. A concrete advantage such as control in some form of German territory up to the Rhine River would, in the event of future conflict, be a tangible contribution to that end. But as this involved a population undeniably German, it was opposed on the basis of the principle of nationality.

The League was obviously not a sufficient answer, a future hope at best, an untried instrument of uncertain possibility. The debate was long, and at times bitter between Wilson and Clemenceau. It was in the end resolved on the basis of compromise: France would not control German territory, but her security would be protected by an Anglo-American guarantee. [3]

3. The Italian Question.

No sooner was the French problem resolved than attention was focused on the Italian.

---

[2] The structure of the League will be analyzed in the next chapter.

[3] This solution, excellent in itself, had the fundamental vice of failing to take into account the realities of the domestic situation in the United States.

The core of the conflict was the clear contradiction between the terms of the Treaty of London and the Fourteen Points. Which should have priority, the sanctity of previous pledges, or the charter of the new order of justice? To Wilson, the issue was a clear case of right against a demand for loot.

Wilson's Manifesto. The Italians, not averse to compromise in the last analysis, badly mismanaged their case. With allies but no friends in 1919, they maneuvered themselves into an impossible position (having entered an additional claim for Fiume) and had to fight it out with Wilson. His frayed nerves and aroused moral sense led him to take the unprecedented step of issuing a public statement of his case, a logically unassailable one within his premises. The result was merely to show Wilson's mistake in thinking that peoples would support him, even against their own governments if necessary, and the Italian issue remained unsolved for the time, neither side able to bend the other to his wishes.

4. Japan and Shantung. The Japanese had quietly and skillfully bided their time. They chose the height of the Italian crisis, in late April, to enter their demands in China. They gathered the results of competent diplomacy.

5. Mandates. In early May the issue was essentially settled of the disposition of the former German colonies and of the non-Turkish areas of the Ottoman Empire.[4] The introduction of the concept of mandate, logical derivative of the League, made it possible to allocate these territories essentially in accordance with the wartime interallied agreements, Russia being of course excluded.

6. Reparations. The question of how much of the damage the enemy (mainly Germany) should and could make good gave rise to much debate. Astronomical figures were bandied about, but no final conclusions reached in 1919.[5]

---

[4] These mandates were of three kinds, A, B, and C, corresponding to the degree of development of the region to which they applied. The distribution of mandates took place in the absence of the Italians, who had temporarily left the conference. One consequence of the annoyance that they had engendered was that the Greeks were asked to occupy Smyrna, initially allotted to Italy by the treaty of London. This episode was one of the less creditable incidents of the peacemaking.

[5] On the Saar, see below, p. 181.

7. The German Treaty. By May, through the process of putting together the various individual parts, a German treaty was produced. A German delegation was invited to Paris, but the observations which it was allowed to make had no significant effect on earlier decisions. Faced with the choice of yielding or resuming hostilities, the German government chose the former alternative.

On June 28, 1919, fifth anniversary of Sarajevo, and in the very same Hall of Mirrors at Versailles where the German Empire had been proclaimed in 1871, the warrant of its defeat and collapse received formal sanction.

8. Unfinished Business. With the signature of the treaty of Versailles, much the most important in the eyes of the majority of nations and delegates, the peace conference in large part disbanded. Much remained to be done, however, mainly the disposition of what had been the territories of the Dual Monarchy. This work, well under way by June, was continued by secondary representatives, foreign ministers, then ambassadors, and lasted another year. In 1920, the new Europe had largely taken shape.

II. THE PEACE TREATIES

A. Treaties with the Enemy States

The charter of the new Europe was embodied in part in the treaties with the five enemy nations. These were

The Treaty of Versailles with Germany (June 28, 1919).

The Treaty of St. Germain with Austria (September 10, 1919).

The Treaty of Neuilly with Bulgaria (November 27, 1919).

The Treaty of Trianon with Hungary (June 4, 1920).

The Treaty of Sèvres with Turkey (August 10, 1920).

1. Pattern of the Treaties. All these treaties follow the same pattern. The first section consists of the Covenant of the League, to membership in which the defeated country would eventually be admitted. This is followed by a description of whatever territorial changes were to take place, with detailed provisions for their enactment (e. g., plebiscites). Then come provisions for the disarmament of the particular country,

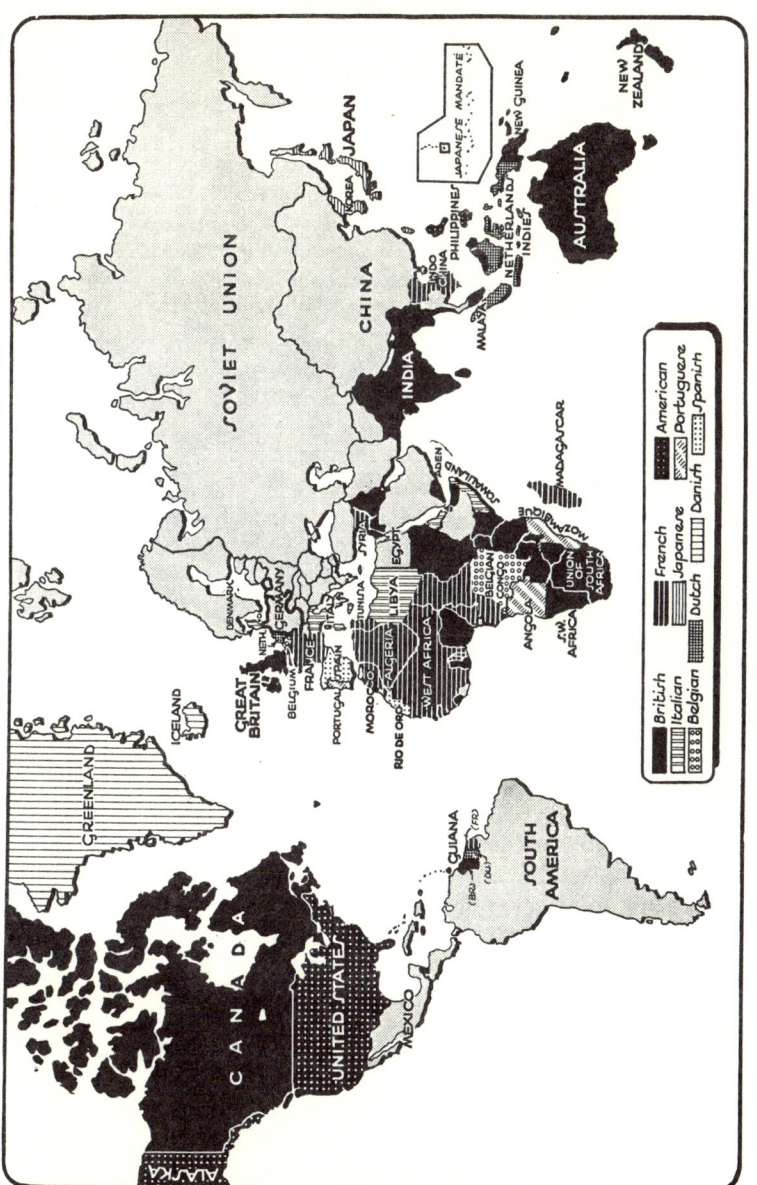

The World of Versailles

followed by economic clauses dealing first with the matter of compensation for damage done, and secondly with the re-establishment of normal economic relations between the belligerents.

2. The War Guilt Clause. Mention must be made, because of its subsequent role, of the famous so-called war guilt clause of the treaty of Versailles. The reparation section of that treaty opens with the affirmation by the Allies (Art. 231) of German responsibility for war damage deriving from the aggressive nature of the war waged by Germany. Such a statement in a treaty of peace was a novel feature, and it had the effect of giving an enormous incentive to the discussion of responsibility, in Germany needless to say, but in other countries as well.

The *Kriegsschuldfrage* has given rise to a whole library of works, and proved a boon to the historian while providing a football for the politician. Interestingly enough, the intrusion of the moral factor, so much criticized in retrospect, was in considerable measure the result of American participation in the war. The unilateral disarmament of the enemy was also based on the theory of his responsibility for aggression: it would eventually be possible, when order and confidence had been restored, for disarmament to become general and world-wide.

B. The Settlements in Eastern Europe

It was within the power of the victorious allies to make settlements with their enemies. But the events centering in Russia were not within their control. From the point of view of the Central Powers, the second Russian revolution of 1917 had had the desirable effect of eliminating Russia as a military factor. [6]

In connection with revolution, defeat, and peace, the new Russian government had given recognition to the principle of nationality. This is what made it possible for the non-Russian peoples incorporated along the western borders of the former Russian empire to emerge into independence. The Allies, also

---

[6] Russia, having withdrawn from the war, was torn by civil war. During the summer of 1918, both sides of the war debated which side to support in this internal struggle. In August, the Germans made an agreement with the Bolshevik government, while the Allies threw their influence on the side of counterrevolution.

espousing the principle of nationality, gave recognition to the new national entities, [7] all of which made directly with the Soviet state treaties which settled their mutual frontiers and laid the bases of their future relations. [8]

Some further, relatively minor, arrangements, such as the direct agreement between Italy and Yugoslavia, the treaty of Rapallo in 1920, went to complete the process of peacemaking.

C. The New Map of Europe

The consequences of the war were therefore registered in a substantial redrawing of the map of Europe. The importance of territorial changes cannot be stressed too strongly. Frontiers have proved much more refractory to change than economic arrangements, for instance; their alteration, in fact, had hardly ever been divorced from war. For that reason, the modifications of the map of Europe resulting from the war deserve careful notice.

1. The Frontiers of Germany.

a. <u>In the West.</u> There was relatively little change in the west. France recovered from Germany the territory of Alsace-Lorraine. During a half century of German rule the complexion of the population had in some measure changed, but the return of these provinces was generally regarded as the simple righting of a wrong, and the population was therefore not consulted. No other territory was acquired by France. But the small territory of the Saar, valuable for its mines, was severed from Germany and placed for fifteen years under League supervision, while title to the mines went to France. This was done under the head of reparation and as compensation for the wanton German destruction of the coal mines in the north of France. A plebiscite was to be held in the Saar at the end of fifteen years to ascertain the wishes of the population. [9]

---

[7] With an eye on future developments, it is important to bear in mind that the first step in the liberation of these states was the defeat of Russia by Germany.

[8] On Bessarabia, see below, p. 183.

[9] The plebiscite was duly held and the Saar fully reincorporated in Germany in 1935.

To Belgium, Germany relinquished the minute areas of Eupen, Malmédy, and Moresnet, on combined ethnic and strategic grounds.

b. IN THE EAST. The chief German loss of territory was in the east. This was inevitable if a Polish state was to be reconstructed, undoing the eighteenth-century partitions. As might have been expected, the precise determination of the boundary gave rise to considerable difficulties. Chief among these was the fact that East Prussia constituted a solid enclave of German territory. The clash between these various desiderata led to a compromise: East Prussia remained part of Germany, but was separated from the rest of it by a strip of

Europe after 1919

Polish territory, the so-called Polish Corridor. Danzig with a little surrounding territory was erected into a Free State, the government of which would be a responsibility of the League.

To the extreme east, a small strip of territory about Memel, eventually seized by Lithuania, brought the frontier between that country and Germany to the Niemen River.

Further south, the valuable industrial region of Upper Silesia was the object of rival claims. A minute portion of it went to Czechoslovakia, but the main part was finally divided between Germany and Poland after a plebiscite, the result of which became the basis of a compromise League award. From Silesia to the Rhine, the southern frontier of Germany remained that of 1914. [10]

2. The New Poland. The frontiers of Poland proved difficult to establish in other respects. Russia had not participated in the proceedings at Paris. She and Poland were at war in 1920-1921. The result was a direct settlement between the two countries, the treaty of Riga of March, 1921, which settled the eastern frontier of Poland at that of 1792.

The city of Vilna, considered by Lithuania her capital, was also claimed by Poland. It was seized and held by the latter country in October, 1920 and the *fait accompli* was eventually recognized.

3. Other Russian Losses. The bulk of the new Poland inevitably consisted of territory of the former Russian empire. From that same empire likewise emerged the three small Baltic states of Lithuania, Latvia, and Estonia. North of them, across the Gulf of Finland, the old Grand Duchy joined the ranks of independent states.

Another Russian loss was the province of Bessarabia, long contested between Roumania and Russia, which the chaos of revolution in the latter country made it possible for the former

---

[10] In addition, under the heading of security, the German territory on the left bank of the Rhine was demilitarized and temporarily occupied by allied forces. A 50-kilometer zone on the right bank of the river was likewise to remain void of fortifications. Neither this arrangement, nor that of the Saar, it should be pointed out, involved permanent losses of territory. In the north, although Denmark had been a neutral, a plebiscite was held (it was supposed to have been held after the war of 1864) as the result of which a part of Schleswig went to that country.

to seize. But in this case Russia refused to recognize the new frontier.

4. The Succession States of Austria-Hungary. The changes along the western border of Russia, while considerable, left in existence the bulk of the Russian state. A far more radical change took place in the case of Austria-Hungary, which simply ceased to exist. As early as October-November, 1918, the two chief partners of the Dual Monarchy went their separate ways; but in addition, the various subject nationalities, whether of Austria or Hungary, secured their independence. Disintegration was an internal fact, but it fell to the Paris conference to settle the numerous conflicting frontier claims of the Danubian countries.

a. AUSTRIA AND HUNGARY. The new Austria, a purely Germanic state of some 6,500,000, consisted of the original Habsburg domain. From Hungary she acquired the Burgenland, and her southern frontier with the future Yugoslavia was settled by a plebiscite in the Klagenfurt area. The former wedge into Italy was removed by placing the northern frontier of Italy at the Brenner as provided in the treaty of London. The Germanic South Tyrol was thereby lost to Austria.[11] Hungary was similarly reduced to a solid Magyar core of some 8,000,000.

b. CZECHOSLOVAKIA. The new state of Czechoslovakia was wholly carved out of Austro-Hungarian territory. It consisted of the ancient Kingdom of Bohemia to which was joined Slovakia, formerly part of Hungary, and the small eastern extremity of Ruthenia. The former Austrian province of Galicia rejoined Poland. The small, but industrially valuable, district of Teschen was divided between Poland and Czechoslovakia.

c. ROUMANIA AND THE SOUTH SLAVS. The province of Transylvania, also formerly Hungarian, became part of Roumania as well as formerly Austrian Bukowina. Roumania also received part of the contested Banat of Temesvar, the rest

---

[11] The treaties of peace with Germany and with Austria forbade the union of the two countries save with allied consent. Simultaneously, with the proclamation of the Austrian republic, a motion had been passed in favor of the *Anschluss,* or union, with Germany.

of which went to the newly organized Kingdom of the Serbs, Croats, and Slovenes.

This last named country was the realization of the South Slav dream. To old Serbia were now joined little Montenegro and the former Austro-Hungarian territory of Bosnia-Herzegovina, Croatia, and Slovenia. The new state thus controlled the whole eastern shore of the Adriatic from Albania to Istria. Its frontier with Italy was essentially that drawn in the treaty of London.[12] But Italy gave up her claims on the Dalmatian coast, retaining only the city of Zara and some islands.

5. Bulgaria. The Balkans were the scene of minor changes only. Bulgaria had to yield to Serbia some small districts by way of frontier rectifications, and lost to Greece that part of Thrace which had given her access to the Aegean.

D. Changes Outside Europe

These changes were a direct consequence of the outcome of the war in Europe. Two countries were affected by them, the Ottoman Empire and Germany.

1. The German Colonies. Germany was shorn of all her colonial possessions. Those in Africa went to the British Empire, France, and Belgium as mandates. German East Africa went to Britain, save for its western section, Ruanda Urundi, adjacent to the Belgian Congo, which became a Belgian mandate. German Southwest Africa was mandated to the Union of South Africa; the Cameroons and Togoland were divided between Britain and France, and France recovered in full title those portions of the Congo she had ceded to Germany in 1911.[13]

The German possessions in the Pacific were mandated as follows: German Samoa to New Zealand; the island of Nauru to the British Empire as a whole; all other islands south of the equator to Australia; those north of the equator to Japan.

---

[12] Slightly modified in Italy's favor. Fiume, claimed by both countries, was erected into a free state, which it remained until 1924, when it was annexed by Italy.

[13] Italy had been promised in 1915 some colonial compensation in the event of British and French gains in Africa. Her Libyan colony was enlarged from a small French cession in the west and a British one in the east, and she also acquired Jubaland, adjacent to her Somaliland colony, from Britain.

Japan also fell heir to the German rights in the Shantung peninsula of China.[14]

2. *The Ottoman Empire.* Like the Austro-Hungarian, the Ottoman Empire dissolved into its component parts. The provisions of the treaty of Sèvres as they affected Turkey need not be considered since they never came into effect.[15] The rest of the empire, the Arab portion, became in part independent (the bulk of the Arabian peninsula), the rest of it, corresponding to the fertile crescent, was mandated to Britain (Iraq and Palestine) and to France (Syria).

III. APPRAISAL AND RECEPTION OF THE PEACE

With the wisdom of retrospect, it is easy to say that the settlements which followed the First World War gave Europe and the world an uneasy and relatively short-lived breathing spell instead of the heralded lasting peace. It is worth considering therefore the quality of these settlements with an eye on the question of how far they are or are not responsible for subsequent developments.

A. The Principle of Self-Determination

One basic principle underlying all treaties is that of self-determination. There is no denying that the espousal of this principle was an asset to the allied cause. The fact of nationalism, however, was no allied invention but rather, for good or evil, one of the vital driving forces of the time. It is also a fact that it was the Central Powers and Russia, and not the western allies, that held under their rule alien and restive nationalities. The combination of Russia's collapse with the defeat of the Central Powers made possible a far wider application of the principle of nationality than would have been the case had Russia shared in allied victory. The new political map of Europe was the closest approximation ever realized to an ethnic map of that continent.

1. *The Minorities.* There were still subject peoples in

---

[14] As a result of this decision, China, also an ally, refused to sign the treaty of Versailles.

[15] For the resurgence of Turkey and the treaty of Lausanne which sanctioned her rebirth in 1923, see Chapter IX.

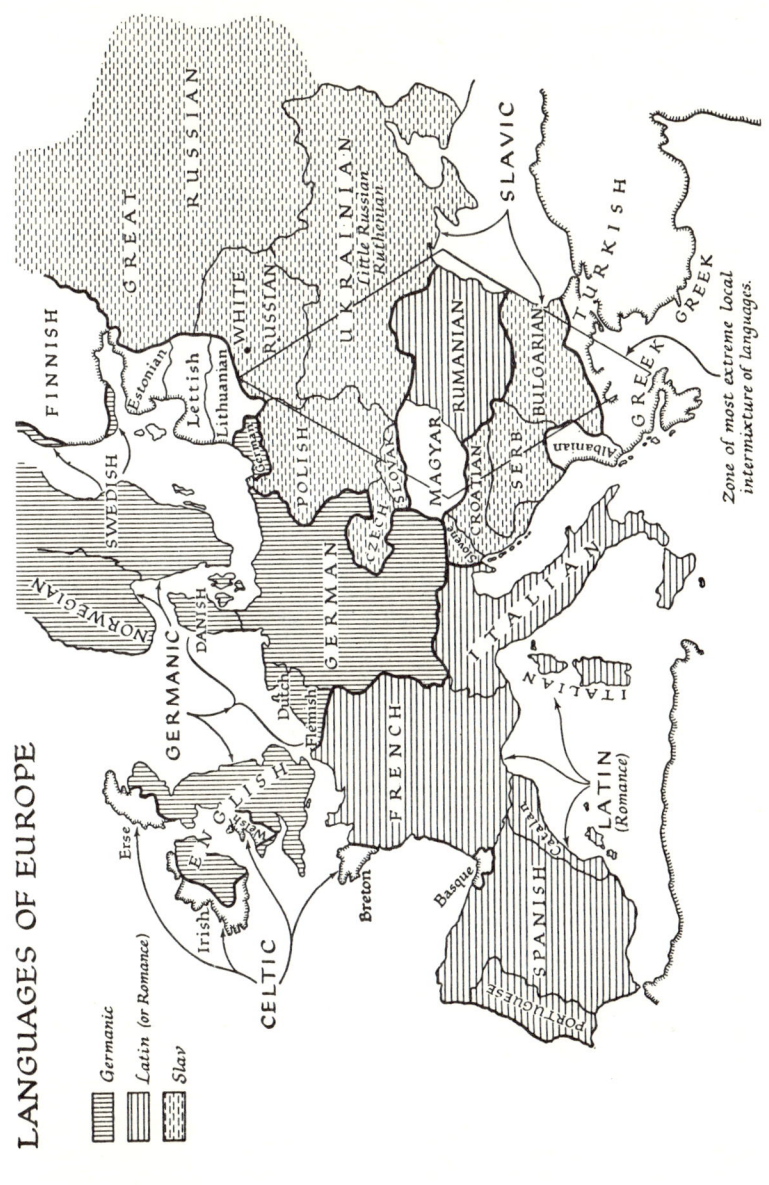

Europe. In some cases, their numbers could and should have been reduced. But it must be pointed out that, short of moving substantial numbers of people—a device not advocated in 1919—there were bound to remain, especially in central and eastern Europe, regions of mixed population, hence minorities. Also, most of the new or greatly enlarged countries of that region were made to undertake special obligations in regard to their minorities. Historic considerations and strategic ones, the latter looming large in 1919, carried considerable weight.

Bearing these considerations in mind, this may be said: Germany had little valid cause for grievance as far as her new frontiers were concerned; the eastern frontier of Poland gave that country too large a non-Polish population; the frontiers between Hungary on the one hand, and Czechoslovakia and Roumania on the other, should not have included so many Hungarians in those countries, though little could be done about the main body of Hungarians in central Transylvania. The other frontiers of Czechoslovakia were justified; Italy should have included fewer Austrians in the Tyrol and fewer Croats and Slovenes on her eastern border. Bulgaria had some justifiable grievance. But, to repeat, had the new frontiers been drawn with the utmost dispassionateness, they would have been little different from those that were drawn. If the validity of self-determination be granted—and how deny it?—the new map of Europe was a vast improvement on the old and represented a great forward step.

B. The Economic Aspects of the Peace

There are other aspects of the matter, however. The fragmentation of central and eastern Europe tended to create a power vacuum and gave rise to a host of problems, political and economic. Among the larger states, as with the smaller ones, the economic arrangements of the peace are subject to telling criticism. Quite apart from any moral questions, the expectations of the victors in the matter of reparations were not founded on any understanding of reality. There were some who, as early as 1919, were aware of this difficulty, but generally it may be said that there was a failure to grasp the economic realities of the moment which the passage of time and the subsequent failures themselves have made so plain to us.

1. The Confusion of Economics and Morality. One aspect of this is important, however, the fact that the whole matter of reparations seemed to rest on a moral foundation of enemy guilt. Reparation was no old-fashioned war indemnity imposed by victor on vanquished, but an implementation of justice. Especially when coupled with the unrealism of the economic aspect of the settlement, this gave a fillip to the discussion of moral responsibility, and the charge of disingenuousness leveled at the Allies received increasing credence, among the vanquished first, gradually among many in the victors' camp.

C. The Treaties and the Fourteen Points

The story of reparations and their consequences, political, economic, and psychological, will be sketched in the next chapter. It will suffice to say at this point that very early, especially in Germany, the peace came to be looked upon as an imposed settlement, the result of allied deceit, and a breach of the Fourteen Points. This was largely a myth. Reparations, like self-determination, had been clearly forecast in that document, which, however, had specified neither particular frontiers nor definite sums of money.

1. The League of Nations. As to the political clauses of disarmament, all would depend upon whether or not the world would settle to an era of peace. The chief innovation of the peacemaking of 1919 consisted in the League of Nations. This was the first attempt in history to formalize the institution of a rule of law among nations in place of the hitherto prevailing anarchy among sovereign states. The attempt was the expression of a hope, the Covenant a novel and untried instrument. That there were deficiencies in it was acknowledged from the first. Much, if not all, therefore, would depend in the future upon the manner in which the instrument would be used.

2. The Mixture of Leniency and Harshness. The contradictory charges have been made that the peace settlements written by the Allies were too harsh and that they were too lenient, or again that their fault lay in an unsound combination of these two qualities. They doubtless could have been far harsher or more lenient, but, again, the decisive test would be found in the manner in which their provisions would be used and in the willingness, or lack thereof, to apply these. The failure of unresolved confusion which characterized the two succeeding decades will be traced in the following chapters.

3. *Deceived Expectations*. But one contributory element in the failure may be pointed out at the outset. The hopes of a bright new world—the phrase "New Order" was common coin in 1919—were in themselves a handicap for the future, for they bespoke a well-nigh universal failure to realize that the havoc of war, physical as well as psychological, is not to be undone by the writing of treaties and charters; more basically still, that wars are likely to create more problems than they settle.

D. Reception of the Peace

1. *General Disillusion*. The reception of the peace was not one of enthusiasm, but rather one of disappointment and frustration.

a. GERMANY. The Germans, who had not known the meaning of war on their own soil, had naively equated the promise of the Fourteen Points with exoneration from the consequences of their deeds. They called the peace a *diktat* and sought escape into the wishful argument that they had been deceived by the Allies, and the more dangerous and less excusable view that they had never really lost the war in the field.

b. FRANCE. There was no elation of victory in France. Realistically, Clemenceau understood that for all the magnitude of the French contribution to victory, that victory had been possible only through the efforts of a mighty coalition of which France was only one member. Peace did not mean the confidence of security for France. Unrealistically, the nation embarked upon the pleasant dream that Germany would make good all the damage.

c. BRITAIN. The British soon discarded the fancies of the khaki election. "Hang the Kaiser" and "squeeze Germany until the peeps squeak" expressed emotion but no serious program for the future. Even before the treaty of Versailles was signed, Lloyd George began to express doubts on the score of reparations. There was in Britain the best economic thinking of the time, and justified concern over the economic future, combined with antiquated concepts of the balance of power.

d. ITALY. In Italy there was soon talk of "lost victory" and "mutilated peace." Partly because of the peculiar nature and handling of the Italian case in 1919, but more fundamentally because of the impact of the war itself on a weak economy and power, Italy was discontented and restless. She was to be, among the victors, the first to break under the strain.

e. RUSSIA. Russia had broken during the war itself. Involved in the chaos of war, civil and foreign, the future of her internal order as well as her relations with the outside world was wrapped in mystery. Russian chaos would some day presumably be resolved. Meantime, of the peace settlements she took the simple view that they were one more manifestation of capitalistic imperialism. Her views carried little weight at the time in the councils of nations, but her very experiment was an important focus of attraction for the unrest of the industrial masses, common in varying degrees to all Europe.

f. THE SUCCESSION STATES. The new Austria and Hungary, heirs to defeat, were deeply critical, especially the latter of her new frontiers. The other succession states, benefiting from victory, were mainly involved in problems of internal reorganization. But how this congeries of weak states, highly sensitive of their newly acquired positions, would adjust themselves and among themselves was one of the great question marks of the future.

2. The United States and the Peace. But the most interesting reaction to the peace was perhaps that of the ultimate artisan of victory. America emerged from the war unscathed, indeed with her power, political and economic, enhanced. The peculiarities of the American behavior stem from the American domestic scene and the American constitutional structure. Wilson represented America at the peace, but an America which, in November, 1918, had to a point refused to endorse his leadership. Short of impeachment or death, however, Wilson could not be removed. Allowing for the nobleness of his ideal, Wilson handled the situation with less than diplomatic skill and political tact. In the end, the matter narrowed down to the specific issue of ratification by the American Senate of the treaty of Versailles and of the tripartite treaty with Britain and France.

The latter instrument never even reached the stage of discussion on the floor of the Senate. As to the treaty of peace with Germany, many felt in America in 1919 that it was too lenient a settlement. But, as it turned out, the chief item of discussion was the Covenant of the League and the issue of the surrender of sovereignty, despite some provisions of the Covenant designed to meet precisely that objection. Wilson undertook a speaking tour of the country in the summer of 1919 and broke under the strain of the effort. Thereafter, his personal feud with Senator Lodge, chairman of the foreign relations committee, the bigotry of the opposition, his own intransigeance, all combined to make compromise impossible.

The treaty of Versailles was never ratified by the United States, which made instead a separate peace with Germany (treaty of Berlin, 1921). This treaty was essentially the same as the rejected peace, save that the Covenant had been deleted.

The provisional and unsatisfactory nature of many features of the peace had been recognized from the beginning, and the argument was often presented that the League was the redeeming feature that would adjust future difficulties. Many specific duties (Danzig, plebiscites, mandates, etc.) had been charged to the League from the first. While not necessarily fatal perhaps to the success of the new order, America's disowning was not the most auspicious beginning for the future of her child.

CHAPTER 9

The False Recovery

I. THE ECONOMIC CONSEQUENCES OF THE WAR

A. The Cost of the War

1. Human Losses. Whatever the qualities, good or bad, of the peace, more fundamental were the wreckage and dislocations caused by the war itself. These were of unprecedented dimensions. Some 9,000,000 were killed, a loss more serious than mere numbers indicate, for—selective process in reverse— they were drawn from the physically most vigorous segment of the population. More than 20,000,000 were wounded. Civilian casualties chargeable to the effects of war, while hard to estimate, were probably as large. The impact of manpower losses was uneven and depended upon the contributions of various national units and their reproductive rates: Russia and France represent opposite extremes in this last respect.

2. Property Damage. Property losses were likewise enormous, whether in the form of direct costs of waging war or of physical destruction. The world's bill has been estimated in the order of $300,000,000,000. These losses, too, were unevenly distributed: active warfare had not been waged on German soil nor on that of some of the Allies. In this connection, it is important to bear in mind that the economy of a highly developed industrial state is more complex and subject to greater dislocations than that of a more primitive agrarian society. As against this, however, the productive and recuperative capacity of modern industry is very great.

3. Financial Burdens. Of necessity again, the war had in large measure been financed by borrowing, so that all the belligerents emerged from it with hugely increased burdens of debt, burdens which, like their other losses, were very unevenly distributed, and the future effects of which would depend upon the magnitude and management of their resources. The gold standard, which had played so useful a role before 1914, had had to be abandoned among European belligerents whose currencies, once the wartime international controls were removed, began to fluctuate and seek new levels of equilibrium.

The nature and magnitude of the problems left as the legacy of war were such as to constitute a wholly new state of affairs, the economic significance of which was generally not grasped at the time.

B. International Financial Obligations

The problem of international financial obligations proved particularly troublesome, and was not disposed of—after a fashion—for more than a decade. It had important political repercussions and served to enhance our understanding and knowledge of economics. It may be best considered under two heads: enemy, and interallied, obligations.

1. *The Story of Reparations*

a. <u>Reparations in the Treaty of Versailles.</u> According to the terms of peace, the defeated enemy—essentially Germany—was liable for the damage consequent upon the war unleashed by his aggression. The extent of the damage was such that its assessment alone was a major undertaking. The treaty of peace had consequently confined itself to making some limited and specific demands (financial and in kind) for immediate delivery, and setting up a Reparations Commission charged with the task of assessing the liability and organizing its discharge.

b. <u>The London Schedule of 1921.</u> Its preliminary report was ready at the beginning of 1921. The total obligation, set at $56,000,000,000, was countered by a German offer of one-eighth that amount. Not until the Allies began to use sanctions was agreement reached on a figure of $33,000,000,000, to be paid in accordance with the so-called London schedule of May, 1921. [1] The French share was to be 51 per cent, the British 22, the rest divided among other claimants.

---

[1] Amounts were specified in gold marks (132,000,000,000), but for convenience figures are given throughout in dollars.

c. THE RUHR EPISODE. Whatever the potential of the German economy, its condition at the time was chaotic. There soon developed difficulties which led to the Reparations Commission (with a dissenting British vote) finding Germany in default.[2] This was followed by the sanction of the occupation of the Ruhr district by the French, with some Belgian participation. French action was based on the belief that Germany was seeking to evade her obligations. The German reply to this action was the resort to passive resistance. Feeling ran high, but economically the occupation of the Ruhr remained unproductive, while it served to complete the collapse of the German financial structure. The stalemate, ultimately equally unsatisfactory to Germany and to France, led to a more realistic approach to the problem on both sides of the Rhine.

d. THE DAWES AND YOUNG PLANS. It was decided to consider reparations as a purely economic problem. Under the leadership of a neutral, hence presumably more impartial chairman, the American Charles G. Dawes, a committee was created to reconsider the whole question. Changes in government in both France and Germany made it politically possible to accept the Dawes Plan in August, 1924. The Ruhr was evacuated, German finances and economy were restored to health, and the provisions of the plan seemed to work satisfactorily. The next five years marked the high tide of European economic and political recovery.

The Dawes Plan had outlined a schedule of payments by Germany, but had not dealt with the issue of her total obligation, hence of the duration of these payments. With a view to settling this matter, another committee, also under the chairmanship of an American, Owen D. Young, set to work early in 1929. Its report, in June, became the Young Plan: Germany was to make thirty-seven annual payments of $512,500,000 followed by twenty-two payments of $391,250,000. With the ratification of the Young Plan in January, 1930, the problem of reparations was ostensibly settled.

2. Interallied Debts. There had been considerable financial assistance of the poorer allies by the richer ones during, and even after, the war. This assistance was largely in the form of

---

[2] There had been a partial moratorium on German payments in 1922.

ordinary international loans. Increasingly, the United States became the great reservoir of credit. At this point, two diametrically opposed views appeared.

a. <u>THE DIVERGENT VIEWS OF CREDITOR AND DEBTOR.</u> The American view was the simple one that the debtors must honor their financial obligations. At most, some relief might be granted in the form of reduced rates of interest. The debtor allies leaned to the view that the war had been a joint enterprise, to the success of which American loans might fairly be regarded as a contribution. There was also the argument, particularly strong in France, that the country could and should discharge her obligation only if she in turn succeeded in collecting reparations. After much debate, between 1923 and 1926, various funding agreements [3] were made between the United States and her various debtors which settled the controversy for a time.

3. *The Mechanism of International Payments.* The United States consistently adhered to the position that inter-allied debts and reparations were wholly unrelated matters. Actually, the Young Plan was made to stretch over a period of years that would coincide with the span of the American-Allied funding agreements.

a. <u>THE BALANCE OF TRADE.</u> Important as the political and moral view of the war may have been, the purely economic aspects of the matter were even more crucial. The British evidenced early sound economic thinking, proposing an all-round cancellation of debts and reparations, even though they were on balance creditors. This proposal was rejected by the United States. The overriding and fundamental question was: how could these huge obligations, whatever their origin and moral justification or lack thereof, be met? The answer in retrospect is clear that, in the last analysis, a favorable balance of trade of debtor toward creditor could alone do this.

b. <u>FURTHER AMERICAN LENDING.</u> In effect, this did not happen; it could not have happened in fact without serious repercussions on the various domestic economies. Yet, for the better part of a decade, the obligations were ostensibly being met. In retrospect again, the answer to how this was done is

---

[3] These were negotiated by the World War Foreign Debts Commission established by the United States Senate in 1922.

simple. At one end of the process, America, the universal creditor, poured out in loans a steady flow of capital. That part of the stream which went to Germany made it possible to finance reparations. In the end, the same American capital flowed back to the United States in payment of her own loans. The process may be described as a huge bookkeeping operation which, from the point of view of extinguishing the debts, accomplished nothing other than a certain amount of shifting of the obligations, and was moreover dependent for its continuation on a continued outward flow of American capital. [4]

4. *The End of an Experiment.* For a variety of reasons, however, mainly concerned with the American domestic scene, the end of the decade of the twenties saw the drying up of the American golden stream. By 1930, economic crisis was spreading over the world.

a. THE HOOVER MORATORIUM. The German situation in particular was becoming increasingly serious. It was appropriate and symbolic that von Hindenburg, president of Germany, the universal debtor, should send an appeal to Herbert Hoover, president of the United States, the universal creditor. The result was the so-called Hoover moratorium of June, 1931, suspending for a year reparation as well as war debt payments.

b. THE LAUSANNE AGREEMENT. But a year later the cleavage reappeared. Weary of attempting the impossible, Germany's creditors were willing to write off reparations. This they did at Lausanne in July, 1932. [5] America took a different view, with the consequence that one by one her debtors, not denying their obligation but arguing the impossibility of meeting it, defaulted on their payments. There the matter rested. The passage of another decade was to show that America, too, had become willing to learn the ineluctable lesson of an impossible economic experiment. [6]

---

[4] This flow of American capital occurred under primarily private auspices, a fact which served to obscure the operation of the international balance of payments.

[5] The final lump sum of $750,000,000 set in this agreement was never paid by Germany.

[6] While basically correct, the above account of the international balance of payments is of necessity an oversimplified picture.

5. *Other Economic Consequences and Readjustments.*

a. <u>America's Place in World Economy</u>. The above has shown how inextricably involved America and Europe had become. The war had had the effect of changing America's position from that of a debtor to that of a creditor nation. But the favorable balance of American trade, instead of being reversed as it should have been if the old equilibrium was to be restored, was and continued to be more favorable than ever. No way of righting this situation has been found to this day. The European economy as a whole, like the American, was that of creditor nations. But Europe had lost much of her trade and her foreign investments. How to reestablish some equilibrium was one of her major problems, the intensity of which varied of course considerably with the circumstances of the various units.

b. <u>Domestic Borrowing and Currency Inflation.</u> Huge internal borrowing and large issues of paper money unsettled all currencies, and all countries were faced with problems of inflation. The universal hope of a return to "normalcy" soon proved to be a dream; the war could not be undone and somehow must be paid for. Yet by the middle twenties a fair degree of stability seemed to have been achieved. Some countries had had to wipe out their currencies altogether, and create new ones; others had achieved stability at some fraction of their former values; England alone succeeded in returning to the old parity.

These devaluations meant wiping out large amounts of savings, and while it would take us too far afield to enter into the question, the fact must at least be mentioned and stressed that such phenomena have profound and unsettling social repercussions.

c. <u>The Russian Experiment.</u> In the east, Russia had deliberately embarked upon the creation of a totally new social structure. The Russian experiment attracted much attention and was the source of, or served to give added point to, the unrest of the industrial laboring class throughout Europe. Labor organization and socialism received a strong impulse from the war, but attempted revolutions outside of Russia failed. Briefly, we shall now look into the developments that took place during this same period of false recovery in the various units of the European complex.

II. THE DEMOCRATIC WEST

Britain and France, the traditional European homes of the democratic idea and practice, were not affected by the war in their constitutional structures, but in other ways both faced major problems.

A. The Course of the United Kingdom

1. The Problems of Britain. The chief domestic problem of Britain was that of economic restoration, which, owing to the nature of the British economy, depended more than any other upon foreign trade. The election of December, 1918 continued Lloyd George at the head of a coalition government, the support of which was overwhelmingly conservative. In opposition were Labor and a group of Liberals led by Asquith. The Unemployment Insurance Act, the commercial agreement with Russia, and the Safeguarding of Industries Act, all passed in 1921, were designed to protect British industry, revive trade, and allay social unrest. The last-named act was especially significant in view of Britain's long-time devotion to free trade.

2. End of the Wartime Coalition. The coalition broke in 1922, and the ensuing election in November returned a clear Conservative majority led by Bonar Law, soon to be succeeded by Stanley Baldwin. Most significant was the fact that Labor for the first time, gaining 142 seats, was the second largest party. The split Liberals were destined never to recover their position in British politics.

3. The First Labor Government. The government's decision to introduce a measure of protection was considered a radical innovation that exceeded its mandate and precipitated another election in 1923. The result, a repudiation of protection, but no clear majority, produced Britain's first Labor government, led by Ramsay MacDonald, actually a Labor-Liberal coalition, in January, 1924.

4. Five Years of Conservative Government. This coalition, hamstrung by fundamental divergencies, soon broke, and a third election took place within two years. Labor's setback and the definitive eclipse of the Liberals (36 members) yielded a clear Conservative majority and a Parliament that lasted its full normal five-year term.

Under whatever dispensation, Britain's basic difficulties remained the same and largely beyond her control. Unemployment, while fluctuating, was rampant, especially in such fields as coal and textiles, which became known as the "sick industries," the locale of which constituted the "depressed areas" of Britain. Trade disputes in coal led to an unsuccessful general strike in 1926, and this in turn produced the preventive Trades Dispute Act. Taxation was very heavy, but, taken as a whole, Britain, half prosperous or half depressed, achieved substantial recovery.

5. The Second Labor Government and the Crisis of 1931. The election of May, 1929 for the first time gave Labor the largest representation in Parliament, though not a clear majority. MacDonald again headed a coalition which soon found itself struggling with the added impact of a world depression. Over the issue of an unbalanced budget as a result of the increased demands of unemployment, there was a split within Labor ranks in August, 1931. Instead of an election, MacDonald succeeded himself at the head of a National Coalition in which, however, the bulk of his own following refused to join; but instead read him out of the party. The electorate was consulted in October and overwhelmingly endorsed the National government; its huge majority (554 out of 615 members) included 471 Conservatives. The government was reorganized under MacDonald's premiership.

6. The Empire. The Statute of Westminster. In matters imperial, the long-term trend of the Dominions toward autonomy continued. From head of the Empire, Britain became a legally coequal member of the British Commonwealth of Nations. This change was formally sanctioned by the Statute of Westminster in 1931; it applied to the Dominions only and did not affect the status of India or of other dependent parts of the Empire.

a. THE IRISH QUESTION. This question had troubled British politics long before 1914. The situation deteriorated during and immediately after the war, so that the provisions of the Home Rule Bill of 1912, or even the more liberal ones of a new bill in 1920, failed to settle the issue. Civil war and anarchy prevailed in Ireland. An Anglo-Irish treaty in 1921 established the Irish Free State, with a status similar to Canada's. Peace began to be restored to the Free State after the more radical faction, led by Eamon De Valera, gave up its tactics of violence in 1923. The six counties of northern Ireland refused, however, to join with the Free State. [7]

B. The French Republic

The war over, French parties and politics soon returned to their pre-1914 complexion and practice, and governments had to be based on fragile coalitions. The postponed election took place in November, 1919, a victory for the National Bloc, but with the election of 1924 the "normal" leftward orientation of the French electorate reasserted itself.

1. The Task of Reconstruction. France emerged from the war with the pressing problem of physical reconstruction of the enormous damage wrought in her northern provinces. The happy illusion prevailed at first that Germany would make good this damage. But in any event reconstruction could not wait and was therefore financed by the state as a charge upon the nation. Reconstruction was successfully carried out, but the burden of debt assumed in the process, on top of the wartime expenditure, had disastrous effects upon French finances. Premier Poincaré's policy of intransigeance toward Germany failed to replenish the French state coffers.

a. STABILIZATION OF THE FRANC. The return of the more conciliatory left to power made possible the acceptance of the Dawes Plan, but accumulating deficits shook the credit of the state. By the middle of 1926, the franc was 48 to the dollar, about one-tenth its former value. In the emergency, a ministry of National Union was organized under Poincaré, whose energetic measures earned him the title of "savior of the franc," which was eventually stabilized at 25 to the dollar. The task had not been too difficult owing to the basic soundness and resources of the French economy.

---

[7] Henceforth the proper name of the United Kingdom is the United Kingdom of Great Britain and Northern Ireland.

There followed a period of economic prosperity, and the country endorsed Poincaré's stewardship in the 1928 election, only to return to a left majority four years later when the effects of the world crisis had not yet been seriously felt in France.

2. *The Problem of Security.* Despite her share in victory France did not feel secure. How to procure security was the other great issue of French politics. The desire for it was unanimous, but two antagonistic schools of thought emerged on how to proceed to that end: one, distrustful of Germany, favored a literal interpretation and enforcement of the terms of the treaty of peace; the other saw better hope in a policy of reconciliation. The latter tendency made gradual but steady headway, especially after 1924. The question of the role and powers of the League of Nations was paramount in this connection, but these developments will be traced together with an outline of the international situation during this period.

C. Weimar Germany

1. *The Republic Established.* One of the slogans of the war had been "to make the world safe for democracy." It looked as if a great success had been achieved in that direction when the Kaiser abdicated and Germany became a republic.

a. THE NATIONAL ASSEMBLY. Following the abdication, the provisional government succeeded in maintaining order against revolutionary attempts of the extreme left, and in January, 1919 a National Assembly was elected, for the first time under unrestricted universal suffrage. This Assembly, like the French in 1871, had the threefold task of carrying on the current business of government, making peace, and drafting a constitution.

b. THE CONSTITUTION. As in other continental countries, there were many parties in Germany, none having alone a clear majority. A left of center coalition of the Majority Socialists, Centrists, and Democrats dominated the Assembly. The constitution was completed and adopted in August, and Friedrich Ebert became the first president of the German republic. Germany was to operate under a system generally similar to the British and French. The President, elected by popular vote for seven years, had normally little power, but a special provision (Art. 48) of the constitution conferred upon him wide powers in the event of an emergency. The real power lay in the hands of the chancellor and his cabinet responsible to the Reichstag. The Reichsrat, corresponding to the former Bundesrat, represented the states, for the German republic retained the federal structure of the empire. There was in Germany a radical constitutional change, but no revolution in the real sense.

c. WEAKNESSES OF THE REPUBLIC. If military defeat had brought the downfall of the Empire, it could hardly be expected, once the first shock had passed, that the old regime would lose all its supporters. The Republic, moreover, was heir to the troubles that war and defeat brought in their train, and these troubles were great and many. The mere passage of time made it possible increasingly to associate the former Empire with prosperity, power, and glory, while the present Republic floundered in impotence and misery. Understandably, the peace itself was universally unpopular.

2. *The Course of the Republic.*

a. THE EARLY YEARS. The early course of the Republic was troubled, and it barely more than survived its first years. Having weathered storms from the left it was attacked from the right (Kapp putsch in 1920).[8] The first regular election under the new constitution took place in June, 1920. The Weimar coalition lost about 100 seats, and the new government rested on a new coalition in which the People's party took the place of the Majority Social Democrats. Like France, Germany now was subject to ministerial instability. The same trend was evidenced in the 1924 election, and eventually a Center-People's-Nationalist coalition was able to organize a government.

b. COLLAPSE OF THE CURRENCY. Most concretely in evidence was the fate of the currency. In May, 1921 the mark was worth 60 to the dollar (4.2 at par). Eighteen months later, the

---

[8] The Ludendorff-Hitler "beer hall" putsch of November, 1923 in Munich seemed at the time to contain more fantasy and ridicule than power.

rate had gone to 7000. The occupation of the Ruhr gave it the *coup de grâce*. Worth 160,000 to the dollar at the end of January, 1923, there followed an accelerating debacle and a wholly fantastic situation. Repudiation of the currency was the only possible outcome. It should be noted that such a phenomenon did not impoverish the nation as a whole, but within it effected the most arbitrary, sudden, and capricious redistribution of wealth which had inevitably widespread social repercussions.

c. THE PERIOD OF STABILIZATION. Following the chaos resulting from the currency collapse, the advent of Stresemann inaugurated a new policy of fulfillment and reconciliation. With the return of economic stability, this policy held for a time good promise of success. During the second half of the twenties, the mark was stable, foreign obligations were met, and the consequences, political and economic, of the war seemed on the way to liquidation. This relaxation of tensions was reflected in the 1928 election marked by a shift away from the right. A broad coalition, presided over by a Socialist, Müller, assumed control.

d. THE PRESIDENTIAL ELECTION OF 1925. Meanwhile, the death of Ebert precipitated a presidential election in 1925. Paul von Hindenburg, Germany's wartime leader and symbol of all that imperial Germany had stood for, won the election by a narrow margin. Hindenburg, once in office, belied the fears of those who thought he would undermine the Republic. But the period of hopefulness was short-lived. The coalition of 1928 broke up in 1929 and was replaced by a narrower one, excluding the Social Democrats, and led by Brüning, of the Catholic Center party.

e. EMERGENCY GOVERNMENT. By 1930, economic and budgetary difficulties were such that Hindenburg dissolved the Reichstag and resorted to the emergency provisions of the constitution to enact the budget. From this point on, the next two years are a story of the inability of the Republic to withstand the additional stresses put upon it by economic distress. The tale of gradual political disintegration belongs in the next chapter by way of preface to the emergence of the Nazi state.

III. NEW POLITICAL EXPERIMENTS

The heralded spread of the democratic ideal and practice was to receive major challenges before many years had passed after the end of the war. It took some time before the nature of the Russian experiment, initially welcomed by the democracies, was to become apparent. The Fascists, from the first, avowed their contempt for democracy. Under outwardly sharply contrasting appearances, these two new systems had much in common, representing responses to the stresses born of war and attempted adaptations to new conditions and problems. That is what makes these experiments so important.

A. The Soviet Union

In brief summary, the empire of the Tsars had not been capable of sustaining the impact of modern war. There lay the fundamental reasons for the revolutions of 1917.

1. The Revolutions of 1917. Revolution first occurred in March, when the Tsar abdicated and a provisional government was organized. But the March revolution resulted in a double misunderstanding. The provisional government rested on the uneasy alliance of the relatively moderate Duma revolutionaries with a much more radical Petrograd Soviet. In addition, the new government was officially dedicated to the continuation of the war alongside Russia's allies, whereas the temper of the country was predominantly one of weariness born of war-induced defeats and privations. At a time when determination and strong leadership were needed, the prospects of a government founded on misunderstanding and divergent purpose could not be very bright. To make assurance doubly sure, the German government had conveyed Lenin from Switzerland to Russia. The result of these circumstances was the Bolshevik *coup d'état* of November 6-7, from which emerged a new government, the Soviet of People's Commissars, of which Lenin was chairman.

2. The Struggle for Survival. The Bolsheviks were revolutionary Marxists, henceforth known to history as Communists. Their seizure of power in Russia was an accidental deviation from the predicted sequence of development, for agrarian Russia had little industry and correspondingly few industrial workers. The revolution having preceded industry and lacking a broad industrial basis, some important consequences followed from this situation.

One, the power of the state must be firmly in the hands of those who knew how and where to lead the revolution. There would be a (presumably temporary) period of dictatorship of the proletariat, which dictatorship would in turn be held in trust by the revolutionary leaders. Secondly, the revolution could be successful only if it spread beyond the borders of Russia, else outside forces of reaction would crush it in Russia as well.

From this, in turn, further consequences followed. The support of the Russian masses, innocent of Marxism, would be sought on the basis of the simple and readily understandable slogan "land, peace, and bread." The old ruling and owning classes would be forcibly expropriated and "liquidated," and peace would be made. The terms of peace would be relatively unimportant, for the only basically significant issue was the survival of the revolution in Russia, and its extension as soon as possible beyond.

a. WORLD REVOLUTION AND CORDON SANITAIRE. Peace was made with the Central Powers at Brest-Litovsk and on their terms. The Allies undid Brest-Litovsk, but the new Soviet state found itself beset by both civil war and foreign intervention. The Allies soon abandoned the thought of overthrowing the new regime by their own efforts and confined themselves to giving assistance to the White Russian armies fighting the revolution. If the Russian masses had little understanding of Marxism, they had no desire to reinstate the old regime: the counterrevolution was eventually put down.

By 1921, even the war with Poland had been liquidated on a basis of compromise, and, along with the new Poland, the Soviets had also recognized the independence of the new states that emerged along the Baltic. These new states, from Finland to Poland, were recognized and supported by the Allies, especially by France, and with Roumania formed the "cordon sanitaire" whose purpose it was to contain the spread of

Bolshevism.[9] By 1921, an equilibrium had in fact been reached: the Soviet state had not been destroyed, but neither had it spread its influence beyond the reduced domain of Tsarist Russia.

3. Organization of the Soviet State

a. THE CONSTITUTION. Even while in the midst of the chaotic struggle for survival, provision had been made for the organization of the new regime. As early as 1921 a new constitution was enacted. Further decisions in 1922 and a new edition in 1924 completed the process of constitution making. The result was to create a federal structure, the Union of Soviet Socialist Republics (U.S.S.R.). The number and dimensions of members of the union has varied in the course of time, but Russia proper, the R.S.F.S.R., has maintained overwhelming size and importance.

The federation was presided over by the All-Union Congress of Soviets, elected on a popular basis.[10] This body seldom met, save to elect the Central Executive Committee, a bicameral body consisting of the Soviet of the Union and the Soviet of Nationalities, wherein resided the exercise of executive and legislative power. From this committee emerged in turn the Council of Commissars, Soviet version of a western cabinet. It will be noted that the principle of separation of powers was deliberately rejected.

b. THE COMMUNIST PARTY. This description alone gives an erroneous impression of the reality of things. The revolution had been made by a small minority imbued with the correctness of the Marxist view of history and of the state. Eventually, the state would "wither away," but a transitional period of dictatorship was foreseen. The Bolsheviks had no intention of submitting their tenure of power to the test of unhampered elections. The Communist party was the tool through which the secure retention of power was reconciled with the formal process of representation.

---

[9] The *cordon sanitaire* was the post-First World War version of what, after the Second World War, came to be known as containment.

[10] Some categories of the population were disfranchised. The voting age was 18 for both sexes. Elections were usually by show of hands, and representation was weighed five to one in favor of industrial workers.

The party was always small and deliberately kept such through the enforcement of stringent requirements for admission and for continued membership.[11] It consisted of the highly politically conscious and active section of the citizenry, blindly devoted to the Marxist gospel and to the most rigid discipline. Party members filled in overwhelming proportion the important positions in the state.

c. THE PARTY AND THE STATE. THE POLITBURO. The party had its own organization and hierarchy, theoretically distinct from those of the state. But since, in actual practice, no opposition was allowed in this one-party state, the same individuals were to a large extent holders of party as well as state offices. The close identification of party and state was thereby effected. Thus the Politburo, chief and central organ of the party organization, became in effect, though unofficially, the most important organ in the state. In it differences were threshed out, policies took shape, and final decisions were made. This small body, of some dozen men, was the real seat of power in the Soviet Union.

d. DICTATORSHIP AND INDOCTRINATION. On the plea that the new regime must insure its safety against unreconciled dissenters, all opposition was suppressed. The police, continuing the tradition of Tsarist days, became more than ever one of the chief props of the state. On the further plea of the need of education, all expressions of opinion were rigidly controlled. Most important was the attention given to molding the minds of the rising generation. An enormous amount was done in spreading literacy and hugely enlarging the opportunities for free education which was at the same time the most effective instrument of political indoctrination.

4. The First Decade of the Soviet Union.

a. WAR COMMUNISM AND THE N.E.P. From the first four years of its existence the Soviet Union emerged undefeated but in a chaotic state. The attempt to enact communist theory in practice had been premature; this, along with the failure of world revolution to materialize, called for a tactical revision of plans. Lenin inaugurated the N.E.P. (New Economy Policy) which temporarily would allow some scope to a freer

---

[11] Around 1 per cent of the population. Periodic purges served to enforce strict discipline.

working of the economy. This policy was essentially successful in its purpose of restoration.

b. <u>The Succession of Lenin.</u> From 1922, Lenin's influence, owing to illness, declined, and his death in 1924 initiated a bitter struggle for his succession. The chief contenders were Leon Trotsky, to whom went much of the credit for the successful survival of the revolution, and Joseph Stalin. In addition to temperamental differences, the points at issue between them were two: different estimates of the relative importance to be given at the time to the prosecution of world revolution as against Russia's internal development, and divergences as to the rate at which true communism should be forced upon the country.

c. <u>The Triumph of Stalin.</u> The struggle was long and ruthless. In the end, the slogan "socialism in one country" was to win out, and with it Stalin over Trotsky, who was forced into exile, first in Siberia, eventually outside the Soviet Union. The country meantime continued to recover from the devastation of war and revolution. Concentrating on its internal development, the international situation having reached a state of stability, in 1928 a vast program was inaugurated with the main purpose of industrialization.

d. <u>The Five-Year Plans.</u> The first five-year plan, dating of that year, was to be followed by a succession of others. The endeavor was to prove in large part successful, making Russia an important industrial state, but the fact explains much of the Soviet development that the revolution preceded the appearance of industry which it set about to create, thereby reversing the correct Marxist sequence. By the end of the twenties, the possibility seemed to exist that the Soviet Union, wrapped up in her own growth, might return to the position of one among the family of nations.

B. Fascist Italy

1. The Period of Transition, 1918-1922. The war and its aftermath produced in Italy, as elsewhere, much disillusion. Italian losses had not been too great, but in contrast with Britain or France, for example, the weak Italian economy was less able than the British or the French to stand its smaller absolute, but in relative terms greater, losses. Hence the very considerable economic stresses after 1918.

Italy, in addition, did not have the longer political experience and practice of Britain and France. With a similar organization, the roots of her democracy were planted in shallower soil. This was reflected in the nature of Italian politics, suitable enough in conditions of normal peaceful growth, as from 1870 to 1914, but now subject to abnormal pressures. There were no strong leaders at this critical juncture. The wartime coalition, broken in June, 1919, gave way to a succession of cabinets that proved incapable of supplying the needed leadership and direction.

The prevailing malaise of the body politic constituted an atmosphere suitable for novel experiments and ideas. The Russian example had considerable attraction, but the threat of communism was not serious at this time, though some thought it such. There were, however, much unrest, numerous strikes, and the famous episode of the occupation of the factories in 1920. Elections in 1919 and 1921 greatly strengthened the Socialists and brought into existence the *Popolari*, a new Catholic democratic party.

a. <u>Mussolini and the Appearance of Fascism</u>. In these circumstances, Mussolini appeared upon the scene, but his first entrance was hardly impressive. Before the war, Mussolini had been one of the more radical leaders of Italian Socialism. But in the autumn of 1914 he broke with the party, having become an advocate of Italian intervention in the war. He was pursuing a lonely course and commanded little influence when he organized the *fasci di combattimento* in 1919. In the election of 1921, the Fascists obtained 35 seats. Their program, in so far as they had one, was a strange mixture of socialism and nationalism, but they appeared increasingly as the opponents of the left in politics, against which they resorted to tactics of violence.

It is a measure of the degree of impotence of Italian parliamentarianism that a new cabinet crisis in October, 1922 resulted in Mussolini being appointed prime minister. [12]

---

[12] The so-called March on Rome was a threatening gesture which might easily have been dealt with by the armed forces. However, the military were not unsympathetic to Fascism and the King refused to sign a decree of martial law. Much has been made of this "unconstitutional" intervention of the crown, but more fundamental was the abdication of Paliament as shown by its endorsement of the new cabinet. The episode is a prime object lesson in the suicide of a democracy in accordance with its own rules of procedure.

2. Shaping the Fascist State. This was a revolution, if it was one at all, very different from the Russian. The constitutional forms of the Italian state were respected, and Mussolini received a vote of confidence in Parliament. Fascism, moreover, had no solid philosophy comparable to Marxism behind it, but represented a confused jumble of ideas that could mean all things to all men.

a. THE PERIOD OF CONSOLIDATION. Consequently, the Fascist state took shape relatively slowly and gradually, to a considerable degree as the result of adaptation to the circumstances of its tenure power. An election in 1923 [13] endorsed the new government, though opposition to it continued both active and vocal. It was indeed the violent voicing of this opposition that resulted in the assassination of the Socialist deputy Matteotti in 1924.

b. CONSTITUTIONAL CHANGES. This murder shook the regime, which in the end, partly because of the continued divisions of its opponents, emerged from the trial more securely established than ever and proceeded to entrench itself. After 1925, no open opposition was allowed and new constitutional laws made the prime minister, henceforth head of the government, no longer responsible to Parliament. Elections thereafter were the inevitable farce that they cannot help being in a one-party state.

c. THE PARTY AND THE STATE. While far less ruthless in application than in the Russian case, the Fascist state, which had fairly taken shape by the late twenties, was totalitarian in form. The Fascist party and its machinery, ostensibly distinct from, came in practice to coincide largely with, the state organization. The Grand Council of Fascism, formally integrated into the constitutional structure in 1929, was the real center of power. Mussolini decidedly dominated that body: the *Duce* was truly a dictator. As in Russia, there appeared the same necessity to control all means of public information, and above all education.

---

[13] Parliament enacted the Acerbo law which provided that the party receiving the largest vote—provided this were at least 25 per cent—would receive two-thirds of the seats. This was a device for translating a plurality into a majority and thus provide stability of government. As it turned out, the scheme was unnecessary, for the Fascists received a clear majority.

d. THE CORPORATE STATE. But, unlike Russia, the outward form of society was not altered, and the break with the past was much less sharp and apparent. One basic reason for this was the fact that the private basis of ownership of property was not changed. Nevertheless, the economic thinking of Fascism was important and found expression in the corporate state. In place of the Marxist concept of the class struggle, the modern state should stress the community of interest among those engaged in a common enterprise, steel production for instance, regardless of their position as owners, managers, or workers. The various segments of the national economy, or corporations (there were 22 eventually) should moreover become the basis of political representation in place of the old-fashioned and out of date geographical divisions. [14]

e. THE NATION AND THE STATE. Unlike Communism again in theory, though there was much that was common in practice, Fascism avowedly exalted the state for which the individual existed. Mussolini and Fascist theorists never ceased to deride the inadequacy and weakness of the democratic belief and practice which they regarded as decadent. Fascism was undeniably a form of response to the urgent problems of a modern society which are undoubtedly different from those envisioned by eighteenth-century constitution makers.

Nationalism was ever a strong component of Fascism, which had early absorbed the small but able group of Nationalists in Parliament. This was consistent with the exaltation of the state. In practice, however, during the first decade, Fascist Italy seemed to belie the fears engendered by the aggressive attitude and pronouncement of her leaders. Many came to feel that Fascist Italy was not a disturber of the peace, and that Fascism had succeeded in restoring order in the nation whose prestige it had enhanced.

3. *The Roman Question*. One of the feathers in the Fascist cap was the liquidation of the Roman question in 1929. The Roman Church could not acknowledge the supremacy of the state, but toward the authoritarian tendency of Fascism it was rather sympathetic than otherwise. Relations between the

---

[14] The Corporate State took shape only slowly and gradually. Not until 1938 was the Chamber of Deputies superseded by a Chamber of Fasci and Corporations.

Italian state and the Vatican, not unsatisfactory in practice, were formally regularized: the creation, within Rome, of the one-hundred acre sovereign state of Vatican City made possible mutual recognition, and a financial settlement with the Pope was made concurrently. The episode redounded mainly to the prestige of Fascist Italy, but did little to settle basic divergences, which were in fact soon to become apparent.

IV. THE POWER VACUUM OF THE SUCCESSION STATES

The most significant fact in central and eastern Europe after the First World War was the emergence of a number of new states carved out in the main from the former Russian and Austro-Hungarian Empires. But while the bulk of former Russia continued to exist, complete fragmentation was the fate of the Habsburg domain. This disintegration, it must be emphasized, was an internal development that took place formally in October-November, 1918. Three wholly new states, Austria, Hungary, and Czechoslavakia were carved out of the territory of the Dual Monarchy, large areas of which went to other countries. This entire region of Europe has in common the characteristic that it is overwhelmingly agricultural, hence relatively undeveloped, economically as well as politically. Also, it had difficulty supporting its large and fast-growing population. [15]

A. The Inheritance of the Habsburgs

1. The Republic of Austria. This purely Germanic core of the Habsburg empire had 6,500,000 inhabitants in an area of 32,000 square miles. One-third of its population was in Vienna, a city geared to the management of a country of 50,000,000. The resulting unbalance was in itself a problem, for Vienna was a stronghold of socialism, along with other industrial centers, while much of the country was controlled by clericals: the cleavage between red and black was particularly sharp in Austria.

After some initial uncertainty, the election of February, 1919

---
[15] This generalization needs qualification in the cases of Austria and Czechoslovakia.

put the moderate Socialists in a position of leadership. Under the constitution of October, 1920, Austria emerged as a federal republic with a democratic parliamentary government of western type, the Habsburgs having meantime been banished.

The difficulties of economic readjustment were inevitably enormous. By 1922 Austria was in serious financial straits, to such a degree that the League undertook the task of rehabilitation. The success of the operation made possible removal of supervision in 1926, and for some years thereafter there seemed hope that little Austria, like her Swiss neighbor of older standing, would achieve political and economic stability. And so indeed it might have had not the whole world become engulfed in crisis.

a. THE ANSCHLUSS. There was one problem wholly peculiar to Austria. The purely Germanic character of the population, in addition to the difficulties of economic readjustment, caused many Austrians to feel that the only hope of salvation lay in union with Germany. The *Anschluss* was however forbidden by the treaties of peace, but the issue could not be permanently disposed of in so simple a fashion. The feeling for *Anschluss*, always substantial in Austria, was difficult of accurate measure, and it tended to fluctuate according to the circumstances, economic and political, of the Reich.

2. Hungary. Having broken loose from Austria, Hungary, owing to the desire for independence of her subject peoples, emerged as a purely Magyar state of 8,000,000 in a territory of 36,000 square miles. Many Magyars were excluded from her borders, and Hungarian revisionism was intense.

For a brief time, in 1919, Hungary set up a soviet regime under the leadership of Bela Kun. Internal opposition and foreign intervention restored the old order. From that time, conservative forces were firmly in control, and Hungary proclaimed herself a monarchy. The opposition to a restoration of the Habsburgs, especially on the part of some of Hungary's neighbors, in addition to a lack of popular support in the country, resulted in the failure of Charles' attempt at establishing himself on the Hungarian throne in 1921. From March, 1920 Admiral Horthy filled the post of Regent.

The economic problem of Hungary, an essentially agricultural country, was relatively easier than Austria's. But Hungarian finances also ran into difficulty, and, as with Austria, there was League assistance and supervision in 1922, followed by restoration of stability. Little was done in Hungary by way of land reform.

3. Czechoslovakia. Newly emancipated Czechoslovakia found herself on the side of the victors. She proved to be the most successful, in every respect, of the succession states, and the one that preserved to the last the democratic institutions under which she began her independent existence. Much credit for this goes to her founding fathers and early leaders, outstanding among whom was the scholar-statesman Thomas G. Masaryk.

Though not burdened with the consequences of defeat, the problems of Czechoslovakia were considerable, essentially the organization and integration of the new state. There were differences between the more advanced Czechs and the less-developed Slovaks, but these were minor by comparison with the existence of some 3,000,000 Sudeten Germans around the western fringe of the country, and about 1,000,000 Magyars on the southeastern border. The reasons which led to the incorporation of so large a minority in Czechoslovakia were several.[16] Despite some complaints on the part of the ethnic minorities, and even of the Slovaks and Ruthenians, there seemed reason to believe that, provided there was no outside interference, the Czechoslovak state might develop into an integrated nation.

A thoroughgoing program of land reform was enacted, limiting the size of land holdings. For the rest, Czechoslovakia was favored by the good balance of her economy, comparable with the French, between agriculture and industry, a fact which had much to do with the successful operation of her political institutions.

B. The New Balkans

A large section of the former Habsburg domain went to two Balkan states, Yugoslavia and Roumania. In these, and the other Balkan countries, the low economic standard, combined with and related to, political backwardness, made the democratic frameworks under which they formally operated very fragile structures. The future alone could tell how much reality there was in the spread of democatic institutions in this part of Europe as in the other new countries bordering on Russia.

1. Yugoslavia and Albania. The central problem of the newly formed Kingdom of the Serbs, Croats, and Slovenes was, like that of Czechoslovakia, one of national integration. The more economically advanced and predominantly Catholic

---

[16] The strategic factor carried understandable weight in 1919. It was the most important single consideration in the decision to maintain the boundaries of the historic Kingdom of Bohemia.

Croats in the north were now joined to the Orthodox Serbs. The union was of their free volition, but the prior independent existence of Serbia gave Serbs an advantage in the operation of the political machine and the filling of its posts. This was resented by Croats who expected at least equality in a looser union. Time and the quality of management would supply the answers. At first, the constitution of 1921 provided for a centralized structure.

Pashitch, the grand old man of Serbia, continued to head the government, while the Croat opposition led by Radich refused for a time to sit in parliament (the Skuptchina). The murder of Radich in Parliament itself led to a renewal of the Croatian boycott and resulted in such stresses that King Alexander in 1929 dissolved Parliament, abrogated the constitution, and made himself virtual dictator. Yugoslavia, as the official name had been since, did not seem quite ready for the successful operation of the democratic process.

Most backward Albania re-emerged from the war. Distinct from her neighbors, her continued existence was in large part a result of their and greater powers' rivalries. One of her tribal chieftains became President in 1925 and assumed the title of King, as Zog I, in 1928. Albania was the object of a contest for predominant influence mainly between Yugoslavia and Italy. [17]

2. Greece. The political life of Greece presents a picture of utmost instability and confusion. In large measure owing to Venizelos' skill, the whole Aegean including some Asiatic territory around Smyrna was to be Greek. This last situation led to war with Turkey [18] while at the same time King Constantine, ousted during the war, was recalled upon the death of his son and successor Alexander. The unfortunate course of the war in Asia Minor led to Constantine's second resignation in favor of his son George in 1922. By 1924, a plebiscite re-

---

[17] The southern sector of Albania, northern Epirus, was also claimed by Greece.

[18] While the government of the Sultan signed the treaty of Sèvres, Kemal Pasha had raised the standard of revolt in Anatolia. The Turkish National Pact of January, 1920 proclaimed the independence of Turkey and refused to recognize the treaty of Sèvres. Kemal, favored by differences among the powers, chiefly Britain and France, was able to make good his challenge. The treaty of Sèvres as a consequence was stillborn, and the new Turkey was recognized by the treaty of Lausanne in 1923.

sulted in the proclamation of a republic, but not the inauguration of greater stability in government, beset by the operation of parliamentary politics mixed with an occasional seizure of power, as by General Pangalos in 1925. Venizelos, ever a dominant figure, was at the helm again in 1928.

Defeat in Asia Minor in 1922 resulted in a drastic but lasting settlement. Reversing the colonizing movement of 2500 years ago, the Greek population of Asia returned to Greece proper, over 1,000,000 persons being involved. Despite the difficulty of absorbing so large a number into Greece's life and economy, the refugees proved on the whole an asset and served to increase the Greek character of Macedonia and Thrace. The traditional Greco-Turkish enmity gave way to henceforth relatively cordial relations.

3. Bulgaria. Bulgaria was saddled with the consequences of defeat, which resulted in King Ferdinand's surrender of the crown to his son Boris III. A strong agrarian party, led by Alexander Stambolisky, dominated the political scene after 1920. Its repressive methods, little short of dictatorship, resulted in its overthrow by a coup in 1923. But Bulgaria's political life, though less volatile than Greece's, continued to be plagued by the use of violent methods. The Communists constituted a substantial menace. A large influx of Macedonian refugees were fertile ground for agitation which led to the verge of war with Greece in 1925. The IMRO (International Macedonian Revolutionary Organization) was an important factor in the domestic affairs of Bulgaria until weakened by internal dissensions. A *coup d'état* in 1934 resulted in the abolition of political parties and a virtual royal dictatorship the following year.

4. Roumania. Roumania emerged from the war with large territorial acquisitions, especially Transylvania and Bessarabia, which meant in turn substantial alien minorities. The introduction of universal suffrage resulted in the emergence of a powerful Peasant party, especially in newly acquired Transylvania, which, however, was not allowed to dominate the government. A thoroughgoing agrarian reform was enacted in 1921, but the pressure of peasant discontent finally forced the acceptance of the peasant leader, Julius Maniu, at the head of the government.

Roumanian politics were complicated by the private affairs of the crown. In 1925, the heir Prince Carol, renounced his rights, and his young son, Michael, succeeded King Ferdinand upon the latter's death in 1927, while the country was ruled by a regency. Carol, however, had much political and military support in the country. Having supposedly broken with his mistress and about to be reconciled with his wife, Carol returned in 1930 to be retroactively recognized as King as from 1927. Despite the failure to modify his personal relationships, Carol remained as King. Under the existing electoral law, an election in 1931 gave the Peasant party a majority at the polls but a minority in Parliament, and in Roumania also, the government came close to being a personal dictatorship of the king.

C. Poland and the New Baltic States

1. Poland. Reconstituted Poland, with a population of some 30,000,000 was much the largest of the new states of Europe, a fact which was the basis of some claim to great power status.

Essentially, Poland had had no separate independent existence since the end of the eighteenth century. The Polish people had successfully resisted all efforts at assimilation by their neighbors, thanks in part to the vigor of their own national feeling. Much had happened, however, in the course of 125 years, and the problems of new Poland were the basic ones of definition and integration.

a. THE PROBLEM OF FRONTIERS. The frontiers of Poland were difficult to establish and remained to a large extent in dispute. That with Russia was the outcome of war in 1920-1921, and Vilna was obtained through an act of force. The result was that between one-fourth and one-third of the population consisted of non-Polish minorities, if the Jews are included as such. If the German minority was the most vocal, far the largest was in the east. It should be pointed out that differences between Poles, Ukrainians, White Russians, and Lithuanians are often less clear than those found farther west in Europe. One consequence of the long suppression of Poland was the intransigeance of Polish nationalism toward its alien minorities. The nature and location of the country, with open and indefensible frontiers in most directions, combined with her historic experience, made the problem of security particularly important and acute.

b. <u>Organization of the State.</u> The problem of organizing the new state out of three sections long under different rulers was one of great difficulty. A constitution, similar to the French, was drafted in 1921, and under it emerged a series of weak administrations. Strong direction was needed, but Poles seemed to have lost none of the divisive individualism which had once led to their undoing. In the circumstances, Pilsudski effected a coup which ousted the existing government in 1926. Thereafter, whether in political office or out, Pilsudski dominated the government in relatively mild, semidictatorial manner until his death in 1935.

Poland, devastated by war, made a substantial recovery. Largely an agricultural state, the demand for agrarian reform was met to some degree. Industry was gradually restored and expanded and the new port of Gdynia, designed to avoid dependence on Danzig, was created.

2. *The Baltic States.* Between Poland and the Gulf of Finland there arose the three small states of Lithuania, Latvia, and Estonia. With a population ranging from one to two million each, the appearance on the map of these minute political units endowed with sovereignty represented an extreme application of the principle of self-determination. For all three, the most significant fact was that they were diminutive entities standing between the huge bulk of Russia and the sea. In this respect the clock had been set back two centuries.

By way of access to the Baltic, only Peter's window remained to Russia, for across the Gulf of Finland from Estonia appeared an independent Finland. Large in extent but with a population of less than 4,000,000, Finland had more in common with the Scandinavian countries than with Russia with whom she had been linked for a century. [19]

---

[19] The Scandinavian countries, Holland, Switzerland, and Spain, which had remained neutral during the war, have not been discussed in this chapter for their course continued comparatively unaltered as a result of their non-participation in the war. During the thirties, Spain was destined to play an important role in international affairs. This will be considered in the next chapter.

V. THE EUROPEAN COMMUNITY OF NATIONS

Until 1914, Europe as a whole had operated under the aegis of a constellation of so-called great powers whose shifting relations and interests had determined their varying alignments and, in the last resort, the issue of war and peace. The consciousness of common elements in European cultures had given the Concert of Europe a degree of reality.

The First World War radically altered the picture. The Ottoman Empire and the Dual Monarchy had ceased to exist. Russia and Germany still existed and would presumably some day resume their place, but for the moment and for some time to come revolutionary chaos in the former, complete defeat for the latter, eliminated them as significant factors in terms of power. Thus the task of leadership in the immediate future would devolve upon the former great powers that were among the victors. There was in addition a greatly increased number of powers of the second, third, or lower order of magnitude.

A. The League of Nations

There was another innovation. The United States had played a new and for the first time decisive role in the affairs of Europe. It was appropriate that the United States should father the concept which, for the first time in history, was written into a peace settlement. The Covenant of the League of Nations appeared as the first section of all the treaties of peace made in Paris in 1919-1920.

1. Structure of the League. The Covenant was the constitution of the League, which was to function in the manner of a bicameral legislature. The Assembly, in which every member had one vote, could take cognizance of any matter falling within the purview of the League but had no real powers of decision, being more in the nature of a forum of world opinion.

Real power resided in the Council. This body consisted of permanent members—representatives of whatever great powers belonged to the League at any one moment—and nonpermanent members, elected by the Assembly. The number of the latter gradually increased from the original four to ten, and thus was effected a compromise between the reality of power and the ideal of democratic representation.

A permanent secretariat was the functioning instrumentality of the League. The Permanent Court of International Justice, or World Court, [20] may be considered an agency of the League. The International Labor Organization, also incorporated into the peace treaties, while distinct from the League, worked in close association with it. Both bodies became established in Geneva, while the World Court sat in the Hague.

2. Function and Operation of the League. The League was entrusted with certain specific tasks, such as the supervision of the administration of mandates through the requirement of annual reports of the mandatory power to the Mandates Commission. It was also the guardian of the minorities treaties, and it engaged in numerous other activities, such as the rehabilitation of Austria and of Hungary and the transfer of populations between Turkey and Greece.

But the essential function of the League was to insure the

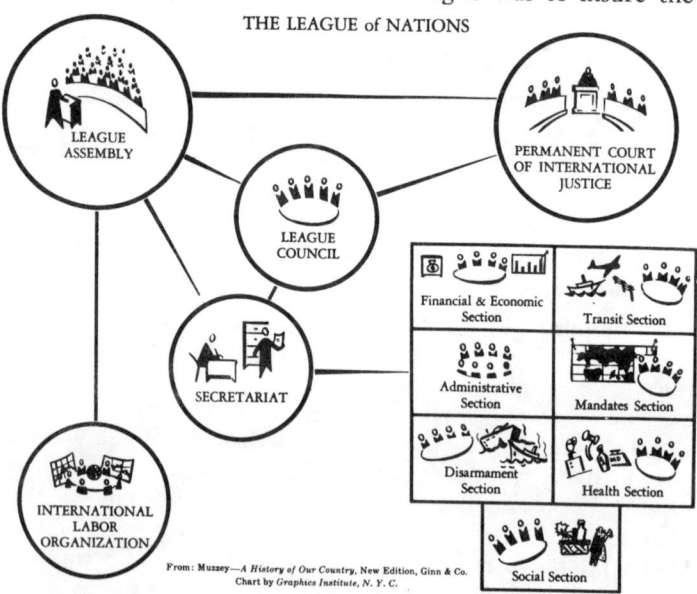

THE LEAGUE of NATIONS

From: Muzzey—*A History of Our Country*, New Edition, Ginn & Co. Chart by *Graphics Institute*, N. Y. C.

---

[20] Not to be confused with the Hague Court of Arbitration established in 1899.

preservation of peace. The League was to be universal in its character. Initiated by the victors, all states could become members, even the enemy after a period of probation. Initially, neither Russia nor Germany belonged to it, and it was the crowning irony that the United States should refuse to join. These limitations were doubtless a major shortcoming, making the League to a large extent an association of the victors, with its vital core in Europe. Time alone could tell how it would evolve. Germany became a member in 1926.

a. <u>The Issue of the Power of the League.</u> More important perhaps than initial limitations of membership was the issue of the law-enforcing powers of the League. In the last analysis, there is an irreconcilable inconsistency between the principle of national sovereignty and the establishment of a rule of law among nations. Within the state the individual is not and cannot be sovereign. The world's nations were not ready in 1919 to surrender their sovereignty, hence the initial vice in the Covenant. This original deficiency was recognized from the first, but the argument ran that in the course of time the League might acquire sufficient prestige and power to command respect for its decrees. The failure clearly to define the power-enforcing instrumentalities of the League was probably the most serious cause of its ultimate failure.

During the first decade of its existence the League was not faced with any major crisis. It was able to resolve some conflicts, but they were mainly issues between minor powers. In other cases it bowed to a *fait accompli* resting on force.

B. The Problem of Security

1. The Debate of Security versus Disarmament. As early as 1919, during the discussions surrounding the drafting of the Covenant, it had been pointed out that for the League to have significance and to inspire confidence as a peace-preserving agency, it must have law-enforcing powers that should be clearly specified in advance. This view, of which the French were the chief exponents, may be regarded more broadly as the view of the continental or land powers. Opposed to it is the position of the naval powers, America and Britain, reluctant to make rigid and specific prior commitments, laying stress on the factors of moral force and world opinion. The two views represented honest differences of opinion stemming from differences of geographic position and historic experience. They were hardly reconcilable or susceptible of meaningful compromise.

From these differences there grew out a long, and in effect never-resolved, debate. It was widely felt that armaments should be reduced, both because of the economic burden that they entailed, and because of the danger to peace inherent in their very existence. France, as the leading land power after 1919, headed those nations whose position may be summed up as: we shall disarm when and to the extent that our security is assured.

2. Attempted Solutions. These discussions led to the drafting of a treaty of mutual assistance in 1923, [21] which in turn led to a demand for the definition of aggression. An attempt to find a way out of the impasse was produced by the British and French premiers, MacDonald and Herriot, in 1924, by introducing the concept of compulsory arbitration. But the Geneva Protocol, as this was known, failed to command general acceptance, even the new Conservative British government rejecting it.

a. THE LOCARNO PACT. A less ambitious, but more successful, effort dealt with the Franco-German problem. In 1925, Gustav Stresemann, seeking to carry out his policy of conciliation, met a favorable response in his French counterpart, Aristide Briand. The outcome was the treaty of Locarno. The frontier between Germany on one side and France and Belgium on the other was to be the object of a guarantee by Britain and by Italy, and Germany was to be admitted to the League. This was an attempt to create conditions of security in a particular area, pending the League's ability to assume broader responsibilities for general security. [22]

b. THE PACT OF PARIS. Three years later, Briand's initiative led to the signing of the Pact of Paris, or Kellogg-Briand Pact, by some fifty nations. This was a simple statement renouncing

---

[21] Outstanding among those opposed to the treaty were Great Britain and non-League members like the United States, Germany, and Russia.

[22] The Locarno pact, and arrangements of this nature in general, raised the important question whether such regional pacts strengthened or weakened the general peace-preserving function of the League.

war as an instrument of national policy. Devoid of effective means of enforcement, such an agreement could have but little value; it was rather an expression of the degree of hopefulness and reconciliation which prevailed at the time, counterpart of the material recovery from the effects of war which seemed to have taken place.

3. The Problem of Disarmament. In this favorable atmosphere the discussion of ways to insure the reduction of armaments was going on. The long, unfruitful debate bogged down in technicalities, but the underlying difficulty was that already mentioned, the insistence of many states on conditions of guaranteed security as a prerequisite to their acceptance of any thoroughgoing scheme of disarmament.

When they participated in these debates, the defeated countries in general, and Germany in particular, took the simple, and for them logical, position that what they were primarily interested in was equality of status. For their own reasons, Italy and the Soviet Union tended to support this stand. Eventually, a disarmament conference convened in Geneva in 1932 at a time and in circumstances which foredoomed it to failure.

a. NAVAL DISARMAMENT. The limitation of armaments at sea had somewhat better success. The Washington conference in 1921-1922 resulted in the acceptance of the 5:5:3:1.67:1.67 ratios for capital ship tonnage by the United States, Great Britain, Japan, France, and Italy, respectively. Japan and France, however, agreed only under pressure, a fact which vitiated the results and prevented the extension of naval disarmament.

It must be pointed out that, after the war, those countries possessed of armaments reduced them very substantially. The real difficulty lay in the fact of continued fear and distrust: whether on land or sea, the holders of superior armaments felt that their security was best served by the continuation of this state of affairs.

C. The Realities of Power: the Foreign Policies of the Powers

Whatever the future of the League might be, it had not succeeded, during the first decade of its existence, in becoming a substitute for the old game of power politics. The behavior of the powers in the circumstances therefore constitutes the reality of international relations during this period.

1. *The French System of Alliances.* France did not feel that the peace gave her adequate safety, especially after the United States and Britain had refused to ratify the treaty of reinsurance of 1919. Security through the League was an attractive concept, but it could only take the place of superior power if made really effective, a problematical outcome at best.

. a. THE NETWORK OF FRENCH AND RELATED ALLIANCES. Highly conscious of her own power deficiencies, France therefore turned to a policy of alliance with those states who shared with her the desire to perpetuate the status that had emerged from the war. As early as 1920, a treaty was made with Belgium, followed by a Polish alliance the following year. In 1924, Czechoslovakia was brought within the system. These three agreements were directed against the German danger.

But Poland and Czechoslovakia were equally interested in eastern and central Europe. Three bilateral treaties among the latter country, Roumania and Yugoslavia, for whom Hungarian revisionism was a common focus, in 1920-1921, brought into existence the so-called Little Entente. These agreements were reinforced by a Franco-Roumanian treaty in 1926 and one between France and Yugoslavia in 1927.

The common interest of Poland and Roumania in retaining their gains from Russia found expression in a treaty between them in 1921. France was the chief exponent of a policy of German impotence and Russian containment, a policy expressed in the structure of alliances just enumerated and of which France, the chief member in terms of military, economic, and financial power was the keystone. This structure, under the aegis of which Europe was to operate until 1938, has sometimes been described as French hegemony. It may be regarded as such, but only with the important qualification that the system was a fundamentally defensive one.

2. *German Policy.* It was only to be expected that Germany and the Soviet Union should have little sympathy for this system and should seek to undermine it. Their common outlook found expression in the treaty of Rapallo which they signed in 1922. But the consequences of the Ruhr episode induced Germany to adopt a western oriented policy of fulfillment and reconciliation. Stresemann was the exponent of this policy, and its fruit, Locarno, emphasized Russia's isolation. Concurrently, Germany signed treaties of arbitration with Poland and Czechoslovakia, but refused to extend to them the type of guarantee contained in the Locarno Pact.

3. *The Policy of the Soviet Union.* As to the Soviet Union, it found itself in an anomalous and unforeseen position. Unfriendly capitalists had failed to destroy it, but neither had the Third International, or Comintern, established in 1919, succeeded in spreading the revolution throughout the world. There was nothing left but attend to the enormous task of internal reconstruction. Foreign policy became negative and defensive, the Soviet Union was gradually recognized by most other states with whom her relations became relatively normal though always tinged with a measure of mutual distrust. The mere passage of time raised the possibility that the Soviet Union would resume the Russian role of one among the community of states. Revolutionary opportunities, as in China, were exploited when assistance was given to the Kuo-Min-Tang in gaining control of the country.

4. *British Policy.* The wartime Franco-British alliance did not long survive victory. The chief reason for this was the fact that British diplomacy returned to the concept of the balance of power, and, misreading the situation, was inimical to what it considered too great a French preponderance. The result was much bickering, a half-hearted opposition to French policy, and an equal half-hearted and ineffectual support of Germany, best calculated to perpetuate differences. Britain was naturally very interested in German economic recovery. Again, Locarno was the high-water mark of apparently successful reconciliation, recovery, and compromise. [23]

5. *Italian Policy.* Italian policy had best profited in the past from a shrewd exploitation of the balance of power. The

---

[23] Britain and France differed strongly on the score of reparations, but the more specific and immediate cause of their breach was the divergence of their policies in the Near East, where Britain supported the Greeks while France backed the Turks in the Greco-Turkish war.

treaty of London of 1915 was a prime instance of such policy. But Italy found the outcome of the war unsatisfactory. Aside from her failure to receive all the expected benefits in the Adriatic, her policy in Asia Minor ended likewise in frustration. There was no balance of power in Europe in 1919. A position of satellite in the French system of alliances held little attraction, and Italian disgruntlement thus took an anti-French tinge: like Britain, Italy favored the restoration of the balance of power in Europe. In the throes of domestic turmoil, Italy's foreign policy was very weak at first. Not only did she emerge with little by way of colonial benefits, but she barely held on to her Libyan possession.

a. <u>The Corfu Incident.</u> The advent of a highly nationalistic Fascism introduced a question mark. The assassination in 1923 of an Italian member of the Greco-Albanian boundary delimiting commission was the pretext for a blustering assertion of power against Greece and the unnecessary bombardment and occupation of the island of Corfu. The issue was eventually composed peaceably through Greek amends, and thereafter Fascism set about belying in practice the fears engendered by its aggressive reputation. In 1924, the Free State of Fiume was annexed, and from 1925 an effort was made to establish better relations with Yugoslavia.

b. <u>Franco-Italian Rivalry in Central Europe and the Balkans.</u> Italy entertained ideas of dominance in the former Austro-Hungarian domain. Like France, she opposed the *Anschluss*, but Yugoslavia and the other victor succession states joined the French camp. Italy succeeded in establishing a predominant influence in Albania from 1925. Balked by French influence elsewhere, she turned increasingly to the former enemies, Hungary and Bulgaria and, from 1928, began to advocate revisionism—provided it were not at her expense. The twenties were a period of consolidation when the main energy of Fascism was absorbed in establishing itself firmly in control of the Italian state in preparation for greater future adventures.

At the opening of the second decade after the First World War one could make a good case for an attitude of moderate optimism that the consequences of the war had been largely liquidated and that the world had returned to the path of peace and progress on which it had thought it had been set before 1914. The false bases of such optimism were soon to be exposed and give strength to the opposite view that 1914 was the close of an era and the opening of a long period—our own—of uneasy transition to a future the outlines of which are not yet discernible through the surrounding murkiness of conflict.

CHAPTER 10

The Return To War

In simplest form, the reason why the last years of the twenties turned out to be a transitory and misleading period instead of initiating the return to continued peace and progress is to be found in the fallacious basis on which the world was operating. The fallacies now became exposed.

I. THE WORLD ECONOMIC CRISIS

A. Nature of the Crisis

Within less than two years, the world economic picture had changed from high prosperity to depression of unprecedented depth. The cycle of prosperity and depression was considered normal in the functioning of a free capitalist economy, but the magnitude and duration of this depression had in turn such political and social repercussions, nationally as well as internationally, as to induce increasing degrees of control and planning in the various economies. Whether this was done with alacrity or reluctance, the trend in varying degrees was universal.

In some respects, the crisis was one of distribution rather than of production. Overproduction and underconsumption are relative terms; the free play of the market produced a maladjustment of prices, between agricultural and manufactured products for instance, which interfered with the exchangeability of goods. This was clearly manifest within a country like the United States, but also affected profoundly the primarily agricultural states of eastern Europe. As against this, agricultural countries did not have the problem of unemployment in the form that beset industrial ones.

1. Position and Role of the United States. The emergence of the United States from the position of a debtor nation to that of the world's foremost creditor called for a readjustment that was not made. The economy of Britain and of industrial Europe had successfully operated on the basis of an unfavorable balance of trade, what might be called a "natural" equilibrium. But the United States, her productive capacity expanded by the very war, was anxious for foreign outlets. Her favorable balance of trade became larger than ever and her increased tariffs (Ford-McCumber in 1921, Hawley-Smoot in 1929) were calculated to magnify it further still. This balance must now be added, instead of working against as formerly, to the payments due on account of foreign loans and investments.

The only possible solution was a continuation of the outward flow of American capital, in the form of new lending, an indirect device for subsidizing the purchase of American goods, but hardly a system in equilibrium. One consequence of this state of affairs was the accumulation of a major proportion of the world's gold in the United States, a condition which, if continued, could only lead to the breakdown of the gold standard, as in fact it did. Whether she would or no America was a capital factor in world trade and economy.

2. *East to West Spread of the Crisis in Europe.* Because of internal economic maladjustments—security speculation, for instance, a sensational manifestation rather than a fundamental cause—the flow of American capital began drying up toward the end of the twenties, and foreign capital in general ceased to flow into Germany. These are the underlying reasons for the Hoover moratorium in 1931.[1] The German banking crisis, immediate background of Hindenburg's appeal to Hoover, may be said to have reached the crucial stage with the threatened collapse of the Viennese Creditanstalt.[2] A "standstill agreement" froze short-term loans for six months.

The central European crisis had repercussions in London, where it led to the abandonment of the gold standard by England in September, 1931. Because of Britain's importance in world trade and finance, many countries followed the British example, constituting the sterling bloc. Others re-

---

[1] See Chapter IX.
[2] This was in turn partly due to difficulties in the eastern countries, such as Roumania.

mained on gold for a time.[3] As mentioned in the preceding chapter, the Hoover moratorium initiated the end of reparations payments, finally liquidated in 1932. It was also, in effect, the end of the allied war debt payments to the United States, although not until 1934 were all debtors in default.[4]

3. The London Economic Conference. Quite appropriately, the new American administration of Franklin D. Roosevelt, inaugurated in March, 1933, took the initiative of calling a world monetary and economic conference which met in London in June. The action of the United States in changing the gold content of the dollar was fatal to the success of the meeting. This action had been taken under the pressure of domestic necessities. It was typical of the tendency, indulged in by all nations, to resort to measures that seemed of immediate value to themselves. Currency manipulations, tariffs, and quotas were all instances of economic nationalism, which in turn tended to make worse a state of affairs that called for international concerted action.

4. Political Repercussions. Large and persistent unemployment inevitably called for state intervention. Most European countries had provisions for unemployment, but the extent of it put an unforeseen burden on national budgets already unbalanced owing to falling revenues resulting from decreased economic activity. The less wealthy and politically experienced the country, the greater the strain on its institutions. The economic crisis did not alone create dictatorship, but it helped considerably the trend away from democratic institutions.

B. The Soviet Union

The Soviet Union was presumably immune to the fluctuations of an unplanned economy. It was nevertheless affected, in its foreign trade, by the disproportionate decline in world agricultural prices, but internally proceeded on its appointed path. The N.E.P. had, by 1928, largely served its purpose of economic restoration, and the state embarked upon the launching of ambitious plans of directed development. In reverse order, the revolution set about creating industry. The first five-year plan,

---

[3] Such as the United States, France, Switzerland, and Holland.

[4] With the exception of Finland, whose insignificant obligation gave rise to no transfer problem.

to be followed by a succession of others, was aimed at endowing the union with a large heavy industry. This was done by diverting much of the productive effort of the country into capital rather than consumer goods. This meant hardship and deprivation for the people, but the nature of political institutions made it possible to enforce the policy. Future generations would presumably benefit from the sacrifices of the present.

Alongside this it was decided that the time had come to extend the practice of communism to the peasantry. A vast program of collectivization of the land was launched, which met with much opposition, especially in the Ukraine and Caucasus. The policy was ruthlessly enforced, however, even at the cost of deporting large numbers of "kulaks" (the better off, hence more recalcitrant, peasants) and of famine in 1932.[5] The havoc was such that the attempt was slowed down for a time, though not abandoned. It had, in addition, repercussions within the inner circle of control. Having eliminated Trotsky, Stalin now emerged in more absolute control than ever. In 1929-1930, so-called "rightist deviationists" were defeated and more of the original leadership of the party were expelled in 1932. The Soviet Union was soon to devote much attention to developments taking place in Germany.

II. THE RISE OF NAZI GERMANY

The budgetary and parliamentary difficulties of Germany in 1930 had resulted in the use of presidential emergency powers and an election in September. The election failed to clarify the situation, but the most significant feature of it was the appearance in the new Reichstag of 107 National Socialist members. There had been only 12 before this, and within a little over two years their party was to be in full control of German destinies.

A. National Socialism

1. Adolph Hitler. The National Socialist, or Nazi, party had come into existence during the early twenties. It was the

---

[5] When the peasants' opposition took the form of curtailing their crops, the government extracted from them the allotted quotas regardless of consequences. The figure of casualties induced by this policy varies widely, but it was very large, ranging in the millions.

creation of Adolph Hitler, a man of Austrian birth, scanty education, and no achievements save discontent. The disgruntlement of failure found an outlet in strong feelings which came to focus in a fanatical desire to restore the greatness of Germany. Unlike Mussolini, Hitler had no socialist background, but, of similar origin and understanding the importance of the mass in the modern state, his effort to canalize popular discontent and hopes into national instead of class conflicts betoken a shrewd appraisal of the modern world. Thus Nazism came to have much in common with Fascism, which Hitler genuinely admired. The name National Socialism, hitherto a contradiction of terms, was much more apt and enlightening than the nondescript label Fascism.

2. *Racialism*. Like Fascism, Nazism believed in the rightness of force and its ruthless use, and in the role of an élite in society. . There were, however, two important differences between the two movements and regimes. Operating in the German, instead of the Italian, context, Nazism was considerably more efficient and brutal in practice; also, unlike Fascism, it derived its nationalism from the concept of race. Belief in racial superiority was hardly a Hitlerian invention, but the manner and the degree to which the assertion of Nordic, or Germanic, pre-eminence was to be translated into actual practice was indeed novel. A pseudoscientific, carefully graded classification was elaborated: white was superior to colored, and within white, Nordic to Mediterranean. At the bottom of the scale were Jews, a deleterious element, fit only for destruction.

3. *Mein Kampf*. The futile Munich beer hall putsch of 1923 had earned Hitler a prison term which gave him leisure in which to write down his thoughts and his program. The result, *Mein Kampf*, a curious mixture of shrewd perception and inept fancy, devoid of intellectual or literary standard, turned out to be one of the important books of mankind.

4. *Bases of Nazi Support*. The Nazis made little progress until the election of 1930. They had little success among those who normally voted anywhere between the Central party and the extreme left; their support came for the most part from the disgruntled middle class, victims of inflation particularly responsive to the idea of the glory of the second Reich. From 1930 on, the progress of the Nazis made rapid strides.

B. Germany from 1930 to 1933

Despite moratoria and standstill agreements, the economic situation of Germany did not improve. There were 6,000,000 unemployed in 1932. In order to keep the government functioning, continued use of the emergency provisions had to be made.[6] In 1932, also, President Hindenburg's term came to an end. The contest for the office narrowed down to one between himself and Hitler. Hindenburg was re-elected by a rather narrow margin and found himself at 85 the candidate of those who wished to preserve the republic against the onslaught of the Hitlerian hordes. A parliamentary election in the spring of 1932 returned a bloc of 230 Nazis, the largest representation for a single party in German parliamentary history.

As one chancellor succeeded another, the situation came to resemble that of Italy ten years earlier, in the sense that Parliament seemed unable to produce an administration capable of governing. As a last resort, despite a slight Nazi setback at an election in November, 1932, President Hindenburg appointed Hitler chancellor on January 30, 1933.

1. The Nazis in Power. That date may be taken as that of the demise of the Weimar Republic. Like democratic Italy, Weimar Germany signed her own death warrant. Hitler's accession to power was undeniably constitutional and received the sanction of the Reichstag. The evolution thereafter was similar to the Italian, save that the pace of it was far swifter. By an overwhelming majority, on March 23, 1933, a newly elected Reichstag ratified an enabling act that made Hitler virtual dictator. Adhering to the rules of its own constitution, another democracy had committed suicide.

C. The Nazi State

1. The Organization of Controls. The Reichstag elected in March, 1933 contained the usual representation of non-Nazis. Its transformation was rapid. To sum up the process briefly, the left was outlawed while the right was absorbed. Hitler's

---
[6] The budget, for instance, had to be enacted by decree.

Germany, the Third Reich that was to endure a millennium, became a one-party state, the Reichstag meeting at rare intervals to act as rubber stamp and sounding board. Subsequent elections, as in Italy, were meaningless endorsements of the regime.

The various aspects of the one-party state, observed in Italy, were largely duplicated here: the party's own military formations, the Brown Shirts, or S.A. (*Sturm Abteilung*); the all-important role of the secret police, or Gestapo; the increasing coordination of all aspects of the life of the nation, whether economic or cultural. The party and the state, though existing as distinct entities, were increasingly identified with each other. At the head of both stood the *Führer*, who assumed in effect the functions of head of the state in 1934, upon the death of Hindenburg, who was not replaced in his office.

a. <u>RACIAL LAWS.</u> There were in addition the racial laws, directed in the main at the elimination of all Jewish influence. Jews were not numerous in Germany; some 1 per cent of the population, though their influence, especially in some fields, was out of proportion to their numbers. To the astonishment of an incredulous world, in the great modern civilized state that Germany was supposed to be, these laws were ruthlessly enforced, as was the suppression of any opposition. Had it not been a fact, such aberration would have passed belief.

2. The Course of Nazi Germany to 1935. The basic aims of Nazism and the reasons for its success were two: the promise to cure Germany's economic disorder and to restore her position among nations. [7] Withdrawal from the disarmament conference and from the League in October, 1933 might assuage German pride but brought few concrete benefits. The period from 1933 to 1935 was one of intense preparation. Dr. Schacht's skillful, if sometimes less than scrupulous, financial manipulations; the use of credit to finance public works and rearmament, did much to alleviate unemployment. [8] With memories of the First World War blockade, Germany em-

---

[7] In this connection, the myths about allied deceit in the conclusion of the armistice, and the socialist "stab in the back" of undefeated armies, were widely broadcast and exploited.

[8] The budget was not published after 1934.

barked upon a policy of economic self-sufficiency, or autarchy, sacrificing in the process butter in favor of guns.

In 1935, Hitler took the first step in seriously challenging the postwar structure of Europe. Unilaterally, Germany denounced the disarmament clauses of the treaty of Versailles. The challenge went in effect unanswered; Germany had embarked upon the path from which there was no turning.

D. The Reaction to Nazism Abroad

The peculiar personality of the Führer and the even stranger contents of *Mein Kampf* made it difficult to appraise the real nature and aims of Nazism.

1. The Italian Reaction. Mussolini was flattered by what he considered imitation; Hitler's regard for him was and remained sincere. A restoration of German power—within limits —as a counterweight to irksome French "hegemony" was suitable enough to Italy. Never enamored of the League, Mussolini proposed a "realistic" solution: the constitution of a four-power directorate of Europe, the four powers to be Britain, France, Germany, and Italy.[9] But no sympathy was expressed for the more peculiar vagaries (e. g., the racial laws) of Nazism, and the first formal meeting of *Duce* and *Führer* in 1935 in Venice was somewhat less than satisfactory.

a. THE ASSASSINATION OF DOLLFUSS. On one point, Italy was adamant: the position of Austria, which she sought to bring increasingly into her own dependence. When, in 1934, an internal coup by Austrian Nazis resulted in the assassination of Chancellor Dollfuss but was successfully put down, Italy was the only power that reacted with determination; she mobilized her forces on the Brenner. Germany disowned the Austrian Nazis, and Austria, if she were to survive in independence, must more than ever fall within the Italian orbit.

The Rome Protocols in 1934, economic agreements involving Italy, Austria, and Hungary, were designed precisely to this

---

[9] The principle of the Four Power Pact, if realistic, was the very denial of the concept of the League. The small countries were aroused by the proposal, and when the pact was signed in June, its content had been voided of significance. Even the "realism" of it is questionable, since it ignored the Soviet Union.

end of strengthening Italian influence in central Europe. Italy was ever more avowedly revisionist and was seeking the leadership of a league of the discontented. In this she had hitherto been confronted by French influence; but now Germany was beginning to emerge as a potential rival in central Europe. Whether this would lead to opposition between herself and Germany, or to some sort of amicable division of spheres of influence, was still uncertain in 1934.

2. *The Renewed Search for Security.*

a. THE SMALLER STATES. The smaller states of central Europe had few illusions in regard to Germany. On the whole, they would have liked to see Italian influence counterbalance German, but Mussolini's Four-Power Pact of 1934 aroused their deep suspicions. At the beginning of 1934, Poland signed a ten-year agreement with Germany. This event, somewhat surprising in view of the circumstances and background, was an indication of Poland's reduced confidence in France's power and determination.

b. THE SITUATION OF FRANCE. France had hitherto been the main prop of the postwar European structure and was the country that might be expected to react most strongly to the threat of German resurgence. But France's reaction was very weak. The reason for this lay in her domestic situation. The world economic crisis was late in reaching France; the "normal" left coalition won the election of 1932. Eventually, depression came to France, and along with it political problems.

These took a form that went beyond the customary manifestation of ministerial crises. There appeared in France groups that questioned the very fundamentals of the regime, which however was not seriously endangered as in Germany. The riots in Paris in February, 1934, though not serious, created a profound sensation, for they showed that the threat to the democratic system had reached to its very birthplace and first home on the European continent.[10] Wrapped up in this domestic crisis, financial to a large degree but to a point also constitutional, the country did not pursue a strong foreign

---

[10] It is in the same February, 1934 that rioting, more serious than in Paris, broke out in Vienna. The result in this case was the suppression of the Austrian socialists.

policy. German rearmament in 1935 elicited no more than paper protestations.

c. BRITISH POLICY. Britain, too, was wrapped up in her domestic concerns and, unlike France, fundamentally not averse to German rehabilitation (within limits also), in which respect her policy somewhat resembled Italy's. She, however, increased appropriations for the air force, and her prime minister, Stanley Baldwin, went so far as to state that her frontier was on the Rhine.

d. THE SOVIET UNION. The Nazis had made wide use of the red bogey. Up to 1933, they could at the same time cooperate with Communists in undermining the Republic and fight it out with them in the streets. Once in power, however, they lost little time in dealing with communism at home, and the Soviet Union, alarmed at the prospect of an aggressive Germany turning eastward for compensations, began to reverse her views on the general iniquity of the peace settlements and was now willing to join those who would maintain the *status quo*.

The means for this were at hand. In 1934, Russia was admitted to the League, where she became a staunch advocate of collective security. She also signed a nonagression pact with France in 1935 and made agreements with Poland and with other neighboring states. But the attempt to set up in eastern Europe a multilateral system of guarantees, similar to that instituted at Locarno for the west, failed: for readily understandable reasons, Germany preferred the system of bilateral treaties. Some others, mistakenly, also accepted this view.

e. RENEWED ACTIVITY OF FRENCH POLICY. The French system of alliances was still in existence in 1934, whatever doubts might be entertained about its solidity. Because of these very doubts, France sought to bolster her connections. Her foreign minister, Barthou, went the rounds of friendly eastern and central European capitals, and in October, 1934 King Alexander of Yugoslavia landed in Marseilles on a state visit, outward symbol of renewed friendship and collaboration.[11]

---

[11] A Balkan Entente, comparable to the Little Entente, was in process of formation at this time, involving Yugoslavia, Roumania, Greece, and Turkey.

While driving through the city, both King Alexander and Barthou were shot by fanatical Croatian nationalists. The incident was in some ways reminiscent of Sarajevo, especially as both Italy and Hungary were implicated in having furnished assistance to Croatian malcontents. The results were very different from those of the Sarajevo assassination. The last months of 1934 and the beginning of 1935 mark an important turning point in our story, the beginning of that chain of interrelated events which in continuous sequence led to the renewal of general hostilities.

III. THE END OF THE LEAGUE

France had been consistently the advocate of a strong and effective League. The idea of collective security was gaining ground in Britain, and Russia had just joined the ranks of its supporters. Italy had always been lukewarm toward the League, and Germany was out of it. The three powers first mentioned, plus their allies, still enjoyed in 1934 an overwhelming preponderance of strength. It is one of the crowning ironies of this story that through the actions of Laval, Barthou's successor, France should now proceed to weaken the League.

A. The Manchurian Episode

Already before this the League had suffered a major setback in connection with Manchurian affairs. Japanese interests in and designs on Manchuria were of long standing, having caused at one time open war with Russia. By 1931, the Japanese government, fallen into the hands of aggressive militarists, used the pretext of a local incident to initiate action in Manchuria. China, relatively impotent militarily, appealed to the League, which, after much tergiversation, had no choice but to find Japan guilty of aggression, the area of conflict having meantime spread to China proper. The League, however, was unable to prevent Japan from securing the fruits of her aggression, and in 1933 Japan resigned from it.

This episode had been enacted far away from Europe and need not have been mentioned here save for the fact that, the issue having come before the League, Japan's success could not but redound to the discredit of that institution and correspondingly weaken the confidence in the efficacy of its protection. Some comfort was derived from the thought that the League was essentially a European institution whose failure to perform effectively in the Far East might not be conclusive. True, neither the United States nor the Soviet Union, prime factors in the Orient, were members of the League at the time of the Manchurian episode.

B. The Abyssinian Affair

1. Background and Preparations. The fallacious base of this comforting view was soon to be exposed. The conjunction of two widely separated developments was to give the League its *coup de grâce*.

a. ITALIAN DESIGNS. One, Fascism, whose foreign policy had been quite mild during the first decade of its existence, was carefully observing the rapidly shifting scene under the impact of German resurgence. It had by now achieved secure control of the Italian state and found itself beset by economic pressures common in varying degrees to all countries. As early as 1932, Mussolini had decided that the time for action was near. Not desirous of provoking a general conflict, his solution was to take action in the colonial field in the hope that by rapid success he could forestall collective action against himself and be free again to take whatever steps might be called for in Europe. Taking up the Crispian dream of empire of forty years earlier, he proposed to absorb Abyssinia, partly surrounded by the old but largely worthless possessions of Eritrea and Somaliland. Before acting, some reinsurance was desirable, which brings up the second factor.

b. THE REORIENTATION OF FRENCH POLICY. It has been pointed out that the same element of Germany's resurgence was causing France to bolster her existing alliances. Having succeeded in adding Russia to the list, she thought likewise to enlist Italy in her camp. This was particularly Laval's policy. To implement this policy meant a broad liquidation of the long-standing Franco-Italian differences. Abyssinia provided the meeting ground and the solution.

Having minimized any possible Italian implication in the assassination of King Alexander, Laval went to Rome where, in the first day of January, 1935, the conclusion of a thorough-going Franco-Italian understanding was effected. The proclaimed and specific bases of the Laval-Mussolini agreement were a common policy for Austrian independence, and the liquidation of some relatively minor colonial issues.[12] But more important, though not publicly announced, was the French giving of a free hand to Italy in Abyssinia. The precise meaning and extent of the "free hand" was to become a matter of dispute between the makers of the agreement.[13]

2. *Abyssinia and the League*

a. <u>Italy Begins to Act</u>. Already in 1934, Italy had begun intense military preparations for the Ethiopian adventure, for which a border incident in December provided the diplomatic starting point. As with Manchuria, the League was apprised of the matter, and in this case again its action may be summed up in delay, tergiversation, and procrastination. It will be noted that Germany's announcement of her rearmament (March, 1935) took place in the midst of this situation. Also, that the Stresa meeting of Britain, France, and Italy, called in response to that announcement, ended in innocuous verbal condemnation of Germany's unilateral action but took no cognizance of the Ethiopian problem.

b. <u>The Position of Britain and France.</u> For obvious reasons, France was especially anxious to find some compromise that would obviate the clear taking of position in the League. Taking advantage of this condition, Mussolini proved quite intractable to various proposals and offers presented by France and Britain. For Britain, though not committed like France, was also anxious to avoid a break with Italy and to preserve the "Stresa front." For other reasons as well, the British position became as difficult as the French.

The growth in Britain of pro-League sentiment that advocated a policy of collective security under League auspices

---

[12] A strip of territory in the Fezzan, to the south of Libya, was ceded by France, as well as a minute section of French Somaliland and a block of shares in the French-owned Jibuti-Addis Abeba railway.

[13] The contents of a letter written by Laval to Mussolini and the nature of their verbal exchanges have never been satisfactorily clarified. Possibly, there was simple misunderstanding growing out of mental reservations.

has been mentioned. The Peace Ballot of 1935, an informal but extensive polling of opinion, clearly showed this. In June, Ramsay MacDonald had yielded the premiership to Stanley Baldwin. An election took place in November which sought to capitalize on this pro-League feeling. Nominally continuing under the "national" label, the government that issued from the election was in substance Conservative.

c. THE LEAGUE TAKES ACTION. Meanwhile, in October, Italian forces began the actual invasion of Ethiopia. Faced with this naked act, the League had no choice but to declare Italy guilty of aggression, and, under Article 16 of the Covenant, proceeded to draft proposals for the application of sanctions which were adopted on November 18. Under mainly French and British pressure the application of sanctions was made qualified and limited. Trying a final effort, these powers produced in December the famous Hoare-Laval scheme which offered Italy substantial territorial and economic concessions at Abyssinia's expense.[14] The plan, equally unacceptable to Mussolini and to a large section of British opinion, resulted in the resignation of Sir Samuel Hoare, the foreign minister.

d. ITALY DEFEATS THE LEAGUE. Of the course of the war itself it will suffice to say that those who had hoped that it would be a long and difficult undertaking and that even limited sanctions might be effective were proved mistaken. Modern weapons and skillful tactics brought the Italian forces to the Abyssinian capital in May, 1936. Economic sanctions having failed of their purpose, it was clear that no one was going to use military force against Italy. Sanctions were gradually abandoned, and one by one most powers proceeded to give *de jure* recognition to the situation of fact.

Not only had Fascism established an empire, formally proclaimed in May, 1936, but it had also withstood with success the united opposition of some fifty nations. Though vastly exaggerated in Italy, this fact could not help redound to the prestige of Fascism, both at home where its hold was con-

---

[14] Abyssinia had become a member of the League in 1923, curiously enough with Italian support and over British opposition. The implied myth that Abyssinia was a modern state was an underlying weakness and complication of the situation. The fact remains, however, that Abyssinia *was* a member, juridically on a par with others.

solidated [15] and abroad. The League was correspondingly discredited.

3. *Repercussions of the Episode in Europe.* Not only was the League discredited, since it would obviously henceforth be foolish for any small nation to put its trust in it, but in a more limited sense, the Stresa front was broken. Germany, outside the League, had watched the whole proceedings with considerable satisfaction. Though not bound by the League decision on sanctions, there had been no planned or organized cooperation between herself and Italy. But the very turn of events was bound to suggest the idea, if it had not already occurred, that cooperation between the two kindred regimes might prove most advantageous to both.

a. <u>Remilitarization of the Rhineland</u>. Repeating her tactics of a year earlier, in March, 1936, Germany removed one more of the shackles imposed upon her at Versailles by sending military forces into the demilitarized Rhineland, repudiating both Versailles and Locarno at once. More verbal condemnations were the only answer. Not even France reacted. In Britain and elsewhere, many, though concerned over future German intentions, found cause for comfort in the consideration of Germany's "moral" justification for her action. Others, more realistic, were appalled at the extent of French abdication.

IV. FRANCE'S FINAL SURRENDER OF LEADERSHIP

A. The Condition of France

The situation in the spring of 1936 was confused but still fluid. Concern over Germany was growing in many quarters, and even antagonism in some. Italy had blocked the attempted Austrian coup two years earlier; now a "satisfied" power, according to the Duce's own declaration, she might join the forces of conservation. Her position and the consequences of her decision were therefore of great significance at this moment. France's position had been weakened and made awkward by the Abyssinian imbroglio; more serious from the international

---

[15] The episode of League sanctions was probably the high point of domestic popularity of the regime.

point of view, France did not try to reassert her leadership, but instead totally surrendered it.

1. Internal Stresses. The reasons for this French abdication are to be found in the domestic scene. The economic and fiscal difficulties of the country did not diminish with the passage of time and the adoption of deflationary policies. The fact that France is a democracy must be stressed at this point, for it meant that the masses of the French people, being more concerned with the immediate and concrete problems of existence rather than the more remote consequences of foreign affairs, this attitude was reflected in governmental action. The old cleavage of French opinion, heritage of the Revolution, was sharpened by these domestic pressures, while the example of neighboring Italy and Germany gave heart to that tradition in France, authoritarian by predilection, which ever favored a strong executive.

2. The Popular Front. The usual thing happened in France in these circumstances that had happened whenever a serious challenge seemed to threaten the Republic: a rallying of the forces of the left. With a view to defending democracy at home and abroad while implementing a program of social reforms, the Radical Socialists, the Socialists, and the Communists, under the label Popular Front, entered the contest for the election of 1936.[16]

The Popular Front won the election, thereby increasing the bitterness of the opposition and intensifying the internal cleavage of the country. The new government, presided over by the socialist Léon Blum, inaugurated a far-reaching program of social reforms and services. The situation was not unlike that of the United States when the New Deal had been launched three years earlier: in both cases reforms were overdue, and feeling ran high in both cases. But there was this important difference: France had neither the physical resources of the United States nor the protection of two oceans. The consequences of a weak foreign policy, because butter had priority over guns, were to be equally disastrous for France

---

[16] This was the first time that Communists formally entered into collaboration with "bourgeois" parties. This reversal of policy represented Moscow's reaction of fear to the threat of Nazism.

herself and for others. From an unexpected quarter a storm was about to break out, which the action of Italy first, then of others, magnified into a major European issue.

B. The Spanish Civil War

1. *The Spanish Background*.

a. SPAIN UNTIL 1931. Little has been said of Spain in this story for the simple reason that Spain had largely remained outside the main stream of European development, whether internationally or in domestic terms. The ostensible framework of representative institutions was largely a façade. In addition to economic and political backwardness, Spain was also plagued by the fact of regionalism, especially strong in the more progressive north.

The "normal" deficiencies of Spanish politics were put under additional strain as a result of military reverses in Morocco in 1921, wherein high officials, even King Alfonso himself, were thought to be implicated. The solution to the unusual difficulties was sought in the establishment of military dictatorship under Primo de Rivera in 1923. The coup served its immediate purpose, but it was not many years before the dictatorship, never very harsh as modern dictatorships go, had managed to lose the backing of even most of its original supporters.

Rivera resigned in 1930 and the King restored the constitution of 1876. Municipal elections in April, 1931 showed such a decided trend that the King left the country and a provisional republican government was proclaimed. National elections followed and a constituent assembly drafted a new constitution which made Spain into a typical parliamentary democracy with representation in a single house.

b. THE REPUBLIC. The course of the republic was not smooth. The opposition to it, whether the Catholic Church, the army, or the upper layers of society in general, was strong and still powerfully entrenched despite curbing legislation. Equally dangerous were the divergences among its supporters, ranging over a large section of the political spectrum and apt to lay stress on disparate aspects of change: political reform, land tenure, regionalism. The election of November, 1933 showed a swing to the right; after a little over two years, the Cortes was dissolved and the ensuing election in 1936 was a victory for a coalition of left parties, a Popular Front comparable to the French.

c. THE ARMY COUP OF 1936. The new government's determination to rid the army of unreliable elements was answered by outright rebellion which broke out in July, 1936. The rebel scheme was a prompt seizure of power using the element of surprise. Despite large support in the army, the resistance of labor groups aiding loyal troops prevented complete success of the rebellion, which on its side was not completely crushed. What started as a coup degenerated into civil war which was to last for the better part of three years. The story of it may be summed up as that of the slow but steady subjugation of the whole country by the rebel forces—or Nationalists as they called themselves—until General Franco, the *Caudillo*, was at the head in Spain of a regime patterned after those of Mussolini and Hitler. Spain and the Spanish people paid a heavy price for being the proving ground of new weapons of war and the arena in which rival powers and ideologies first met in open clash.

2. *The Powers and the Civil War.*

a. THE MYTH OF NONINTERVENTION. From the first it was clear that Fascist Italy was giving assistance to the rebels. This assistance was predicated on the assumption that a little of it would suffice and that thereby a situation would be created where Spain would be amenable to Italian, in place of French, influence. Fresh from his Ethiopian triumphs, Mussolini would at little cost extend Italy's sway over the western Mediterranean. [17] This attractive calculation miscarried. Italian intervention was followed by that of others, in smaller and varying degrees, and there was obvious danger that the Spanish conflagration might spread.

This above all must be avoided in the eyes of Britain and France. The Popular Front government of Premier Blum proposed that all should abstain from interference in the Spanish war, and eventually a nonintervention committee was set up in

---

[17] Strategic considerations were involved in this policy. France was being encircled, and her lines of communication with North Africa were being threatened.

London. The story of nonintervention is tortuous, yet easily summed up: it served as a safety valve and was used, mainly by Italy, as a device for preventing action while herself proceeding with assistance to Franco. Denying intervention at first, after a while Mussolini took to boasting of it; in any event his prestige was at stake, and nothing short of Franco's victory would serve. Germany likewise aided Franco; Russia's and France's help to the legally constituted government merely served to prolong the struggle. In the last analysis, Britain and France were willing to pay the price of Spain rather than face a conflict.

b. <u>France Surrenders Leadership to Britain</u>. This may seem strange. But Britain, or at least her government, was not averse to the overthrow of a government supposedly too amenable to Communist influence. Britain was also hoping to prevent the formation of too close a German-Italian connection. France, divided and weakened by internal quarrels, made one correct decision: to pursue a common policy with Britain. From this sound premise she drew, however, the incorrect conclusion that British initiative must be followed uncritically. The proposal by France of nonintervention, and especially the manner in which nonintervention was allowed to operate, mark the real abdication of France, and her surrender to Britain of European leadership.

c. <u>The Rome-Berlin Axis.</u> This leadership Britain seemed willing to assume. If its aim was to make possible Italian victory in Spain while avoiding a wider conflict it was quite successful. But in so far as the justification for this peculiar diplomacy was the prevention of German-Italian collaboration, it was a dismal failure.[18] Partly because she found herself in a certain amount of difficulty in Spain; partly because it began to seem as if the standard Fascist patter about decadent democracies might after all be true, in which case unlimited horizons of expansion might be contemplated; and partly also because the adventitious dovetailing of German and Italian action had proved hitherto so rewarding, Italy entered in October, 1936 into the partnership henceforth known as the Axis.

---

[18] There was much respect in Italy for British and French armed power. Britain's policy of appeasement was completely misunderstood by Italy as weakness, or alternatively as subtle duplicity.

This association, ostensibly dedicated to the defense of European civilization against Communism, more narrowly to Italo-German collaboration in matters of parallel interest, particularly the maintenance of the Danubian *status quo* and the integrity of (Franco) Spain, may in more homely language be described as a partnership for plunder. Its name, the Axis, was supposed to express the fact that leadership had passed to the new vigorous nations around whose Rome-Berlin Axis Europe would henceforth revolve. In the light of British and French supineness, there was validity in the assertion.

Forgetful for a moment of Aryan superiority, within a month Hitler followed the Axis agreement with an anti-Comintern pact with Japan. A year later, in November, 1937, Italy joined the anti-Comintern. The Axis had grown into the Rome-Berlin-Tokyo triangle.

d. THE SOVIET UNION. Should it come to a test of force, Britain, France, and Russia still enjoyed a preponderance of power. The Soviet Union, as pointed out, had thrown her lot on the side of collective security. Unfortunately, suspicion continued to prevail within the partnership. This distrust had a long and deep-rooted background, but the British and French reaction to German and Italian aggressiveness was calculated to reinforce and renew Russian doubts and weaken within Russia the supporters of the policy of cooperation with the west expounded by Litvinov in Geneva.

<u>Trials and Purges in Russia.</u> On the other hand, developments within the Soviet Union served to nourish doubts about her aims and her reliability. Internally, the Soviet Union was making progress in shaping the new industrial society. The first five-year plan was followed by a second, which somewhat slackened the pace of industrialization in favor of a larger share of consumer goods production. Albeit at huge human cost, the program of land collectivization was also pursued. In 1936, a new constitution was put into effect; formally more democratic, it had little effect on the real location of power within the Union.

Despite this progress, there was cause for questionings. From the middle thirties, the government seemed to feel concerned with the danger of remaining opposition. New purges, both extensive and drastic, were effected. The outside world could only be bewildered at the spectacle of a succession of trials where old trusted Bolshevik leaders and the highest army officers confessed to a variety of offenses reaching the length of plotting with foreign powers (unnamed, but clearly Germany) for the overthrow of the regime. Andrei Vishinsky earned wide fame as the prosecutor in the Moscow trials. The secrecy and mystery of Soviet procedure, so alien to western judicial methods, raised considerable doubts in regard to the solidity of the regime, more specifically the value of its army. As it turned out, ruthlessness proved effective, but the continued cleavage between east and west created conditions most suitable to the successful pursuit of Axis aggression.

V. THE END OF THE VERSAILLES SYSTEM

Hitler's Germany had so far turned to good account the divisions among her potential victims, and was aided in this by the fact that many, especially in the west, willfully sought comfort and shelter in the thought that German aims limited to the recovery of Germany's legitimate place in Europe. This hope Hitler exploited to the full. He had solved Germany's economic difficulties by the resort to devices of an essentially transitory nature. The forced pace of rearmament and the economy of guns instead of butter must soon lead to the acquisition of butter, else recoil into a novel set of difficulties. Germany's was already a war economy.

A. The Greater German Reich

1. The Anschluss

a. ITALY, BRITAIN, AND FRANCE. At the beginning of 1938, the Spanish Civil War was still unfinished. Italy, committed to the ultimate success of Franco, was finding it necessary to pour a steady stream of resources in order to insure this outcome. Even British patience was tried when an agreement aimed at avoiding disturbances in the Mediterranean was grossly abused by Mussolini. [19] But Neville Chamberlain, the prime minister,

---

[19] The appearance of "piratical" submarines in the eastern Mediterranean for once provoked a determined British reaction, whereupon the "pirates" promptly disappeared. Such reaction Mussolini understood far more easily than the general policy of appeasement.

was so set on the policy of courting Italy that he preferred the loss of his foreign minister, Anthony Eden, to a modification of his course. Needless to say, such action was calculated to boost Italy's self-confidence and price. France was by now docilely following the British lead. The New Deal type of social reforms inaugurated by the Popular Front were not, as in the United States, accompanied by a bold governmental policy of deficit financing, but rather by an attempt at a deflationary policy of budget balancing. There occurred again a phenomenon often observed in France: a left government running into fiscal difficulties, being overthrown on that score, and giving way to a more conservative and financially "sounder" administration, all within the framework of the same parliament. Confronted with budgetary difficulties and the necessity of devaluation, the Popular Front coalition began to disintegrate. If the depression had come late to France, its manifestations were unusually prolonged.

b. <u>Germany Begins to Move.</u> Taking advantage of these conditions, Germany decided that the time had come to move, for the first time outside her borders. Austria had for some time been the scene of increasing internal unrest, assiduously nourished by the Nazis, and the ruthless suppression of the socialists in 1934 lessened the possibility of withstanding the Nazi pressure and intrigues. A domestic crisis, synchronized with German threats, produced in Vienna a new government which promptly "invited" the Germans to send troops for the preservation of order. On March 12, 1938 the Nazis occupied the country, which they proceeded to integrate into the Reich.

c. <u>Consequences of the Anschluss.</u> Britain and France did not act, and Mussolini, too busy elsewhere, thought it best to pretend satisfaction. Within the Axis partnership, Hitler had taken skillful, if ruthless, advantage of his associate.[20] The lesson was not lost on central Europe. The Italo-German equilibrium had been broken and Italy could no longer be relied upon to offset Germany's growing influence. It might be wise to climb on the Nazi bandwagon, or at least to come

---

[20] From partner, Italy had become a prisoner in the Axis. A measure of her subservience may be seen in the enactment of racial laws, similar to the German, upon which Mussolini had earlier poured his scorn.

to terms with the Nazis, while there was still time. As by-products of these changes, the rearmament of Hungary was consented to by the Little Entente, and that of Bulgaria by her Balkan neighbors.

The prevailing tendency in London was still to regard the *Anschluss* as awkward in enactment but fundamentally not an aggressive act. Nevertheless, as a precaution, Britain and France drew closer. Britain still courted Italy, and another Mediterranean agreement was made, but Mussolini decided to continue to cast his lot with the Axis.

There were two countries for which it would be particularly difficult to come to terms with Nazi Germany—Czechoslovakia and Poland. The remaining eighteen months of peace were in large part taken up with the destruction of one and preparations for the undoing of the other.

B. The Destruction of Czechoslovakia

Following a pattern that was beginning to become familiar, Hitler at the time of the *Anschluss* had given strong assurances that he intended to respect Czech integrity. It was not long, however, before he became aware of the impossibility of resisting the earnest appeals of "oppressed" Sudeten Germans.

1. The Sudeten Problem. This population, over 3,000,000, was spread along the fringe of Czechoslovakia where she bordered on a Germany by which she was now in large part encircled. The reasons for the inclusion of this minority, historic and strategic, went back to 1919. Events were soon to demonstrate their soundness. As minorities went, the Sudeten had some, but neither many nor serious, causes for complaint. To a large extent, they were in fact becoming reconciled to their membership in the new Czechoslovakia; but the advent of the Nazis changed all this. With the stress on Germandom, its superior rights and claims, an element of unrest appeared in the Sudetenland. Not, however, until the direction of the movement was taken over by Berlin did it become a serious issue.

The *Anschluss* was the signal for more intensive and organized agitation on the part of the Sudeten, who began to make demands for concessions from Prague, demands which as soon as met created a request for more. A mounting press campaign in Germany was a forewarning of Nazi intentions. The summer passed in uneasy peace and growing international tension, until in a speech on September 12, Hitler demanded for the Sudeten the right of self-determination, adding the threat of German intervention.

2. The Crisis of September, 1938. This was tantamount to a demand for the cession of Czech territory, and indeed was intended as such. At this critical point, Prime Minister Chamberlain intervened by going to discuss the matter personally with Hitler. For all the concessions made to him, Hitler proved difficult to satisfy; actually, he was anxious for war. Another visit had to be made by Chamberlain to Hitler, and not until negotiations seemed on the point of collapse was peace preserved as the result of a dramatic meeting in Munich of Hitler, Chamberlain, Daladier, and Mussolini. At the eleventh hour the Duce had thrown his influence on the side of compromise.

a. THE MUNICH SETTLEMENT. The ostensible basis of the Munich settlement was the application of the principle of self-determination: those areas of Czechoslovakia with a predominantly German population were to be incorporated into the Reich. The strength of the moral case, fully exploited by Germany, was especially useful to those who still insisted on remaining blind to the reality of the German development. Chamberlain was the leading exponent of this view and seems to have sincerely believed that he had insured "peace for our time" as a result of the Munich agreement. To a large extent British opinion endorsed him at this time. There were many, however, who saw Munich for what it was, and the repercussions of it were immeasurable.

3. The Consequences of Munich

a. DESTRUCTION OF THE FRENCH SYSTEM OF ALLIANCES. Little mention has been made of France in this episode for the reason that the initiative of negotiations rested wholly in British hands; France acquiesced and followed. Unlike Britain, however, France had a formal alliance with Czechoslovakia. When she joined Britain in putting pressure on Czechoslovakia to yield or take the consequences alone, she was clearly and publicly renouncing the bases of her policy for the past twenty years. Perhaps the chief significance of Munich was the German success in finally breaking the French system of alliances, the solid reality of the European international situation since 1920. From now on, it was a case of each one for himself among the smaller states; how best to curry Nazi favor, either to avoid destruction, or alternatively to secure advantages at the expense of neighbors.

b. <u>THE NEW ALIGNMENT OF EUROPE.</u> Not only was the French system of alliances destroyed, but its newest recruit, the Soviet Union, had been excluded from Munich. Russia was exonerated from taking action in support of Czechoslovakia on account of France's prior refusal to act. But to exclude Russia from the deliberations leading to the settlement was something else again, and another signal German success. For all the justified doubts that there were of Russia among the western powers as a consequence of the recent peculiar developments within the Soviet Union, this suspicion could not but be reciprocated.

In the last analysis, Munich marked a change from the system under which Europe had functioned since the war to one in which three large units of comparable order of magnitude could compete and line up in different ways: the western Anglo-French bloc; the central European Axis; and the Soviet Union. It was a great enough victory for Germany to have restored herself to the full status of great power. Had this been her real and sole aim, a balance might have been established in Europe comparable to the one under which peace had long reigned before 1914. But there was now a basic difference in the fact that the pre-1914 powers had all operated within a mutually understood framework of limited aims. The western combination alone continued this tradition, modified only in the sense of having become dangerously devoted to the negative preservation of peace and the *status quo*, hence its policy of appeasement and peace at any price.

But neither the Nazi-Fascist Axis nor the communist Soviet Union shared this negative, if civilized, outlook. They represented forces of change with an inner dynamism of aggression. There was in a fundamental sense no common ground for real understanding. Munich may be regarded as the curtain raiser for the tragedy that was to begin eleven months later.

C. The Last Phase: Unlimited Horizons of Change

The settlement of Munich had been followed by attempts at Anglo-German and Franco-German understanding; Hitler, once more, professed to have no further designs. But it took little time to bring out that Germany was dissatisfied with the operation of these agreements.

1. From Munich to Prague. In the more limited sense, the Munich settlement meant that Czechoslovakia, hitherto keystone of the Little Entente, was now militarily inconsequential and at the mercy of the Reich. It took a bare six months for the logical consequences of this state of affairs to come to fruition.[21] In March, 1939, adopting a somewhat different technique, President Hacha was summoned to Berlin where he "agreed" to place the fate of the Czech people in German hands. The next day Prague was occupied, a Protectorate of Bohemia and Moravia organized, and separate Slovakia became an independent state, vassal of Germany.

By way of footnotes to this last change, Hungary established a common frontier with Poland through the acquisition of Ruthenia, and Germany "redressed" another wrong by incorporating Memel. Also, not to be altogether outdone, on April 28, Mussolini occupied Albania, whose royal title was assumed by the Italian King.

2. The Pact of Steel. Italy was being treated rather cavalierly by her ally, who did not feel called upon to consult her before taking action. Her position was becoming one of having to consider how much of her influence she could preserve and how to do this. The French opposition she had encountered earlier across the Adriatic had been benign by comparison with the methods of her ostensible ally. Nevertheless, Mussolini decided to burn his bridges and tied himself to Hitler more securely than ever with the Pact of Steel of May,

---

[21] Further consequences of Munich were the incorporation of Slovak territory in Hungary, and the seizure of Teschen by Poland. A little later, Czechoslovakia was transformed into a loose federation of her three ethnic components: Czechia (Bohemia-Moravia), Slovakia, and Sub-Carpatho Ruthenia.

1939. This instrument was one of aggression—for all the subsequent Italian complaints of the premature German use of it. Nothing would do but a thoroughgoing upsetting of the whole European map and structure; the time was past for minor claims and territorial readjustments.

3. *From Prague to Danzig*

a. <u>The Policy of Appeasement Reversed.</u> The German occupation of Prague was a logical step on the road to complete German control of central Europe. But it also made untenable the pretense behind earlier German moves that they fell within the compass of "legitimate" claims based on self-determination. Clearly, there was no appeasing Germany since she had now overstepped the bounds within which she ought to have remained on the basis of any reasonable and fair interpretation of her demands. Such at least was the British reaction: Chamberlain, the champion appeaser, and British opinion with him, made a sudden and sharp about face in their policy. Sufficient force would alone deter Germany, whose next aggression might be expected in the direction of Poland. [22]

At the end of March, Britain announced that she would defend Poland against German aggression. [23] Similar guarantees were extended to Greece and to Roumania following Italy's seizure of Albania. Agreements were made with Turkey to secure the Mediterranean. [24] Under British leadership this time, this was a last-minute attempt to bring to life a new version of the defunct French system of alliances.

b. <u>Russia and the West.</u> To complete the circle, British and French approaches were made to Russia, who, although she had not formally denounced the French alliance, considered it in effect inoperative; after Munich, Russia suspected that Britain and France might be seeking to divert German aggression against herself. There were going on in Moscow at the

---

[22] The ten-year pact of 1934 with Poland had meantime been denounced by Germany.

[23] The British guarantee to Poland was, initially, unilateral, an unusual procedure in diplomacy.

[24] As the price of a Franco-Turkish agreement, Turkey exacted from France's Syrian mandate the cession of Alexandretta.

same time open and half-hearted negotiations with the British and French, and secret ones with the Germans.

c. <u>THE NAZI-SOVIET PACT, SIGNAL FOR WAR.</u> Consistent in her course, Germany began to raise the Polish question, in general terms through a press campaign, more restrictedly over the Polish Corridor and the city of Danzig. In their negotiations with the Russians, the Nazis had a considerable advantage for they found no difficulty in meeting the conditions that Russia would consider alone as evidence of earnest intent: control of the three Baltic states south of the Gulf of Finland, and a partition of Poland. It was not within the power of the western democratic regimes, controlled by their public opinions, to meet such terms, even if Poland were excluded.

The outcome of the situation was the announcement to a startled world of the conclusion of a Nazi-Soviet nonaggression treaty on August 22, 1939. After the long record of mutual vituperation and antagonistic action, such an agreement was possible only between such regimes as the German and Russian, not responsible to opinions and parliaments. Specific territorial arrangements were of course secret. The real significance of the pact was that, for a price and for a time at least, Stalin had granted Hitler a free hand against Poland and the assurance that Germany would not have to fight a war on two fronts.

Short of a Polish surrender, war could not be avoided, and the Nazis were anxious to make actual use of their military machine. The mounting tempo of the campaign of a controlled but unrestrained press and impossible demands on Poland were the prelude to a German invasion launched without declaration of war on September 1, 1939. In view of their past record, there was some skepticism abroad about British and French behavior. These powers did in fact attempt some futile last minute negotiations. Receiving no reply to her ultimatum, on September 3 Britain formally declared war on Germany, followed a few hours later by France. The Second World War had begun.

PART IV
Europe in the Modern Age

Partition of Poland (1939)

CHAPTER 11

The Second World War and After

I. THE EUROPEAN WAR

A. The Initial Phase: September, 1939 - April, 1940

1. The War in Poland The Second World War, by contrast with the First, was slow in getting under way. To be sure, the *Wehrmacht* had its way in Poland with greater ease and in less time than many had expected. Within three weeks Poland had been conquered; the resistance of Warsaw was a heroic gesture that could not affect the outcome. The invasion of Russian forces from the east was the last blow, and by the end of September Poland was no more. Her fifth partition had taken place, a Russo-German treaty implementing the secret clauses of the Nazi-Soviet pact of August. The Soviet Union absorbed roughly a third of the country, Vilna went to Lithuania, and Germany took the rest, setting up a small dependent Polish state in the Gouvernement General around Warsaw.

2. The "Phony" War. But the end of the Polish campaign was not the signal for intensified hostilities in the west. From the first, there had been virtually no action along the Franco-German frontier; the Allies did not feel strong enough to launch a major offensive, and it suited the German book to be able to concentrate on Poland. The continued inactivity through the autumn and winter—even the dreaded air war failed to materialize—led to the characterization of this unusual conflict as the "phony" war. Many suspected that the western allies and Germany would come to terms on the basis of the *fait accompli*.

a. THE SOVIET UNION. Acting the part of a loyal ally, the Soviet Union gave the world the strange spectacle of joining her propaganda to the German in an effort to sap the morale of the western democracies. More concretely, she took advantage of the stalemate further to enhance her own position. The small Baltic states of Lithuania, Latvia, and Estonia were forced to grant special privileges to the Soviet Union, preliminary to their occupation by Soviet forces and to their final incorporation as Soviet Republics in 1940. Finland proved less amenable, and was attacked by the Russians in November, 1939.

The Russo-Finnish War. This aggression led to the expulsion of the Soviet Union from the League, and Finland's stubborn resistance earned her widespread respect and sympathy. The Russians had seemingly miscalculated, but the ultimate outcome could not be in doubt once they decided to make the necessary effort. In March, 1940 Finland had to accept the Soviet terms of peace. [1]

These Russian gains were not welcome in Germany, where it was felt, however, that they could not be opposed. The western allies contemplated the possibility of assistance to Finland, and even made some preparations to that end. They were using the lull to build up their deficient military power in being and to mobilize their vast resources, but their attitude was one of unjustified confidence. Their complacency was about to receive a rude shock.

B. The Spread of the War in Europe: April, 1940 - June 1941

1. The Conquest of Denmark and Norway. The Nazis were not hampered by any regard either for the niceties of law or the feelings of public opinion. In this respect, though with more callousness and crudity, they took the same position as the Germany of 1914: necessity is the higher law, and victory would justify the means used to achieve it. [2]

In April, 1940, the world was startled by the news of German

---

[1] Finland had to cede territory that placed Lake Ladoga wholly within the Soviet Union, and her second largest city, Viborg (Viipuri), islands in the Gulf of Finland, some territory farther north, and part of the Rybachi peninsula giving access to Petsamo. Finally a thirty-year lease of Hangoe, that was to be converted into a Soviet naval base.

[2] There was this difference that, in 1914, Germany acknowledged the moral wrong as well as claiming the "necessity" of invading Belgium.

landings in Norwegian ports, while Denmark was being overrun. The coup was well planned, Norwegian resistance could not be of any duration, and an Anglo-French expedition could not prolong hostilities beyond June, by which time the whole country was subdued and a puppet government under Vidkun Quisling had been established.[3]

Perhaps the most significant consequence of the Norwegian episode was the fall of the regrettable Chamberlain government in Britain.

2. *The War in the West*. Winston Churchill became prime minister of Britain on May 11, 1940. On May 10, the Germans had finally unleashed the war in the west, to which the Norwegian episode had been a preliminary introduction.

a. THE LOW COUNTRIES OVERRUN. The German plan of action in 1940 was basically similar to the Schlieffen Plan of 1914: to strike at the allied forces from the north, avoiding the French fortifications along the German frontier.[4] In 1940, both Belgium and Holland were invaded. The Dutch resistance was brief. It provided Germany with an opportunity to test the virtues of brutality in the wanton air bombing of Rotterdam. Meanwhile, Luxembourg had also been overrun and the Belgian defenses breached.

Franco-British forces were unable to stem the German advance; Brussels and Antwerp were abandoned. More serious was the breakthrough in the French lines at Sedan. Using to excellent advantage the new methods of warfare, made possible by the combined use of air power and mechanized land power, the German armies poured through the gap, making a dash for the Channel.

b. DUNKIRK. The Channel was reached and the bulk of the British forces, together with substantial French, were trapped in Belgium. They fought a retreating action to the beachhead of Dunkirk. The British had husbanded their air force, which was able to provide sufficient cover while naval forces and the weirdest conglomeration of craft from England succeeded in

---

[3] The King and his government went to England, where they set up a government in exile.

[4] The Franco-German frontier was heavily fortified and there was much confidence in France in the impregnability of the Maginot line, which, however, did not extend along the Franco-Belgian frontier.

conveying a large part of the trapped force to Britain, minus, however, all its equipment. Dunkirk was a sad blow to the Allies, yet in some ways a moral victory, for it steeled the British to utmost endeavor. They were fortunate in their leader Churchill who, in those trying days, became the very incarnation of the spirit of resistance to which he gave expression in some of the most stirring prose in the language.

c. T̲h̲e̲ ̲F̲a̲l̲l̲ ̲o̲f̲ ̲F̲r̲a̲n̲c̲e̲. Less than three weeks had elapsed from the opening of the campaign to the closing of its first phase. The Dutch government had fled into exile in England, but King Leopold of Belgium chose to ignore the advice of his ministers. He ordered his armies to surrender and remained in his country, a decision that was to prove in retrospect a mistake.

The French were now alone, but, despite their losses, many refused to believe the situation past retrieving. A brief lull, during which the French command was reshuffled, was followed by a German attack along the Somme front. This was soon broken, and there ensued complete disintegration. Isolated actions proved futile and the Germans advanced through the country virtually at will. Paris was entered on June 14 and the Maginot line taken from the rear.

The French Armistice and the Vichy Regime. At this juncture, the government was divided in its counsels between the advocates of continued resistance from Africa and the overseas empire, and those who felt that such a gesture would be futile, owing to the impossibility for Britain alone to retrieve the military situation. In the context of 1940, especially as it appeared in France, the latter view was perhaps the more rational, the former in the nature of an act of faith.

Such an act of faith did occur in Britain, still unharmed behind the Channel moat. The British offer of complete merger and joint citizenship with France, while designed to secure the remaining French resources for the struggle, was a dramatic and imaginative gesture, an opportunity that was allowed to pass. Paul Reynaud, the French prime minister and advocate of continued resistance, resigned in favor of the aged Marshal Pétain.

Pétain, symbol of French resistance during the First World War, was, according to his limited lights, a patriotic Frenchman;

he believed, however, that the war was irretrievably lost. The prestige of his name helped weaken and confuse the nation overwhelmed by disaster. Pétain sued for an armistice which, after some delay, was granted.

Three-fifths of the country, including the entire Atlantic seaboard was to be under German occupation. Vichy, in the unoccupied zone, became the temporary capital, where Marshal Pétain, now Head of the State, taking advantage of the prevailing disorganization and stunned acquiescence of the French people, proceeded to set up a new regime modeled after Italian Fascism. Pierre Laval was the driving force in the new government.

On June 10, Mussolini had finally declared war upon both France and Britain. The French collapse resolved his lingering hesitations: Italy must be in at the kill if she was to share in the spoils. [5]

3. Significance and Consequences of the Fall of France

a. GERMAN DOMINATION OF THE CONTINENT. The French debacle, especially the rapidity and thoroughness of it, was a shock to the world. Whatever its causes, it brought out in full light the greatness of the vacuum that it created. Hitler's Germany was now supreme in Europe, which it could set about reorganizing under the guidance of the Nazi new order. Hitler showed scant regard for his Italian ally, not allowed for the time to share in the spoils of victory.

Even in defeat, France retained some bargaining power, mainly her fleet and her colonies. Hitler dared not press too hard, lest these go over to the Free French movement, initially a small group led by General de Gaulle who, in London, proclaimed that a battle, but not the war, had been lost, and refused to recognize the arrangements of the Vichy regime. The latter, however, was undoubtedly the legal government of France and generally recognized as such. [6]

---

[5] As in 1914, Italy was neutral at the outset. Her neutrality was perhaps more useful to Germany than her intervention. Mussolini had no objection to war, but he felt that Italy was not ready for it in 1939, and there was some annoyance on his part at Germany for having precipitated it at so early a date.

[6] Albeit under the pressure of defeat, the Vichy government came into existence as a consequence of an act of the French Parliament.

But before the Nazi new order could safely be organized, peace must be fully restored. The situation was in some ways reminiscent of that in Napoleon's time, with the continent in control of one power and Britain alone standing against that power. For the moment, Britain could at best survive and many thought that she might come to terms. Hitler would indeed "guarantee" the British Empire, but the British people were now fully aroused, and Nazi blandishments carried little conviction in the light of past record. Churchill infused new vigor into a reorganized government; his promise of "blood, sweat, and tears" struck the precisely appropriate note of somber resolution. This resolution was atonement for past blunders, and the world that has remained free owes a large debt to Britain.

b. <u>THE BATTLE OF BRITAIN.</u> If Britain would not come to terms, an effort must be made to destroy her at home. In the lack of sea power, the air provided a possible answer. Through the summer of 1940 the air battle raged over the British skies. Less undiscriminating frightfulness, and more concentration of selected vital industrial targets, might have accomplished Hitler's purpose. But the greater skill, quality, and management of the Royal Air Force (radar played an important role in this) enabled it to inflict such losses on the *Luftwaffe*, while British morale and industrial production held up, that after a time the attempt must be written a failure. Churchill, as usual, gave the performance apt expression: "Never have so many owed so much to so few."

Despite heavy losses at sea from the activity of German submarines, Britain managed to maintain sufficient control on the water to keep her people and her industries supplied. But the British was a negative victory, comparable to the Marne in 1914. It had enabled Britain to survive but done no injury to the Nazi control of the continent. The war again was a stalemate.

4. *Consolidation of the German Control of the Continent.* For all that Hitler was supreme on land, much of the continent was still not under direct German rule. That situation could now be righted, especially as there were signs of restlessness in these areas.

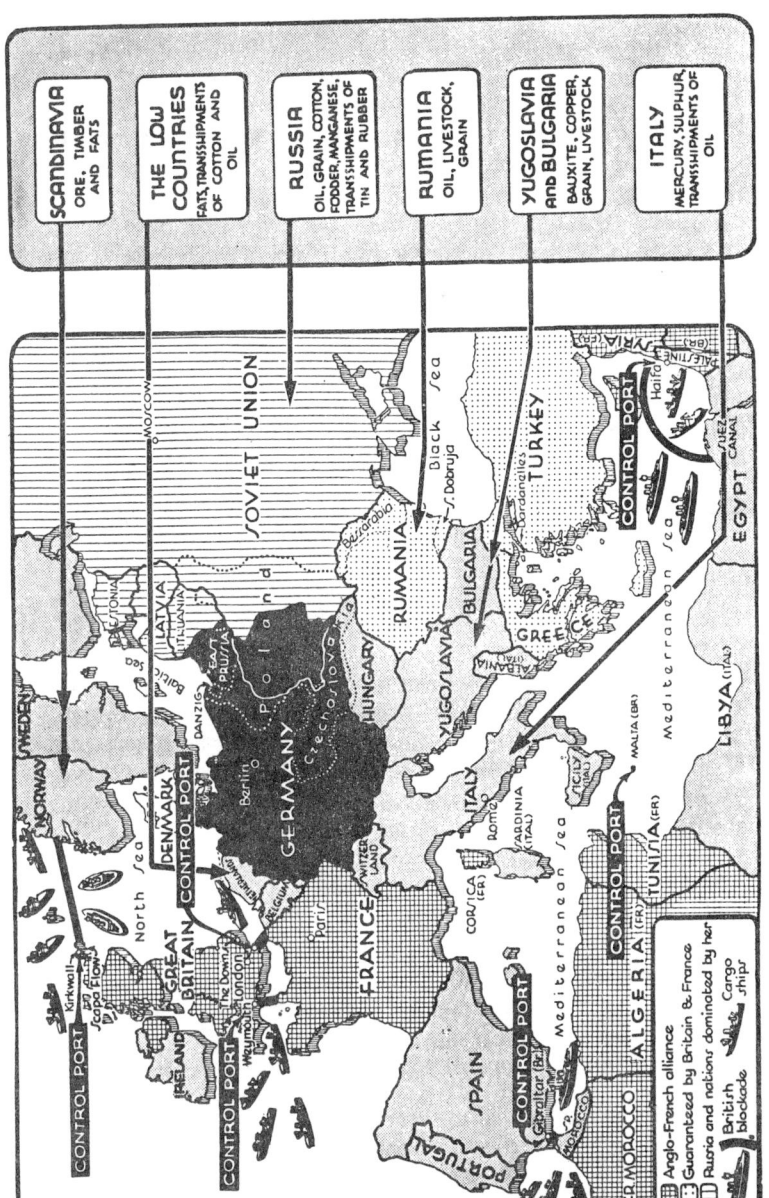

The Allied Blockade

a. ROUMANIA. As early as June, 1940, Roumania, following German and Italian advice, yielded Bessarabia and Bukowina to Russia in response to an ultimatum from that country. Hungary and Bulgaria were next with their demands. Desirous of avoiding a separate war in Europe, Hitler and Mussolini summoned representatives of the three countries and issued an award in Vienna. Bulgaria recovered the Dobrudja, lost in 1913, and Hungary about half of pre-1914 Transylvania. Roumania had been partitioned. She, too, like Poland, had been the object of an Anglo-French guarantee. In 1940, such guarantees took on the flavor of the kiss of death.

The remainder of Roumania became a complete Nazi satellite, and German troops were "invited" to occupy the country in October, after King Carol had once more abdicated in favor of his son and fled the country. The presence of the Germans on the Black Sea pointed to possible Russo-German differences. Tsar Alexander I and Napoleon had also been unable to agree over Constantinople.

b. GREECE AND YUGOSLAVIA. In October, 1940, also, frustrated Mussolini took the initiative of launching an attack upon Greece from Albania. There was laughter abroad when the Fascist legions were thrown back by the Greeks, and the Greco-Italian war went on inconclusively through the winter.

Nazi pressure was meanwhile being exerted on Hungary, Yugoslavia, and Bulgaria to induce them to join the Axis. Hungary maintained a shadow independence, but Bulgaria yielded completely and was occupied in March, 1941.

There remained Yugoslavia, where at the end of March, a *coup d'état* overthrew the government of the Regent Prince Paul and put the heir, Prince Peter, on the throne. This defiance of Nazi wishes brought a taste of German frightfulness to Belgrade, and the country was overrun by mid-April.

With Yugoslavia conquered, the German forces pushed on into Greece, which was simultaneously attacked by Bulgaria. An end was thus put incidentally to Mussolini's inglorious war.

5. *The War in the Mediterranean and the Near East.*
The conquest of Greece brought the Germans to the Mediterranean which Hitler kept reassuring Mussolini was Italy's preserve—an ever-shrinking preserve it seemed. A British force

which had come to the aid of Greece had to be evacuated, first from the mainland, then even from Crete, where the Germans gave the first demonstration of the use of air power in capturing an island with airborne troops.

a. THE WAR IN THE DESERT. The shaky British hold on the Mediterranean was thus further threatened. If Franco had shrewdly declined to join the Axis in war, thereby assuring the safety of Gibraltar, the Italian declaration of war in June, 1940 had brought Malta under attack, while from Libya an offensive was launched against Egypt, where a woefully inadequate British force was established.

The Italian performance in north Africa was in a category with that in Greece. But the war ranged widely in the desert. The initial Italian advance was stopped near the Egyptian border, and was followed by a British penetration of Libya as far as Tobruk. The British assistance to Greece, drawn largely from North Africa, made possible an Italian advance which was eventually contained again. [7]

6. *The Soviet Union Brought into the War*

a. RUSSO-GERMAN DIFFERENCES OVER THE BALKANS. From the beginning, Russia had pursued a policy of benevolent neutrality toward the Axis while exacting substantial advantages for this neutrality. Trusting neither side in the conflict, she was quite content to see them exhaust each other while enjoying the position of *tertius gaudens*.

But if Germany had not defeated England, her own power had not suffered materially, and she had besides much of the resources of Europe to draw upon. After the failure of the air war against England, Hitler sought a far-reaching settlement with Russia that would bring her into partnership with himself, Italy, and Japan.

The Balkans proved the chief point of difference, and, by the end of November, 1940, the Russian counterproposals

---

[7] In May, a *coup d'ètat* in Iraq installed a government favorable to the Axis. This produced British intervention, which restored the pro-British government. At the same time, French Syria, loyal to Vichy, was also overrun by British and Free French forces. Egypt remained neutral throughout the war, watching events and ready to align herself with the victors, whoever they might be.

caused the negotiation to fail. Before the year was out, Hitler, following again the Napoleonic pattern, had ordered operation "Barbarossa," preparations for an attack on Russia. The Balkan developments in the spring of 1941 caused some delay in launching the Russian campaign, which finally opened on June 22.[8]

b. THE ATTACK ON RUSSIA. Here was land war at last on a colossal scale, with millions involved on both sides.[9] The German plan was predicated on exploiting the factor of speed to break through, surround, and destroy the Russian armies. The Germans registered marked successes, reaching Leningrad, penetrating close to Moscow, and overrunning the Ukraine. The Russian losses were staggering, but Russian fortitude and totalitarian control could bear them.

More important, Russia was able to maintain a sufficiently large industrial output in her eastern centers, and to trade again space for time as she had done on other occasions. Despite her losses, her armies were not destroyed, and despite Hitler's boast in October that Russia was broken, it soon appeared that the German plan had so far been a failure. Offensives to capture Moscow in October-November led only to retreat; a winter campaign had to be faced by the Germans, and in December Hitler assumed personal command of the army, perhaps not the best thing that could have happened to that well-tempered tool of Nazi policy.

Once more the war was a stalemate, but its character had altered and the Russian phase opened up vast new possibilities.

II. THE WORLD WAR

A. The Intervention of the United States

1. *The United States and the War.*

a. AMERICAN ISOLATIONISM. Allowing for certain differences, the Second World War reproduced the pattern of the first where the United States was concerned. The disillusion which had followed 1918 had resulted in a strong revival of

---

[8] Preparations had been in progress in Russia apparently in expectation of this attack, and Stalin himself had for the first time assumed the premiership, thus taking control in name as well as in fact.

[9] In this war Germany was assisted by Roumania, desirous of recovering Bessarabia. With a similar motivation, Finland also re-entered the war.

isolationism, in the form of the naive belief that the country had been tricked into an enterprise in which it had no stake; from this it followed that any repetition of 1917 must be avoided at all costs. As the situation had begun to deteriorate in Europe, especially with the Abyssinian war, legislation was passed with the purpose of immunizing the country from conflict. The Neutrality Acts were basically an attempt of the American people to convince themselves that they could pursue their own course in divorce from the rest of the planet.

The Nazis had lost for Germany much good will in America, though a deliberate effort was made to discount as propaganda much that was heard about their doings. When war broke out in 1939, American feeling was generally sympathetic to the western democracies, but the determination remained strong to avoid involvement; further barriers were erected which hampered their ability to draw upon American economic resources, and even the controversy over the rights of neutrals was revived.

b. <u>AMERICAN AID TO BRITAIN</u>. The Democratic administration of President Roosevelt was not isolationist, and within the limits of its power and of existing legislation did its best to assist the allies. The fall of France was a rude shock to American complacency resting in part on the assumption of superior Anglo-French strength. The prospect of a Nazi victory gave assistance to the growing opinion that such an eventuality was not a matter of indifference to American interest.

The administration stretched legality to the utmost in its effort to assist Great Britain. In September, 1940, fifty overage destroyers were turned over to her in exchange for the use of naval and air bases in Britain's Atlantic possessions, while at the same time compulsory military training was adopted by Congress and the naval establishment began to be enlarged. America was becoming the arsenal of democracy, in doing which the Lend Lease Bill in March, 1941 provided a skillful way to obviate the handicap of neutrality legislation. In August, 1941, President Roosevelt and Prime Minister Churchill, meeting at sea off Newfoundland, proclaimed the Atlantic Charter, a document reminiscent of Wilson's Fourteen Points, though less precise in content.

Lend Lease in War Strategy

c. Pearl Harbor. The emphasis was still on aid "short of war," and the debate went on interminably and inconclusively between interventionists and isolationists. It was resolved in unexpected fashion by the impact of circumstances outside American control.

The outbreak of war in Europe had provided Japan with an opportunity to intensify the pursuit of the program of expansion on which she had embarked since 1931. Britain was fully occupied nearer home and, after her collapse, France could not resist the steadily increasing demands on Indochina. The United States alone, though militarily unprepared, was able to oppose Japan. Having cemented her alliance with Axis powers in September, 1940, and concluded a nonaggression pact with Russia in April, 1941, Japan carried on for a while negotiations with the United States. But, as it appeared that the gap between the wishes of the two countries was too wide to bridge by compromise, Japan decided that the time was opportune for action. On December 7, a series of operations was launched at various points in Asia and in the Pacific, the most sensational of which was the attack on Pearl Harbor.

The American reaction was one of anger and dismay. Will or no, the United States was at war with Japan. As Germany and Italy took the initiative of declaring war, the United States was catapulted into the Second World War.

2. *The Nadir of Allied Fortunes.* The vast American potential of resources and skills did eventually turn the tide of war, but it would take time to translate this potential into force in being. Meanwhile, a holding operation was the most that could be envisioned, and the year following Pearl Harbor saw allied fortunes at their lowest ebb.

a. The War in the Pacific. In the Far East Japan overran French Indochina, Thailand and Burma, the Philippines, Hong Kong, and British Malaya, where the powerful base of Singapore proved but a minor obstacle. The Dutch East Indies and many of the Pacific islands similarly fell under the control of Japan, which from New Guinea, was knocking at the gates of Australia. The "Greater East Asia Co-Prosperity Sphere" seemed to be taking shape.

But the naval and air engagements in the Coral Sea and at

Midway in May-June, 1942, and the successful holding of Guadalcanal in the summer, marked the beginning of successful containment. The effects of American and European setbacks and of Japanese occupation were, in some respects however, never to be reversed, for Japanese defeat did not undo the legacy of Asia's revolt against the west.

b. THE MIDDLE EAST, FOCUS OF GRAND STRATEGY. While these events were taking place in the Far East, the Germans renewed their offensive in Russia, and although not successful in breaking Russian resistance, they inflicted great additional losses and gained much new territory, reaching the Volga at Stalingrad and the Caucasus in the south. An offensive from Libya, where control of the war had passed from Italian to German hands, reached to within fifty miles of Alexandria. It looked as if the grand strategy of the Axis might be successful: a huge pincer movement from Egypt and the Caucasus to seize Suez and the Near East, and an even more grandiose operation effecting a junction with the Japanese at the gates of India.

3. The Turning of the Tide. These very successes had in themselves, however, strained the resources of the Rome-Berlin-Tokyo triangle. German losses in Russia were also substantial, and ever-lengthening lines of communication created problems of their own. As against this, American potential was beginning to be realized. The menace of submarines in the Atlantic was sufficiently mastered to make possible an increasing flow of supplies to the various theaters of action.

a. EL ALAMEIN AND STALINGRAD. At the end of October, 1942 General Montgomery launched an offensive at El Alamein, which, after a few days, succeeded in breaking General Rommel's front. The pursuit of the Axis forces across North Africa that began at this time did not halt, save momentarily, until they had been driven back to Tripoli.

Simultaneously, Anglo-American forces under the command of General Eisenhower landed in French Morocco and Algeria, which were quickly secured. It did not prove possible, however, to effect a junction with the allied forces coming from the east before the winter. But in May, 1943 the last remnants of the Axis armies were cornered and captured in Tunisia.

North Africa was free and securely in allied hands.

By October, 1942, also, the German failure to capture Stalingrad could be rated a major, if negative setback. The Russians were moreover able to muster sufficient strength for the launching of a counteroffensive which they sustained through the winter. Substantial territory was regained by them but, perhaps more important, a large German army was surrounded and captured before Stalingrad. Stalingrad, El Alamein, and Guadalcanal clearly marked the turning point of the war.

B. Politics, Diplomacy, and War

Axis successes had been due not only to initial greater preparedness and equipment, but to unity of command as well: from the beginning the war in the west was essentially in German hands. Allied unity and cooperation were equally desirable, not only for purposes of warfare, but, even more important, for the future organization of peace. The wartime aspect of the effort was successful; the aftermath a failure.

1. The United States, Great Britain, and the Soviet Union.

The clearer urgency of war helped simplify the efforts at cooperation. Anglo-American understanding was a relatively easy matter, but where it came to Russia mutual suspicion was hard to overcome. In addition to political differences, Russia felt that she was carrying the main burden of the land war, which for a long time was the case, and kept clamoring for the establishment of a second front in the west, perhaps oblivious of the difficulties of amphibious operations. The supplies generously sent from the United States, despite great difficulties, through Murmansk in the north and Persia in the south, helped her resistance and somewhat softened her suspicions, for a time at least. But trust never approached the confidence and free exchange that characterized Anglo-American relations. [10]

---

[10] A series of conferences to coordinate the war effort and lay plans for the peace took place in Washington (June, 1942), Casablanca (January, 1943), Moscow (June, 1943), Quebec (August, 1943), Cairo and Teheran (November, 1943), Quebec again (September, 1944), and Yalta (February, 1945).

2. The Role of France.

America, Britain, and Russia were inevitably the Big Three, carrying as they did the main burden of fighting. But many other countries had to be considered. France was impotent, yet important to both belligerents. The Vichy regime did not make peace with Germany. When North Africa was invaded, in November, 1942, the whole of France came under German occupation, while the fleet was scuttled at Toulon. The Vichy regime had been recognized by the Allies, and the problem of their relations with the Free French, led by General de Gaulle, was increasingly difficult. Relations were particularly awkward at the time of the north African invasion, after which a provisional French government was set up in Algiers. Although the German occupation of France was generally "correct," and did not indulge in the wholesale brutality that characterized it in eastern Europe, the Gestapo was active, much labor was drafted for service in Germany, and the resistance of the country became increasingly stronger and more organized. In this resistance, the Communists, after the German attack on Russia, played an important and highly creditable part which was to have considerable consequences in the future.

3. The Italian Situation.

At Casablanca, in January, 1943, the leaders of the western allies laid plans for an invasion of the mainland of Europe, concentrating at first on the weaker link in the Axis, Italy. North Africa having been cleared of Axis forces, Sicily was invaded in July. By mid-August the island had been conquered. But the political repercussions of this invasion were even greater than the military.

a. ITALY IN THE WAR. Italian participation in the war had elicited little enthusiasm in the country, especially when it appeared that the French collapse was a beginning rather than the end. The military performance of the Italian forces did not help the country's prestige in regard to either friend or foe, and the Germans were led to assume increasing direction of the war in the Mediterranean, Italy's own special preserve. As the war showed no signs of ending and brought nothing but an increasing burden of privations at home and setbacks abroad, the Fascist regime lost much of what popularity it had had, and opposition to it and to the German alliance grew correspondingly.

b. <u>THE END OF FASCISM AND THE ARMISTICE.</u> On July 25, 1943, shortly after the Sicilian invasion and after a stormy session of the Fascist Grand Council, Italy and the world were startled by the announcement that Mussolini had been arrested, that the King had appointed Marshal Badoglio in his place, and that Fascism was abolished. In Italy, the news was received with passive relief or active enthusiasm, but no one seemed to stand up for Fascism. Italy was trying to extricate herself from the war, and the new regime, while pretending to adhere to the German alliance, was negotiating with the Allies. An armistice was concluded at the beginning of September.

c. <u>ITALY A THEATER OF WAR.</u> The hope that all of Italy might be secured for the Allies at one stroke did not materialize. By the time they effected a landing at Anzio below Naples, sufficient German forces had moved in to contain the beachhead. The result was that the country fell under virtually complete German control, while the Allies had to fight their way painfully up the whole length of the peninsula. It took two years to do this, during which Italy, instead of escaping the war, became one of its bitterly contested battlegrounds, well suited to the delaying operations conducted by the Germans with skill.

d. <u>THE ITALIAN SOCIAL REPUBLIC.</u> Meanwhile the Badoglio government and the King had taken refuge behind the allied lines, and even declared war against the ex-ally Germany. In addition, the Germans had managed to effect a sensational rescue of Mussolini, who shortly reappeared in the north where he set up an Italian Social Republic, Fascist in constitution and allied to Germany. The story of the Social Republic, in its steadily shrinking territory, is a mean footnote to the main episode of Fascism. It was a certain convenience to Germany, which showed scant regard for it, and Italy was torn by domestic strife in addition to being a battleground.[11]

C. The Last Phase

1. Festung Europa. The invasion of Italy and the collapse of Fascism were omens of the future. But it took another two

---

[11] Mussolini himself was captured while trying to escape during the confusion at the end of the war in Italy. He was executed and gruesomely displayed in Milan, the scene of his initial triumphs.

years to end the war. Although the Russian advance was grinding forward, Germany was still in command of vast resources. Also, Hitler was to make good the boast that if he could not conquer he would bring down with him the house of Europe, by contrast with 1918 when the more rational military, once they had come to the conclusion that the war was lost, sued for the termination of hostilities.

With efficient ruthlessness, Germany proceeded to organize for ultimate defense the fortress of Europe. In addition to her own resources, she made increasing demands upon those of her satellites or conquered countries, and in the process of doing this aroused ever-increasing enmity. The Resistance, as it came to be known, working in close collaboration with the Allies, although it could not by itself achieve conclusive results, became nevertheless a useful and important element in the war. Most significant of all perhaps were the lasting, because irreversible, consequence of life as organized in *Festung Europa*.

2. D-Day

a. THE LIBERATION OF FRANCE. Allied forces entered Rome on June 4, 1944. What would have been a notable event was soon obscured by a greater: on June 6, a huge armada conveyed an army of invasion to the Norman coast of France. A lodgment was established and expanded, into which enormous quantities of men and matériel were poured. By the end of July the beachhead could no longer be contained by the Germans, and from August the war became one of wide and rapid maneuver comparable to the initial German phase. With the assistance of another invading force from the south, moving up the valley of the Rhone, and of the French Resistance (the F.F.I., or French Forces of the Interior), the Germans were rapidly rolled back. On August 25 Paris was liberated.

b. THE RUSSIAN ADVANCE. In the east, the Russians had launched a succession of offensives during the second part of 1944. These offensives gained much territory and had important political consequences as well. In the north, Finland was forced out of the war in September. In the south, Roumania sought to effect an about face even more abrupt than the Italian, and signed an armistice in September. Bulgaria, too, sought to extricate herself from the German connection at this time, but

Russia declared war upon her and proceeded to occupy the country. The Germans' position in Greece was becoming precarious, and that country, too, was virtually rid of them by November. Albania and Yugoslavia, where the Resistance led by Marshal Tito played an active role, were likewise freed from German control. In Hungary, the Germans were still resisting in Budapest at the end of the year.

c. THE END IN GERMANY. As the year 1944 closed, the western allies stood poised on the borders of Germany, having overrun France and Belgium. But Germany herself still controlled, in addition to her own territory, Norway and Denmark, most of Holland, Italy as far as Bologna, Croatia, most of Czechoslovakia, and Poland to Warsaw.

Since Hitler would fight to the bitter end, there was nothing for it but to bring the war into Germany, where considerable destruction was being wrought by the allied air raids. A momentarily successful German counterattack, the Battle of the Bulge, could not change the final outcome. This effort spent, the stage was set for the battle of Germany. While the Russians were advancing from the east, the western allies launched the last offensive. The Rhine was crossed in March, and German resistance began to disintegrate. By agreement with the Russians, the western allies stopped their advance at the Elbe, while the Russians were taking Berlin and Vienna. It was too late for a last German attempt to divide the Allies by surrendering to the west. Resistance was ended first in Italy with the German surrender there. Germany herself was in chaos. Playing his role to the last, Hitler himself perished among the ruins of Berlin, while the German command accepted terms of unconditional surrender.[12] On May 8 hostilities came to an end in Europe.

3. *The Surrender of Japan.* The war was still going on with Japan, however. It will suffice to say that, having reached their maximum expansion during the latter part of 1942, the

---

[12] There has been much discussion and adverse criticism of this arrangement. It was influenced in considerable measure by the situation at the end of the First World War, out of which there arose in Germany the myth that the country had not been defeated but surrendered on the basis of promises implied in the Fourteen Points.

Japanese thereafter were slowly and painstakingly, but steadily pushed back toward their home islands. After the end in Europe, there could be no doubt of the ultimate outcome in Asia. But it was thought that this outcome might yet be delayed and that invasion of the Japanese islands might prove costly. With this in mind, at the Yalta conference in February, 1945, the promise of Russian assistance was secured.

The end was highly dramatic. The role of applied science in the war had been enormous, and both sides strove to secure the prior advantage of new discoveries and weapons. On July 26, 1945 an ultimatum was issued, threatening dire consequences to Japan. Its refusal was followed by the dropping of the first atomic bomb on Hiroshima on August 6. The world was stunned and shocked at such destructiveness. The Soviet Union, in order to participate in the Far Eastern settlement, declared war on Japan on the 8. A second bomb dropped on Nagasaki induced Japan to accept the allied terms. The formal surrender of Japan took place in Tokyo Bay aboard the American battleship Missouri on September 2.

CHAPTER 12

Between War and Peace

Even apart from the fact that our time is one of unprecedentedly rapid change, accompanied by unusual uncertainties and stresses that may easily convey an image of confusion, we are too close to the events that have occurred since the end of the second World War to be able to discern a clear pattern in their unfolding. Nevertheless, in attempting to give some record of contemporary developments, the period since 1945 may be divided into two very unequal segments. The first covers less than a decade, during which time the urgent task of basic reconstruction was accomplished; by 1952 or 1953 Europe had not achieved stability, but the physical damage and the disorganization caused by the war had been made good to the extent of providing some basis for continued orderly functioning.

Moreover, international relations have assumed in our time an unwontedly high importance. That the second World War marked the definite end of the European Age, in the sense that Europe ceased to be the motive power of the planet, has become a trite observation. The demotion of all, save the Soviet Union, and the corresponding emergence of that country and the United States to a category of power unmatched, made the rest to a novel degree sensitive to American and Russian developments and dependent upon the relations between the two superpowers. The nearly simultaneous advent of a new American administration and the passing of Stalin, early in 1953, opened a new chapter in the tale of these relations. Since then Europe has followed a course of nearly uninterrupted economic expansion and progress, while her component units, singly and collectively, have groped with the problem of finding their proper place in the world.

The first and shorter period itself falls into two parts. The first two years of it, the immediate aftermath of the war, witnessed the accomplishment of the most urgent task, what might be called the clearing of the rubble and the formulation of treaties that normalized relations between some at least of the belligerents; it was also an interval of transitional uncertainty in American-Soviet relations. By 1947 these sharply crystallized into the rigid antagonism of the Cold War while Europe went about laying new foundations for the future. However, in examining this process it will be convenient to prolong the story somewhat beyond 1953.

Thereafter, the ups and downs of Russo-American relations, the fluctuations of relaxation and intransigence within the Communist milieu, the uncertain fate of European integration, the tendency to reassert greater independence by those other than the great two, make a continuing story which will be best outlined as a whole.

I. THE WORLD AFTER THE WAR

A. The Aftermath of the War

1. The Psychological Aftermath. The huge armies of our time inevitably consist in the main of civilians drafted for an emergency. Inevitably also, to the vast majority in these armies, as well as to their relatives at home, the termination of hostilities is synonymous with the restoration of peace, in turn equated with the desire to resume interrupted peacetime activities. Nowhere more than in the United States was the enormous pressure "to bring the boys back home" felt, a pressure which was only too successful, and the results of which have been extremely onerous.

Nevertheless, it is of interest to note the difference in the climate of the two postwar periods where the desire for a return to "normalcy" was concerned. After 1918 the desire took in large measure the form of contemplating a simple return to 1914; if the wish to return to peacetime occupations

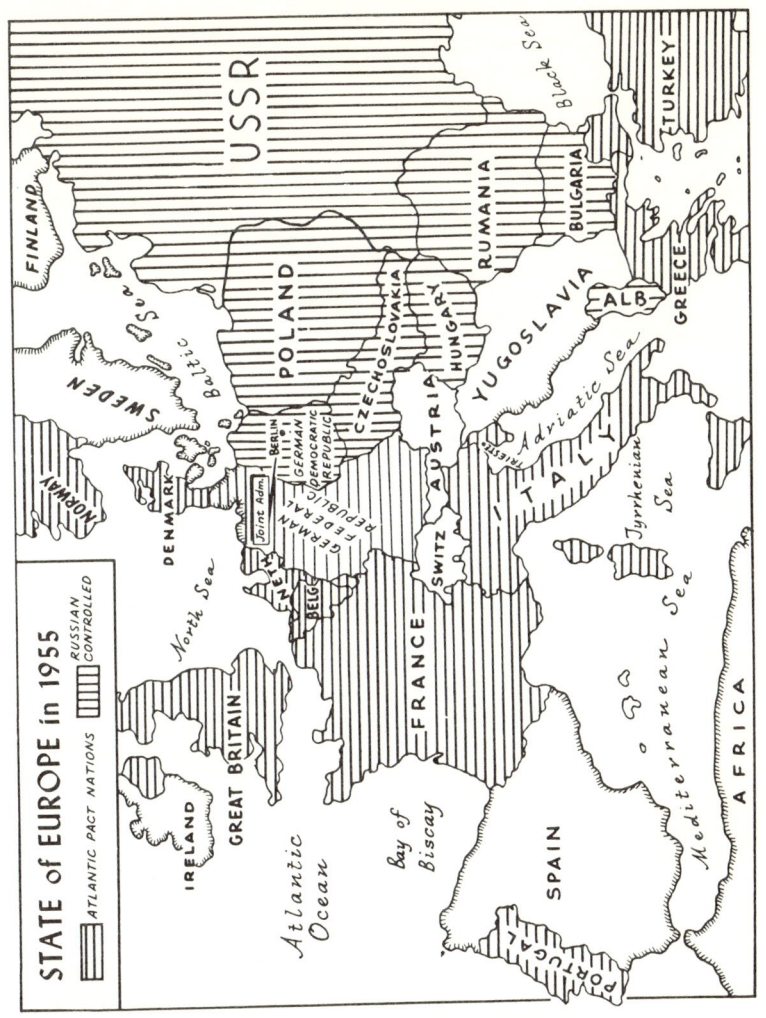

Yugoslavia and Albania both have Communist regimes, but the former is not attached to the Communist bloc, while Albania follows in the wake of Communist China.

was no less in 1945, especially in Europe, there were few who envisaged a mere restoration of the circumstances of 1939. The memory of that period held no magic and few shed tears over its vanishing; whatever the future held in its lap it would have to be other. That it would be better than the past was a hope shared by many, but the record of the last twenty-five years has also served to induce not a little scepticism.

2. *The Economic Aftermath.* Two sets of considerations stand out which may be broadly distinguished as economic and political. As to the first, the destruction wrought by the war created an immediate need for reconstruction. From a purely economic and statistical point of view, as against a human, the loss of life was perhaps the least serious and the most easily made good.[1] The physical destruction of houses, factories and transportation systems called for greater exertion and outside assistance.

The United States was, among the belligerents, the only country that had benefited economically from the war, since its productive capacity had been greatly expanded during its course. It took the leadership in mobilizing the food resources of the world. The peoples of Europe were fed, and there were no substantial outbreaks of epidemics after the war. Such agencies as UNRRA (United Nations Relief and Rehabilitation Administration) played a large role in procuring this result.

Beyond the immediate need for food there was the one, scarcely less urgent, for raw materials and equipment to set the wheels of industry turning again. This, too, was done with eminent success, even if one allows for numerous flaws in the detail of execution and for ill-managed actions such as the abrupt termination of lend-lease, which created dismay abroad.

a. <u>THE DOLLAR GAP AND THE MARSHALL PLAN.</u> But it soon became clear that Europe could not establish an equilibrium of trade with the United States. The situation, already apparent after the first World War, was greatly intensified by the second. The futility of loans such as had been made after the first World War was now widely recognized, but the

---

[1] In addition to the casualties directly or indirectly traceable to the war, there were large forced transfers of populations, mainly in response to and in retaliation for German wartime practices.

termination of lend-lease threatened to create an awkward situation.

It was at this point that Secretary of State Marshall made the proposal out of which grew the plan bearing his name, or the European Recovery Program. The success of this undertaking may be judged by the fact that European industrial production achieved far greater heights than those of 1938.

Nevertheless, if the injection of large supplies of American capital into the European economies proved highly successful and advantageous to all, it was by its nature a temporary device. Subsidizing the sale of American products abroad, if momentarily useful to both the American and the European economies, could hardly constitute the basis of sound economic relationships; the dollar gap, the unbalance of trade between Europe and the United States, could not indefinitely continue. The system must eventually come to an end, but one thing had become clear, the enormous importance of the United States in the world's economy and the extent to which the fluctuations of the American economy have repercussions abroad.

3. *The Political Aftermath*

a. Issues of Domestic Politics. The very failure of the hopes held out to peoples during the first World War was a sobering experience. But the second World War, like the first, had the effect of fostering considerable unrest among the masses; this was markedly so in Europe, virtually all of which had felt the heavy weight of German exactions.

The occurrence of revolution in Russia in 1917 had exerted considerable attraction on much of labor, long familiar with the socialist outlook. The Soviet state had not only survived the second World War, but had come out of it with the enhanced prestige that its role had earned it; at all levels of political opinion admiration and sympathy for the Russians were widespread among their allies in 1945. Moreover, following the Nazi attack in 1941, the Kremlin had mobilized Communists everywhere, and the Communists, throughout the occupied lands of Europe, had assumed a role of leadership in the Resistance. Their performance had been highly creditable —they had paid without stint the blood tax—and this redounded to their credit as individuals and, in some measure and to the confusion of others, to that of their ideology. Loyal adherents of the Soviet fatherland, they sought to exploit this advantage for political ends, posing as the best, if not the sole, spokesmen of the peoples and upholders of the ideal of national independence. The dubious behavior of many bourgeois elements, collaborators in varying degrees as they had been, further contributed to the plausibility of the Communists' contention. The result was a great surge of Communist strength in the politics of European countries; it was especially marked in France and in Italy where the Communists held important positions in the initial postwar administrations. Commanding between one-fourth and one-third of the popular vote, the possibility could be envisaged that, through the normal operation of the electoral process, Communist governments would emerge in control in either or both countries. This raised in turn the question of how to prevent such an eventuality from materializing; in other words, how to operate a democratic system with so large a Communist component in the body politic. Here lay perhaps the most acute single issue of the domestic politics of Europe immediately after the war.

b. THE REALIGNMENT OF POWER. Should either France or Italy, or both, fall under Communist control, the consequences would be enormous, for the rest of the continent would likely follow suit, a possibility of truly revolutionary implications. In varying degrees, the former Great Powers of Europe, the Soviet Union always excepted, had all been reduced to second or third rank, while that country and the United States had emerged as superpowers of an entirely different order of magnitude. Britain had played a great role and had a large voice in the war; but the very effort to a degree had weakened her, and her central problem had become the elementary one of economic survival. Germany was thoroughly beaten and destroyed; France's power seemed nonexistent. This state of affairs, brought about with great suddenness, created a novel situation, for, diminished as she might be, Europe still contained the second greatest reservoir of industry and human skills that made her a highly valued prize. Most important of all, from the European point of view, the second World War had had the effect of completing and of making clear beyond possible cavil a process which had been initiated in 1914. From power house of the planet and controller of the destinies of others, Europe, as a whole and in her component parts, had become the object of the policies of greater powers. So drastic a change could not but produce enormous stresses and strains; war, if it settles some problems, is apt to leave a legacy of others no less complicated and urgent.

B. Some Instruments of Peace

The common popular tendency to equate the end of active hostilities with the restoration of peace expresses an illusion. The conditions just mentioned, both domestic and international, have made the formal and complete restoration of peace a will-o'-the-wisp still unattained after a quarter of a century has passed. Peace there has been only in the sense that no open conflict has occurred among the major powers. Nevertheless, certain definite results were achieved that may be put under two heads.

1. *The United Nations.*

In the circumstances, the creation of an international organization that would establish a rule of law among nations seemed more than ever vital. Here also the United States had much of the initiative, and the outcome was the San Francisco conference of April-June 1945, while the war was still being waged, where the United Nations was born. President Roosevelt who, more than any one, made this his own, had insisted that the organization come into existence before and apart from the peace settlements. [2] The result was a but slightly altered version of the defunct League of Nations.

The Security Council, the General Assembly, the various commissions and specialized agencies, largely duplicate similar organs of the former League. Like the old League, the United Nations has been unable to resolve the problem of sovereignty. Five Great, or supposedly Great, Powers—the United States, the Soviet Union, Britain, France, and China—have permanent representation on the Council and the power of veto. That power has been widely used, mainly by the Soviet Union,

---

[2] This was the lesson supposedly learned from the mistake of having inserted the League of Nations Covenant into the treaties of peace following the first World War.

which has resorted to it as a means to avoid the consequences of being often in a minority, especially in the earlier stages.

a. <u>Deficiencies of the United Nations</u>. Like the League, the United Nations has shown itself capable of dealing with relatively secondary issues, where either the major powers were not directly involved, or where they felt that their stake was not vital.[3] The United Nations has also provided a useful safety valve and meeting ground, though the practice of vituperation and vacuous grandiloquence seems a questionable gain.

Realistically, it was recognized that the United Nations could not be effective without force at its disposal. But the attempt to organize such force, like that to control or limit armaments, has led to a so far unresolved stalemate. It should be recognized perhaps that armaments are less a cause than a manifestation of existing tensions, and that to approach the problem of security and peace through disarmament is in the nature of putting the cart before the horse.

An awkward situation also arose from the state of affairs in China. Save for the island of Formosa and small islands off the mainland, which remained under the rule of Chiang Kai-shek, China had fallen under the control of a Communist government. This government, however, was not recognized by the United States, among others, and the Chinese seat on the Security Council continued to be occupied by the delegate from Formosa. Attempts to secure the admission of Red China to the United Nations continued to fail, American opposition playing a large part in this situation, and there was no current indication that a solution to the dilemma was forthcoming.

2. The Treaties of Peace with Germany's Satellites.

Just as the organization of the United Nations was divorced from the process of peacemaking, so, again, by contrast with 1919, that process itself was reversed. It was decided in 1945 to deal first with the minor enemies, leaving the major ones, Germany and Japan, for subsequent consideration.

---

[3] An exception to this statement may be seen in the Suez crisis of 1956 (see below, pp. 316-17) when an *ad hoc* United Nations force was successfully interposed between the belligerents. This episode may yet constitute an important precedent, but the value of it was much weakened by the failure to adopt a similar course in Hungary.

a. <u>Territorial Readjustments.</u> Discussions were elaborate and tedious, but eventually agreement was reached in 1946, and treaties of peace were concluded with Hungary, Bulgaria, Roumania, and Finland. These treaties effected substantial changes in the map of Europe.

Italy's new eastern frontier deprived her of most of her gains after the first World War. Over much-contested Trieste a

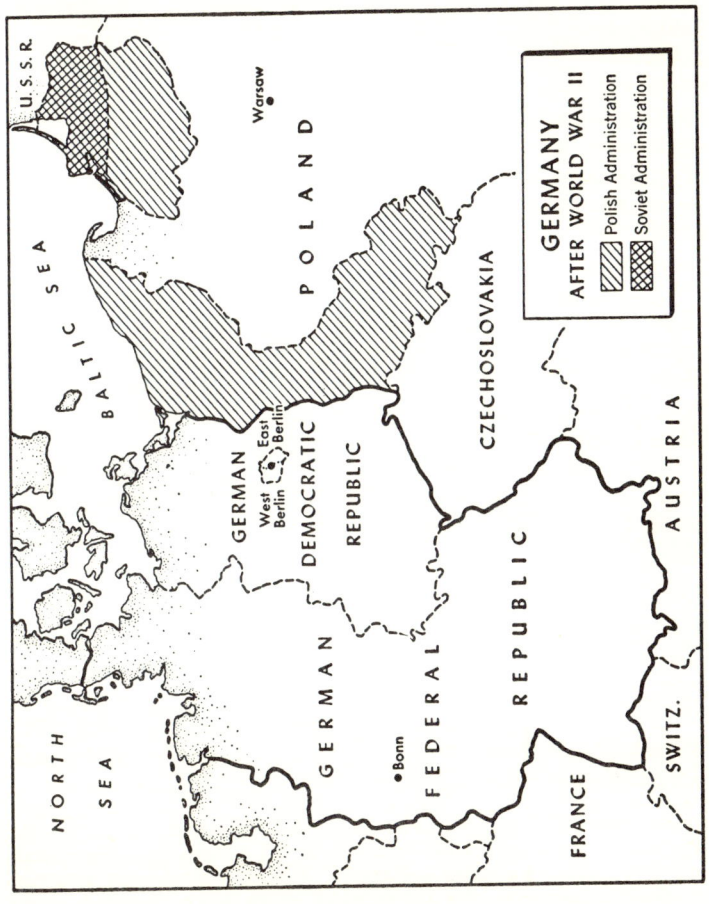

Occupied Germany

compromise was reached by creating a Free Territory of Trieste. A continuing deadlock over the choice of the governor left the territory under partly Anglo-American and partly Yugoslav occupation, [4] until, in 1954, the thorny problem of Trieste was settled with the division of the Free Territory between Italy and Yugoslavia, Italy retaining the city and Yugoslavia most of the rest. Some insignificant changes took place along the French frontier, but none on the Austrian border. Italy was deprived of her colonies, the fate of which was left to the United Nations, except for Abyssinia, restored to complete independence.

Hungary was essentially reduced to her pre-1939 borders, and from Roumania Russia retained Bessarabia and Bukovina. The same applied to the Russian acquisition of Polish territory, and even friendly Czechoslovakia had to yield her extreme eastern section, Ruthenia. The small Baltic states remained incorporated in the Soviet Union, and some Finnish territory was acquired, as well as the naval base of Hangoe. [5]

The former German satellites were, in addition, disarmed and made subject to the payment of reparations.

3. *The Status of Germany, Austria, and Japan.* Pending final peace settlements, the status of Germany and Austria remained provisional. East Prussia was divided between Poland and the Soviet Union, Koenigsberg became Kaliningrad, and the territory between the frontier of 1939 with Germany and the Oder-Neisse line was likewise occupied by Poland, a large part of its German population being evicted. In the West, France established a special regime in the Saar. The rest of Germany was divided into four zones of occupation, American, Russian, British, and French, while Berlin, wholly within the Russian zone, was similarly divided into four sectors and placed under quadripartite administration. A similar arrangement was made for Austria as she had existed prior to 1938, and within Austria for the city of Vienna. These provisions for Austria lasted until 1955, when it proved possible to reach agreement

---

[4] In 1948 the United States, Great Britain, and France issued a declaration favoring the return of the Free Territory to Italy. This was done with an eye on the coming Italian election and did not help reach ultimate agreement.

[5] This last was relinquished by the Soviet Union in 1956.

on her score among the wartime allies; formal peace was concluded with her, restoring her full sovereignty and putting an end to foreign occupation.

Japan, like Germany, was left in a state of suspense. Pending final peace she was reduced to the home islands, but in her case the occupying force was entirely American. Subsequent developments in the Far East, to be mentioned later, led to the drafting of a treaty of peace by the United States in 1951, an arrangement in which, however, the Soviet Union declined to participate.

II. THE COLD WAR

A. Two Worlds Instead of One

The fact that it had been possible to enact formal treaties of peace with the minor enemy countries in 1947 betokened at least a modicum of cooperation among the wartime allies. But even while these limited understandings were reached signs had been multiplying of increasing divergence. The ideological struggle between Communism and a more or less qualified capitalism, more concretely the contest between the Soviet Union and the United States, in fact became the dominant issue of the postwar period; the clear and open break may be situated in 1947. However, before dealing with that aspect of things, it will be convenient to survey briefly the condition and the course of the component parts of Europe in the years that immediately followed the war.

1. The Reconstruction of Western Europe. The task of reconstruction faced all, for the destruction and the dislocation that were particularly intense during the later stages of the conflict had been immense, and the danger of chaos, political and economic, was considerable. That the existence of individuals and nations was insured in relatively orderly fashion is credit to Europe's own vitality and to American assistance which, in combination, procured this result. Within their common plight the various countries faced conditions that differed.

a. <u>THE UNITED KINGDOM.</u> The fact that, unlike others, Britain had not known invasion and occupation by the enemy put her in a special position. An election took place as early as July 1945, and, despite the success of the wartime coalition under the leadership of Winston Churchill, the result was to give Labour, for the first time in Britain's history, a clear and large majority that enabled it to enact its own program without the need of compromise. The basic difficulties of the British economy were beyond the power of any political party to right. Within, therefore, the relatively narrow limits of the inescapable, Labour embarked upon a program of gradual nationalization and of increased social security and services. Most of the changes instituted may be regarded as permanently acquired, but the fundamental problem of economic adjustment remained in precarious balance. Labour was returned to office by the slenderest of margins in 1950 and a barely larger Conservative majority was produced by the election of 1951, as a result of which Sir Winston Churchill became once more Prime Minister. He finally withdrew in 1955 and the Conservatives were confirmed in office with a somewhat larger majority in 1956.

King George VI died in 1952, being succeeded by his daughter Elizabeth II. The ceremony of her coronation, in June 1953, was made an impressive occasion, reminder of the glory that had been England's. The evolution of the Commonwealth, after 1945, followed the established trend of allowing increasing scope to the centrifugal tendencies it contained. A major step was taken in 1947 with the grant of independence to India which, as two states, India proper and Pakistan, retained a connection with the Commonwealth, as did also Ceylon, while Burma rejected such a link. Something more will be said later, [6] in connection with the dissolution of all the European empires, about further changes that have taken place in the British domain.

b. <u>FRANCE AND ITALY.</u> The French situation was politically more involved than the British. Vichy had killed the Third Republic, and Vichy in turn went down into suitable oblivion. A Fourth Republic came into existence, and, after some lengthy debate, a new constitution was ratified by the French people. In all major respects the Fourth Republic was a close replica

---

[6] See below, pp. 322-23.

of the Third. French politics, however, operated in a somewhat different context.

There had been hopes that the wartime Resistance, which the provisional government of General de Gaulle represented, might yield a renewed national cohesion. The Communists emerged in post-war France as the party with the largest popular following, between one-fourth and one-third of the electorate. A new party, the *Mouvement Républicain Populaire*, a Christian democratic group, also appeared. The Communists at first participated in the government, but, after their eviction from it in 1947, went into opposition. In 1946, General de Gaulle resigned as head of the government and another group, the *Rassemblement du Peuple Français*, made up of his rather heterogeneous following, was organized.[7] Between these extremes the Fourth Republic managed to lead an uneasy political life under the guidance of precarious coalitions of middle parties and to the accompaniment of a kaleidoscopic succession of ministries.

But the picture of political instability concealed some fundamental changes of lasting significance. Most important perhaps, for the long term, was the reversal of the demographic situation of the country, with the consequence that France in this respect no longer constitutes an exception in Europe;[8] most of all she has become sharply transformed from an "old" into a "young" country, a fact the consequences of which are inevitably far reaching.

The second World War wrought greater physical damage in France than the first. The problem of reconstruction therefore loomed large in the postwar economy and finances of the country. But more than simple reconstruction was attempted. Under the guidance of a group of men, among whom Jean Monnet stood out, ambitious plans were sketched already during the war for the modernization of an economy which, among the developed ones, had remained relatively backward. Under the chaotic surface of political instability the Commis-

---

[7] In 1952 the R.P.F. membership in parliament split into two groups which showed signs of becoming integrated into the normal operation of the French party system.

[8] The French population remained virtually unchanged between 1870 and 1940. Since the war it has risen from 40 to 50 millions.

sion instituted for the purpose was encouraged to proceed with the implementation of its plan. Marked success attended its endeavors which enabled France to travel an appreciable distance toward entering the world of twentieth-century economics, though little attempt was made to control inflationary pressures. A substantial sector of the economy was nationalized, the state playing an important role in the direction of the rest. This mixed economy, half free half nationalized, successfully laid the bases of future expansion, for all that much remains to be done. As in Britain, great strides were made in the direction of instituting the welfare state.

One peculiar problem for France was that of readjusting her place among nations, owing to the very great discrepancy of her positions before and after the war. The Fourth Republic was fertile in initiatives, especially in regard to the solution of the German problem and the organization of Europe. More will be said of these presently as of France's imperial difficulties. [9] In considerable measure it fell to the Fifth Republic to gather the fruits of much that had taken place under the Fourth.

The Italian case presents certain similarities with the French, but also notable differences. Fascism had come to an end in 1943, but new arrangements had to wait for the end of the war. In 1946 Italy gave herself a new constitution and by a narrow margin of the popular vote abolished the monarchy. The Communists commanded an even larger following than in France and the bulk of the Socialists, under the leadership of Pietro Nenni, generally collaborated with them.

As in France, they were evicted from participation in the government in 1947, but thereafter there was greater political stability in Italy than in France. This was due to the emergence of the Christian Democratic party, successor to the old *Popolari*. Under the able guidance of Alcide de Gasperi, the Christian Democrats were strong enough to govern virtually alone after the disintegration of the wartime and immediate postwar coalition. They emerged from the election of 1948 with an absolute majority in parliament, but lost that position in the consultation of 1953, following which they continued to govern at the head of a more fragile coalition. One difficulty

---

[9] See below, pp. 324-25.

lay in the fact that the Christian Democratic party itself covers a very wide range of tendencies; this centrifugal situation made itself increasingly felt, especially after the resignation of de Gasperi in 1953.

From the devastation of war Italy made an excellent recovery. To be sure, she remains subject to the deficiencies of her native resources on which the pressure of population continues to exert itself. The difference between North and South has been little attenuated, despite some efforts, of which the *Cassa del Mezzogiorno* is an illustration, to deal with the condition of the latter. However, there has been a very substantial outburst of industrial activity in the North which has accomplished two results: on the one hand, Italy is being launched into the world of twentieth-century economics; on the other, the increasing demands of industry for labor have resulted in a very large internal emigration from the South to the North, and have substantially mitigated the employment situation. The rate of growth of the Italian economy has been sustained and has been among the highest. Italian finances have been managed on a sound, if conservative, basis, but the inequalities of the social structure remain a major problem, grist to the Communist mill. The continental frontiers of Italy were settled in the manner indicated before, and the loss of imperial possessions as a consequence of the war was an advantage rather than a handicap.

c. <u>DIVIDED GERMANY</u>. When the allied leaders met at Potsdam in the middle of 1945, German power had been annihilated and much of Germany lay in physical ruin. She was at first divided in the manner that has been described,[10] but the sharpening of the cleavage between the East and the West led to the emergence of two main distinct parts. Eventually, the zones of occupation of the Western powers were virtually merged, first the American and the British, to which the French was added later. Having suffered as they had at the hands of the Germans, the Russians adopted a policy of

---

[10] In addition, because of the nature of the Nazi regime and its actions, trials of war criminals were instituted. However justified retribution may have seemed, the Nuremberg trials raised a host of troublesome issues, not least in the domain of law, and the wisdom of them has been the subject of much debate.

THE UNITED NATIONS SYSTEM

The United Nations

The Specialized Agencies and IAEA

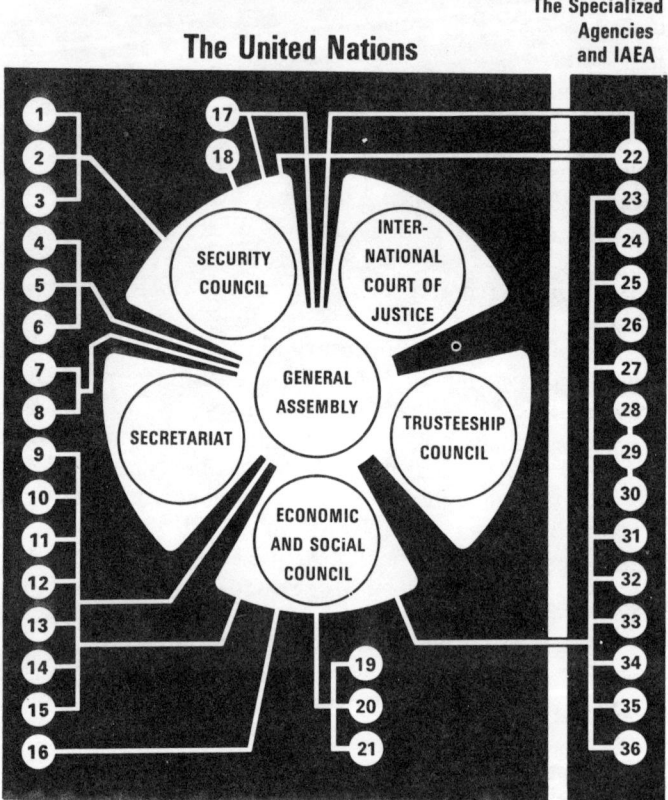

The United Nations

1 United Nations Truce Supervision Organization in Palestine (UNTSO)
2 United Nations Military Observer Group in India and Pakistan (UNMOGIP)
3 United Nations Peace-keeping Force in Cyprus (UNFICYP)
4 Main Committees
5 Standing and Procedural Committees

6   Other Subsidiary Organs of General Assembly
7   United Nations Relief and Works Agency for Palestine Refugees in the Near East (UNRWA)
8   United Nations Conference on Trade and Development (UNCTAD)
9   Trade and Development Board
10 United Nations Development Programme (UNDP)
11 United Nations Capital Development Fund
12 United Nations Industrial Development Organization (UNIDO)
13 United Nations Institute for Training and Research (UNITAR)
14 United Nations Children's Fund (UNICEF)
15 United Nations High Commissioner for Refugees (UNHCR)
16 Joint United Nations–FAO World Food Programme
17 Disarmament Commission
18 Military Staff Committee
19 Regional Economic Commission
20 Functional Commissions
21 Sessional, Standing and *Ad Hoc* Committees

The Specialized Agencies and IAEA

22	IAEA	International Atomic Energy Agency
23	ILO	International Labour Organisation
24	FAO	Food and Agriculture Organization of the United Nations
25	UNESCO	United Nations Educational, Scientific and Cultural Organization
26	WHO	World Health Organization
27	IMF	International Monetary Fund
28	IDA	International Development Association
29	IBRD	International Bank for Reconstruction and Development
30	IFC	International Finance Corporation
31	ICAO	International Civil Aviation Organization
32	UPU	Universal Postal Union
33	ITU	International Telecommunication Union
34	WMO	World Meteorological Organization
35	IMCO	Inter-Governmental Maritime Consultative Organization
36	GATT	General Agreement on Tariffs and Trade

Courtesy: United Nations Press

ruthless exploitation in their own zone while seeking to extract from the rest a maximum of reparation. The Western powers showed greater concern for the restoration of the German economy, if only to lessen the need of their own assistance. A drastic currency reform in 1950 was the beginning of an economic recovery that has been astounding in the degree of its success, until, among major currencies, the Deutsche Mark became one of the most solid. Absorbing more than 10,000,000 refugees, Western Germany built up a large favorable balance of trade to the extent of creating in turn new problems in the operation of European and world trade. In 1961 the gold value of the mark was slightly increased.

Politically, Western Germany became organized as a Federal Republic with the seat of government in Bonn. Konrad Adenauer, leader of the Christian Democratic party, became Chancellor and, despite his age, vigorously led the country on the path of recovery and of cooperation with the other Western states.[11] The election of 1957 gave the Christian Democrats an absolute majority in the Bundestag and raised the possibility that a two-party system might emerge in Germany. As in the case of Italy, the Christian Democrats subsequently lost this position but continued to govern with the support of some other smaller groups. The two major parties, Christian and Social Democrats, have been close to each other in strength.

In view of the Nazi record, it was no more than natural that many, especially in Europe, should view German recovery with alarm and suspicion. Like Stresemann thirty years earlier, Adenauer saw in cooperation with the West the best prospect of restoration for Germany; in pursuing this policy he was greatly aided by the Russo-American conflict. Germany found herself in the anomalous position of being divided into two distinct states, formally still not at peace with her former enemies, yet at the same time each part of her a member of one of the two rival coalitions. In and outside of Germany lip service has been paid to the desirability of German reunification, while neither side will agree, in and outside again, to the conditions that the other sets for the realization of that end.

---

[11] Chancellor Adenauer finally stepped down from office in October, 1963, at the age of 87.

Clearly, this situation contains an element of instability, while the ultimate fate and mood of the German people remain question marks. The Bonn Republic recognized neither the legitimacy of its eastern rival nor the permanency of frontier arrangements in the East. [12]

d. THE REST OF WESTERN EUROPE. In the Low Countries and in the Scandinavian ones no very large Communist groups appeared, nor were new constitutions drafted and, broadly speaking, the British pattern obtained. [13] Spain, generally unpopular with postwar European regimes, continued under the rule of General Franco who had been shrewd enough to resist Axis blandishments during the war. Increasing American interest, primarily strategic, and the passing of time helped the country resume to a point its place among European nations; despite improvement, the Spanish economy remained in difficult condition. Portugal pursued an even course under the relatively benevolent and mild dictatorship of Salazar, whose long tenure of office did not come to an end until 1968 as the result of age and illness.

2. *The Soviet Union and its Satellites*

a. THE U.S.S.R. The hurt that the Soviet Union suffered from the war, whether in the form of material losses or human, staggers the imagination. The ultimate success that crowned its fortitude could not, however, but redound to its prestige; within the Soviet Union itself it served to strengthen the hold of the regime and of its leaders, Stalin above all. The crying need was reconstruction and, despite the lack of outside assistance—Russia herself refused to join the Marshall Plan—the

---

[12] The period following the second World War, like that after the first, witnessed an attempt on the part of France to detach the Saar from Germany. Unilateral French action first, then protracted negotiations and a series of agreements, finally ended with the French acquiescence in 1956 in the outright incorporation of the Saar into Germany.

[13] A special issue arose in Belgium owing to King Leopold's behavior during the war. In the end the monarchy was retained, but King Leopold abdicated in favor of his son Baudouin. Belgium is one of the few countries that have not been troubled by exchange difficulties. The Congo, possession of which she retained undisturbed, was a substantial asset; by contrast Holland had a very difficult problem of readjustment as a result of the loss of her East Indian empire.

nature of the political controls made easier the organization of the task; the Russian state, ever willing to deal ruthlessly with opposition, could with relative ease commandeer its resources and peoples and impose upon them sacrifices that would have endangered the life of a democratic regime.

These sacrifices were even greater than they need have been, for, ever suspicious of the outside, Russia continued, despite her economic plight, to divert a very large share of her resources into the maintenance of military strength. Continuing the device of five-year plans, the task of restoration was successfully accomplished; having returned to pre-1941 levels, Russian production went on toward higher goals, ever stressing the expansion of heavy industry at the expense of amenities, consumer goods. What internal stresses this policy may have caused is difficult for outsiders to know; though Stalin seemed in firm control there was apparent need for the time-honored device of purges, of which that associated with the so-called "doctors' plot" in 1952 were perhaps the most startling.

However, in January 1953, the world was apprised of the death of Stalin. In view of the duration of his rule and of the extent of his power the issue of his succession raised a large question mark. For a time no one definitely filled his place, and out of the unfathomed mysteries of the Kremlin emerged a picture of intense rivalries that the phrase "collective leadership" poorly concealed. One possible candidate for Stalin's succession, Beria, found himself early, and physically, eliminated. Malenkov, Molotov, Khrushchev, and others, had their ups and downs, all surviving until the last-named emerged in apparently unchallenged control. His speech, secret at first but soon revealed, in 1956, a violent attack on the Stalin regime, and the seeming subsequent toleration of discussion and criticism, were unexpected jolts. Perhaps the surface change was less significant than the underlying permanence of controls.

b. THE SATELLITES OF THE U.S.S.R. Whether Soviet or Tsarist, and whether under the banner of Marxist ideology or of national interest, the tendency of the Russian state toward expansion has altered little. Victory in the second World War made possible the acquisition of substantial territories, the three small Baltic states, half of East Prussia, the eastern third of Poland, formerly Czech Ruthenia, Bukovina, and Bessarabia. But beyond this, in central and eastern Europe an entirely new situation developed. East Germany, Poland, Roumania, Hungary, Czechoslovakia, and Bulgaria had been overrun by Soviet armies. These countries remained in occupation and gradually all had forced upon them exclusively Communist regimes, controlled in effect from Moscow. In all of them, save in Czechoslovakia, the native strength of Communism was small; they had merely changed masters, Moscow taking the place of Berlin.

Despite complete control by their Communist parties and their total subservience to Moscow, or perhaps just because of those reasons, these countries offered the familiar spectacle of a succession of purges in their leadership. To a considerable extent, also, their economies were integrated into that of the Soviet Union, often in disregard of the local interest.

In Greece, the presence of allied forces frustrated the attempted establishment of a Communist regime.[14]

The Case of Yugoslavia. Yugoslavia did not fall under direct Soviet control, Russian forces having withdrawn from the country. But Marshal Tito, leader of the wartime Resistance, managed to achieve complete control and the country was aligned with the rest of the Soviet satellites until a breach occurred in 1948 between Tito and the Kremlin over the issue of domestic versus foreign control of policy. As a consequence, Yugoslavia presented the unique example of a "national" Communist regime pursuing its independent course apart from the rest of the Communist world.

Following the break with Moscow, Yugoslavia increased her contacts with the West whence economic and financial assistance was forthcoming. After the death of Stalin the Soviet Union began to relent toward Yugoslavia and there ensued a marked relaxation of tension, culminating in the startling spectacle in 1955 of a visit to Belgrade by Bulganin and Khrushchev, on which occasion the latter offered rather abject apologies for past Russian deeds and behavior. The impact of such developments could not but be far reaching and they

---

[14] Albania, contiguous to Yugoslavia, also fell under Communist rule, although not under occupation by Soviet forces.

gave Yugoslavia importance and interest far beyond what her own power could command. For Moscow to acknowledge that it might not have the exclusive monopoly of Marxist truth has the same implications as for a church to accept heresy on a par with orthodoxy. It is little wonder that the example of Tito's Yugoslavia should not have been lost on the other satellite states where Communist control lacked a wide and solid basis of consent. The revolt of the workers of East Berlin in June, 1953, was a failure, and an outbreak of greater proportions in Hungary in October, 1956, was brutally put down after a virtual civil war in which the Russians found it necessary to intervene. But the Poles seemed at first to have better success in restoring a measure of national, though still Communist, control of their own affairs under the determined and skillful leadership of Gomulka.

Successful heresy breeds further heresy, and though Tito has successfully retained power in Yugoslavia, he found himself confronted with the effects of independent thought and expression, of which the demotion and imprisonment of Milovan Djilas is a good illustration. "National Communism" is a contradiction of words, in logic if perhaps not in politics and history, and the case comes to mind of the French Revolution which, starting from a universalistic outlook, ended by giving nationalism its greatest fillip.

B. Two Worlds in Opposition

1. The Break Between East and West. If the physical recovery of war-ravaged Europe was generally both rapid and successful, for Europe and for the world at large the overriding consideration was the breach between East and West, more concretely between the United States and the Soviet Union. Despite the precipitate dismantling of the American military machine, a state of equilibrium obtained, unprecedented and unique in its form, owing to the exclusive possession of the atomic weapon by the United States for some years. The division of Germany and of Europe into two spheres increasingly appeared to have been based on a misunderstanding, for in the eastern section the Russians equated "friendly" with subservient governments, and "free" elections were interpreted to mean freedom for Soviet adherents alone. Protests against this situation were unavailing; the Russians may well have believed that their allies had merely used the expression "free elections" as a convenience while in effect being prepared to accept their methods of control.

It was otherwise in the portion of Europe where Russian forces were not physically present. But the great success of Communism, especially in France and in Italy, raised a large question mark for the West. In both countries the Communists participated in the government in the immediate postwar period and it was a delicate operation to govern while preventing them from obtaining control of crucial positions in the state. In any case, these conditions in both the east and the west of Europe were conductive to increasing American concern with and opposition to Communist activity in general. The open breach may be placed at 1947.

a. THE TRUMAN DOCTRINE. Already in the spring of that year the Communists were maneuvered out of the government in both France and Italy. In fact, the main Soviet antagonism seemed at first directed toward the British Empire, perhaps because of its presumed weakness. Britain was no longer strong enough to maintain her hold by force on unwilling outlying possessions. She withdrew from India and Burma. After a time, she announced that she was no longer able to sustain the cost of maintaining a force in Greece where civil war was raging.

It is at this point that, with little preparation, the United States decided to take over the British responsibility in that quarter. The Truman Doctrine, limited initially to an appropriation for assistance to Greece and Turkey, was in reality notice to the world that America was embarking on a policy of containing Russian, or Communist, expansion, specifically in this case toward the Mediterranean. [15]

From that time the lines have been drawn with increasing clarity. A coup in Czechoslovakia, still insufficiently "coordinated," put the Communists in complete control of that country in 1948. A Russian attempt to force the Western powers out of Berlin through an economic blockade was frus-

---

[15] Likewise, the Russian attempt to secure a foothold, in the form of trusteeship, in Libya had been successfully resisted.

trated by the Anglo-American ability to supply the city by air. From Stettin to Trieste the "iron curtain" was drawn, and the division of Germany hardened in the manner already indicated.

b. THE KOREAN WAR. On the opposite side of the Soviet Union, in the Far East, a situation somewhat comparable to the German had come into existence with the division of Korea into two parts along the 38th parallel of latitude, a decision also made at Potsdam. Here again it soon appeared that there was no possibility of agreement on the holding of elections in the whole country and the reunion of its parts. Two distinct entities emerged instead, a People's Republic in the north, of the customary Communist-dominated type, and a Republic of Korea in the south, from which after a time the American occupation forces were withdrawn.

During the summer of 1950 there took place the invasion of southern Korea from the north. Immediately, acting through the United Nations, the United States took up the challenge. [16] The fighting in Korea was bitter and underwent varying fortunes; apart from South Korean forces, the burden of it was carried by the United States, though a number of other countries sent token contingents as symbols of their participation. After long and wearisome negotiations an armistice was finally concluded in 1953 which essentially restored the situation to the pre-1950 condition.

2. *The Integration of Western Europe.* The consequences of the Korean episode went far beyond the immediate locale of its occurrence. Under American leadership new life was put into the United Nations. Where Europe was concerned Korea brought into clearer focus the reality of the Soviet danger—might not the East German satellite act in the same manner as the North Korean? The result was to give added point to the desirability for Europe, or at least that part of her that was outside the sphere of Soviet control, to reconstruct her shattered power, whereas the stress had been, understandably,

---

[16] What the Russian role may have been in determining the North Korean action is difficult to establish with certainty. The temporary absence of the Soviet representative made possible the decision of the Security Council without incurring a Soviet veto.

on the prior need for economic reconstruction while relying for security on the shield of American protection.

a. Economic and Political Integration. The idea of a united Europe is old, but time and again it has foundered on the rock of rival nationalisms embodied in sovereign states. However, the common plight of defeat, devastation, and vastly diminished power created certain common problems which such an undertaking as the Marshall Plan, for instance, endeavored to meet on a common basis. Already in 1950, even before the outbreak of Korean hostilities, French Foreign Minister Robert Schuman proposed the setting up of an international authority that would integrate the coal and steel industries of France, the German Federal Republic, and the Benelux countries. After protracted negotiations the Coal and Steel Community came into effective existence in 1953. The plan was intended to provide a basis for the expansion of these industries and a model for the integration of other aspects of economic life. It was also intended, through the "scrambling" of these basic elements of the economies, to make future resort to war impossible; in this respect it represented an attempted solution of the problem of Germany.

An inclusive European market would offer possibilities comparable to those of the American, and concrete proposals for its creation reached the point of formulating treaties that subsequently came into force. Plans were also drawn up for the common development of atomic energy, an initiative to which the rapidly growing demands for energy, combined with the European deficiency in power and the consequent dependence on external sources, Middle Eastern oil in particular, created an added incentive. In these endeavors, "little Europe," France, Western Germany, Italy, and the Benelux countries, constitutes the central core; their success would make that core a powerful center of attraction to others. To be sure, these were tentative steps, attended by not a little reticence and difficulty, not the least of which was the traditional British reluctance toward continental involvement.

The Organization for European Economic Cooperation (OEEC) had the same objective of facilitating intra-European exchanges, while the Council of Europe is intended to achieve a comparable result in the political domain. The United States gave its blessing and support to all these efforts at European integration. So far, greater success has attended the economic than the political aspect of these endeavors.

b. MILITARY INTEGRATION. Difficult as economic integration may be, any attempt of a similar nature in the military field is even more delicate, for the armed forces of the state, by their nature, constitute the most sensitive point of its sovereignty. The emphasis, therefore, in this field was on contrast between the European outlook and the American approach to Europe. Alliances, however, are an old tale in Europe.

N.A.T.O. Already in 1948, the Brussels Treaty Organization joined Britain, France, and the Benelux countries in a fifty-year pact of mutual protection. The concept of union for common defense was shortly enlarged with the signature in Washington in 1949 of a pact that created the North Atlantic Treaty Organization, NATO for short.

In addition to the signatories of the Brussels Treaty, NATO included the United States, Canada, Iceland, Norway, Denmark, Portugal, and Italy. Greece and Turkey were added in 1951. The heart of the agreement lay in considering an attack upon one or more of its members as an attack against all.

The European Defense Community. With the conclusion of the NATO agreement, and especially after the outbreak of the Korean War, the United States shifted its effort from economic recovery, by now well under way, to the creation of military strength in Europe. Pressing for the formation of a European army, the Council of NATO established in Paris in 1951 a Supreme Headquarters Allied Powers, Europe (SHAPE), at the head of which was placed General Dwight D. Eisenhower, the American wartime commander.

In order to increase the military power of Europe, consideration was also given to the rearmament of Germany, even though formal peace had not yet been made with her. Such a suggestion inevitably revived among many in Europe wartime memories of German power and deeds. A French proposal for the integration of Europe's armed forces, including the German, led to the arrangement known as the European Defense Community (EDC). After many delays, the French Assembly refused to ratify the EDC arrangement in August, 1954. Subsequent negotiations sought for an alternative way to provide for the rearmament of Western Germany, looking to her joining NATO while ending the occupation status and restoring her sovereignty. This was eventually accomplished. No formal treaty of peace has been concluded with Germany, or a part of Germany—on the plea that such an arrangement can only be made with a reunited country—but, to all intents and purposes, the Federal Republic enjoys unfettered sovereignty and is a member of the western alliance.[17] With little speed and great deliberation, not to say some qualms, Western Germany embarked on the process of recreating an army.

There has been, on the American side, some impatience with European tergiversations, but the legacy of centuries of conflict and suspicion is not readily overcome. Much is bound to depend on the course of German developments and the mood of the German people, primarily domestic German issues, that many view as question marks.

III. EUROPE IN THE WORLD TODAY

In closing this survey a glance may be cast at the record of the immediate past with a view to appraising, in obviously tentative fashion, the current direction of change. Speaking of Europe, the fact must be stressed above all that it is no longer possible, as for some time it has not been, to consider that continent in isolation. Though not in the sense expected by those who hoped that, from the second World War, One World would emerge, in the sense of intricate and inescapable interdependence, One World is certainly apt characterization of existing circumstances. It will be convenient to focus attention in succession on the relations between the two great rival blocs, then on the significance of that part of the world that would eschew absorption by either, and finally on the more narrowly European aspects of change and adaptation, always bearing in mind that each of these aspects is intimately related to the others.

A. The Changing Pattern of Relationships

While the position of the United States and of the Soviet Union as superpowers has remained unchallenged, there have

---

[17] Similarly, Eastern Germany occupies a like position in the eastern counterpart of NATO, the Warsaw Pact.

been some important changes in the world situation during the past two decades. Much of the world, including Europe, would prefer not to be entangled in the contest between the two, and there has been much talk of neutralism and of third forces. Some scope has been given to these tendencies by the Russo-American stalemate, which in some degree has neutralized both powers, but American and Russian developments and American-Soviet relations remain in the last resort crucial for all; they are the background which others could never forget and for that reason something, if only briefly, must be said of them.

1. *The United States; Its Problems and Position.* The paramount fact about the United States has been its acceptance, after a brief hesitancy, of a world role commensurate with its power. Mention has been made of the Truman Doctrine, the Marshall Plan, NATO, and the Korean War. The United States had little desire to make acquisitions for itself, but, for reasons of its own security if no others, found itself opposing what it regarded, rightly or wrongly, as Soviet designs of expansion. This led it to assert its influence everywhere in the world, and, leaving aside the superogatory debate of whether and to what extent American policy has been imperialistic, that America has become a world empire may fairly be granted. Across the Atlantic and the Pacific American influence asserted itself as the just mentioned items clearly indicate. Empires have a way of behaving in accordance with the dictates of an inner logic of their nature.

Yet that role, on a world scale at least, was a novelty to the American people, all the more felt for the suddenness of its occurrence. The election of General Eisenhower to the presidency of the country in 1952 was less the assertion of a military mood than the expression of a widely felt desire for a pause in a too strenuous endeavor. Appropriately, one of the first accomplishments of the new administration was to put an end to the fighting in Korea. The rest of the decade, covering the two Eisenhower administrations, was to a point a period of retrenchment, of taking stock and shifting the focus of attention to domestic issues.

Not that the outside was forgotten—it could hardly have been—as witness the activity and the determined stance of

Secretary of State John Foster Dulles. But even the concern with the Communist problem—or bogey—found expression in the phenomenon of which Senator Joseph McCarthy became the most blatant embodiment at home. The deeply rooted American tradition of individual rights eventually brought an end to the witch hunt, which for that matter did not impede more creditable developments, those in the domain of civil rights for example. All the while, through ups and downs that in retrospect appear like minor fluctuations, the American economy was rising to ever greater heights of production.

In 1960, by the narrowest of margins, John F. Kennedy was elected president. His youth and the new style he introduced in the conduct of affairs were apt symbols of an altered climate, perhaps more significant than the concrete accomplishments of his administration. He captured the imagination of many, no less abroad than at home, a fact to which the reaction to his tragic death bears adequate witness. His administration deliberately sought to insert itself into the tradition of which earlier Democratic presidents had been spokesmen, Wilson's New Freedom and Roosevelt's New Deal. The domestic focus of care, the creation of a more just society, was large, but this did not interfere with an equal concern with the outside, a role of world leadership for America. The country was powerful and rich enough not to have to face the necessity of a choice between guns and butter, but could easily afford both, and use them both for its own and the general good.

Guns, as it happened, would be needed increasingly, for it was during the Kennedy administration that were planted, unwittingly perhaps but planted none the less, the seeds of the American involvement in Southeast Asia, more specifically in Vietnam. The administration of President Johnson, though with a different style, essentially continued the policies of its predecessor, chalking up substantial domestic achievements.

American prosperity did not grow less, but a more sceptical mood crept in. On the one hand, the opening of the door to the redressing of the legitimate enough grievances of the Black section of the population had the effect that might have been expected: granting concessions often does not so much create gratitude as it gives rise to hope that easily becomes impatience, hence to dissatisfaction. The rising mood of Black militancy, the long hot summers, have been in recent years a rising cloud on the American horizon. And that mood of disillusion, despair, and bitterness to a degree has matched that other source of dissatisfaction, the stalemate in Vietnam.

That the United States is pursuing in Vietnam imperialistic aims of a classical nature is a gross misrepresentation. Yet it is not unfair to say that America has found itself confronted with other empires—whether Chinese or Russian, and whether Communist or other matters little—and has been reacting in the classical manner of empires. The traditional background of isolation explains at once the manner of involvement—a fit of absentmindedness comes to mind—and the reaction of frustration of a people not accustomed to not having its way. The mood has been particularly marked among the young who, in addition, have been finding out that an affluent society does not necessarily answer all the aspirations of man.

Mention is made of these aspects of the American scene because of the importance of the American role in the world, hence the necessity of understanding the mood of America and its problems. Lest one lose a proper sense of perspective, it may also be pointed out that, taking an overall view of twenty-five years, America's foreign policy has been characterized by an unusual rapidity of adaptation, moderation, and not a little success.

2. *The Soviet Union and Its Problems.* For similar reasons of power and importance something must be said of the Soviet milieu. The imperial tradition is no novelty to Russia, which, whether Tsarist or Soviet, has tended to pursue the same goals in this respect. This does not mean that the impact of ideology and revolution can be disregarded.

What the ultimate judgment of history may be—there probably will be no such but lasting controversy instead—of the importance of the figure of Stalin there can be little question. The fact is that under his rule Russia was launched into industrial modernity and won the war. His demise in 1953 and the subsequent period of hesitancy culminating in the emergence of Nikita Khrushchev have been mentioned. The year 1956 is an important landmark which witnessed on the one hand the famous speech he delivered at the Twentieth

Party Congress, on the other the harsh suppression of the Hungarian revolt. These two events, which may be read as signs of uncertain direction, properly illustrate in juxtaposition the fundamental issue that has beset the Soviet state.

The degree of development of the Soviet economy did not allow the Soviet people to have both guns and butter as the Americans could. To maintain armaments on the American scale, with a gross national product roughly half the American, was an accomplishment that the nature of the regime alone made possible. The lower Russian living standard contributed as well, though pressures began to be felt from the increasing desire of the people for a greater share of amenities. The allocation of resources between heavy industry and the production of consumer goods has been one of the major problems of the directors of the Soviet economy. And so likewise has agriculture, ever a stepchild in a Marxist milieu. An ambitious program for the opening up of virgin lands to grain production was unwisely launched by Khrushchev but before long backfired, until grain had to be imported from abroad.

An equally ambitious and grandiose Seven-Year Plan, which among other things proposed to overtake the United States by 1970, fell far short of realization, and a more moderate and realistic Five-Year Plan was launched in 1956. Khrushchev seemed to have taken on the mantle of Stalin, though he refrained from resorting to the latter's harsh methods of control; his opponents were removed to minor posts rather than physically eliminated. A shrewd and flamboyant extrovert, more given to practicality than to strict adherence to dogma, he none the less aroused discontent because of his methods and of some of his failures. He overcame an attempt to remove him in 1958, after which he seemed in firm control more than ever. But in 1964 a new attempt succeeded which reduced him to the status of a private citizen.

He was accused, among other things, of being guilty of Stalin's crime, the cult of personality—read personal dictatorship. Collective leadership was the ostensible answer, and the team of Leonid Brezhnev and Aleksei Kosygin took his place. Far less colorful, more pedestrian, perhaps no more than high class bureaucrats, the new leaders adopted what might be called a middle of the road and business approach to the problems of the Soviet economy. The very growth of it had the effect of minimizing the stress on ideology, until many of the devices familiar to a capitalist economy—the market, productivity, profitability, cost accounting—began to be rediscovered under the prodding of such economists as Liberman and Varga, now given greater freedom of expression. For that matter, economic planning is a world-wide tendency which reflects modern technological conditions independently of ideological predilection.

The general tendency toward relaxation of centralized controls, the ups and downs of that trend, have been accurately reflected in the cultural domain, nowhere more than in literature, which has been a sensitive barometer of the prevailing climate. As early as 1954, Ilya Ehrenburg, ever a dependable weather vane, published a novel, *The Thaw*, an expression of the change that followed the passing of Stalin. It became quickly apparent that a large reservoir of suppressed discontent existed among the intelligentsia. Such works as Dudintsev's *Not by Bread Alone* or Solzhenitsyn's *A Day in the Life of Ivan Denisovich*, this last depicting conditions in Siberian labor camps, attracted wide attention, both at home and abroad, sometimes as much because of the change their appearance revealed as because of their literary merit.

The results have been a source of embarrassment to the political leadership, which responded with an alternation of permissiveness and repression. A measure of the still prevailing Soviet climate may be gathered from the episode of Pasternak, author of the widely read *Dr. Zhivago*, being prevented from going to Stockholm to receive the award of a Nobel prize, which he thereupon proceeded to decline; or the case of Sinyavsky and Daniel, sentenced in 1966 to seven and five years at hard labor respectively for having allowed the publication of some critical works abroad.

One peculiar problem which has confronted the Soviet leadership has arisen out of the ideological factor. Moscow long and successfully claimed and maintained the position of being the sole fount of the correct interpretation of the Communist doctrine. This was easier to do so long as Russia was the only Communist state, but with the appearance of other Marxist states it was not long before heresy raised its head, of which the above-mentioned case of Yugoslavia in 1948 was the first successful illustration. Excommunication had little effect; instead of which, as might have been expected, the virus spread.

Most important of all has been the case of China. Stalin himself had been of two minds about the spread of Communism to China, but, by 1949, Mao Tse-tung had gained control of the country. Sino-Soviet relations continued friendly for a time, China receiving assistance from the Soviet Union. But it would have been utopian to expect that the vast entity of China, so diverse from Russia in many respects, economically and culturally, would long remain subservient to Muscovite direction. The breach may be placed around 1960 and matters have deteriorated since. Russian attempts at reestablishing friendly relations failed, until there are two rival centers of leadership whose manner of dealing with each other, so far mainly in words, despite some armed border clashes, reminds one of the Catholic-Protestant relationship at the time of the Reformation.

Clearly, there could be no question of dealing with China as was done with Hungary in 1956. One form of the Russian reaction has been to try to enlist the backing of other Communist parties. A world congress of such parties, called by the Russians in 1966, was cancelled. After long preparations, such a congress met in Moscow in 1969, when it turned into a predictable anti-climax. Not only did the Chinese and some others refuse to attend, but even some of those present, the Italians for example, representing the largest Communist party outside the Communist world, would not be coerced into full adherence to the Muscovite orthodoxy. Little more than meaningless generalities and platitudes were the final outcome of the meeting.

From the standpoint of the outside, not a little irony may be seen in the Russian assertion of the untouchability of the sacred soil of the Soviet fatherland, countered by Chinese claims to Russian-held territories. The two may be brother socialist states, but there is no denying that an appreciable portion of the Soviet fatherland is the result of Tsarist imperial activity.

a. THE PROBLEM OF THE EUROPEAN SOVIET SATELLITES. For all that most of the states of eastern central Europe were ostensibly brother socialist states of the Soviet Union, the hand of the Kremlin lay heavy upon them. The wholly understandable Russian concern with security and economic reconstruction was at first the determinant of Soviet policy toward its European satellites. Rigid political orthodoxy and ruthless economic exploitation were the earmarks of the Stalinian period, which Tito's Yugoslavia alone succeeded in escaping, and the changes that followed the passing of the Russian dictator in his own country inevitably had repercussions in the satellites.

There was correspondingly economic relaxation in answer to the latent demand of the people. This was especially notable in the domain of land policy, where collectivization became substantially qualified and even a degree of private enterprise was allowed. East German reparations were abandoned and an effort at more fairly organized multilateral cooperation found expression in the attempt to put new life into COMECON, the Council for Economic Mutual Assistance,[18] which would now come closer to what its name expressed. The effort met with but moderate success, while the hopes raised by political relaxation were cause for concern to the Kremlin. The skillful and courageous stance adopted by Gomulka alone saved Poland in 1956 from armed Soviet intervention, while Hungary had poorer success, as previously indicated. The normally dreary and sordid tale of changes in the local leaderships, to the accompaniment of the customary deviationist charges, need not be gone into in detail.

The contemporary judgment of the *Manchester Guardian* on the Hungarian episode of 1956 is apt: "The Soviet empire stands stripped of all pretense that what knits it together is an endeavour for the common good. It joins King Bomba and all the other common despotisms that have had no thought but to perpetuate themselves and no ultimate means other than force. Like them it has lost all directing hope, and like them it will go the way of dismemberment and unwept dissolution."

"Dismemberment" may seem premature, but the centrifugal tendency has persisted, despite shifts of emphasis in Moscow and the reluctance to repeat the 1956 performance in Hungary.

---

[18] This had been organized in 1949 to include the entire Soviet bloc except Yugoslavia, but in effect was largely used as an instrument of Soviet exploitation.

Thus, for example, Albania, ever at odds with Yugoslavia under any ideological dispensation, welcomed the 1948 break between Tito and the Kremlin, but the Soviet attempt to restore the relationship with Yugoslavia caused Albania to become the oddity of a minute outpost of Chinese influence in Europe. The Czechs, who had remained quiescent and subservient during and after the 1956 crisis, rather unexpectedly embarked on a program of far-reaching liberalization at the beginning of 1968. The "Spring dawn" was of brief duration. Following a period of negotiations and hesitancy on the part of the Soviet Union, Czechoslovakia was invaded in August. Little violence occurred, although there was great bitterness, the invasion being cloaked under the guise of brotherly assistance to a regime threatened by the intrigues of capitalist-imperialist reaction. In Czechoslovakia the Russians have adopted, with apparent success, the subtler tactics of gradual erosion, but the ultimate end is the same. *Gleichschaltung* is not a new practice.

The coercion of Czechoslovakia had from the Soviet point of view the advantage of not being a purely Soviet operation, for it was joined in by most of the members of the Warsaw Pact. That pact, which dates from 1955, was the Soviet response to the accession of Western Germany to the western security pact that was NATO. The Russian concern with security is at once strong, clear, and legitimate; Russia did not feel that it could allow any of her satellites to stray from her control and possibly become a tool of western, especially American, designs.

The case of East Germany is noteworthy. After the passing of Stalin, Russia adopted a new line toward that section of Germany, the German Democratic Republic. Efforts were now made to create better conditions and greater satisfaction for its people. To staunch the steady flow of escapes through West Berlin, in 1961 the city was physically divided into two sections through the erection of a wall in its midst. But at the same time conditions have been improved in East Germany, which has become an important industrial state in its own right. The issue of Poland's western frontier, the Oder-Neisse line, unrecognized by many states, to a considerable extent put Poland in a reliably dependent position vis-à-vis the Soviet Union.

For a time Gomulka was a popular figure in Poland for having stood up to Russian pressure in 1956, and Poland became the locale of greater freedom of expression. But the passing of time showed these hopes to have been an illusion. Kadar in Hungary, presumably a dependable Soviet agent, maneuvered with skill between the Charybdis of repression and the Scylla of popular resentment; the course of Hungary has been relatively smooth.

It was Roumania's turn to kick against the traces. The emergence of Ceausescu in 1967, to the accompaniment of the usual purges and rehabilitations in the leadership, was an assertion of national independence, comparable to the Polish one in 1956. Ceausescu, too, maneuvered with skill, not challenging the ideological orthodoxy. Roumania escaped the Czech fate of invasion, continued to profess loyalty to Moscow, yet refused to condemn China and even disapproved the occupation of Czechoslovakia. Like other Soviet satellites, Roumania has sought to enlarge economic exchanges with the non-Communist world. This has proved easier for more independent Yugoslavia, which has traveled an appreciable distance toward the establishment of a mixed economy.

3. *The Changing Face of the Cold War.* These circumstances have played the simultaneous roles of cause and effect in the relations between the Soviet Union and the West, more specifically the United States. The centrifugal tendencies at work in the Communist world have had their counterpart in the free, not least in the American-led coalition. Nevertheless, Soviet-American relations have continued crucial for all, and something must be said of them and of some landmarks in their evolution.

In 1953 the possibility of new initiatives between the two superpowers seemed open. A four-power meeting in Berlin in January 1954 foundered on the issue of the German problem. The two segments of that country seemed to be drifting even farther apart, each more closely integrated than ever into the rival alliances that were NATO and the Warsaw Pact. But a few months later, when a meeting took place in Geneva for the liquidation of the French position in Indochina,[19] both the

---
[19] See below, p. 324.

United States and the Soviet Union were present as observers. A year later it finally proved possible, ten years after the war, to agree on a treaty for Austria, now formally at peace again and a sovereign state, though forbidden to join any alliance. [20] Little was accomplished at a summit meeting in July 1955 beyond agreement on allowing a number of states to join the United Nations.

The following year provided an interesting test of relations. The British difficulties in dealing with Egypt, the French annoyance at the latter's support of the Algerian rebellion, and Israeli fears merged in a joint attack of those three countries against Egypt. [21] The Egyptians were easily defeated, mainly by the Israeli forces, but the ill-contrived Anglo-French operation dragged on. Meanwhile, in the United Nations, where the breach of the peace was considered, the U.S. and the U.S.S.R. for a moment joined hands in condemning the presumed aggressors, while the Soviet Union muttered dark threats of nuclear intervention against them. Hostilities were ended with the agreement of all to a United Nations intromission.

This pointed to a common Russo-American interest in preserving the peace. But it is highly significant that the episode occurred simultaneously with the above-mentioned Russian intervention in Hungary. Despite much sympathy for the Hungarians in the West, no assistance to them was forthcoming, a situation which could be interpreted as a tacit American acknowledgment that eastern Europe belonged in the Soviet sphere of interest while the Middle East was more uncertain ground. [22]

The interpretation of reciprocally acknowledged spheres of

---

[20] The return to the Finns in 1955 of the base of Porkalla was another sign of the Soviet mood of accommodation.

[21] The specific precipitant of the crisis was Nasser's nationalization of the Suez Canal Company, in turn a response of his disappointment at his failure to obtain western, mainly American, credits for the Aswan Dam. The war was initiated by an Israeli attack, the British and the French pretexting intervention for the purpose of interposition between the belligerents.

[22] In 1957 Congress authorized the President to use American armed forces in resisting Communist aggression in the Middle East (Eisenhower Doctrine). Under this grant of power American supplies were sent to Jordan in 1957 and United States troops temporarily went to Lebanon in 1958.

interest received added support from the crisis that arose in Berlin in 1958 out of a renewed Soviet attempt to evict the western powers from that city. In the face of a determined American stance, the Russians "forgot" what had seemed like an ultimatum and the issue evaporated. Relations improved for a time, but a summit meeting in Paris in 1960 broke up in recriminations as a result of the U-2 incident.[23] When the Berlin wall was erected in 1961 the western reaction did not go beyond expressions of verbal indignation.

Meantime a new administration had taken office in Washington. One of the problems it faced was the overthrow of the Cuban regime of Batista by Fidel Castro. Latin American revolutions are familiar occurrences, but after a period of hesitation, when it appeared that the new Cuban regime was Communist oriented, relations with the United States deteriorated badly, little helped by the ill-contrived episode of the Bay of Pigs, an attempt to overthrow the Castro regime with limited American assistance, a bungled failure from which Washington came out with little credit. The meeting in Vienna between Kennedy and Khrushchev in the spring of 1961 unfolded in a somber mood.

But the latter misjudged badly when, in 1962, under the pretext of protecting Cuba from American invasion, he decided to install Soviet missiles on the island. In the face of a virtual American ultimatum, directed to Moscow rather than to Havana, the missiles were withdrawn. It was a serious Soviet setback, which contributed to Khrushchev's later downfall, but also served as a clarification: the American acknowledgment that eastern Europe was in the Soviet sphere had for its counterpart the recognition by the Soviet Union that the American continent fell in that of the United States.

a. <u>THE ARMS RACE.</u> Thus continued competition also contained in it possibilities of accommodation. The word containment fairly describes American policy in the fifties toward the Soviet Union, an updated version of France's post-World War I *cordon sanitaire*. But Russia was now powerful, and the fundamental motivation on both sides was one of suspicion

---

[23] An American espionage airplane was shot down over the Soviet Union, and President Eisenhower, though assuming responsibility, refused to make the apologies demanded by Khrushchev.

and fear. American actions, of defensive intent in American eyes, could easily take on aggressive color when viewed from Moscow. And, to be sure, a look at the map was calculated to confirm these suspicions. Thus NATO was supplemented by SEATO (Southeast Asia Treaty Organization), designed for the containment of Communism, Chinese as well as Russian, in Asia, even though SEATO turned out to be a diluted and ineffectual version of its European equivalent.[24] CENTO (Central Treaty Organization), successor to the Baghdad Pact, joining Turkey from NATO and Pakistan from SEATO with intervening Iran, was intended to complete the ring of encirclement. It has been equally ineffectual.[25] One is reminded of the pre-1914 *Einkreisung*, outcome of fear of German designs which fed in turn German fears. And the parallel could be pushed further. Thus, even in 1961, when the Soviet party program asserted the possibility of coexistence, it also reiterated the Soviet endorsement of "the sacred struggle of the oppressed peoples and their just anti-imperialist wars of liberation." Was Cuba attempting to liberate itself any more than Hungary had been?

The period between the two World Wars witnessed prolonged, if ultimately futile, attempts to deal with armaments. The belief that arms constitute a danger to peace is not wholly devoid of foundation; yet, as already pointed out, it also amounts to putting the cart before the horse, for arms are in the last resort more the expression than the cause of insecurity. The tendency after the second World War has been, as was the case before the first, to honor the ancient maxim *si vis pacem, para bellum*. We now call it the balance of terror, a highly unstable condition, and there has been considerable similarity between the interwar discussions and those of our time. The heart of the matter, and the central difficulty, is best

---

[24] The United States, Britain and France, as well as Australia and New Zealand, were members of SEATO. Among Asiatic countries the Philippines, Thailand and Pakistan joined it, but India, Burma and Ceylon abstained. The Far Eastern situation in the sixties has been dominated by the American intervention in Vietnam and the Sino-Soviet rift.

[25] The Baghdad Pact initially included Iraq, but that country withdrew from it following the revolution of 1948, after which CENTO was created. The United States has not been a member of CENTO, participating in it as an observer.

summed up in what was then the position primarily expounded by France and now taken by the U.S. and the U.S.S.R.: we shall disarm when and to the extent that we feel secure.

This should not be interpreted as implying inevitable repetition of historic occurrence. For there are novel factors in the present situation which derive in the main from the fact of technological advance. American superiority in the nuclear field in particular for a time induced overconfidence and complacency. This attitude received a severe jolt from the launching of *Sputnik*, the first earth satellite, in October 1957, an event from which much prestige accrued to the Soviet Union. The exaggerated American reaction of depression and self doubt did not last very long. Resurging American confidence was perhaps best expressed when a new President, John F. Kennedy, launched an ambitious program and asserted that America would put a man on the moon by 1970. [26] In any case a great boost was given to the arms race. But at the same time awareness of the destructive possibilities of modern weapons was a sobering thought which induced a strong and real desire to control their development. The wish is shared by both chief participants, but the problem for both is how to institute controls or limitations while making sure that no advantage accrues to the adversary. The harnessing of science and technology to military purposes may be bemoaned, yet no one has seriously suggested that scientific and technological development might be controlled; even if one ignores its martial possibilities, the fact remains that our culture is firmly wedded to the assumption that scientific progress must and will go on.

One factor is that of cost. Even apart from the fact that military budgets have soared, much of the new technology, even for peaceful purposes, can only be afforded by those with enormous resources. This has had the effect of accentuating the discrepancy between the superpowers and the rest. Two developments must be noted. One is the effort of the two to put a stop to the spread of nuclear weapons among possibly less responsible hands. Geneva was the seat where discussions were held, reminiscent of those of thirty years before, but the tacit agreement on a ban to nuclear testing was broken by the Soviet

---

[26] This was done in July 1969.

Union in 1961, with the consequence of renewed American tests. Discussions were subsequently resumed and finally led to the signature in Moscow in August 1963 by the United States, the Soviet Union, and Britain of a treaty banning nuclear tests in the atmosphere, though not underground. In 1967 another treaty extended the ban to outer space.

The test ban treaties were steps on a road whose ultimate destination was the control of nuclear weapons, more immediately the prevention of their spread among those not yet possessing them. There is no denying that even a small nuclear armory puts the possessor of it in a different category from others. That is the reason why Britain, who had shared in the development of these weapons, did not renounce them, although she did endorse the test ban treaties.

It was otherwise with France. Disgruntled at what she regarded as discrimination, and partly under the impact of the aftermath of the Suez episode, she embarked on a program of nuclear armament. The first French nuclear test took place in the Sahara in 1960 and has been followed by others. China has pursued a similar course, and the rapidity of her progress has caused surprise in view of her technological and economic backwardness.

In July 1968, with the backing of an earlier United Nations resolution, the United States and the Soviet Union signed a non proliferation treaty, to which a number of states have subsequently adhered, Britain among them. A number of countries have at present the possibility of producing nuclear weapons, which have so far refrained from doing so. To freeze the nuclear club is an obviously invidious undertaking so long as there are those who do not feel sufficient trust in their allies or in the value of international institutions; this explains the reticence of such countries as West Germany, Japan, and Israel.

There is foundation for the widespread feeling that the issue of the control of armaments deserves priority over all others. Russo-American discussions, in which others participate, continued despite the setback—seemingly no more than a passing setback—that was a consequence of the Soviet occupation of Czechoslovakia in 1968. In November 1969 Strategic Arms Limitation Talks (SALT) were initiated in Helsinki between the United States and the Soviet Union.

B. The Non-Committed World

The point has already been made that one of the major consequences of the second World War was clearly to write *finis* to the European Age. Nowhere has this been clearer than in the imperial domain. It will be convenient to consider individually the various European empires.

1. The British Case.

Empire has been for Britain of greater significance than for any other country, at once source and appropriate symbol of the power that was hers. That empire evolved into a Commonwealth under the aegis of a flexible and permissive policy, which made possible its peaceful transformation, and it was thought that the evolutionary process might continue, allowing growing scope to the autonomy of its parts while preserving among them a connection beneficial to all.

This has proved an illusion in the face of too strong a centrifugal tendency. In the case of the Dominions the decline of British power, economic and military, and the corresponding rise of the American, has resulted in a gravitation toward some connection with the latter. This applies in particular to Canada, Australia and New Zealand, which however retain their formal link with the British crown. The result is a vicious circle which redounds to the further diminution of the British position. The South African case has been a special one. The policy of *apartheid*, or racial segregation, has caused the Union of South Africa to quit the Commonwealth. So did Rhodesia in 1969, following an earlier Unilateral Declaration of Independence (UDI) after some unfruitful negotiations.

The Indian empire was relinquished in 1947, split into two, India and Pakistan, to the accompaniment of large displacements of population and a high toll of casualties. The unresolved issue of Kashmir has poisoned the relations between India and Pakistan, degenerating into a brief war in 1965. The fact that the conflict was settled in Tashkent, under Soviet auspices, is a measure of the tenuousness of the Commonwealth link, though the British economic interest in the subcontinent has not diminished.

Out of the rest of the British imperial domain a number of

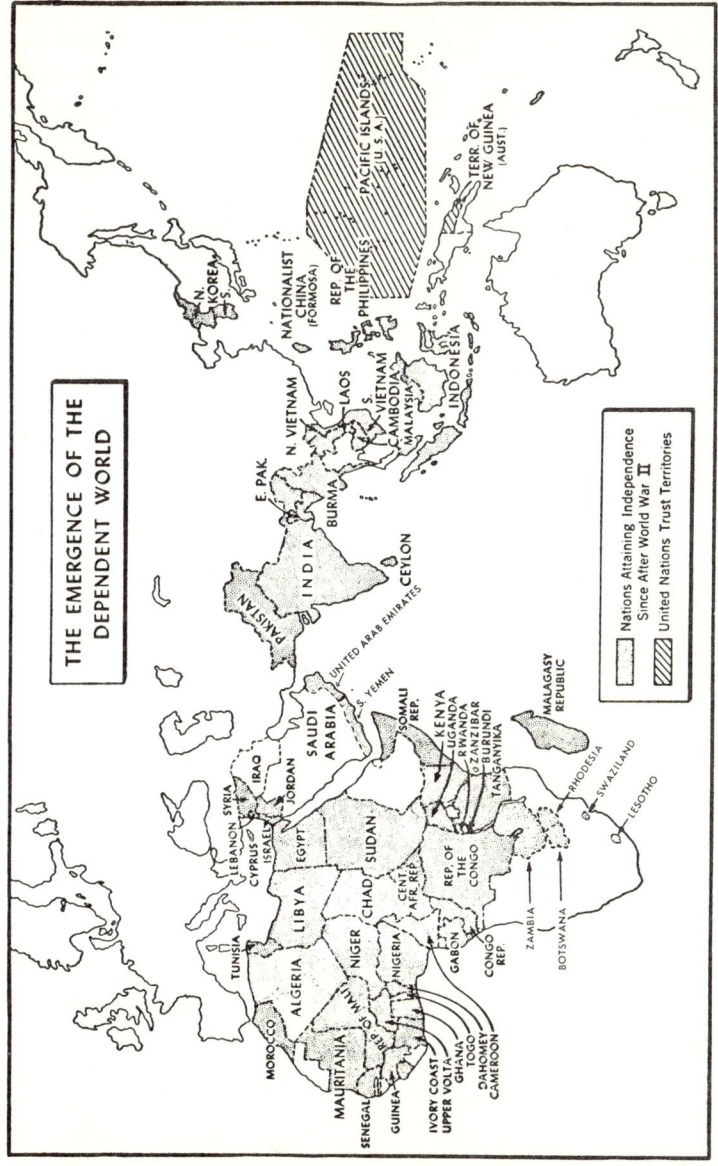

Most of Britain's Caribbean possessions and British Guyana have also attained independence, still qualified in the case of the former. The scattered remnants of European empires still under colonial rule are striving to achieve the same status.

states have emerged, Ghana (the former Gold Coast), Nigeria, several East African states, and many others, some of them of diminutive dimensions, most of them retaining the link with the Commonwealth, whose representatives have periodically met in London. In this representation the majority is no longer white. One particular aspect of the process of imperial devolution has been the British attempt to create large units in the form of federations. These have generally failed, as shown by the examples of East Africa, the Rhodesias, and the Caribbean; even unitary Nigeria, held for a time as a model, has had a civil war. A final measure of the process of imperial retreat may be seen in the announced decision to withdraw British forces from East of Suez by 1971.

2. *The French Case.* The French approach to empire has stood in contrast with the British, characterized by strong centralistic and integrating tendencies. The attempt of the Fourth Republic to organize a French Union, giving colonial peoples representation in the French parliament, was not a success. A number of individual Africans for example have indeed been turned into authentic Frenchmen, but the injection of French egalitarian ideas has also backfired into a demand for independence.

The failure to make timely concessions in Indochina led to a rebellion under the leadership of Ho Chi Minh. The war was unpopular in France and the leadership of Paris was confused, until the episode of Dien Bien Phu presaged the end. A new government, led by the energetic Mendès-France, liquidated the East Asian situation in the spring of 1954: Vietnam, on the Korean model, was divided into two parts along the 16th parallel, while Laos and Cambodia achieved full independence. [27]

It was the same Mendès-France who laid the bases for the relinquishment of Tunisia and Morocco, finally sanctioned in 1956. This was relatively easier owing to the fact that both were formally protectorates. But the intervening North African section, Algeria, proved far less tractable. Constitutionally, Algeria was an integral part of France and some 10 percent of its population was European. France was unable to put

---

[27] The United States, in perhaps not dissimilarly bungling fashion, eventually involved itself in the succession of the French position in Vietnam.

down the rebellion in Algeria; the unorthodox war that resulted, a protracted and dismal operation, eventually had repercussions in France herself, where it led to the downfall of the Fourth Republic in 1958.

Under the leadership of de Gaulle, its successor, the Fifth, finally relinquished Algeria, although it took four more years of difficult negotiations to accomplish that end. De Gaulle, meanwhile, had launched the process of decolonization with a vengeance. In connection with the adoption of a new constitution in France, her remaining possessions, mainly in sub-Saharan Africa, were given the option of total independence or of retaining, within independence, some connection, economic and cultural, with France. Most of them—Guinea was an exception—elected the second course, which has insured them very substantial assistance. France is the country which, in proportionate terms, has made the largest contribution to the underdeveloped world, most of her aid being directed to her former possessions. Though not neglecting economic, the French have placed great stress on the factor of language and culture. This policy may be regarded as one of intelligent adaptation to the transformation of empire, neo-colonialism in a different language. The ultimate outcome is uncertain, and France, like Britain, still retains some shreds and tatters of empire over which direct control is exercised.

3. Others. Like French Indochina, the Dutch East Indies were overrun by the Japanese during the second World War. The efficient but paternalistic rule of the Dutch could not be re-established. Faced with native rebellion and under outside prodding, American for one, after some attempts at constitutional reorganization, the Dutch had to accept total eviction. Indonesia emerged as a fully independent state of more than 100,000,000 people.

Unlike the Dutch, the Belgian empire, the Congo, was a recent creation; moreover, very primitive conditions prevailed in that large region, where also a paternalistic policy had been adopted. But even the primitive Congo could not remain immune to the prevailing winds of change. With considerable precipitancy the Congo achieved independence on July 1, 1960. The immediate consequence was chaos, a mutinous army, and secessionist tendencies, of which that of Katanga, a region of important mining (copper) wealth, under the able leadership of Moise Tshombe, was the most stubborn. The government appealed for assistance to the United Nations, of which the Congo was a member. Various countries contributed contingents, while the Congo became a bone of contention between rival great power influences. The American financial contribution to the United Nations operation was large, while others, mainly the Soviet Union and France, pointedly refused to assist in an operation of which they disapproved. By the end of 1963 a measure of unity and order, though fragile, had been restored to the Congo.

Spain and Portugal had initially led on the road to empire though they were little active in the late nineteenth-century competition. Interestingly, they seemed to retain their possessions longer than others. Following the French withdrawal from Morocco, Spain relinquished her own Moroccan holdings and seems to have embarked on the final relinquishment of what little remains in her control. Portugal has more stubbornly clung to her own though faced with latent rebellion in Angola and Mozambique, regions in which the proximity of the South African and the Rhodesian states are complicating factors.

4. *The Troubled Middle East.* This region deserves special attention. The demise of the Ottoman Empire as a consequence of the first World War opened the door to two developments: the reorganization and revival of the Turkish state was one; uncertain possibilities in the Arab world was the other. Apart from the fact that the latter presents a very broad range of diversity in the degree of its development, ranging from the fairly modern to the feudal, it also contains the divergent tendencies of distinct and rival centers of power and of unitary yearnings. Arab unity, mainly based on religion and culture, is largely a myth, in some ways comparable to the non-existent unity of Christendom; in considerable measure it is a negative emotion, fed by the factor of opposition to outside influence or control.

Throughout the Arab world the desire for independence has asserted itself and the second World War gave it an additional boost. The French lost their Syrian and Lebanese mandates, while Egypt increasingly loosened her British connection. The emancipation of French North Africa has been mentioned, and

Libya, lost to Italy, also achieved independence after a period of trusteeship. In their gropings toward modernity, the Arab states have been beset by the usual struggle between the new and the ways of the past and their record has been one of high political instability.

Finally, despite its formal independence, the fact that the Arab world contains enormous oil resources has made it a continuing focus of outside interests, among which the American has been increasingly significant. The Russian interest in the region is old, primarily political, with the consequence that the Middle East has become one of the sensitive foci of Russo-American competition.

Into this complex situation the conjunction of the Zionist drive and of the German wartime performance in regard to the Jews introduced an additional complication. The outcome of it was the creation, in 1947, through a United Nations decision, of the state of Israel. From the Arab standpoint this was but a modified version of the old imperial activity; why should they be made to provide alleviation for Christian wickedness and folly? The Jewish hope is equally understandable. How to reconcile the two is the problem.

The immediate result was war, in which the Arabs were worsted, and the state of Israel was confirmed, essentially a modern western state, highly efficient and progressive, but endowed with absurd boundaries. The unresolved dilemma exploded in the following decade into the war and the above-mentioned Suez episode. The match between 50,000,000 Arabs, spread over vast territories, and 2,000,000 Israelis cramped in an exiguous area may seem highly uneven. The condition finds adequate expression in the observation that the Arabs can afford to loose any number of wars but that the loss of a single one would settle Israel's fate. The irreconcilable dilemma exploded into open hostilities once more in 1967. The six-day war was a brilliant Israeli performance, admiration for which, at the technical level at least, could hardly be withheld. But it brought an accommodation no nearer.

The Arab states, Egypt most of all, have striven to exploit the rivalry between the greater powers and secured what assistance they could from any of them. More recently, the Soviet Union has tended to support the Arabs, Israel putting her reliance on the United States. The two superpowers, the British and the French to a lesser degree, have striven to maintain their influence, the most dangerous form of this effort being the supply of arms to one side or the other, or both, though there have been some signs of awareness on the part of the greater powers of the danger implicit in such tactics. Some have envisaged the possibility of a settlement imposed by the great powers, in the manner of Concert of Europe decisions of earlier days, a prospect of limited possibilities in the face of the irreconcilability of the prime movers.

5. Some Consequences of the Devolution of Empire. The emergence to independence of a host of new entities may be regarded as a manifestation of the nationalistic force, exported from its initial European home to the rest of the world. Certainly the trend of the times favors the cry for freedom, arguments against which appear difficult to sustain. Yet the removal of even legitimate grievances has raised as many questions as it has solved.

For one thing, the emergence of the national entities of Europe has been the result of a long historic evolution, as has likewise been the development of governmental institutions. Many of the new states, especially in Africa, are wholly synthetic creations, legacies of colonial administrative arrangements that bring together disparate groups or cut across existing affinities. It is a case of the state preceding the nation. In a number of instances only very small numbers are involved, even when the state is territorially extensive; economic viability sometimes remains an open question and backwardness of development is the norm.

The tendency of the new states has been to copy the political institutions of their former masters while rejecting their rule. But the trappings of representative institutions, in the lack of adequate roots, has often resulted in a travesty. Military coups have been frequent, often the work of high-minded, if inexperienced, men. Assistance from the outside, foreign aid, has been an important factor in the economy of the new states, at once desired and a source of suspicion, and it has become apparent that the mere injection of money was a poor substitute for local competence, even in many instances but an added source of corruption.

This has not prevented the new states from seeking to play a role on the world scene. Their desire to escape involvement in the quarrels of the greater powers is both legitimate and understandable, but their attempts at creating some sort of united front, a Third force, have met with little success. The Bandung conference in 1955 could produce unity in condemning imperialism, but that cry has become in the nature of beating a dead horse. Also, the new states have tended to conform to the normal behavior of states. Among them there are differences, conflicting claims and rivalries, not to say tendencies that can only be described as imperialistic. The pretended brotherhood of India and China has been sorely tested, the issue of Kashmir between India and Pakistan has proved as intractable as that of Alsace between Germany and France. The manner in which India took possession of Portuguese Goa, however much rationalized, can hardly be described as other than aggression. Examples could be multiplied.

Most of the new states have achieved membership in the United Nations. The consequences have not been of the best, emphasizing the distinction between words and the reality of power, with the absence of which often goes a lack of responsibility. The five great, or so-called great, powers may resort to the veto in the Security Council, but Israel has disregarded well-nigh unanimous Assembly resolutions; Israel, not without justification, puts no trust in resolutions, nor even for that matter in great power promises. Overwhelming condemnation of South Africa and Rhodesia has proved equally ineffectual. The proliferation of membership in the United Nations has been in the nature of a logical *reductio ad absurdum* which has served to impede rather than enhance the primary and fundamental purpose of the institution.

It has been easy for the Soviet Union to endorse so-called "wars of liberation," but the position of the United States has been quite difficult. From its own origins in anti-British rebellion, the United States has tended to be sympathetic to any claim for emancipation. To say nothing of the fact that this has put it in an embarrassing position vis-à-vis its foremost allies—the British and the French, who also happened to be the chief imperial powers—the realities of the situation, the consequences of independence, have increasingly been brought home.

The Congo was an enlightening experience and Vietnam a calamity; in both instances, in the latter especially, priority has been given to the national interest, interpreted rightly or wrongly as the necessity to block Communist expansion.

As to the European states, with the possible exception of Britain, the loss of empire has rather been for them an advantage. Certainly the French wars in Indochina and Algeria were no enhancement of the French position of power, and with France as with others the loss of world mastery has coincided with a remarkable resurgence. We shall close this survey with some consideration of the most recent developments in Europe, in free Europe particularly, since something has already been said of the situation in the Soviet bloc.

C. The Resurgence and the Reassertion of Europe

We may consider first the more important developments in the various countries of Europe, then turn to some considerations which have broader application.

1. *The Individual Countries of Europe*

a. THE UNITED KINGDOM. The Conservatives ruled Britain during the fifties, confronted with the same basic and related problems with which any British government must deal: establishing the bases of a functioning economy, finding Britain's proper place in the world. The urbane Anthony Eden took over Churchill's succession upon the latter's final retirement in 1955. As a consequence of the Suez fiasco, and of poor health, he was replaced in turn by Harold Macmillan in 1957.

The economy seemed to thrive for a while, but the slogan "you never had it so good" was misleading, for all that the Conservatives were endorsed by a larger majority in 1959. The fundamental problem remained that of "catching up" with a world that was progressing faster than Britain, the discrepancy being well illustrated by Britain's smaller rate of growth. [28] The sharpest manifestation of Britain's difficulty was the deficit in her balance of trade and in the dilemma of the allocation of

---

[28] The figures of average increase in per capita productivity during the decade 1955-1964 are as follows: Britain 2.3 percent, France 4.7, West Germany 4.8, Italy 5.8.

In 1972 a treaty was signed in Brussels which looks to the admission of the United Kingdom, Ireland, Norway and Denmark to the Common Market community.

resources. The too expensive production of missiles was abandoned, American Polaris missiles taking their place. In her search for position Britain had looked to the empire, to the "special connection" with the United States, to Europe as a last resort. Despite words of encouragement for European unity of some sort, Britain clung to her separateness and took a highly sceptical view of the Common Market. It was only as a last choice that, having turned down the initial opportunity to join that combination, Britain applied for membership in it in 1961. She met a sharp rebuff from France in 1963, after long negotiations, and under Lord Home, who had succeeded Macmillan later in the year, her economic difficulties grew no less. Labour was returned to office in 1964 with a bare margin of four under the leadership of Harold Wilson. The majority became 97 in 1966, but Labour found the problems of the national economy no more tractable than had its adversaries. The policies adopted to redress the balance of trade have been of the same kind in both cases, leading to discontent among the following of Labour. The pound was threatened, Britain found herself repeatedly in need of outside financial assistance, and the currency was finally devalued by 14 percent in November 1967. A renewed application for membership in the Common Market led to another French rebuff, even if less sharp than in 1963, and the search for an elusive equilibrium has continued, to the accompaniment of a domestic mood of combined complacency and passivity. [29]

b. <u>THE FIFTH FRENCH REPUBLIC.</u> The Fourth French Republic jogged along, a picture of political instability on the surface, less ostensibly laying the bases of reconstruction. [30] But it finally met its fate over the imperial problem, more specifically the war in Algeria; in the spring of 1958 France was on the verge of civil war. By general consent, General de Gaulle was seen as the only possible savior of the situation. He became Prime Minister in June, 1958, received a grant of power from parliament, and a new constitution was enacted with overwhelming popular endorsement. Thus the Fifth Republic was born, the Fourth, like the Third, having quietly abdicated—or committed suicide. Apart from the immediate issue of Algeria, the more fundamental problem that France faced was the same as it has been since the Great Revolution, the location and the distribution of power in the society. For nearly two centuries crises have repeatedly brought strong men to the fore, who in turn have been subsequently rejected; the fear of the dictator is deeply rooted in the French body politic.

Broadly speaking, the new French constitution bore some resemblance to the American, characterized by a division of

---

[29] The contention that the economic policies of the Labour government were bearing fruit was not verified while that government lasted.

[30] See above, pp. 293-94.

powers. Whether this would introduce stability, or open the door to abuse on the part of the executive as on earlier occasions, time alone could tell. The imperial problem was settled in the manner that has been indicated. For the rest, a 20 percent devaluation of the franc proved to be a judicious measure which initiated the introduction of order in the financial domain and assisted the competitive position of the French economy, at least for some years. General de Gaulle was undoubtedly a strong personality, one of the outstanding figures of our time; he has, not inappropriately, been characterized as an unusual combination of the eighteenth and the twenty-first centuries. His wartime record bore witness to his patriotism and his courage; believing in the national state as the solid reality of our day, he tended to scorn humanitarian vaporings and international institutions. Himself an aristocrat, an odd combination of romanticism and cold calculation, he could play politics with the best and excelled at turning his high-handed cantankerousness into an asset, both at home and vis-à-vis the outside.

For a decade, until defeated in a referendum in May, 1969, he ruled with a strong hand, although, despite certain abuses, France remained a free country. She enjoyed stability and sound finances, while the seeds of economic progress planted under the Fourth Republic bore fruit. As a consequence, French stock rose in the world, a result to which de Gaulle attached the highest importance. There was no aggressive nationalism in France, but the exaltation of the national value had the effect of putting a brake on the movement for European integration, at the political level at least, though at the economic the Common Market continued to prosper.

One particular aspect of Gaullist policy was its handling of the German problem. Interestingly enough, the second World War did not leave the same legacy of rancor as the first, but rather a tendency toward reconciliation between the long-time foes. Immediately after the war, de Gaulle had taken the traditional French view in regard to the curbing of German power, favoring the fragmentation of Germany. After his return to power, he did not seek to undo the work of the Fourth Republic, but instead endeavored to improve upon it. Meeting a congenial response from Chancellor Adenauer, he extended to Germany, especially in 1962, the hand of friendship and forgetfulness. The treaty of friendship, rather too hastily drawn up in 1963, did not however bring all the fruits that were expected of it.

Under such a regime domestic policies were given second place. The parliamentary election of October, 1962, following the appointment of Georges Pompidou to the Prime Ministership and a dissolution of the Assembly, gave the Gaullists a clear majority, an unprecedented situation in France. In 1965 de Gaulle was re-elected to the Presidency of the country, though only on a second ballot. The very success of the regime and the facts of stability and prosperity gave a fillip to critics of de Gaulle's olympian ways, but the divisions of the Left made its opposition ineffectual. Finally, in May, 1968, starting with student troubles, a mass strike developed in the country. The situation for a moment seemed to be out of control and to contain revolutionary possibilities. It was handled with supple determination by Pompidou, who was shortly thereafter dismissed.

In May, 1969, over yet another referendum,[31] de Gaulle met a setback, whereupon he resigned. In the presidential election of June, Pompidou was elected, again on a second ballot, and to a point owing to Communist abstention, perhaps justifying the judgment that the French people want Gaullism without de Gaulle. At the age of 78, though still quite vigorous, General de Gaulle could hardly be expected to return to power though he continued to cast a long shadow over the politics of France. He went into retirement while the French people decided whether the constitution of the Fifth Republic has finally succeeded in making them a governable people.[32]

c. MID-EUROPE. The Italian scene after the passing of de Gasperi bore resemblance to that of the Fourth French Republic: political instability combined with economic progress. The Christian Democrats continued to dominate the scene but were torn by internal dissensions, depending on unstable coalitions with smaller parties to the Right or the Left of themselves. A shift in the former direction after 1957 was followed by one in the opposite under Amintore Fanfani.

---

[31] It advocated a reorganization of the country on a regional basis, but combined this with a proposal for the virtual abolition of the Senate.

[32] The economy began to deteriorate around 1966. The events of 1968 greatly accentuated these difficulties.

The Socialists had tended to work closely with the Communists, but the Hungarian episode in 1956 created strains in that alliance. The advent to the Papacy of Pope John XXIII aided the liberal tendency within the Christian Democratic group where there was increasing talk of an "opening to the Left." This was finally realized in 1963 when some Socialists entered the government, among then the veteran Pietro Nenni. It was an uneasy coalition, and one of its effects was to increase the appeal of the Communists among the electorate. The coalition was broken, renewed, and broken again, its vicissitudes being paralleled by those of the Socialist factions.

As to the Communists, though outside the government, they have become increasingly integrated into the political life of the country and have been in control of numerous local administrations. Their able leader, Palmiro Togliatti, displayed both skill and moderation; after his passing in 1964, the tendency continued to assert increasing independence from the dictates and policies of Moscow, in the Czechoslovak episode of 1968 for example. In many respects, the Italian Communists, like the French, have striven to create the impression of being a party of order. Certainly a large part of their following and not a little of their leadership has placed increasing emphasis on concrete and specific workers' grievances in place of revolutionary zeal. This was notably the case in France during the events of May-June, 1968, when stress was marked between the more enthusiastic student leadership and the sober one of the Communist party. Yet the fear of Communism dies hard among many bourgeois; the instability of Italian politics has led some to fear, while others hope for, the return of strong government, especially as the memory of the Fascist experiment becomes attenuated.

The German Christian Democratic party has shown greater cohesion than the Italian, and so has German Social Democracy, making German politics correspondingly more stable. In the election of 1957 the Christian Democrats achieved an absolute majority of the popular vote, 50.2 percent, and in the Bundestag they had 270 out of 497 members. The German Social Democrats firmly set their face against Communism and have been staunch adherents of the Bernsteinian reformist tendency. The authoritarian and high-handed manner of Chancellor Adenauer antagonized even some of his own following, and the Christian Democrats lost ground in the 1961 election. Adenauer finally resigned in 1963, but made little attempt to conceal his dislike of his successor, Ludwig Erhard, chief architect of the Germany economic "miracle."

Despite the latter's success in the election of 1965, mounting criticism led to his resignation the following year and to the accession of the smoother Kurt-Georg Kiesinger; under his Chancellorship a grand coalition of Christian and Social Democrats was achieved, the foreign office post going to Willy Brandt, the leader of the latter. [33]

Passing and temporary setbacks have barely halted the progress of the German economy, which has been plagued by the problem of an enormously large favorable balance of trade. The German mark has been in great demand and Germany only with difficulty resisted pressure by some other countries —the United States, Britain, and France in particular—for an upward revision of its value in 1968. This finally occurred in October, 1969.

Germany, too, has been faced by the problem of finding her place in the world. She still labors under certain disabilities— the ban on nuclear weapons for example—legacies of the Nazi performance, the memory of which lingers outside of Germany, with the consequence that she has not carried political weight commensurate with her economic. Adenauer played the French card, while Erhard favored the American, and Franco-American differences during the Gaullist period created for Germany an impossible dilemma. West Germany has claimed to be the sole representative of all Germans, denying the legitimacy of the German Democratic Republic. But hopes of reunification, if not abandoned, have been put off to the Greek kalends, and the Hallstein doctrine [34] has been tacitly ignored. The question whether or not all the German people

---

[33] The election of October, 1969 resulted in a gain for the Social Democrats although the Christian Democrats remained the largest party. The small Free Democratic party, despite substantial losses, was put in an arbitral position and a government was organized on the basis of a coalition between it and the Social Democrats, whose leader, Willy Brandt, became Chancellor.

[34] The refusal to have dealings with states that would grant recognition to the German Democratic Republic.

are to be under one single state or several, one of the major issues of nineteenth-century European politics, still remains unresolved. Rumblings of neo-Nazi revival, as of neo-Fascist in Italy, tend to alarm good domestic democrats and all outsiders, in the German case especially, but such revival has so far not been very significant.

2. Broad Tendencies and Common Problems

a. THE ISSUE OF EUROPEAN INTEGRATION. The recovery of the states of Europe has exceeded all expectations. Yet the fact of their demotion remains, and the problem for them, till yesterday great powers, important still but unquestionably of second rank, is the common one of finding their place. The ancient quarrels of Europe, the Franco-German for example, have lost much of their sting. The nationalistic virus has lost much of its strength in the lands of its origin, its manifestations far more vigorous elsewhere.

Even in the days of the aberrant vagaries of European nationalisms the sense of community of culture and purpose had never wholly died. In the face of the rise of the two superpowers, European unity might provide an answer for all to the question of their place in the world. Europe outside the Soviet sphere still contains after all, next to America, the greatest reservoir of wealth, human resources and skills. The very fact of common defeat might have been an opportunity to be seized by the forelock. Britain, injured but possessed of the prestige of victory, was the one state in a position to assert leadership in such an imaginative undertaking. But her insular tradition proved too strong for her to overcome.

The above-mentioned initiative that was the European Coal and Steel Community (ECSC) was of more modest scope. Yet it was also an attempt to assert French leadership—at its best. Continued economic growth during the fifties made possible the taking of another step; the Treaty of Rome, which came into effect on January 1, 1958, created the European Economic Community. Six states, France, West Germany, Italy, and the Benelux countries, joined in the commitment to do away with tariff barriers among themselves. The comparison inevitably comes to mind with the role played by the nineteenth-century *Zollverein* in the Germanic world.

The combination of the six, Little Europe, is also reminiscent of Charlemagne's empire. The British reaction of almost sneering scepticism was regrettable, especially in the light of the subsequent success of the EEC. The British answer that was EFTA, seven peripheral countries [35] joined in a free-trade association, was a pale copy of the EEC. The creators of the latter were fully awake to the political implications of their action, wisely electing to proceed in gradual fashion. Thus two questions arose: the further development of the combination of the Six, in political terms especially, was one, the relations between the EEC and EFTA was the other; the fusion of the two groups would indeed make Europe, a free western Europe at least. The key to the situation was obviously Britain, but the peculiar problems of the British economy put her in the disadvantageous position of a demandant when she turned to the Common Market as a last resort. The result was the above-mentioned French veto.

b. THE AMERICANIZATION OF EUROPE. This touches on another problem. One ostensible reason for that veto was General de Gaulle's contention that Britain was not sufficiently European, that her clinging to the American connection cast her in the role of Trojan horse of American influence. That influence, first American aid and the shield of American power above all, had been universally welcome in free Europe immediately after the war. But with recovery, with the reversal of the problem of the dollar gap, with the penetration of American capital giving rise in some quarters to the cry of American colonization of Europe, American power and influence also came to be increasingly resented. The feeling has been widespread in Europe, even if de Gaulle elected to give sharpest expression and unnecessarily obnoxious form to the wish for independence.

In the more restricted but vital military domain the ambiguity arose of the continuing desire for the protection of American nuclear power on the one hand, and the suspicion of the possibility of Russo-American accommodation on the other. In simplest form, could America be depended upon to risk the wiping out of New York for the sake of saving London or

---

[35] The United Kingdom, the Scandinavian countries, Switzerland, Austria, and Portugal.

Paris from a similar fate? States are states after all, for all of whom the national interest properly has first priority.[36] These uncertainties were reflected in the discussions centering around the fate, or the reorganization, of NATO. Here again de Gaulle's France took the most extreme position, severely curtailing her participation in the alliance, quitting NATO, while simultaneously developing her own policy of rapprochement with the U.S.S.R.

In these developments one may see a proper reflection of undoubtedly changing circumstances, but their fluidity also gave rise to confusion. France alone obviously does not have the power to perform a balancing act between the U.S. and the U.S.S.R.; united Europe might. French leadership in the accomplishment of European unity could be acceptable to others, the suspicion of a desire for dominance was not, and the pronouncements of the French President, not least the style of them, were well designed to nurture such suspicions. Hence the British plight and the above-mentioned German dilemma. To a degree one may speak of a revival, even if in attenuated form, of a long existing competition among the three leading states of Western Europe. Yet in the competition for primacy among Britain, France and Germany, or in the possible dominance of a combination of two out of the three, the prospect of open conflict remains highly improbable. The future alone can disclose the fate of European integration, the hopes for which have undoubtedly suffered a setback.

In Europe as elsewhere the prevailing *zeitgeist* has been fast changing. Affluence, most marked in the societies bordering on the North Atlantic, has brought with it an increasing awareness that it is not alone the ultimate answer to man's quest. Elsewhere as well, in the Soviet domain for example, the growing complexity of existence has given increasing importance to the operation of technology and correspondingly devalued the significance of political action and dogma. Nowhere is this better reflected than in the restlessness of the young, whose often negative and unfocused agitation yet expresses with adequacy a profound and not illegitimate discontent.

Europe has been the home of Christianity, and for all the

---

[36] European doubts about the dependability of America's purpose have been matched by American dissatisfaction at the unwillingness of European countries to assume their proper share of the burden of defense.

warranted talk about the de-Christianization of the Christian world, the influence of the Christian ethos remains strong. But the impact of change could not leave the churches unaffected. To many, the sectarian divisions of Christendom have taken on the color of a superseded legacy of the past, petty differences in contrast with which the broad grounds of agreement have the greater significance. The ecumenical movement has had wide attraction. Some Protestant sects have shown a tendency to merge and even the more rigid and hierarchical Catholic Church has responded, especially under the guidance of Pope John XXIII (1958-1963); the second Vatican Council gave rise to hopes that may have been premature. His successor Paul VI has been more cautious. It would be rash to expect that the burden of centuries of dissension, strife, and mutual suspicion can be shed in a day. Even between Christians, Catholics especially, and Communists, supposedly irreconcilable enemies, a most interesting dialogue has been adumbrated. The world is changing fast; a technology that evolves at a fantastically accelerating rate, operating in the context of a slow-changing human condition, creates stresses with explosive possibilities.

All the while the "Americanization" of Europe has been proceeding apace, a tendency criticized and bemoaned by many Europeans. But this is little more than nostalgia, regret for an irrecoverable past. For the Americanization of Europe means little more than its modernization; the simple fact is that the United States, in part owing to Europe's suicidal course, has been cast in the role of leadership in the ways, desirable or infamous as they may be, of the modern world. For all its overwhelming weight and influence America has not by deliberate plan sought to impose its ways on others; the imitation of them is overwhelmingly their own choice.

3. The Turn of the Decade.

Mention has been made of the events of 1968 in France. They were expression of an unrest that in many of its aspects was world wide. From San Francisco to Tokyo, by way of New York, Paris and Rome, the young gave vent to their dissatisfaction. Lacking adequate organization and a thought out program of action, they accomplished little that was concrete.

In the French case in particular, the students and the striking workers gave a severe jolt to the regime; as also mentioned,

General de Gaulle quit power in 1969.[37] The system of the Fifth Republic was not changed, but his work—the restoration of internal order and of the French position abroad—had been done. The more grandiose aspect of his purpose had proved to be utopian in the face of the concrete reality of French resources and power. His successor, Georges Pompidou, adopted a more supple stance and even the franc was devalued once more.

One consequence of this change was its impact on the British situation. Misjudging the augurs—the polls—Prime Minister Wilson called a general election in June 1970. It resulted in a Conservative victory and his replacement in office by Edward Heath. It was he who had conducted the initial negotiations for Britain's accession to the Common Market, almost a decade before. He had not lost his faith in the desirability of a Europe larger than that of the Six and returned to the charge. His efforts eventually bore fruit, and after lengthy negotiations the treaty was signed in Brussels in January, 1972 that sanctioned Britain's admission to the EEC. Not only Britain, but Ireland, Norway and Denmark also signed the treaty. It is worth noting that, in the British case, the outcome was accompanied by a widespread attitude of resigned acceptance of the inevitable rather than by a positive reaction of enthusiasm.[38] If the four join the six, the new Europe of the Ten will doubtless wear a different complexion and the possibility exists of resuming the initial impulse that had motivated the launchers of the European movement.

The new British government was confronted with the same problem as its predecessor, mainly that of the state of the economy, struggling with the classically unorthodox phenomenon of inflation combined with rising unemployment. Britain has also been troubled by a resurgence of the Irish problem. The situation in Ulster has been reminiscent in some of its manifestations of that immediately before the first World War, the sparking factor being now the grievances of the Catholic minority in Ulster. Rhodesia had quit the Commonwealth and had been subjected to economic sanctions. As usual, these

---

[37] He died in 1970, leaving his memoirs incomplete.

[38] The problem remains of enacting the necessary domestic legislation and it is of interest that the leader of the Labour Party has reversed his own earlier attitude while in office to one of opposition.

proved little more than an ineffectual inconvenience, and discussions dragged on between its regime and the British government in an attempt to regularize relations.

Needless to say, the Soviet Union regarded the enlargement of the European community with an unfriendly eye. The range of its own commitments, the Far Eastern situation in particular, caused it to favor stability on its western, European flank; but the prospect of a European security conference met with a qualified response at best. This condition lay at the root of the discussions with the United States, the SALT talks, which proceeded at a leisurely pace in Helsinki and Vienna. The German situation remained of paramount importance in this connection, and the regime of Chancellor Willy Brandt showed signs of adopting an increasingly supple attitude. This took the form of a willingness to acknowledge the validity of the Oder-Neisse frontier and of establishing closer relations with the Soviet Union and its European satellites. Agreements were concluded with Poland, and even with the German Democratic Republic. After the resignation of the intransigent Walter Ulbrecht, exchanges pointed in the direction of mutual recognition and the prospect could be entertained of both Germanys becoming members of the United Nations.

This relaxation of tensions between the Federal Republic and the countries of eastern Europe, West Germany's *Ostpolitik*, raised an important question. It could be interpreted as paralleling the American and Russian desires for normalization and stabilization of their mutual relations. It also contained the possibility that in the negotiating process the United States and Germany—free Europe for that matter—might each undercut the bargaining position of the other. Hence there was a degree of reciprocal suspicion while repeated professions of loyalty to the Atlantic alliance were expressed by both.

Italian politics have been more confused and unstable than ever, complicated by the enactment of a divorce law. This condition was reflected in the difficult and protracted process of electing a president for the country in 1971 to succeed the socialist Saragat.

Italy, like Germany, witnessed a slowing down of her rate of economic growth. This problem has been very acute in the United States as well. The United States also experienced a very large unfavorable balance of payments, even on purely trade account. Speculation on gold and the dollar resumed until, in August 1971, President Nixon took a sharp initiative that amounted to a renunciation of the oft repeated American stand in monetary matters. As in 1933 the dollar would be detached from gold while a ten percent tax was imposed on imports and domestic economic controls were introduced. The manner, judged by many unnecessarily brutal, yet had the effect of bursting an abscess. Moreover, whatever American economic difficulties might be, the American place in the economy of the whole world remains too large for anyone to ignore its impact. Negotiations, difficult at times, by the end 1971 led to a lifting of the American import surcharge in connection with an agreement to devalue the dollar and a realignment of currencies. [39]

This American reversal in the domain of economics was, however, no more startling than another in the political, the announcement that the American President would visit Peking in 1972. It took the world by surprise, especially in view of President Nixon's earlier pronouncement; here was an example of unusual flexibility at the very least.

The consequences of this changed American position were both considerable and numerous, not the least of them being the very awkward position in which it put Japan. Clearly the American opposition to the admission of Red China to the United Nations could no longer be sustained. Indeed Red China was admitted amid general rejoicing in November 1971, while Chiang Kai-shek's Taiwan was unceremoniously evicted. [40] In the world as a whole the new American stand was generally welcome as a belated and overdue acknowledgment of reality. What it signified most of all was an opening of new possibilities, the Big Two becoming the Big Three,

---

[39] The American action was mainly directed at Germany and Japan, whose currencies were judged to be especially undervalued. Japan's economic expansion has been altogether remarkable, making her the third industrial power in the world.

[40] That Taiwan is part of China was about the only point of agreement between the rival regimes of Mao Tse-tung and Chiang Kai-shek. In the circumstances, the two-China proposal—membership in the United Nations for both mainland China and Formosa—even though formally supported by the United States, had little chance of adoption. In theory, Chinese membership in the United Nations has simply continued, but with a different representation, a position that raises some fine points of international law.

even if China has a long distance to travel before her potential is translated into effective power comparable with that of Russia and the United States.

The Russians had no choice but to put a good face on the event, but it was not long before what had been hitherto intra-Communist party quarrels were elevated to full international status. The occasion was immediately at hand. Differences between the two widely separated portions of Pakistan led to an attempt by the government to coerce the eastern section, East Bengal, by armed force. This led in turn to the claim to full independence on the part of the latter, while millions of refugees, in appalling conditions of misery, poured into India. Was this a domestic or an international problem? In the face of the impotence of the United Nations and of the inaction of the great powers, it came to war between India and Pakistan. A mere two weeks sufficed to settle the issue and in the outcome a new nation, Bangladesh, was born.

But the episode had wider international repercussions, for the Soviet Union supported India while China favored Pakistan. In the forum of the United Nations the world was treated to the spectacle of two Communist states indulging vis-à-vis each other in unrestrained accusations and the use of the veto in blocking contrary resolutions. The United States was embarrassed, having at an earlier stage sought to build up India as a counterweight to China in Asia, yet at the same time pursued a friendly policy toward Pakistan, the hinge between SEATO and CENTO. Momentarily at least, the United States and China found themselves in the same camp. The final outcome, India's victory and the emergence of Bangladesh, inevitably constituted a success for the Soviet Union and a corresponding setback for its opponents.

All this is a long way from Europe whose role in the affair was indeed minimal, and it confirms the passing of the European Age. The sensitive foci of conflict in the present world are to be found primarily in Asia, be it the Middle East, the Indian subcontinent, or Southeast Asia. The United States has been going through the process of reexamining the range of its commitments in the light of its power, which to be sure is great but not unlimited. Thus we are faced with a state of affairs which, on a world wide scale, is reminiscent of the earlier European. As there were before 1939, there are now three main centers of power, the United States, the USSR, and China. The same possibilities of dual combinations exist, which each of the three fears, suspects, and seeks to prevent. But the current state of military technology is altogether different from what it was thirty years ago. Yet it may also be observed that the state system, originally a European creation, has survived; the Communist ideology, like the earlier one of the French Revolution, has been absorbed by, or succumbed to, the vitality of the national factor.

Only in union can the former great powers of Europe other than the Soviet Union hope to join the club of the present day great. What matters above all in regard to the future of Europe is the relationship among the three chief centers of powers in it, what might be called the North Sea triangle, Britain, France and Germany. Britain is still uncertain and groping, France has made a striking recovery and is striving to insert herself into the modern world of the twentieth century. Germany, even the Federal Republic alone, carries the greatest economic weight of all; she has been knocking at the gates of recognition, but has given indication of understanding that the weight of her past can only be gradually overcome. The present and future relations among the European powers, formerly great and formerly small, are a continuation of their former record. But they operate in a novel context: the present state of technology; the intrusion of the Communist ideology, a diminishing influence; and the legacy of national differences. This last is a much attenuated factor, for the violent nineteenth-century nationalism of Europe has been effectively exported. The European Age is gone beyond recall, yet Europe remains full of a rich ferment of vitality and her role in the world is not finished.

INDEX

Abdul Hamid II, 116
Aberdeen, George, 21
Abyssinia, 96, 241-243
Adenauer, Konrad, 335
Adowa, battle of, 134, 140
Adrianople, Treaty of, 14
Aehrenthal, Alois von, 146
Africa, partition of, 131-134
Agadir Incident, 148
Aix-la-Chapelle, Congress of, 9
Albania, 119, 150, 185, 217, 255, 268, 279
Alexander, Tsar I, 5-7, 10, 18, 118
Alexander, Tsar II, 52-53, 109-110
Alexander, Tsar III, 110, 125
Alexander I, Serbia and Yugoslavia, 217, 239-241
Alfonso, King of Spain, 246
Algeciras, Conference of, 144-145, 147
Algeria, 126, 274
Algiers, 276
Alliances, French system of, 226; World War I, 125-127, 137-147
Alsace-Lorraine, 62, 101-102, 152, 181
Anschluss, 184, 215, 228, 250-252
Antisemitism, 93, 236
Anzio, landing of, 277
Armistice, World War I, 171; World War II, 277, 279-280
Arms Race, 318-321
Asia, imperialism in, 134-135
Asquith, Herbert, 199
Association Law, 93, 94
Atlantic Charter, 271
Ausgleich, 51-52, 77, 105
Australia, 89
Austria, (1815-1848), 4-6, 12; (1848-1852), 32-33, 35; (1852-1870), 47, 50-52; (1919-1930), 214-215; postwar, 178
Austria-Hungary, (1852-1870), 51-52; (1870-1914), 105-107, 213; (1930-1939), 237, 251; (1945-1952), 290-291; post-World War I, 184; revolution of 1848, 32-35
Austro-German alliance, 125
Austro-Prussian War, 50-52, 59
Austro-Sardinian War, 34, 47

Bach, Alexander, Baron von, 51
Badoglio, Pietro, 277
Baghdad Pact, 305
Baldwin, Stanley, 199, 239, 243
Balfour, Arthur J., 87; declaration, 169
Balkans, (1815-1848), 12; (1852-1870), 53-54; (1870-1914), 117-119; (1919-1930), 216-219; emancipation of, 116-117; revolts, 116-118; wars, 118-119, 149-150; World War I, 269-270
Baltic States, 220, 262
Bangladesh, 344
"Barbarossa," operation, 270
Barthou, Louis, 239-240
Belgian Congo, 99, 142; independence of, 325-326
Belgium, 98-99, 261; independence of, 16-17
Bentham, Jeremy, 26
Berlin, Colonial Conference of 1884-1885, 133; Congress of, 117, 124-126; Treaty of, 146, 192; Crisis, 318; Wall, 315
Berlin-Bagdad railway, 141, 152, 161
Bernadotte, Jean Baptiste, 7, 100
Bessarabia, 183, 268
Bethmann-Hollweg, Theobald von, 104
Bey, Enver, 116, 117
Bismarck, Prince Otto von, 48-51, 53, 59-64, 76, 91, 102-104, 121-128, 137-139
Björkö Episode, 144
Black Sea Convention, 63
Blanc, Louis, 30, 39
Blocs, France, 93

INDEX

Blum, Léon, 245
Boer War, 89, 133
Bohemia, 36, 217, 255
Bolsheviks, 169-170, 180, 205, 207, 250
Boris III, Bulgaria, 218
Bosnia-Herzegovina, 117, 124, 145-147, 185
Bosporus, strait, 12
Boulanger Episode, 92, 93
Bourgeoisie, 15, 29, 74, 94, 107, 245
Boxer Rebellion, 136
Brandt, Willy, 336, 342
Brest-Litovsk, Treaty of, 167-169, 206
Briand, Aristide, 224
British North America Act, 89
Brüning, Heinrich, 204
Bucharest, Treaty of, 150, 167-169
Bulgaria, 118-119, 124-125, 178, 218, 268, 278, 289
Bulge, battle of, 279
Bülow, Prince Bernard von, 104, 139-140, 143-144
Bundesrat, 101, 102
Byron, Lord, 13

Cairo Conference, 275
Cambon, Paul, 151
Campbell-Bannerman, Henry, 87
Canada, Dominion of, 55, 89
Canning, George, 11
Capitalism, 71
Caprivi, Count von, 104
Caporetto disaster, 166
Cape-to-Cairo railway, 133
Carbonari, 9, 31
Carlsbad Decrees, 8
Carol II, Roumania, 218
Casablanca, Conference of, 275, 276
Castlereagh, Robert Stewart, 5, 10-11
Catholic Center Party, 103, 204
Cavaignac, General, 31-32
Cavour, Camillo Benso di, 44, 46-49, 64, 96
Centrists, 104
Chamberlain, Joseph, 86-87, 139
Chamberlain, Neville, 250, 253, 256
Chambord, Count of, 91
Champollion, Jean Francois, 27
Charles Albert, 10, 34, 38
Charles I, Austria, 118, 215

Charles X, France, 14-15, 20
Chartists, 25
Chaumont, Treaty of 1814, 4
China, Japanese aggression in, 240-241; penetration of, 135-136
Christian Democratic Party, Italy, 294-295, 334
Christian IX, Denmark, 49, 100
Churchill, Winston, 263, 264, 266, 271, 292
Civil War, America, 58-59, 82
Clemenceau, Georges, 92, 174-176, 190
Clericalism, 92
Cobden, Richard, 23
Cold War, 291-307
Colonialism, 92, 135
Colonial movement, 129-130, 138
Combes, Emile, 94
Common Market, *see* European Economic Community
Commonwealth of Australia Act, 89
Commune, Paris, 91
Communism, 207-209, 233, 239, 245, 276, 285; in France, 286; in Italy, 286
Communist Manifesto, 39, 74
Comte, Auguste, 26, 27, 65
Concert of Europe, 9-10, 44, 120, 123, 150
Concordat of 1801, 94
Congo Free State, 99, 133, 316
Conservative Party, British, 25, 54, 85-87, 199, 200, 330, 341
Constantine I, Greece, 217
Cordon Sanitaire, 206, 207
Corfu Incident, 228
Corn Laws, 23, 25
Council for Economic Mutual Assistance (COMECON), 314
Couza, Prince Alexander, 53
Cretan rebellion, 54
Crete, 118
Crimean War, 42-44, 46, 52, 109
Crispi, Francesco, 96, 140, 149
Cuban Crisis, 318
Custozza, battle of, 34, 36
Czechoslovakia, 183, 184; after World War I, 215-216; after World War II, 290; destruction of, 252-255; the "Spring dawn," 315

Daladier, Edouard, 253
Danzig, free state, 183; occupation of, 256-257
Dardanelles, 12
Darwin, Charles, 65, 80
Dawes Plan, 195, 201
D-Day, 278
Deák, Francis, 52
"Decembrists," 11
Descent of Man, 65
De Gaulle, Charles, 265, 276, 293, 325, 332-334
Delcassé, Theophile, 138-140, 142, 144
Democracy, 75, 76
Denmark, 7, 49, 100; war with Prussia, 36-37, 50; World War II, 262, 263
Depretis, Agostino, 96
Dickens, Charles, 24
Disarmament, 223-225
Disraeli, Benjamin, 54, 86, 124, 131
Dollfuss, Engelbert, 237
Dostoevsky, Feodor M., 108
Dreikaiserbund, 125
Dreyfus, Alfred, 93; case, 93
Duma, 111-112, 166, 205
Dunkirk, battle of, 263-264
Durham, Lord John, 25, 55

Ebert, Friedrich, 202, 204
Economic liberalism, 23, 24
Eden, Anthony, 251
Education Act, 86
Edward VII, Britain, 139
Egypt, 13, 19-20, 90, 269, 317
Eisenhower, General Dwight D., 274; as President, 308
El Alamein, battle of, 274, 275
Elgin, Lord, 55
Ems Despatch, 61
Engels, Friedrich, 39
England, *see* Great Britain
Entente Cordiale, 21, 139-140
Essay on Liberty, 26
Estonia, 183, 220, 262
Ethiopia, 241-243
European Economic Community (EEC), 331, 337-338, 341
European Economic Cooperation, Organization for (OEEC), 305
European Free Trade Association, (EFTA), 331, 338

European Recovery Program, 285
Extinction of Poverty, 31

Fascism, 210-212, 234, 241, 243, 245, 277
Fashoda Incident, 138-139
Ferdinand I, Bulgaria, 218
Ferdinand I, King of Italy, 9-11
Ferdinand VII, Spain, 21
Ferry, Jules, 92; school laws, 92
Festung Europa, 277-278
Fifth French Republic, 325, 332-334
Finland, 6, 111, 183, 220, 278
Fiume, 169, 177, 185; free state annexed, 228
Five year plans, 209, 232-233, 249
Foch, Marshal, 167
Fontainebleau, Treaty of, 4
Fourier, Charles, 26
Four Power Pact, 237, 238
Fourteen Points, 170-171, 173, 177, 189, 190
Fourth French Republic, 292-294, 324-325
France, (1815-1848), 3-9, 14-15, 20; (1848-1852), 29-32, 40-41; (1852-1870), 55-63; (1870-1914), 90-94; (1919-1930), 201-202; (1930-1939), 238-241, 244-246, 248, 250-251, 253-254; (1945-1952), 292-294; (1953-1972), 324-325, 332-334; African colonies, 133-134; Algerian rebellion, 324-325; form of government in, 84; imperialism in Far East, 135-136; liberation of, 278, politics in, 85; post-World War I, 176, 190, 226; Vichy Regime, 264-265; World War II, 264, 276, 278
Francis Joseph, Austria, 51, 106
Franco, Francisco, 247, 248, 250, 269, 299
Franco-Prussian War, 48, 60-63, 69, 120-121
Franco-Roumanian Treaty, 226
Frankfort, Treaty of, 62
Frederick III, Germany, 104
Frederick William III, Prussia, 5
Frederick William IV, Prussia, 35-37
Free trade, 23
French Revolution, 14-15, 26, 74-77

INDEX 349

Gambetta, Léon, 92
Garibaldi, Giuseppe, 47, 57, 63
Gastein, Convention of, 50-51
Geneva Disarmament Conference, 225
George II, Greece, 217
George III, Great Britain, 8
George IV, Great Britain, 8, 15
German Confederation, 6, 8, 32-33, 35-36, 50
German Republic, 202-204
Germany, (1815-1848), 8; (1848-1852), 35, 37; (1852-1870), 48-50; (1870-1914), 101-105; (1919-1930), 202-204; (1930-1939), 235-238, 251-257; (1945-1952), 290; (1953-1972), 295-299, 335-337; African colonies, 133-134; imperialism in Far East, 136; occupation of, 290; postwar (1918-1919), 178, 180-182, 185-186, 190; post-World War I policy, 226-227; revolution of 1848, 33, 35; unification of, 48-51, 63; World War II, 261-270, 278
Gioberti, Vincenzo, 46
Giolitti, Giovanni, 96, 97, 148-149
Gladstone, William E., 54, 62, 85-86, 88, 131
Great Britain, (1815-1848), 5-8, 11, 15-16, 24-26; (1852-1870), 54-55; (1870-1914), 88-90; (1918-1930), 199-201; (1930-1939), 239, 242-243, 248, 250-251; (1945-1952), 291-292; (1953-1972), 330-332; African colonies, 133-134; Commonwealth of, 292, 322-324; dominions of, 89-90; form of government in, 85; imperialism in Far East, 135-136; politics in, 85-87; postwar (1918-1919), 176-177, 190; post-World War I policy, 227; World War II, 263-265, 271, 275, 276
Greco-Italian War, 268
Greece, 6, 19, 53-54, 117-119, 217-218, 301, 303; independence of, 13-14; World War II, 268, 279
Greek Revolution, 13, 118
Grey, Charles, 16
Grey, Edward, 151
Guadalcanal, 275

Guarantees, Law of, 97
Guizot, Francois, 20-21, 29

Habsburg Empire, (1815-1848), 6; (1848-1852), 32, 33; (1852-1870), 51; (1870-1914), 106, 108, 213, 214; post-World War I, 184
Hacha, President, Czechoslovakia, 255
Haldane, Richard, 152
Herriot, Edouard, 224
"Higher Criticism," 28, 80
Hindenburg, Paul von, 197, 204, 231, 235-236
Hiroshima, 280
Hitler, Adolph, 233-237, 251-253, 255, 257, 265-266, 268, 270, 278
Hoare, Samuel, 243
Hoare-Laval Plan, 243
Hohenlohe, Prince, 104
Hohenzollerns, 33
Holland, 5, 99, 263
Holy Alliance, 7, 9, 18
Home Rule Bill, 88, 201
Hoover, Herbert, 197, 231
Horthy, Admiral Nicholas, 215
House, Edward M., 164, 173
Hundred Days, 4, 6, 9
Hungary, 36, 255, 279, 290; post-World War I, 178, 215; Russian intervention in, 314; World War II, 268

Imperialism, 21, 77-78, 104, 128-142
India, 21, 89
Industrial Revolution, 22-24
Intellectual climate, 26-28, 65-66, 78-82
International, The, 75
International Labor Organization, 222
Ireland, 54, 55; land problem, 54-55
Irish Free State, 201
Irish Nationalist Party, 87, 88
Isabella, Queen of Spain, 21, 60
Israel, 327
Italia Irredenta, 48
Italian Revolutions, 33, 34
Italo-Ethiopian War, 241-244
Italo-Turkish War, 148-149

Italy, (1815-1848), 6, 9-10, 18; (1848-1852), 33-34, 36-38; (1852-1870), 44-48, 63; (1870-1914), 94-97; (1918-1919), 176-177, 190-191; (1919-1930), 209-213; (1930-1939), 247, 250-251; (1945-1952), 289-290, 294-295; (1953-1972), 342; acquires Rome, 63; African colonies, 133; anticlericalism in, 97; form of government, 84; politics of, 95-97; post-World War I policy, 227-228; *ralliement*, 93; reaction to Nazism, 237-238; revolution of 1848, 33-34; unification of, 44-48; World War II, 268, 269, 274, 276-277
Izvolsky, Alexander, 146

Japan, 111, 177; imperialism in China, 136, 240; surrender of, 279-280; World War II, 273-274
Jaurès, Jean, 94
Jellacich, Joseph, 36
July Days, Paris, 25
July Monarchy, 29
Jutland, battle of, 162

Kapital, Das, 74
Karageorgevitch family, 118
Kellogg-Briand Pact, 224
Kemal Pasha, Mustapha, 115-116, 217
Kennedy, John F., 309
Khrushchev, Nikita, 311-312
Kitchener, Horatio H., 138
Korean War, 301
Kossuth, Louis, 36, 52
Kotzebue, August F. F. von, 8
Kriegsschuldfrage, 180
Kulturkampf, 103
Kun, Bela, 215
Kuo-Min-Tang, 227

Labor Party, British, 87, 199-200, 292
Laibach, Congress of, 10
Laissez faire, 23, 29, 54-56
Land Acts, Ireland, 88
Latvia, 183, 220, 262
Lausanne Reparations Agreement, 197
Lausanne, Treaty of, 186, 217

Laval, Pierre, 240-242, 265
Laval-Mussolini Agreement, 242
Law, Bonar, 199
League of Nations, 174-178, 181, 189, 192, 214, 221-223, 236, 240-244
Legitimists, Conservative, 91
Lend Lease Bill, 271
Lenin, Nicholas, 166, 205, 208-209
Leo XIII, 74, 80, 93, 97
Leopold I, Belgium, 17
Leopold II, Belgium, 99, 133, 264
Leopold of Hohenzollern, 60
Lesseps, Ferdinand de, 64
Liberalism, 23-26, 35, 38, 65, 80; in France, 57; in Great Britain, 25, 26, 86-88; in Italy, 33; "new," 86, 87
Liberal Party, 85-87, 199, 200
Liberal Unionists, 86, 88
Libya, 149; war of 1911-1912, 130
Life of Jesus, 80
Lithuania, 183, 220, 262
Little Entente, 239, 252, 255
Litinov, Maxim, 249
Lloyd George, David, 87, 163, 174, 175, 190, 199
Locarno Pact, 224, 227
Lodge, Henry C., 192
London, Treaty of, (1827), 14; (1840), 20; (1915), 169, 177, 184-185, 227
Louis XVIII, France, 4, 9, 14
Louis Napoleon, *see* Napoleon III
Louis Philippe, France, 15, 17-18, 20, 29, 30
Ludendorff, Eric, 168, 171
Lusitania, 162
Luxembourg, 60, 99, 263

MacDonald, Ramsay, 199-200, 224, 243
MacMahon, Marie Edmede, 61, 91
Macmillan, Harold, 330
Maginot line, 263-264
Mahmoud II, Turkey, 20
Malthus, Thomas R., 24
Manchurian Episode, 240, 241
Mandates, 177, 185-186
Manin, Daniele, 34
Maniu, Julius, 218
Marchand, Jean Baptiste, 138
Maria Cristina, Spain, 21

INDEX

Marne, battle of, 159
Marshall Plan, 284-285
Marx, Karl, 24, 39, 65, 74-75, 80
Marxism, 39, 166, 206-209
Masaryk, Thomas G., 216
Materialism, 79-80
Matteotti, Giacomo, 211
Maurras, Charles, 77
Maximilian, Mexico, 58
"May Laws," 103
Mazzini, Giuseppe, 37, 45-46
Mehemet Ali, Egypt, 13, 19, 20
Mein Kampf, 234, 237
Menschikoff, Aleksandr Sergeyevich, 43
Metternich, Era of, 8-11; defeat of, 35
Metternich, Prince Clemens, 4-6, 8-11, 13, 17-18, 32-33, 35, ˆ6, 45
Mexico, intervention of Napoleon III, 57-58
Miguel, Don, 21
Militarism, 77-78
Mill, John Stuart, 26
Milner, Alfred, 133
Modernism, 80-81
Moltke, Helmuth von, 48
Monarchists, 94
Monroe, James, 11
Monroe Doctrine, 11, 59
Montenegro, 117-118, 124, 150, 185
Montgomery, Bernard, 274
Monumenta Germaniae Historica, 27
Moravia, 255
Morocco, 140, 143-144, 147-148
Moscow, conferences, 273; trials, 250
Müller, Wilhelm, 204
Munich, beer hall putsch, 203, 234; Conference of, 253-254; settlement, 253
Murat, Joachim, 6
Mussolini, Benito, 210-212, 237-238, 241-243, 247-248, 250-253, 255, 268, 277

Nagasaki, 280
Nanking, Treaty of, 21, 135
Napoleon I, France, 3-8, 22, 45
Napoleon III, Louis, 31-32, 38, 40-41, 43-44, 47, 50, 53, 55-57, 59-61, 121
Napoleonic Ideas, 31
Napoleonic Wars, 6, 69

National Assembly, France, 30, 31, 91; Germany, 35, 202
National Socialism, *see* Nazism
National workshops, 30, 31
Nationalism, 7, 33, 42, 64, 76-78, 117; as cause of world war, 186; economic, 232
Navarino, battle of, 14
Nazism, 233-240, 245, 251-254; new order, 265, 266
Nazi-Soviet Pact, 257, 261
Netherlands, 5-6, 98-99
Neuilly, Treaty of, 178
Neutrality Acts, 271
New Deal, 245, 251
New Economy Policy (N.E.P.), 208, 232
New Zealand, 89
Nicholas I, Russia, 11, 13
Nicholas II, Russia, 110, 144
North Africa, 269, 274-276
North Atlantic Treaty Organization (NATO), 306; French withdrawal from, 339
North German Confederation, 50
Norway, 7, 262, 263
Novara, battle of, 38
Nuclear Test Ban Treaties, 321

Obrenovitch, Milan, 118
October Manifesto, 111
Ollivier, Émile, 57
Olmütz, Treaty of, 37
Opium War, 21, 135
Orange, House of, 99
Origin of Species, 65
Orlando, Vittorio, 174, 175
Orleanists, Liberal, 91
Otto I, Greece, 14, 53
Ottoman Empire, (1815-1848), 6, 12, 19; (1852-1870), 42-43, 53; (1870-1914), 113, 115-119, 124, 148; (1918-1919), 177, 185-186
Owen, Robert, 26

Palmerston, Henry, 20-21, 34, 54, 131
Panama scandal, 93
Pangalos, Theodore, 218
Pan-Slavic Congress, 35-36
Paris, Congress of, 44, 56
Paris, Louis Philippe, 91

Paris Peace Conference, 172-176, 221
Paris, Treaty of, (1814), 3; (1815), 4; (1856), 56
Parliament Act, 87
Parnell, Charles Stewart, 88
Pashitch, Nikola, 118, 217
Pasternak, Boris, 312
Paul, Regent Prince, Yugoslavia, 268
Pearl Harbor, 273
Peel, Robert, 16
Permanent Court of International Justice, 222
Pétain, Henri, 264, 265
Peter I, Serbia, 118
Peter II, Yugoslavia, 268
"Phony" War, 261
Piedmont, 45
Pilsudski, Josef, 220
Pius IX, 37, 65, 80, 97
Plehve, Venceslas de, 110-112
Plombières Agreement, 47
Pobyedonostsev, Konstantine, 110
Poincaré, Raymond N. L., 201-202
Poland, 5-6, 17-18, 53, 100, 182-183, 219-220, 238, 255, 290; revolt of 1863, 110; World War II, 261
Polish Corridor, 183, 257
Politburo, 208
Popular Front, 245, 246, 251
Pompidou, Georges, 341
Portsmouth, Treaty of, 111, 136
Portugal, 7, 98
Positive Philosophy, 65
Prague, occupation of, 256
Proletariat, 75, 107
Prussia, (1815-1848), 5-6, 8; (1848-1852), 32-33; (1852-1870), 48-50, 60-63; (1870-1914), 101-103

Quadruple Alliance, 7, 9
Quebec, Conferences of, 275
Quisling, Vidkun, 263

Racconigi Agreement, 147
Radetzky, Joseph, 34, 36
Ralliement, 93
Ranke, Leopold von, 27
Rapallo, Treaty of, 181, 226
Rasputin, Grigori Y., 113

"Red Sunday," 111
Reform Bill, (1832), 15-16, 18, 25; (1867), 54, 85
Reformists, Marxian, 75
Reichstadt, Duke of, 31
Reichstag, 101, 102, 204, 236
Reinsurance Treaty, 127-128, 137
Religion, 42-43, 66, 81, 108, 115; and science, 80
Renan, Ernest, 80
Reparations, World War I, 177, 188-189, 194-197
Rerum novarum, 97
Revolutions, (1830), 14-15; (1848), 29-36; (1905), 111-112; (1917), 165-166, 180, 205-206
Reynaud, Paul, 264
Rhodes, Cecil, 133
Riga, Treaty of, 183
Risorgimento, 45, 94, 96
Rivera, Primo de, 246
Rome, annexed to Italy, 63
Rome-Berlin Axis, 248-249, 251-252, 254
Rome-Berlin-Tokyo Triangle, 249, 274
Rommel, General Erwin, 274
Roon, Albrecht von, 48
Roosevelt, Franklin D., 232, 271, 287
Roumania, 53, 117-119, 216, 218, 289, 290; postwar (1918-1919), 183-184; World War II, 268, 278
Royalists, France, 91
Ruhr Episode, 195
Russia, (1815-1848), 6, 11-12, 14; (1848-1870), 52, 53; (1870-1914), 108-113; (1917-1930), 205-209; (1930-1939), 239, 249-250, 256; (1945-1952), 285-286, 290, 299-300; (1953-1972), 310-313; expansion of, 108-109, 135-136; March Revolution, 165; October Revolution, 166; political parties, 112; postwar (1918-1919), 180, 183-184, 191; post-World War I policy, 227; World War II, 261, 262, 269-270, 274-276, 280
Russo-Chinese Tensions, 313
Russo-Finnish War, 262
Russo-German Treaty, 261
Russo-Japanese War, 111-112, 136

Russo-Turkish War, (1827), 14; (1875), 123-125

Saar territory, 181, 183
Sadowa, battle of, 50
Safeguarding of Industries Act, 199
St. Germain, Treaty of, 178
St. Jean de Maurine, Treaty of, 169
Saint-Simon, 26
San Francisco Conference, 287
San Stefano, Treaty of, 124
Sarajevo, 150, 155
Sardinia, 6, 43
Sardinian Charter, 34, 38, 46
Schacht, Hjalmar, 236
Schleswig-Holstein, 36, 49
Schlieffen Plan, 158, 159, 263
Schliemann, Heinrich, 27
Schuman Plan, 305
Schwarzenberg, Felix, 36, 37, 51
Science, 78-79; and religion, 80
Second French Republic, 30-31, 38
Sedan, battle of, 61, 90
Sepoy Mutiny, 134
Serbia, 117-118, 124-126, 155-156, 185, 217
Serbo-Bulgarian War, 126-127
Sèvres, Treaty of, 178, 217
Shimonoseki, Treaty of, 136
Silesia, 10, 183
"Six Acts," 8
Slovakia, 255
Smith, Adam, 23
Social Democrats, Germany, 104, 107; Russia, 112
Social Republic, Italy, 277
Socialism, 39, 74, 75, 103
Somme, battle of, 162; in World War II, 264
Sonnino, Sidney, 176
Sovereignty, concept of, 120
Soviet Union, 205-209; *see also* Russia
South Africa, 89
South America, 11
Southeast Asia Treaty Organization, (SEATO), 319
Spain, (1815-1848), 7, 10-11, 20-21; (1852-1870), 60; (1870-1914), 98; (1919-1939), 246-248; (1945-1952), 299
Spanish-American War, 98
Spanish Civil War, 246-248, 250

Stalin, Joseph, 209, 233, 257
Stalingrad, 274-275
Stambolisky, Alexander, 218
Steel, Pact of, 255-256
Stein, Heinrich, 8
Stolypin, Peter, 112
Straits question, 12, 20, 145
Strategic Arms Limitation Talks (SALT), 321
Stresa, 242, 244
Stresemann, Gustav, 204, 224, 227
Suez Canal, 317
Supreme Council, League of Nations, 174
Sweden, 7
Switzerland, 100
Sykes-Picot Agreement, 169
Syllabus of Errors, 65

Taaffe, Eduard F. J. von, 107
Taff Vale decision, 87
Taiping rebellion, 135
Talleyrand, 4, 5
Tardieu, André, 175
Technology, 78-79
Teheran, conference, 275
Thiers, Adolphe, 20, 29, 61, 91
Third French Republic, 90-94, 130, 138, 292
"Three F's," 88
Tientsin, Treaty of, 135
Tisza, Stephen, 155
Tito, Marshal Druz, 279, 301
Toulon, battle of, 276
Trades Dispute Act, 200
Trades Union Act, 86
Trianon, Treaty of, 178
Trieste, free territory of, 289-290
Triple Alliance, 126, 140-141, 145, 147
Triple Entente, 145
Tripoli, 140, 148-149
Troppau, Congress of, 10
Trotsky, Leon, 209, 233
Truman Doctrine, 303
Tunis, French occupation of, 126
Turin, Treaty of, 47
Turkey, 12, 14, 118-119, 303; post-war (1918-1919), 178, 186
Twenty-one demands, 170

Ukraine, 268
Ulster district, 88

Unemployment, 30
Unemployment Insurance Act, 199
Unified Socialist Party, 94
United Nations, 287-288, 296-297; admission of Red China, 343
United Nations Relief and Rehabilitation Administration (UNRRA), 284
United States, 11; (1919-1939), 230-231, 251; (1945-1952), 302-304; (1953-1972), 308-310; and peace, 191; isolationism, 270-271; war debts, 196-198; World War I, 164-165; World War II, 270-273, 275-276
Unkiar Iskelessi, Treaty of, 20
Urbanization, 73
U.S.S.R. (Union of Soviet Socialist Republics), 207; *see also* Russia
Utopian Socialism, 26, 39

Valera, Eamon De, 201
Vatican City, 213
Venizelos, Eleutherios, 118, 217-218
Verdun, battle of, 162
Verona, Congress of, 10
Versailles, Treaty of, 178, 180, 186, 190-192, 194
Vichy Regime, France, 264-265, 276, 292
Victor Emmanuel, 10
Victor Emmanuel II, 38, 47, 63
Victoria, Queen of England, 25, 89
Victorian Compromise, 25, 54
Vienna, Congress of, 4-8, 12, 100
Vietnam War, 309-310
Villafranca, truce of, 47
Vishinsky, Andrei, 250

War guilt, 157-158, 180
Warsaw Pact, 315

Washington Conferences, (1921-1922), 225; (1942), 275
Waterloo, 4
Watt, James, 22
Weimar Constitution, 202; Republic, 235
Wellington, Arthur W., 16
Weltpolitik, 138-139
Westminster, Statute of, 200
White Terror, 9
Wilhelmina, Holland, 99
William I, Netherlands, 16, 17
William I, Prussia, 48, 63, 100, 102, 104
William II, Germany, 104, 128, 138-139, 141-142, 144
William III, Holland, 99
Wilson, Woodrow, 164, 167, 170, 171, 173-177, 191, 192
Windischgrätz, Alfred, Prince zu, 36
Witte, Sergei, 110-112
World Court, 222
World War I, 155-171; background of, 143-154; consequences of; 193-229; outbreak, 155-157; settlements following, 172-190
World War II, aftermath, 282-287; background of, 232-257; outbreak, 261-280; territorial readjustments, 289-290

Yalta Conference, 275, 280
Young Plan, 195
Young Turks, 81, 116
Ypsilanti, 13
Yugoslavia, 216-217, 268, 279, 301

Zeitgeist, 80
Zemstvos, 53
Zog I, Albania, 217
Zola, Émile, 93